Cognitive-Behavioral Therapy for Sexual Dysfunction

Cognitive-Behavioral Therapy for Sexual Dysfunction provides clinicians and graduate students with a comprehensive biopsychosocial model of useful, practical, empirically-based strategies and techniques to address common sexual dysfunctions. It is the most comprehensive volume describing the couple cognitive-behavioral approach to assessment, treatment, and relapse prevention of sexual dysfunction. The focus is on sexual desire and satisfaction with an emphasis on the Good Enough Sex (GES) model of sharing sexual pleasure rather than intercourse as an individual perfect performance test. This title reflects the contributions of Mike Metz to the field of couple sex therapy.

Michael E. Metz, PhD, was a psychologist and marital and sex therapist, and researcher in private practice in Minneapolis/St. Paul, Minnesota. He published over 60 professional articles and 4 books, including *Enduring Desire*, which received the AASECT 2011 Best Book Award. He was a leading advocate for the integration of couple therapy, sex therapy, and spirituality. He passed away in 2012. This book, *Cognitive-Behavioral Therapy for Sexual Dysfunction*, is a tribute to his professional legacy.

Norman B. Epstein, PhD, is a professor of family science at the University of Maryland, College Park and director of the department's nationally accredited Couple and Family Therapy clinical training program. He is an author or editor of 4 prior books, has published 62 journal articles and 58 chapters in edited books on aspects of couple and family relationships and therapy, and has presented over 120 research papers and 90 training workshops on couple and family therapy at national and international professional meetings.

Barry McCarthy is a professor of psychology at American University, a diplomate in clinical psychology, a diplomate in sex therapy, and a certified couple therapist. He has published over 105 professional articles, 26 book chapters, and 14 books. He has presented over 400 professional workshops nationally and internationally. In 2016, he received the Masters and Johnson award for lifetime contributions to the sex therapy field.

Cognitive-Behavioral Therapy for Sexual Dysfunction

Michael E. Metz, Norman B. Epstein, and Barry McCarthy

Routledge
Taylor & Francis Group

NEW YORK AND LONDON

First published 2018
by Routledge
711 Third Avenue, New York, NY 10017

and by Routledge
2 Park Square, Milton Park, Abingdon, Oxon, OX14 4RN

Routledge is an imprint of the Taylor & Francis Group, an informa
business

Library of Congress Cataloging-in-Publication Data
A catalog record for this book has been requested

ISBN: 978-0-415-87407-6 (hbk)
ISBN: 978-0-415-87408-3 (pbk)
ISBN: 978-0-203-86345-9 (ebk)

Typeset in Bembo
by codeMantra

Contents

Preface

Cognitive-Behavioral Therapy for Sexual Dysfunction honors the professional legacy of Michael E. Metz, Ph.D. and provides a guide for the practice of sex therapy in a relational context, based on sound empirical evidence and the authors' extensive clinical experience. At its core is the comprehensive couple biopsychosocial approach that Mike emphasized for assessment, treatment and relapse prevention with sexual dysfunctions through his extensive clinical practice, writings, and professional training workshops. Initially, Mike and Norman Epstein designed the structure and content of the book, and Mike wrote first drafts of the chapters, with input from Norm, especially regarding the cognitive-behavioral and couple dynamic aspects. After Mike passed away in 2012, the book project stalled, but eventually Barry McCarthy, Mike's longtime co-author on widely disseminated self-help books on male and couple approaches to treatment of sexual problems, joined the project to provide his rich knowledge and experience with Mike's biopsychosocial approach. Norm and Barry emphasized building on Mike's foundational work and also updating the material based on current research in the field. Staying true to Mike's thinking and clinical methods was a challenge at times, as there were many instances when we dearly wished we could sit down with Mike and talk through issues in the writing, to share his company and friendship again as well as his expertise.

Mike's unique perspective on the role and meaning of sexuality in people's lives integrated cognitive-behavioral factors (individuals' thinking about themselves and their relationships, their emotional responses regarding sex, and their behavioral patterns and skills) with core human needs for intimacy, playfulness and spirituality, the importance of the couple as intimate and erotic allies, and the crucial ability for couples to manage differences and conflicts constructively. Mike emphasized sexuality as a couple relational process in which partners' subjective desire and satisfaction are influenced by biological, psychological and interpersonal factors. The integrative biopsychosocial model described in this book represents the maturation of the sex therapy field, the history of which we summarize. Although the book emphasizes cognitive-behavioral concepts and clinical methods, the strategies and techniques are relevant for therapists using a variety of theoretical models. We focus on psychological processes and couple dynamics, but bio-medical factors are recognized throughout as crucial for understanding sexual function and dysfunction. Social and relational factors, as well as partners' cognitions and emotional responses, certainly have been addressed in the sex therapy literature, but they often have been downplayed. From Mike's perspective those are crucial for understanding human sexual response. Sexuality is not only about physical function, as physical responses and subjective satisfaction are influenced strongly by the meanings that partners attach to their sexual and overall relational interactions, as well as the couple's emotional responses and behavioral patterns. Consequently, the assessment methods described in this book pay a great deal of attention to individuals' cognitions, emotional responses, and behavioral skills (for communication, problem solving and eroticism/sexual pleasuring). We also emphasize systematic assessment of couple interactions, such as demand-withdraw patterns, that may develop in response to a sexual problem or that may cause and maintain a dysfunction. Likewise, the treatment approaches described in this book emphasize conjoint interventions that target reduction of couple interaction patterns contributing to sexual dysfunction and enhance eroticism and sexual pleasure. Thus, cognitive-behavioral couple sex therapy is a consistent integration of approaches to individual functioning and couple dynamics. It calls for knowledge and skills for both individual and couple therapy, reducing both individually-based and relationally-based barriers to joyful sexual relationships.

Mike Metz was a well-respected clinician, researcher, and educator who cared deeply about assisting couples to develop satisfying sexual and overall relationships. He believed that the concepts and methods of cognitive-behavioral couple sex therapy have great potential to empower diverse couples, in terms of sexual orientation, race, ethnicity and partner status, to experience healthy and fulfilling intimate sexual relationships. It is a strengths-based approach that encourages and guides couples to collaborate as a team to enhance their relationships. Although couples typically enter therapy focused on problems and emotional distress regarding sexual dysfunction, the clinician's optimistic and straightforward approach helps instill hope and positive motivation. The therapist plays an active educational role but collaborates consistently with the couple to achieve their personal goals for their relationship. Mike's therapeutic style was empathic and respectful of individual, couple, cultural and value differences. We have attempted to weave those qualities that we share as well throughout this finished version of Mike's labor of love. This book adds to the major contributions that Mike Metz made as a professional model for the study of human sexuality and the sensitive treatment of sexual dysfunction. Sexual problems offer unique opportunities for psychological, relational and sexual growth, as couples' initial focus on physical function is broadened and satisfying emotionally intimate sexuality becomes a cornerstone of their personal bond. The dyadic focus of cognitive-behavioral couple sex therapy simultaneously produces benefits for individual mental health and relationship quality.

We hope that this book will motivate seasoned clinicians and academicians, as well as new professionals, to integrate sex therapy into the mainstream of the mental health field. Sexual function problems are among the most common and distressing concerns facing the general population, whether they are a primary complaint presented by clients or surface through a clinician's assessment. This book honors Mike Metz's legacy by presenting the theoretical approach and clinical methods that he played a central role in developing and championing.

Norman B. Epstein and Barry W. McCarthy

Chapter 1

Understanding Sexual Dysfunction and Sex Therapy

Cognitive-Behavioral Therapy for Sexual Dysfunction (CBCST) provides a detailed description of assessment and treatment strategies for sexual dysfunction (SD) for experienced clinicians and graduate students. This book addresses the lack of sex therapy training that is common in psychology, marriage and family therapy, social work, and other mental health programs. Most clinicians receive very little practical training in this crucial area. Our goal is to provide a realistic and authoritative foundation in CBCST concepts, assessment, and interventions that facilitate clinician comfort and confidence.

We focus primarily on CBCST with married and partnered couples, both opposite and same-sex. In the absence of a partner, this approach can be modified for use with individuals. CBCST is a subspecialty of couple therapy. It is grounded in strategies to promote skills for sexual and relationship function and satisfaction, as well as interventions to reduce relational conflict and distress that subvert sexual function and satisfaction. The psychoeducational component of this approach is required because many adults, regardless of intelligence and education level, have limited knowledge and comfort with sexual physiology and psychosexual skills. CBCST interventions focus on the complex interplay among partners' cognitions, emotional responses, and behavioral interactions that subvert the sexual relationship.

CBCST is an artful *blending of sexual science and clinical practice*. In behavioral terms, SD involves absent, inhibited, or feeling a lack of control of sexual response. It also involves a variety of non-sexual behaviors (e.g., couple communication) that influence sexual function. The behavioral patterns in a couple's overall and sexual relationship are important targets for clinical interventions. Cognitive components of SD involve thought processes that interfere with sexual desire, pleasure, eroticism, and satisfaction. Emotional components of SD involve both chronic and transitory emotions (e.g., depression, anxiety, anger, shame) that block sexual satisfaction. CBCST incorporates assessment and intervention with cognitive, behavioral, and affective components within a comprehensive biopsychosocial model. In this book we:

- describe methods for assessing behaviors, cognitions, and emotions within a relationship context;
- detail therapeutic interventions focused on sexual pleasure and function;
- provide clinical "coaching" regarding common processes in sex therapy; and
- offer case vignettes as well as psychosexual skill exercises, handouts, and educational materials.

Roots of SD include characteristics of the two clients (e.g., sexual beliefs they learned in childhood) and their relationship. We emphasize dyadic formulations of SD that take both partners and their interaction patterns into account, incorporating evidence-based procedures and providing guidance for best clinical practices.

Sex Therapy as an Exceptional Clinical Opportunity to Benefit the Relationship

Couples find it difficult to view SD as similar to other challenging relationship issues (e.g., finances, conflicts with relatives, work commitments, parenting) because of the sensitivity of sexual issues. SD invariably is a relationship problem, if not in origin, then in impact. Many couples and therapists wrongly fear that SD signals irreconcilable "incompatibility." Couples and clinicians overlook the exceptional therapeutic opportunity available for promoting sexual health and couple intimacy by improving the quality of the sexual relationship. Effective sex therapy not only allows the professional to help relieve individual emotional distress and enhance self-worth; it also has great potential to increase emotional closeness. Regardless of a clinician's primary theoretical orientation (e.g., psychodynamic, humanistic, family systems, feminist) and professional discipline (psychiatry, psychology, social work, marriage and family therapy, pastoral counseling, professional counseling, nursing), CBCST provides a wealth of resources, strategies, and interventions that can be integrated with diverse approaches. Clinicians with a variety of professional backgrounds can use CBCST as a clinical modality that offers exceptional opportunities to reduce distress and enhance an intimate relationship.

Usually individuals and couples do not seek assistance for SD. Often they present concerns associated with medical and mental health conditions (e.g., cancer, generalized anxiety disorder, grief over a parent's death, parenting problems, depression), which seem unconnected to sexual problems. In other cases, they present global relational issues (e.g., frequent arguments, feeling disconnected from each other) without any specific reference to sexual problems. However, sexual concerns are often in the background of these diverse problems. "I suffer daily anxiety, so I avoid sex." "Since my father died, I don't have any interest in sex." "I'm receiving chemotherapy, so I have no sexual desire." "We don't talk much, and rarely show affection." Sexual concerns are present in a wide variety of clients' presenting complaints even though they may be hidden or secondary.

Sexuality is personal and sensitive, causing clients and clinicians hesitation and discomfort, so they avoid talking about or even thinking about sexual issues (Risen, 2010). Our objectives are to increase clinicians' comfort with discussing aspects of sexual functioning, as well as to provide guidelines for sexual history taking, assessment and diagnosis, and CBCST interventions. With increased comfort and confidence, clinicians can help individuals and couples with SD and sexual concerns.

Sexual Dysfunction as a Relationship Problem

Sexual problems have multiple causes, dimensions, and effects on the individual, the partner, and their relationship. Effective treatment integrates medical, pharmacological, psychological, and relational components (e.g., Althof, Rosen, Rubio-Aurioles, Earle, & Chevret-Measson, 2006; Binik & Hall, 2014; Metz & Pryor, 2000). SD can have a profound detrimental effect on the overall quality of a couple's relationship (Levine, Risen, & Althof, 2016). Difficulties with SD become relational problems when they are sources of embarrassment, conflict, dissatisfaction, or avoidance.

The Interplay of Sexual Dysfunction, Individual Psychological Function, and Relationship Problems

SD is a source of significant psychological distress and relationship problems. It commonly results in couple conflict, confusion, alienation, and dissatisfaction. SDs are classified as individual psychiatric disorders in the Diagnostic and Statistical Manual 5 (DSM-5; American Psychiatric Association, 2014), even though they are expressed in relationships and are influenced by interpersonal processes. Individual pre-existing health and mental health problems and couple relationship conflicts can contribute to the development of SD (Metz & Epstein, 2002). Thus, SD offers an exceptional opportunity for the helping professional to provide support and enhance the quality of life of the individual and couple, promoting personal and relationship health and satisfaction.

Core Sex Therapy Competencies

In addition to general clinical proficiencies that all therapists need (e.g., excellent listening skills and empathy), there are three core proficiencies in sex therapy: (1) accurate, evidence-based biopsychosocial information about sexual behavior and function; (2) comfort with discussing sexual details and addressing sexual difficulties; and (3) knowledge of strategies for the assessment, formulation, and treatment of SD. Equipped with specialized knowledge, personal and professional comfort, and practical skills for assessment and intervention, a clinician can feel confident providing CBCST.

Our aim is to provide clinicians with best practices for assessment and treatment based on the findings of clinical research on SDs and couple relationship factors that influence them.

Relevance for Heterosexual and Same-Sex Couples

The vast majority of knowledge about SD has been gathered from research and clinical practice with heterosexual married couples. However, these concepts and methods are highly applicable with same-sex couples. Characteristics of individuals that contribute to SD (e.g., performance anxiety, sexual trauma, depression) operate similarly regardless of sexual orientation. Although there are important factors in the lives of same-sex couples that differ from those in heterosexual couples (e.g., discrimination, gaps between partners in their stages of coming out), dyadic aspects of SD (e.g., power struggles and avoidance) are similar. Where sex researchers and therapists have found differences by sexual orientation—for example, dyspareunia among heterosexual couples occurs with vaginal intercourse whereas among gay men it occurs with anal intercourse; low sexual desire occurs more often among lesbian couples than either gay male or heterosexual couples—it is important to address factors unique to sexual orientation (Nichols, 2014). Otherwise, sex therapy competencies are applicable across sexual orientation.

Sexual Dysfunction and Sexual Health

The Diagnostic and Statistical Manual (DSM-5) is a primary source for classifying SD.

The DSM-5 Sexual Dysfunctions are:

- Hypoactive Sexual Desire Disorder—males.
- Sexual Interest/Arousal Disorder—females.
- Inhibited Arousal—difficulty with sexual arousal.
- Inhibited Orgasm—delay or absence of orgasm.
- Premature Ejaculation—rapid ejaculation.
- Genito-Pelvic Pain/Penetration Disorder—persistent genital pain or spasms of the vagina that interferes with intercourse.

However, the DSM-5 classification system views sexual problems from an individual perspective, ignoring relationship dynamics that influence each partner's sexual cognitions, emotions, and behaviors. Aubin and Heiman (2004) and Weeks and Gambescia (2015) examine SD from a relationship perspective, which we strongly support. Clients often present difficulties such as couple conflict regarding frequency of sex and preferred behaviors (e.g., oral sex, anal intercourse). These relational aspects of sexual problems can cause significant individual and relationship distress.

Descriptions of SD include three components: (a) a condition that is chronic or persistent (in contrast to occasional difficulties with sexual desire, arousal, or orgasm that are normal); (b) the sexual condition causes personal distress, and (c) it causes relational problems. The latter two components are crucial for understanding the impact of SD and the need for treatment.

Sexual problems may be comorbid with other psychological issues (Rosen, Miner, & Wincze, 2014). SD commonly occurs with mood disorders, generalized anxiety disorder, obsessive-compulsive disorder, and sleep disorders. Common interpersonal causes of sexual problems include relationship distress and alienation, psychologically and/or physically abusive behavior, and attachment injuries and broken trust (Johnson, 2008). These problems need to be addressed either before or concomitant with CBCST.

CBCST seeks to promote *sexual health* for individuals and couples. The United Nations World Health Organization described sexual health from an integrative biopsychosocial perspective:

> Sexual Health may be defined as a dynamic and harmonious state involving erotic and reproductive experiences and fulfillment, within a broader physical, emotional, interpersonal, social, and spiritual sense of well-being, in a culturally-informed, freely and responsibly chosen, and ethical framework; not merely the absence of sexual disorders.
>
> (World Health Organization, 1975)

Thus, the goal is not only to reduce distress, but also to enhance positive experiences.

There is no set definition of a "normal" sex life. Individuals and couples vary widely in terms of how often they engage sexually and what behaviors are involved.

Table 1.1 Sexual Difficulties Involving Discrepancies in Preferences

---

- Frequency of sex—a discrepancy in partners' preferences is very common
- Expectations of intercourse (e.g., length, style, positions, eye-contact)
- Variety of sexual practices (e.g., preference for types of pleasuring, oral sex, anal sex, sex videos, BDSM activities, sexy apparel, erotic scenarios)
- Sexual interaction (e.g., who initiates, arousal styles, orgasm patterns)
- Acceptability of masturbation with/without partner
- Acceptability of sexual fantasy
- Acceptability of sex "toys" (e.g., dildos, paddles, vibrators)
- Acceptability of substances to facilitate sexuality (e.g., alcohol or marijuana)
- Adaptation to sexually transmitted infections and medical problems
- Communication regarding sexual preferences and concerns

For some couples, once a week, twice a month, or even a few times a year may be acceptable. A couple's sexual behaviors may vary considerably from one encounter to another (e.g., a heterosexual couple may not always have penile-vaginal intercourse, and partners do not have an orgasm every time). Satisfaction depends on the expectations and meanings that the individuals attach to their sexual experiences, and the degree to which there is a good match between partners' goals and personal standards. Individuals experience variations in their level of sexual interest, degree of physical responsiveness, sexual satisfaction, and the degree to which they accept these variations as normal influences their satisfaction.

Sexual Difficulties

A common sexual issue that does not involve an SD involves *discrepancies between partners' preferences*. Table 1.1 lists types of preference discrepancies.

It is normal for individuals to experience occasional problems with desire, arousal, or orgasm. Many factors (e.g., life stresses, fatigue, relationship conflict, illness) cause fluctuations in sexual response. Clinicians help clients assess the frequency and severity of sexual difficulties as well as conditions that influence their occurrence. The danger is when clients interpret transitory difficulties as evidence of SD, have catastrophic thoughts about the severity of the problem, and blame themselves or each other. Emotional distress and avoidance of sex based on predictions that problems will persist can produce a self-fulfilling prophecy in which normal difficulties develop into a full-fledged SD. A key role of the sex therapist is to educate clients about normal variations in sexual response, the variety of factors that can contribute to transitory problems, and constructive ways to respond to difficulties.

Prevalence of Sex Dysfunction

Findings regarding frequency of SD vary considerably. Methods from the past 50 years include using an availability sample (Kinsey, Pomeroy, and Martin, 1948, 1953) and surveys using non-representative samples (e.g., Aschka et al., 2001; Ende, Rockwell & Glasgow, 1984; Metz & Seifert, 1993; Schein et al., 1988; Spector & Carey, 1990) report SD rates for men, women and couples ranging from 10% to 95%. Masters and Johnson (1970) estimated that approximately 50% of couples experience SD. A classic study by Frank, Anderson, and Rubinstein (1978) of happily married, sexually satisfied couples found that 80% occasionally experienced sexual difficulties. The occurrence of sexual difficulties does not mean that couples will be dissatisfied with their relationship. Rather, the subjective meanings that people attach to their sexual experiences play a major role in the quality of sexual relationships.

The best representative study regarding the occurrence of dysfunctions conducted in the United States (Laumann, Paik, & Rosen, 1999) found that approximately 45% of couples at a given time experience a male (31%), female (43%) or couple (45%) SD that created relationship distress. Nevertheless, it is common for couples to think that they are among the "very few" who experience sexual problems, in part because people do not disclose sexual problems.

The National Health and Social Life Survey (NHSL) study (Laumann, Gagnon, Michael, & Michaels, 1994) provided empirically validated information. The frequencies of female and male sexual problems they found are in Table 1.2.

Many clients mistakenly believe that erectile dysfunction (ED) is more prevalent than premature ejaculation (PE), due to the widespread marketing of medications for ED. In fact, PE is much more common than ED, although the meaning of the SD for the couple and the level of distress varies considerably. ED presents a greater challenge to relationship satisfaction because it is more likely than PE to result in a non-sexual relationship.

Public and professional awareness of SD has increased with the marketing of PDE-5 medications (Viagra, Levitra, Cialis), with developments in sexual medicine offering distressed couples increased hope. However, in the last decade there has been an imbalance in approaches to treating SD, with an inordinate emphasis on the biomedical approach to individual sexual performance, especially for males. Increased attention to a biomedical approach to female SD has involved a pill to enhance desire, testosterone enhancement, and the search for a "female Viagra."

Table 1.2 Female and Male Sexual Dysfunction Prevalence: National Health and Social Life Survey (1994)

Female Dysfunction Prevalence	(%)
Low desire	33.4
Inhibited orgasm	24.1
Sex not pleasurable	21.2
Pain with intercourse	14.4
Performance anxiety	11.5
Lubrication problems	10.4
Climax too soon	10.3
Male Dysfunction Prevalence	(%)
Premature ejaculation	28.5
Performance anxiety	17.0
Low desire	15.8
Erectile dysfunction	10.4
Ejaculatory inhibition	8.3
Sex not pleasurable	8.1
Pain during intercourse	3.0

Source: Laumann et al. (1994). Permission to republish granted by University of Chicago Press.

The failure of biomedical interventions (Brock et al., 2002), as well as the significant psychological placebo benefit associated with medications (Berry & Berry, 2014), highlight the over-simplification of focusing on individual sexual function and disregarding the couple's psychological and relational well-being. It is crucial to understand the important meanings that couples attach to their own and their partners' sexual responses, as well as to the role of intimacy in a couple's relationship. SDs involve complex intrapsychic responses involving thoughts and emotions, and interpersonal behavioral responses between partners. Clinical experience demonstrates that SD is rarely a simple problem with a simple medical cure, in spite of people's longing for a "quick fix."

SD is an important relationship problem that often causes emotional distress. It can be a secondary manifestation of psychological and/or relational problems as well as sexual problems such as compulsive sexual behavior and a history of sexual trauma (Levine et al., 2016; Metz & Epstein, 2002; Weeks & Gambescia, 2015). Consequently, it is crucial that clinicians look beyond a bio-medical conceptualization and solution. A comprehensive assessment of the individuals and their relationship is crucial to evaluating an SD and designing an appropriate treatment plan.

What Is Distinctive about Couples with Sexual Dysfunction?

Some individuals are disgruntled with their sex lives even though for the most part they are sexually functional (Kleinplatz et al., 2009). On the other hand, in Frank et al.'s (1978) study of a community sample of couples who reported satisfaction with their relationship, the prevalence of difficulties was high. Laumann et al. (1994) also found that many couples reported satisfaction with their sex life despite experiencing sexual difficulties and SD.

The importance of individuals' subjective appraisals of their sexual difficulties also was evident in Byers and Grenier's (2004) community sample of 150 heterosexual university-educated couples experiencing PE, in which men but not women reported lower sexual satisfaction. When partners are dissatisfied with the time of ejaculation, they still can develop internal sexual scripts or scenarios that allow them to experience sexual pleasure and satisfaction. Two couples may experience the same sexual problem, with one couple developing a diagnosable SD because one or both partners perceive the sexual problem negatively, whereas the members of the other couple accept the problem as a tolerable nuisance and focus on positive aspects of their sexual relationship.

Satisfied Couples Have Realistic Sexual Scripts

Sexual satisfaction is influenced by "meaning" more than by sexual function. Many couples who experience low sex desire, ED, PE, non-orgasmic response, or sexual pain are able to maintain sexual satisfaction. It is less the sexual response and more the thoughts and associated emotions that determine the subjective quality of couple sexuality. A key cognition that the CBCST model applies to understanding sexual response and satisfaction is the concept of the "script." A script is a cognitive schema that involves the person's basic beliefs about characteristics of people and events in the world, including sequences of events that occur in particular types of situations (Dattilio, 2010; Epstein & Baucom, 2002). Beginning early in childhood, individuals develop schemas based on internalizing information from experiences with family members as well as exposure to messages through mass media. Some schemas involve characteristics associated with a particular role (e.g., the characteristics of a loving partner), whereas others involve scenarios such as an exciting sexual interaction. These schemas become templates that the individual uses to understand and evaluate current experiences.

Epstein and Baucom (2002) differentiate between an *assumption*, a schema about characteristics that a person or sequence of events *has*, and a *standard* about the characteristics that a person or event *should* have. For example, a client may hold an assumption that an individual who is physically attracted to a partner automatically becomes sexually aroused by touching the partner. This script involves an assumption about how sexual responses naturally occur. In contrast, a client may hold a standard that an individual who loves her should demonstrate that level of caring on a daily basis by asking about her thoughts and feelings. An individual's assumptions and standards become problematic when they are rigid and inaccurate or involve unrealistic views of individuals and relationships, which lead the person to be upset when real-life does not happen as desired.

The script concept has received considerable attention from sex therapists (Rosen, 2007; Weeks & Treat, 2001), and couple therapists (Dattilio, 2010; Epstein & Baucom, 2002). Those clinicians assess and intervene with partners' views of an intimate relationship and sexual patterns. A sexual script involves thoughts and visual images about sexual interaction—what one would prefer to occur and what one predicts is likely to occur. Weeks (2004) emphasizes the influences that family-of-origin experiences, particularly with key attachment figures, have on an individual's sexual script. Individuals with an insecure attachment style want intimate sexual involvement but expect rejection. Other sexual scripts involve perfectionism, in which an individual imagines engaging in intense sex as portrayed in R-rated movies—a standard that is very difficult to attain.

A second way in which standards are problematic is when the partners have different "shoulds." They battle over whose standard should prevail, with each person feeling certain that he knows the "right" way. The resolution needs to be authentic for each partner—a "win-win" outcome. When a couple is able to work out differences—a process described as "bridge-bend-bond"—each feels understood, respected, and valued—open to acceptance and change.

When working with SD, it is easy for therapists to succumb to a couple's unrealistic sexual scripts. Examples include having a goal for a woman to experience orgasm during intercourse every time or a goal for a man with ED to return to 100% predictable sex performance. Unreasonable expectations set the couple up for failure. CBCST adopts the perspective that sexual health and relationship satisfaction are the ultimate goals, rather than any specific sexual standard (Metz & McCarthy, 2010a).

Integrating Evidence-Based Knowledge and Quality-Based Practice

In this book, we draw on empirical and clinical evidence to understand SD and describe integrative treatment that promotes best clinical practices. We explore the science and therapeutic art of sex therapy. Our CBCST approach emphasizes comfort addressing sexual concerns and provides case examples, psycho-educational materials, homework assignments, and coaching. The goal is improved sexual function as well as enhanced individual self-esteem and relationship satisfaction. The most challenging component of CBCST is not the psychosexual skills training, but intervening to make changes in the couple's relationship that they will experience as satisfying. We provide the cognitive/behavioral/emotional/interaction model to equip the clinician with clarity in treatment planning. The therapist then can confidently proceed to help couples enhance their sexual pleasure and satisfaction.

Cognitive-Behavioral Therapy

Cognitive-behavioral therapy (CBT) is a theoretical model and system of psychotherapy that emphasizes the interrelationships among cognitions, behavior, and emotions in individuals' psychological and interpersonal functioning. All three domains contribute to personal functioning as well as the quality of interpersonal relationships. Because the three domains mutually influence each other, changing one of these components leads to changes in the others. Altering cognitions and behaviors can lead to changes in emotions, although direct intervention with emotion can also be effective. Changes in cognition can produce change in behavior, and vice versa.

CBT initially was developed to treat individual psychopathology, and it has been used to treat a wide range of disorders, such as depression, anxiety, eating disorders, and personality disorders. It has its roots in behaviorism of the 1950s, integrated with cognitive therapy models of Beck (1993) and Ellis (1975) and emotion-focused models (Greenberg & Johnson, 2010). Mindfulness components (e.g., Brotto & Woo, 2010) have been added to traditional CBT.

Beginning in the late 1970s, CBT increasingly has been applied to the treatment of relationship problems by integrating its concepts and methods with those of couple and family systems theory. Early versions of CBT for couples (Jacobson & Margolin, 1979; Stuart, 1980) focused on the association between relationship satisfaction and the degrees of positive and negative behaviors exchanged by the couple. In addition to strategies for increasing the proportion of positive to negative actions (e.g., behavioral contracts), therapists taught couples communication and problem-solving skills. Those behavioral components of CBT remain important for altering negative couple interactions, including those associated with SDs. Therapists also identify and intervene with cognitions that are barriers to behavior change (e.g., a standard that one should not have to ask the partner to behave in desired ways), as well as emotions that influence behavior (e.g., anger that leads the client to overlook the partner's attempts to behave positively) (Baucom & Epstein, 1990).

Epstein and Baucom's enhanced CBT model for couples (Baucom, Epstein, Kirby, & LaTaillade, 2015; Epstein & Baucom, 2002) addresses the rich interactions among cognitions, behaviors, and emotions in a close relationship, as well as the contextual influences of life stressors at the levels of the client's individual characteristics, couple dyadic differences, and external environmental demands such as work pressures. In the behavioral domain, it uses a variety of interventions to shift distressed couples' negative interactions toward constructive and satisfying patterns. Cognitive interventions address partners' selective perceptions of events, negative attributions about causes of relationship problems, negative expectancies regarding events that will occur, and inappropriate and unrealistic schemas (assumptions and standards). Interventions for emotions focus on enhancing emotional experience and expression when such feelings are inhibited or regulating volatile emotional responses. Jacobson and Christensen (1996) took another approach to broadening the scope of CBT with couples, developing a model that balances realistic and appropriate changes in couples' behavioral interactions via traditional communication and problem solving skill training with methods that increase partners' acceptance of aspects of each other and their relationship that are unlikely to change.

CBT principles and methods have been applied to understanding and treating SD. Recognizing the role of performance anxiety, Barlow (1986) applied CBT strategies to SD, focusing on distracting negative thoughts. Work on sexual scripts represents another application of cognitive aspects of CBT to SD. Epstein and Baucom (2002) provided detailed guidelines for identifying and modifying problematic cognitions, which are used with cognitions concerning SD. CBT principles have been a component of traditional SD treatments such as sensate focus, which modify couples' behavioral interactions, improve couple communication about sex, and decrease anxiety by reducing the danger and pressure that partners perceive in touching each other. CBT approaches to emotional aspects of SD include other interventions that directly reduce or enhance emotional responses. When clients are unaware of emotions that influence sexuality or are inhibited in expressing those feelings, CBT techniques that focus on emotion cues (e.g., mindfulness exercises) can increase positive emotions. Breathing and progressive muscle relaxation methods can reduce anxiety associated with sexual activity.

Integrative CBCST incorporates cognitive, behavioral, emotional, physiological, and interpersonal factors. Integrative CBCST techniques include in vivo systematic desensitization; keeping a diary of thoughts, feelings, and behaviors; psychosexual skill exercises; reality testing of cognitions; sexual rehearsal; visualization; relaxation training; positive psychology techniques; and meaning making. The complexity of SD is particularly rich and inviting for inclusion of CBCST strategies. The therapist has a wealth of opportunity for creativity to not only ameliorate SD but also to improve the couple's overall quality of life (Table 1.3).

In addition to SD, CBCST addresses problems such as sexual trauma, atypical sexual behavior, and stresses associated with sexual orientation. Unfortunately, the focus in the SD field has shifted more to the individual who has sexual difficulties and away from the couple relationship, particularly with the release of pro-sexual medications and other bio-medical treatments (Winton, 2001). While this gives the impression that SD has a single cause with a simple cure, clinical experience and

Table 1.3 Characteristics of CBCST

- Focuses on cognitive, emotional, and behavioral processes in the relationship
- Therapy process is structured and relatively time-limited
- Therapist collaborates with clients to set clear, measurable goals
- Therapist is moderately directive, using a psycho-educational approach
- Therapist teaches clients new skills (e.g. communication, problem-solving, cognitive restructuring, emotion regulation)
- Couples are assigned psychosexual skill exercises to practice at home

research validate the importance of a comprehensive, integrated approach. Effective treatments involve medical, psychological, and relationship components. This book describes such an integrative approach.

Contemporary Sex Therapy: Cognitive, Behavioral, Emotional, and Relationship Features

CBCST includes components that address cognitive, behavioral, emotional, and relational factors that promote couple cohesion, cooperation, and intimacy (Epstein & Baucom, 2002). Examples of *cognitive* dimensions include a positive attitude toward sex, a commitment to sexual health, and personal responsibility for pursuing developmental (lifelong) sexual growth. *Emotional* features include experiencing, accepting, and constructively expressing one's honest feelings about sex and one's body. *Behaviorally*, couples cultivate cooperation to ground their sexual pleasure in physical relaxation. They learn self-entrancement and role enactment arousal in addition to partner interaction arousal. The couple cooperates as an "intimate sexual team" who prioritize emotional empathy, forgive each other for prior disappointments, and view sexuality as an opportunity for intimacy and cohesion.

In CBCST, men and women develop cognitive, behavioral, and emotional skills that promote sexual health. The therapist utilizes clinical "tools" to assist couples to enhance sexual health, integrate sexual skills, and serve as a map for sexual growth (Metz & McCarthy, 2010b). Whether the clinician uses traditional sex therapy techniques (e.g., sensate focus) or creatively designs individual and couple psychosexual skill exercises, interventions promote affirmation and acceptance of the individuals and couple.

The Process of CBCST

Some sex therapy models focus on the function and meaning of sexuality indirectly through the individuation process, which emphasizes personal sexual responsibility rather than needing the other person's validation (Schnarch, 1991). The core strategy in CBCST is to facilitate change in attitudes, behaviors, and emotions, using psychosexual skill exercises as homework (McCarthy, Bodnar, & Handal, 2004). A vital clinical role is to explain, process, design, refine, and individualize psychosexual skill exercises. The goal is to enhance relationship and sexual satisfaction by improving partner communication, lowering sexual anxiety, developing realistic sexual and relationship cognitions, and increasing psychosexual skills.

CBCST usually begins with a 4-session assessment process, followed by 10–20 conjoint treatment sessions that include 2 sessions focused on relapse prevention. Integrated within CBCST are specific strategies and psychosexual skill exercises for each type of SD. Therapy provides flexibility and creativity so the treatment is individualized.

Sexual homework assignments provide a continuous process to identify tensions and anxieties, inhibitions and blocks, and deficits in relationship and psychosexual skills. The homework assignments provide the clinician the opportunity to conduct ongoing micro assessments of partner comfort, attitudes, cooperation, and emotions that guide the design of subsequent interventions. Blocks to sexual function are discussed, and strategies to promote cooperation and overcome the thoughts and behaviors that impede sexual function are designed.

Table 1.4 Key CBCST Interventions

- Psychoeducation for realistic sexual expectations and function
- Communication (expressive and listening) skills training
- Problem-solving skills training
- Substitution of mutually supportive and respectful interactions for aversive ones
- Enhancement of awareness and expression of inhibited emotions
- Emotion regulation skills training
- Coaching partners in evaluating the validity and appropriateness of their thoughts and sexual interactions

Some couples progress steadily, whereas others require extended therapy (Heiman & Meston, 1999). Couple improvement is easier when dealing with a life-long specific SD caused by sexual anxiety and deficits in sexual skills, and when the couple has a cooperative relationship, are motivated to enhance sexual satisfaction, and experience female SD. More difficult to treat are couples with chronic and unresolved relationship conflict, acquired male SD (especially low sex desire), a pattern of avoiding touch, and a narrow performance "pass-fail" approach to sexual performance (e.g., intercourse resulting in orgasm) (McCarthy & McCarthy, 2014). Table 1.4 outlines the key CBCST interventions.

The Classic Human Sexual Response Cycle

Sex therapy must be based on a model of human sexual response and function. Traditionally, SDs have been classified based on the Masters and Johnson (1966) physiological response model. They divided the sexual response cycle into excitement, plateau, orgasm, and resolution stages. Kaplan (1974) expanded this model to include sexual desire (Figure 1.1).

In reality, sexual response cycles vary for individuals and couples. One time a woman may progress sequentially through excitement, plateau, and have multiple orgasms. Another time she may reach plateau but not be orgasmic. With no muscle

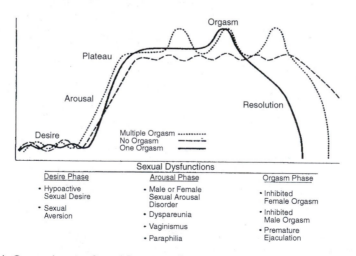

Figure 1.1 Comprehensive Sexual Response Cycle

contractions, congestion lasts longer and resolution occurs more slowly. A third time the same woman may go through excitement, plateau and orgasm quickly. In the treatment of SD, it is important to remember that orgasm is not the prime goal, although many clients have been socialized to focus only on that outcome. Pressure to perform interferes with sexual response for both women and men.

There are similar curves for the male sexual response cycle. Curve "A" is a man going through excitement, plateau, orgasm, and a refractory period. This refractory time becomes longer as he ages. Curve "B" is a man going through the stages without having an orgasm. Contrary to the myth of "blue balls," it is important for therapists and clients to know that women do not have to "service" men in order to avoid a physical problem. There will be congestion until the blood flows into resting circulation, but it naturally resolves. Curve "C" is a man going through the four stages quickly. Men who try to perform on curve "A" all the time experience performance anxiety. As anxiety increases, pleasure and spontaneity decrease, as does satisfaction.

There is an interesting physiological difference in the brains of men and women after orgasm. In men, there is a neurologic discharge from the hippocampus, which makes them sleepy. Women do not have this hippocampal discharge, and after orgasm may feel activated. Consequently, with heterosexual couples it is important to encourage men to stay involved with their partner after orgasm so they can enjoy hugging and non-genital touch before disengaging and going to sleep.

Desire

Desire is the core component of healthy sexuality. The desire phase involves sexual anticipation, fantasy, and yearning, as well as a sense of deserving for sex to be good for the person and relationship. Desire is promoted by positive anticipation, deserving, freedom, choice, and unpredictability. Fear, shame, coercion, and performance anxiety commonly contribute to inhibited sexual desire. In addition, sexual compulsivity or sexualizing emotions results in self-defeating, hyperactive sexual desire (Bancroft & Vukadihovil, 2004).

Excitement/Arousal

During the excitement phase, in addition to a subjective sense of pleasure and feeling turned-on, the man experiences erection and a few droplets of "pre-cum" from the tip of his penis. The woman experiences increased blood flow to her genitals, vaginal lubrication, breast swelling, and vaginal adaptation to increase receptivity to intercourse.

Plateau

The plateau phase is when arousal remains at a moderate to high level. Her body "settles in" (becomes saturated with pleasure). It is normal for his erection to decrease, to "take a break." Not understanding that this is normal, a man may panic, making an inference that he had lost arousal and his erection will not come back. Panic is a huge distraction, disrupting the plateau phase, with the anxiety making arousal difficult to regain. With relaxation and trust in his body, all that the man requires is gentle penile touch and his erection will easily come back from this "break." It is his sexual body's normal "wax and wane" erection process. This also occurs with female sexual excitement and lubrication.

Orgasm

Sexual pleasure peaks during the orgasm phase, accompanied by rhythmic contractions of the pelvic muscles and release of sexual tension. For a man, a sensation of ejaculatory inevitability, the beginning of the orgasm experience, precedes the contractions that result in ejaculation. Orgasm is similar for women, but more variable, flexible, complex, and individualistic. The woman might be non-orgasmic, singly orgasmic, or multi-orgasmic, which can occur in the pleasuring phase, during intercourse, or through afterplay. Men usually experience one orgasm.

Satisfaction

During the afterplay phase, the body gradually returns to the non-aroused state. Both a man and a woman experience "afterglow" and feel sexually satisfied. This can be a time of special emotional connection and build their intimate bond.

A New and Empowering Model of Female Sexuality: Responsive Sexual Desire

The classic physiological response cycle is characteristic of males and younger couples. The Basson model of "responsive female sexual desire" offers a balanced biopsychosocial perspective (Basson, 2001). Male sexual desire is more physiological and "proceptive" (initiating), whereas women's sexual desire is more "receptive" and energized by intimacy and pleasure. The responsive sexual desire/arousal formulation is particularly relevant to women. With aging, especially after 50, the responsive sexual desire model becomes relevant for men and couples. The responsive sexual desire model is what motivates midlife and older couples to value sexuality.

Men and women follow a similar physiological arousal sequence, although psychological and relationship factors are different (Fisher, 2004). Basson (2007) found that in long-term relationships, a woman's sexual desire becomes more integrated into her psychological system. In the beginning phase of a new relationship, romantic love/passionate sex/idealization lead to easy sexual desire and response. In a committed relationship (after 6 months to 2 years), this needs to be replaced by a mature sexual desire/function pattern.

In this model of desire and sexual response (Basson, 2007, 2010), women have a lower biological urge for the release of sexual tension. Orgasm is not necessary for satisfaction and does not need to occur at each encounter. Women's sexual desire is a *responsive* rather than a spontaneous event, influenced by subjective psychological excitement. While a young man's sexual desire may be energized by physical drive, a woman's sexual desire typically develops from her receptivity to sensual and/or playful touch. Touching leads to sexual desire and continues to pleasure, genital stimulation, arousal, and orgasm. Sexual desire develops *after* initial sensual contact.

Female sexual response often begins in sexual neutrality, but sensing an *opportunity* to be sexual, the partner's desire, or an awareness of *potential benefits* that are important to her and their relationship (emotional closeness, bonding, love, affection, healing,

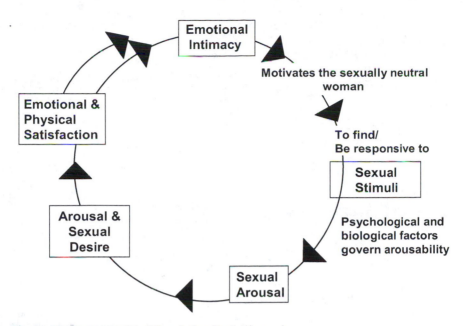

Figure 1.2 Basson Model of Female Sex Desire/Arousal

Source: Basson (2001) Reprinted with permission of the publisher (Taylor & Francis Ltd, http://www.tandfonline.com).

acceptance, commitment), she chooses to seek sensual contact and pleasure. She becomes aware of desire to continue the experience for *sexual* reasons and experiences heightened arousal. This brings a sense of physical well-being with added benefits such as emotional closeness, love, affection, desirability, and acceptance. This model acknowledges that sexual desire for men may be more biologically driven whereas for women it is more psychological and relational. Too often, men mistakenly believe sexual performance is more important than emotional intimacy. In fact, his female partner is likely to highly value personal attention, his presence, touch, and shared pleasure. It is important to note that with aging, more men experience responsive sexual desire. In addition, there are women who seldom utilize responsive sexual desire. Sexual desire patterns are variable, flexible, and individualistic (Figure 1.2).

The Importance of Sexual Function and Dysfunction Models

The model of sexual health and dysfunction that clinicians employ is important because models determine the therapist's assumptions about relationships, sexual health, and SD. This determines the clinical formulation, treatment goals, and therapeutic interventions. Imbedded in the model are fundamental clinical values such as whether the client values sex or views sex negatively, a focus on the individual or couple, as well as treatment objectives of relief of distress vs. promotion of relationship health. CBCST blends these features in a positive approach to sex, addressing both individual and couple aspects of functioning, and whether partners are satisfied with their relationship. Embracing a comprehensive model helps prevent misdiagnosis and shields the clinician from adhering to cultural preconceptions and stereotypes. The CBCST approach is centered within a broader integrative biopsychosocial model. Because clinicians tend to see what they expect to see (Groopman, 2007), it is important to base therapeutic efforts on a comprehensive model that guides assessment and treatment.

CBCST Within an Integrative Model

Understanding CBCST within the broader context of a biopsychosocial model provides the therapist a schema for comprehensive understanding of five basic domains of sexual health and satisfaction. Those domains are portrayed in Figure 1.3.

1. The first domain involves the *developmental* stages and relevant features of sexuality. The developmental feature emphasizes that sexual health is a lifelong process involving age relevant learning, growing, discovering, and integrating. Each life stage requires that individuals and couples adapt to physical and psychological changes that commonly present challenges. For example, sexual desire difficulties vary in meaning for an age 20 person, a middle-aged client of 40, and an aging 60-year-old.

    McKee et al. (2010) identified characteristics that are important for healthy sexual development: freedom from unwanted activity; an understanding of consent; education about biological and physiological aspects of sex; relationship skills; personal agency; lifelong learning; resilience; open communication; sexuality that is not aggressive, coercive, or joyless; self-acceptance; sex as pleasurable; understanding personal and societal values; awareness of public and private boundaries; and experiencing sexual self-efficacy.

Sexual Health & Satisfaction
Features of the Biopsychosocial Integrative Model

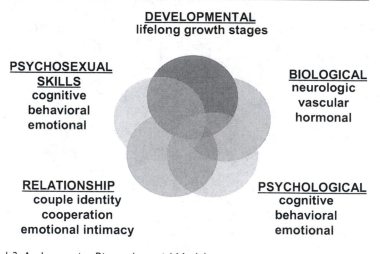

Figure 1.3 An Integrative Biopsychosocial Model
Source: From Metz & McCarthy (2011).

2. The *biological* domain includes the body and physiologic function: vascular, neurologic, hormonal, and health habits. Because the body is the foundation for sexual health, sexual physiology and function is important. A positive, realistic expectation of sexual function is a crucial component for individual and relationship satisfaction. Without reasonable expectations, clients are susceptible to hype, marketing misinformation, and performance pressures.

3. The *psychological* domain includes cognitions, behaviors, and emotions. The couple's cognitive, behavioral, and emotional responses influence their approach to sexual intimacy. Individuals' cognitions can detract significantly from the quality of their sexual experiences and damage a couple's relationship. For example, individuals commonly make negative attributions about the causes of SDs, such as inferring that a male's ED is due to a loss of interest in his partner, when that is not the case. Similarly, once a man has experienced what may begin as transitory ED, he may develop a negative expectancy that the next time he attempts to have intercourse it will recur, which elicits performance anxiety and a self-fulfilling prophecy. Unrealistic standards for sexual response also detract from sexual and relationship satisfaction. "Spectatoring," in which the individual self-consciously monitors and evaluates his response is a common contributor to SD.

   Other psychological factors influencing SD are anxiety and depression. Common symptoms of depression (e.g., low motivation, fatigue, self-criticism, hopelessness) detract from sexual functioning. In addition to specific sexual performance anxiety, disorders such as generalized anxiety and obsessive-compulsive disorder interfere with eroticism, intimacy, and satisfaction.

4. The *relationship* domain represents the partners' blend of cognitions, emotions, and behavioral interactions. Shared *relationship identity*, as well as assumptions and standards about their sexual relationship, affect the ways they behave sexually. In addition, their attitudes regarding *cooperation* and *collaboration* influence their ability to cope effectively with challenges posed by sexual difficulties. The relationship domain also involves the couple's behavioral patterns, including skills and coping styles. Couples who engage in negative conflict styles—such as one partner demanding and the other withdrawing or both avoiding—subvert resolution of issues and attainment of emotional intimacy (Metz & Epstein, 2002). A CBCST approach focuses on avoiding "power struggles," and instead building partner cooperation, altering negative emotions, and replacing them with positive and warm emotions (Table 1.5).

5. *The psychosexual skills* domain includes cognitive, behavioral and emotional lovemaking skills. These encompass the three basic sexual arousal styles, pleasuring skills, erotic scenarios, and intercourse scenarios, as well as flexible sexual techniques. The CBCST approach provides a wealth of practical psychoeducational and behavioral skills for enhancing couple sexual health.

Table 1.5 Cognitive-Behavioral-Emotional Dimensions Applied to a Relationship

Couple "Identity"—the composite of partner cognitions: assumptions, standards, perceptions, attributions, expectancies

Couple "Cooperation"—partner behavioral solidarity, interaction patterns, teamwork: constructive engagement vs. blaming or avoidance

Couple "Emotional Cohesion"—emotional acceptance, compassion, empathy, intimacy, and emotional solidarity

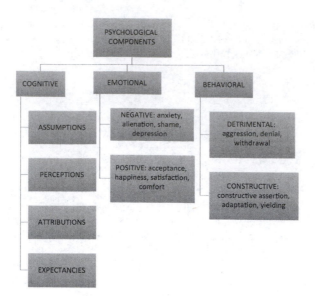

Figure 1.4 Enhanced Psychological Dimensions: The C-B-E Model

Understanding SD with the Enhanced Cognitive-Behavioral-Emotional Approach

The Cognitive-Behavioral-Emotional (CBE) model is based on Epstein and Baucom's (2002) enhanced CBT for couples approach. This provides crucial elements for understanding cognitions, behavioral deficits and excesses, and emotional factors that couples with SD experience. The CBE model recognizes that the cognitive, behavioral, and emotional components constantly interact, both within each person and between the partners. These factors interact—thoughts influencing emotions and behaviors, emotions influencing behaviors and thoughts, and behaviors influencing thoughts and emotions (Figure 1.4).

Cognitions

Epstein and Baucom (2002) describe five types of cognitions that affect sexuality: assumptions, standards, selective perceptions, attributions, and expectancies. These cognitions can be beneficial or detrimental depending on their effects on emotions and behaviors. Cognitions involve the ways that the individual thinks about self, relationship, and sex. It is crucial for partners to think accurately, positively, and reasonably about sex. Otherwise, for example, the client who sets unreasonable standards for sexual performance is likely to feel frustrated and be at greater risk of developing SD.

Behaviors

Behaviors may be constructive or destructive depending on their effect on the individual and couple's sexuality. Constructive behaviors include clear communication, cooperation, playfulness, and yielding. Detrimental behaviors include demanding, physical and psychological aggression, avoidance, and denial of responsibility. Behaviors regarding sex are choices that are moderated by thoughts and emotions, even though at times behavioral responses may seem immediate and impulsive. Epstein and Baucom (2002) differentiate between communication behaviors (which are intended to convey information and devise solutions to problems) and instrumental and expressive acts that serve a function of accomplishing a task or conveying caring. Distressed couples commonly escalate exchanges of aversive behaviors and fail to take actions to repair distress associated with such negativity (Gottman, 1994; 1999). Constructive skills for expressing thoughts and emotions, as well as for listening empathically, are core components of CBT with couples distressed about SD.

Emotions

The experience of emotions is based on a combination of physiological arousal and the individual's cognitive appraisal of the meaning of the physical sensations. The individual's attributions label the symptoms as some form of positive or negative emotion (e.g., fear, sadness, loneliness, anger, frustration, guilt, comfort, happiness, excitement). Emotional states both provide important information to the individual about her life experiences and act as "motivators" that prompt, penalize, or reward action. Emotions influence thoughts (e.g., one feels sad in the presence of a partner and thinks, "I don't love her anymore.") and behaviors (e.g., the sad person withdraws from the partner). Emotions associated with sexuality and one's body (e.g., arousal vs. shame or performance anxiety) (Everaerd, Both, & Laan, 2006) are important foci in CBCST.

The Five Kinds of Relationship Cognitions

Epstein and Baucom (Baucom & Epstein, 1990; Baucom et al., 2015; Epstein & Baucom, 2002) organized the cognitions that influence the quality of relationships into five basic types. Sexually satisfied couples hold reasonable, constructive, and cooperative cognitions, whereas distressed couples manifest detrimental cognitions. Table 1.6 summarizes these five types of relationship cognitions.

The subjective meaning of an experience is determined by each person's standards, assumptions, perceptions, attributions, and outcome expectancies. Partners

Table 1.6 Types of Relationship Cognitions

- **Assumptions**→what each believes people and relationships *are* like
- **Standards**→ what each believes people and relationships *should* be like
- **Selective Attention (perceptual)**→ what each notices about the partner, the relationship, and the emotional state, level of fatigue, prior experiences in similar situations
  - **Filtering, "selective abstraction"** (Beck, 1993), **"negative tracking"** (Jacobson & Margolin, 1979), or **"sentiment override"** (Weiss, 1980)—the selective attention that the partners are unaware of
- **Attributions**→ casual and responsibility *inferences or explanations* for relationship events; this serves to increase an individual's understanding and control over complex relationship events
- **Expectancies**→ *predictions* of what will occur in the future; outcomes or efficacy

---

Source: Epstein, & Baucom (2002). Reprinted with permission.

hold standards about desirable qualities of sex and relationships, assumptions about healthy and unhealthy behaviors, employ perceptual filters in noticing some events that occur while overlooking others (influenced by gender, social roles, and prior experiences), make attributions about causes of positive and negative experiences in their relationship, and make predictions about their own and each other's future actions as well as their power to alter them. We describe in detail how clinicians can assess detrimental cognitions that are unrealistic (e.g., "We should always have perfect sex") or inappropriately negative ("I am a failure as a lover").

Detrimental CBE Features with SD

Clients vary in the degree to which they focus on cognitions, emotions, and behavioral aspects of an SD. One partner may focus on emotional distress, the other on specific sexual behaviors or an expectancy regarding future sexual response. A comprehensive understanding of a couple's experiences with an SD requires assessment of all three domains.

Sex therapists have been known to say that the most important "sex organ" is between one's ears: the brain and one's thought processes. Emotional and behavioral responses can be automatic, occurring quickly without conscious planning. Cognitions play a major role in clients' sexual experiences. This is why we emphasize accurate and reasonable cognitions in CBCST. If a client has a standard that sex should always be perfect (i.e., as portrayed in movies) and does not realize the normal variability of couple sexuality, this sets up unattainable goals. When sex in real life falls short of the standard, she is disappointed and may make negative attributions about the cause, "Our sex life is poor so we've lost the chemistry." "Our relationship is flawed." Similarly, a male partner may hold an assumption that "a normal man always has automatic erections." When ordinary erectile problems occur, he misattributes the cause: "I can't perform because I've lost my virility. I'm over the hill as a lover." He may hold a negative expectancy, "My partner will lose sexual interest in me and be attracted by other men."

Individuals accept these negative thoughts as self-evident "truths," reinforced by the media hype about sex. Good Enough Sex (GES) principles help the couple challenge inappropriate and unrealistic cognitions (Metz & McCarthy, 2007). While we coach clients in using constructive sexual behavioral skills and moderating distressing emotional responses, we consistently intervene with the ways that clients think about sex, its role in their lives and relationship. *Meaning is at the core of relationship and sexual satisfaction.*

Case Illustration: Cognitive-Behavioral-Emotional Scenarios

Interactions among negative cognitions, emotions, and behaviors contribute to sexual distress and impede couple cooperation in solving sexual problems. The following is an example of a common distressed interactive pattern.

When the man has PE with negative cognitions ("failure") and emotions ("shame"), he feels performance anxiety, avoids discussion of the SD, and blames himself or his partner. In response, his partner may engage positively for a while, but when the SD becomes chronic, she feels rejected and avoids him. This creates secondary shame, anxiety, and alienation.

If the female partner experiences non-orgasmic response, she is likely to develop negative cognitions ("inadequate") and feel anxious. She may engage for a while (e.g., talk to her partner, read, talk with a friend, consult a doctor), but when the SD is chronic she increasingly avoids sex because of self-doubt and shame. Her partner also engages positively for a while, but when the SD becomes chronic, he expresses criticism about her sexual avoidance while internally he may be experiencing thoughts of rejection and worthlessness, along with feelings of hurt, loneliness, and anxiety.

Case Illustration: Mark and Sarah

CBE elements are illustrated by Mark and Sarah, a couple experiencing chronic ED. CBCST addresses this with cognitive restructuring and behavior change.

Mark:

Cognition: "I am a failure, I can't please Sarah. She is upset with me. I don't know what to do, sex is supposed to be automatic. I will fail again. What's wrong with me? This is hopeless!"

Emotions: anxiety, shame, frustration, embarrassment, sadness.

Behavior: avoidance, silence, verbal and nonverbal expressions of irritation when Sarah tries to talk about the ED.

Sarah:

Cognition: "I should be responsive. I should turn him on. He's not aroused, so I am a failure. He's quiet so he must be angry with me. I don't know what else to do. He feels terrible and it is my fault. He's going to leave me, punish me."

Emotion: anxiety, frustration, irritation, loneliness.

Behavior: tries to engage (e.g., "What's wrong?"), but eventually avoids, expresses irritation.

A key aspect of CBCST involves the therapist, with input from both partners, identifying circular processes in couple interactions that involve each person's influences on the other. For example, when one person complains about the other's lack of sexual desire, it angers the recipient and leads him to distance himself further, which then confirms the negative attribution that the partner does not care. Although changing the negative behavioral pattern can have a significant positive impact, it is crucial to identify and modify negative thoughts and emotional responses that either elicit the negative behavior or interfere with a shift to more positive interactions. In CBCST, sexual satisfaction is experienced as an *emotional* dimension, grounded in the *cognitive* dimension (the meaning attributed to the *behavioral* dimension).

What Clinicians Need to Know: Sexual Behavior

A core competency for sex therapists is remaining current with research findings regarding sexual behavior. Individuals and couples embrace accurate information to bring perspective on their sexual behavior and feel "normal." It is crucial to guide clients toward appreciating that sexual information in the media commonly involves distortions that undermine accurate understanding of one's functioning and contribute to unreasonable assumptions and standards. Most media information is based on convenience samples (e.g., readers of a particular magazine such as *Playboy*, college students, urology clinic patients, participants in pharmaceutical trials). These data are not representative of the overall population or the population of clients who present with sexual concerns. Solid representative data for the U.S. are available from the NHSL study (Laumann et al., 1994).

Accurate Information Is Powerful

Evidence-based information is an essential feature of CBCST for two reasons: (1) objective data inoculate the clinician from prejudice and preconceived notions; (2) representative data offer the individual and couple factual parameters about sexual problems. Informed knowledge promotes realistic sexual assumptions, standards, perceptions, attributions, and expectancies. Clients who feel stigmatized because of their SDs become more realistic—and hopeful—when they learn that 50% of couples have sexual difficulties. The married man who feels guilty about masturbation learns that the majority of married men (and a significant portion of married women) masturbate, at least occasionally. Representative data offer realistic reference points for clinicians and couples.

The *National Survey of Sexual Health and Behavior (NSSHB)* is a representative survey for persons in the U.S. between the ages of 14 and over 70 (Herbenick et al., 2010). Data about masturbation, oral sexuality, vaginal intercourse, and anal intercourse demonstrate wide variation in people's sexual behaviors. The NHSL study (Laumann et al., 1999), demonstrates the range of sexual behaviors, as well as the prevalence of SDs. Subsequent international studies have provided information regarding the prevalence of SD in countries around the globe (Laumann et al., 2005). Table 1.7 summarizes key research findings that can help clients develop realistic comparison points for their own sexual experiences.

Table 1.7 Sexual Behavioral Normative Data for Adults

- Men on average have had 6 sex partners, and women 5 sex partners
- 75–80% of men are sexually faithful, as are 80–85% of women
- Couple sex frequency is 1–2 times per week, more frequent (2–3 times a week) among younger couples. Regular sexual experiences are a characteristic of a satisfying relationship
- SD is "normal"—by age 40 virtually all men and women experience episodic and brief periods of SD. Distress occurs with prolonged, chronic SD
- Physically healthy men and women are sexually functional throughout their lives
- 68% of single men and 48% of single women masturbate
- 57% of married men and 37% of married women masturbate
- 27% of men and 8% women masturbate at least 1 time per week
- 94% of men and 84% of women have sexual fantasies more than several times per month

---

Source: Laumann et al. (1994) Used with permission of University of Chicago Press.

Frequency and Duration of Sex

Physical health is an important predictor of couple sexual activity. Age has a subtle rather than dramatic influence on frequency. As long as people maintain flexible standards about what constitutes good sex (forms of stimulation beyond sexual intercourse, plus less emphasis on orgasm as the criterion for satisfying sex), they can find a variety of ways to interact sexually that can be highly satisfying (Agronin & Robinson, 2014; Hillman, 2008; Kleinplatz, 2010). The best scientific data regarding couple sex—contrary to media presentations—show that adults do not have a secret life of abundant sex (Laumann et al., 1994). Among Americans between the ages of 18 and 59, one-third had sex as often as twice a week, one-third a few times a month, and one-third a few times a year. The average frequency of intercourse was 6–7 times a month. There is a slight decline in frequency with aging, and yet sexual satisfaction increases with age. For 70% of couples, the sexual encounter (including intercourse) lasted 15–45 minutes.

Love-Making Preferences

There is a wide range of sexual behavior preferences. The NHSL revealed that three-quarters of couples regularly engaged in oral sex (receiving, men = 79%, women = 73%; giving, men = 77%, women = 68%). About one-fourth of couples had engaged in anal intercourse at some time in their lives (men = 26%, women = 20%) and about 10% in the past year (Table 1.8).

Adult Masturbation

Many people learn negative or confusing messages about masturbation and believe that it is "bad," "wrong," or "sick." Masturbation can have a wide range of positive and negative functions and meanings. It is important for men and women to learn to regulate sex drive (including masturbation frequency) so that it supports sexual and relationship health (Table 1.9).

Men and women are very similar in their reasons for masturbating. Individuals masturbate when their partner is not available or is ill. Unfortunately, half of men and women report that they feel guilty about masturbating. In truth, adult

Table 1.8 The Appeal of Sexual Practices to Men and Women

	Men (%)	Women (%)
Vaginal intercourse	95	96
Watching partner undress	93	74
Receiving oral	79	73
Giving oral	77	68
Group sex	46	7
Lifetime occurrence anal intercourse (heterosexual)	45	55
Watching others do sexual things	40	17
Stimulating partner's anus with your fingers	26	15
Using vibrator/dildo	23	17
Anus stimulated by partner's fingers	22	18

Source: Laumann et al. (1994) Used with permission of University of Chicago Press.

Table 1.9 Frequency of Masturbation

Frequency of Masturbation

	Men (%)	Women (%)
Single individuals who masturbate	68	48
Married individuals who masturbate	58	37
Those who masturbate at least 1 time per week	27	8
"Always" or "Usually" orgasm with masturbation	82	61
Masturbation during the past year by education Level:		
+ Graduate degree	80	60
+ Did not complete high school	45	25

Source: Laumann et al. (1994) Used with permission of Edward Laumann.

Table 1.10 Reasons for Masturbation, by Gender

Reasons for Masturbation, by Gender

Reasons for Masturbation	Gender of Respondent (%)	
	Men	Women
To relax	26	32
Relieve sex tension	73	63
Partners unavailable	32	32
Partner doesn't want sex	16	6
Boredom	11	5
Physical pleasure	40	42
Go to sleep	16	12
Fear of AIDS/STD	7	5
Other	5	5
Total *N*	835	687

Source: Laumann et al. (1994) Used with permission of Edward Laumann.

masturbation is normal and healthy. The level of education influences the percentage of individuals who masturbate (better-educated individuals are more likely to masturbate). The most common reason that people report is to relieve sexual tension (Table 1.10).

Sexual Fidelity

Although the popular media report that most men and women are sexually unfaithful, the majority of men and women practice fidelity. The scientific data indicate that about 20–25% of men and 10–15% of women have engaged in extra-relationship affairs (Allen et al., 2005). Affairs typically disrupt a sense of safety, security and intimacy between partners, eliciting trauma symptoms in the betrayed individual. Consequently, when a couple presents with SD and a current or past affair, the effects of the infidelity must be taken into account in the treatment plan.

Orgasm

The NHSL data indicate that during partner sex 95% of men and 71% of women experience orgasm. Although the frequency of sex gradually lessens with age, the frequency of orgasm remains fairly constant, and levels of satisfaction increase. The increase in satisfaction has been associated with individuals' increased knowledge and acceptance of a wider variety of satisfying sexual behaviors that the couple experience (Kleinplatz, 2010).

Use of Erotic Material

NHSL data indicate that 41% of men and 16% of women regularly used erotic materials, including X-rated videos (23% men; 11% women), sexually explicit books or magazines (16% men; 4% women), and visits to a strip club with nude/semi-nude dancers (22% men; 4% women). With the growth of the Internet, access to erotic materials has increased significantly (Cooper & Marcus, 2003). Compulsive sexual behavior is almost exclusively a male problem (Kafka, 2014); the ratio of male to female occurrence is more than four to one. Cooper (1998) estimated that 6–8% of men are "addicted" to erotic materials, and more than two-thirds of people with sexual compulsivity problems use the Internet as a venue. Cooper, Delmonico, and Burg (2000) reported that 20% of "netizens" engage in some sort of online sexual activity, and 15% of Internet pornography viewers have online problems (Cooper & Marcus, 2003). Over-dependence on online erotica has a role in male and female SD (McCarthy & Metz, 2008).

Healthy Sexuality Is Learned

Sex for reproduction is a bio-physiological instinct, but achievement of psychosexual health involves a complex learning process. We learn sexual information, attitudes toward one's body, pleasurable sensations, and sexual scenarios and techniques. As infants and children, unless we experience abusive behavior, we learn that touch and being held is comforting and enhances feelings of safety. We learn that touching parts of our body—vagina, penis, labia, testicles, and anus—produce special pleasure. Sexual curiosity leads us to examine and experiment in a healthy systematic exploratory process. Children and adolescents progress at their own pace, guided by their curiosity and comfort level. A destructive feature of child sex abuse is that it interrupts and subverts the self-determining growth process. Sex, like other life skills, is best learned when the person is ready to learn; psychologists refer to this as "developmental readiness."

There is a variable sequence to growth in sexual health. Each person has her own "pace" of comfort and readiness for experiences of touch and affection as infants and children, curious explorations of touch, and information seeking about genitals and gender differences. Parents provide age appropriate explanations, and boundaries are learned from comfortable, supportive adults. A 4-year-old learns that yes, it feels good to touch her vulva, but that she should do that when she is alone in her room or the bathroom; that it is private. There is respect for the child's "readiness" when adults offer "matter-of-fact" teaching about her body, sensual feelings, and understanding of sexual feelings, going at a pace that responds to cues of comfort from the child.

Step-by-Step Progressive Sexual Learning

Children gain experience and grow, learn words for sexual body parts, self-touch, examine other children's bodies, learn boundaries acceptable to the adult world, and gradually progress in sensual-sexual experiences. To grow from playfully holding hands with a girl at age 3-or 4, to "playing doctor" with a neighbor child as a 6- or 7-year-old, to holding hands and kissing as a 10- or 12-year-old, to experimenting with breast fondling and genital touching as a 12–15-year-old, reflects a "natural progression" that is guided by the level of curiosity and comfort, and progresses in levels of sexual focus (Paikoff, McCormack & Sagrestanol, 2000). When this progression proceeds with self-determined "readiness" and age-appropriate spontaneity, it facilitates sexual health.

However, when this natural progression is interrupted by abusive sexual experiences or if it occurs "out of sequence," the child's sexual development is disrupted, fueled by internal sexual conflicts and broken trust of adults. Approximately one in ten men and one in three women report a history of sexual abuse, either in childhood or adolescence (Finklhor & Browne, 1985; Rellini, 2014). Sex abuse is a significant mental health challenge in general for both women and men, with increased risks for depression, PTSD and other disorders, as well as for SD. There is more stigma for men because "abuse is not supposed to happen to males." They worry about what it means, because the vast majority of sex perpetrators are male (adult or older adolescent). Males are more secretive and ashamed about sexual abuse and deal with it less well than females. It is crucial to confront the stigma and silence. Females and males deserve to have sexually healthy lives. Addressing a history of sex abuse is crucial in comprehensive CBCST. The focus is helping the client be a proud survivor rather than a shameful, anxious, or angry victim (McCarthy & Breetz, 2010; Rellini, 2014).

Childhood Sexual Experience

Studies estimate that the prevalence of childhood sexual experiences with peers ranges from 39% to 87%. Bancroft, Herbenick, and Reynolds (2003) found that 87% of males and 84% of females reported sexual experiences with peers prior to starting high school. Among very young children, this may involve asking to touch the other's genitals or kissing while pretending to be married. Pre-pubertal children "play doctor" and examine each other's genitals, chests, or swap stories about adult sexuality. Late grade school and middle school children frequently engage in kissing and light fondling, including direct genital stimulation. Forty-three percent of males and 30% of females reported there was erotica or pornography in their home as children, while many more—80% of males and 49% of females—reported having access to pornographic materials outside of home.

While parents, teachers, policy-makers, and others worry about childhood sexual experiences, it is important to understand that age-appropriate sexual exploration is part of sexual growth. A question is "What happens to children who have no childhood sexual experiences with other kids?" Males with no history of sexual experimentation found it more difficult in their 30s to experience sexual well-being. This reinforces the beneficial effects of "graduated and sequential" sexual experiences.

Comfort and psychosexual skills are learned step-by-step, over years of experience. Touching, kissing, hugging, fondling through clothes, fondling with clothes partially removed, laying together on a sofa or a towel on the beach, learning how these experiences feel—are healthy when the individuals are ready and it is welcomed, comfortable, and accepted.

When conducting CBCST, it is important to understand the individual's sexual learning experiences, including the positive or negative messages that he or she received about particular types of sexual behavior. The following are three important developmental sexual milestones.

> **Learning to masturbate**. How did the client learn about masturbation? Boys typically learn from talking with other boys and experimentation. Age when he first masturbated is an important developmental marker. Boys typically ejaculate with masturbation between ages 12 and 14 (Bancroft et al., 2003). Myths about the "dangers" of masturbation increase the difficulty of discussing this behavior. The history of masturbation is an interesting study in erroneous thinking, even among the medical community. Shame and silence perpetuate these myths, and are slow to die. Positive attitudes toward masturbation build a foundation for sexual health.

> **First intercourse**. Sexual activity has started at progressively younger ages, and condom use has become more frequent (Bancroft, 2009). Four of five individuals have intercourse before they reach age 21. Reasons for first intercourse include "curiosity" (24% women, 51% men), affection for partner (48% women, 25% men), physical pleasure (3% women, 12% men), wedding night (21% women, 7% men), peer pressure (3% women, 4% men), and wanting to have a child (1% women, 0% men). When first intercourse occurred and the person was not ready or did not want it, peer pressure was an important influence (29% of men and 25% of women), as was alcohol or drugs (3% of men and 7% of women) (Laumann et al., 1994).

> **Sexual problems and dysfunction in adolescence and young adulthood**. Although the vast majority of the literature on SD has focused on adult populations, there is evidence that adolescents and young adults commonly experience sexual problems as well (O'Sullivan & Pasterski, 2014). Because individuals' sexual experiences during their youth shape their sexual schemas and behavioral responses for life, understanding and treating sexual problems among the young is quite important.

Sexual Identity and Orientation

Although media descriptions of sexual orientation tend to focus on discrete categories (heterosexual, homosexual, bisexual, asexual), in reality orientation is complex, and there is evidence that it exists along continua (Morrow, 2006a). There still is much to learn about degrees to which sexual orientation is determined by biological, psychological and interpersonal factors. Orientation *identity* (see Figure 1-5) is best described as the composite of five features—(1) sexual attraction, (2) sex behavior, (3) fantasy arousal, (4) social preferences, and (5) emotional preferences (the gender the client feels most intimate with) (Diamond, 2008). A number of models of sexual identity development have been proposed, all of which describe a progression from earliest awareness of feelings, through some distress and increasing

The 5 Features of Orientation Identity

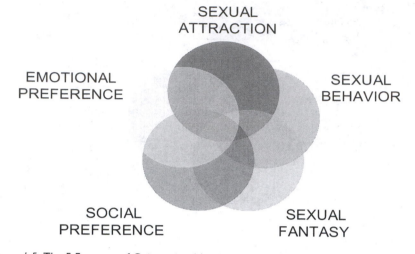

SEXUAL
ATTRACTION

EMOTIONAL
PREFERENCE

SEXUAL
BEHAVIOR

SOCIAL
PREFERENCE

SEXUAL
FANTASY

Figure 1.5 The 5 Features of Orientation Identity
Source: From McCarthy & Metz (2008).

acceptance of the self, to coming out to others and pride (Morrow, 2006a). Lives of gay, lesbian, bisexual, and transgender individuals universally involve discrimination experiences, and it is clear that social support from family of origin, "family of choice," and mental health professionals makes a significant difference in well-being (Cohen, Padilla, & Aravena, 2006; Elze, 2006; Nichols, 2014).

The NHSL study reported that 6% of men were *attracted* to other men, 5% engaged in same-sex *behavior* since turning 18, and 2% same-sex behavior in the prior year. In the NHSL study, 2.8% of men defined themselves as gay. Fear of homosexuality is very common among boys and adolescents (who worry about being "normal"), which adds to the prejudice against gay men.

Same-sex couples experience SD at a comparable frequency as heterosexual couples (Herek & Gernets, 2007), but it is important to avoid applying heterosexual standards for normative sexual responses to members of sexual minorities (Nichols, 2014). Same-sex SD is exacerbated by anti-gay social attitudes (including a myth that gay relationships are doomed to failure) and difficulties with the coming-out process. Sex therapists currently are at somewhat of a disadvantage in working with same-sex clients, particularly lesbians and bisexuals, due to limited research on sexual issues with sexual minorities. Furthermore, in spite of the fact that homosexuality was dropped as a diagnostic category of psychopathology several decades ago, therapists need to be culturally sensitive in examining their own biases toward variations in sexual orientation (Nichols, 2014).

Sex Throughout the Lifecycle

CBCST is based on a model of sexual pleasure and function that accepts changes over the lifecycle. Young adult males learn that sexual function is usually automatic and autonomous, requiring nothing but the presence of the partner. Biological reproduction is instinctive. However, in reality sexual function and satisfaction are subverted by myths and unrealistic expectations. Even in youth, there are multiple factors that can detract from sexual desire, arousal, and orgasm. Healthy sexuality is a biopsychosocial challenge. Furthermore, with aging come a variety of physical and psychological changes (e.g., menopause, systemic diseases such as diabetes and arthritis, life disappointments, role changes such as retirement) that have the potential to disrupt sexual response and satisfaction for both females and males. These changes are risk factors for SD. However, with reasonably good health, older adults continue to enjoy sex, adapt to the normal changes with aging, and report sexual and emotional satisfaction (Agronin & Robinson, 2014; Kleinplatz et al., 2009). In fact, Kleinplatz (2010) describes "lessons from great lovers" that focus on older couples' reports of ways in which they expanded their definitions of satisfying sexuality beyond sexual intercourse and created erotic and sensual shared adventures in their relationships. Psychoeducation components of CBCST are valuable in guiding older clients toward developing more flexible and satisfying sex lives.

Accurate Sex Data Provide Perspective

The elements that promote vibrant sexuality in older couples serve as guides for younger couples, especially a positive attitude toward sex and maintaining good physical health (Table 1.11).

Grounding CBCST on scientific data provides balance and an objective perspective about sexual concerns. Empirical data are value free and portray what people actually experience. Scientific understanding presents a different perspective than the marketing and hype in the media.

Healthy, Satisfying Sex Varies in Quality

Helping couples with SD involves promoting positive, realistic sexual expectations. Valuing variable sexual experiences and abandoning the need for perfect performance guards against SD by overcoming performance pressure and fear of failure. Positive, realistic sexual expectations of GES (Metz & McCarthy, 2012) engender sexual acceptance and immunize the couple from sexual problems with aging.

Table 1.11 Factors that Promote Vibrant Sexuality

- Good physical health
- Positive mental health
- Positive attitudes toward sexuality and body
- Sexual interest and activity
- Expectations of satisfying sexual function with aging (vs. "self-fulfilling prophecy" of sexual loss)
- Embracing the adjustments involved in coping with illness
- Adapting to the sexual attitudes and expectations of the partner
- Following healthy, age-appropriate lifestyle behaviors (e.g., sleep, exercise, weight management)

In well-functioning, satisfied couples, the quality in approximately 35–45% of encounters is very good, in 20–25% it is good for at least for 1 partner, in 15–20% it is okay but not remarkable; while 5–15% of sexual experiences are mediocre, dissatisfying, or dysfunctional (Frank et al., 1978). Embracing GES as normal and healthy is empowering (Metz & McCarthy, 2012).

Realistic expectations, empathy, and flexible cooperation promote sexual acceptance and satisfaction. Couples with SD experience frustration and alienation, leading to arguing and blaming that undermine the relationship. Healthy couples accept that variability in sexual quality is typical in well-functioning, satisfied relationships.

Axioms of Contemporary Sex Therapy

CBCST is enriched by being mindful of the precepts of contemporary sex therapy, as summarized in Table 1.12. These equip the therapist with realistic knowledge and sensitivity.

Cognitive-Behavioral Psychosexual Skills

In the chapters that follow, we describe (1) accurate sexual information to provide the framework for understanding clients' functioning, (2) the causes and effects of female and male SD, (3) guidelines and tools for assessment and diagnosis, (4) the major barriers to effective CBCST, (5) an overview for treatment of SD, (6) clinical management of female and male SD, and (7) strategies for designing an individualized relapse prevention plan. We include psychosexual skill exercises and guided therapeutic interventions, homework assignments, educational materials, individual and couple worksheets, as well as assessment materials.

Table 1.12 Axioms of Contemporary Sex Therapy

1. Sexual difficulties present the clinician an excellent opportunity to relieve distress and enhance quality of life
2. Sexual health is developmental and lifelong. People can be sexually satisfied into their 80s. The aging stage has subtle, important dimensions requiring accurate knowledge and sensitivity
3. SD is multi-causal and multidimensional, with multiple effects on the person, partner, and relationship
4. The ultimate aim of sex therapy is enhanced behavioral function, sexual self-esteem, and emotional satisfaction
5. The individual is responsible for her own sexual function in cooperation with the partner
6. Realistic, age appropriate sexual expectations are essential to individual and couple satisfaction
7. Clinical theory, research, and practice interact and are enriched when embedded in a comprehensive view of sexual health and satisfaction. Sexual health is more than an absence of problems
8. Sex is inherently relational, affecting the emotional life of the couple
9. When sex is a vital energy, it contributes 15–20% to relationship satisfaction. When it is dysfunctional, it contributes 50–75% to the distress
10. Comprehensive understanding of sexuality integrates medical, pharmacological, psychological, relational, and social/environmental factors

Crucial Features of CBCST

CBCST focuses on the interplay of cognitive, behavioral, and emotional factors influencing positive and negative sexual functioning. Physical and mental health are essential parts of the assessment and treatment plan. Biopsychosocial education for clients is important as well, to ensure realistic knowledge about sex function.

Normative sexual behavior guides CBCST. This provides perspective and reference points to anchor clinicians' and clients' realistic, reasonable expectations. In spite of the wealth of sex information available in evidence-based books, respected websites, and school and religious education curricula, even well-educated individuals often are erroneously educated about sexual function.

Summary

The ultimate purpose of CBCST is enhancing the well-being of the couple (Snyder, Castellani, & Whisman, 2006). CBCST is the treatment of choice for treating SD. Evidence supports the importance of the cognitive meanings that partners attach to their sexual experiences, and the complexity of the impacts that those meanings have on individual and couple sexual behavior and satisfaction. While SD is for the most part defined in terms of behavioral indices, the cognitive and emotional components are essential for understanding SD and conducting treatment to promote couple sexual and relationship satisfaction.

Evidence based biological, psychological, and social/relational information is an essential feature of CBCST. Understanding "what people do sexually" provides context for assessing a couple's SD. It protects the clinician from making erroneous assumptions of what is "normal." Knowledge is powerful. Realistic knowledge about one's sexual body, sexual psychology, and relationship health form the context for understanding and treating SD.

Key Points

- SD is very common, although sometimes veiled by other problems.
- SD is an exceptional clinical opportunity to improve quality of life.
- There are three core competencies crucial for conducting effective sex therapy: (a) accurate knowledge about sexual behavior and SD; (b) comfort addressing sexual difficulties; and (c) skills for designing and implementing comprehensive treatment.
- It is important to integrate evidence-based knowledge and quality-based clinical skills. Comprehensive treatment is guided by the biopsychosocial approach. SD is best treated as a couple issue.

Chapter 2

Engaging Clients and Conducting Assessment, Diagnosis, and Treatment Planning

In this chapter, we provide a framework for the clinician to engage clients and to conduct a comprehensive CBCST assessment within the biopsychosocial model. It is crucial that assessment sessions be comfortable for both the therapist and couple. Determining the cognitive, behavioral, and emotional features of SDs, as well as the couple's dyadic patterns, ensures comprehensive assessment, the basis for effective treatment.

Use All Available Biopsychosocial Resources

The CBCST approach is anchored in: (1) conducting a comprehensive biopsychosocial assessment that guides the selection of specific therapeutic interventions for the SD, impediments to healthy sexuality, and, if needed, medical and pharmacologic interventions; (2) ensuring a positive value for sexuality with a focus on sharing pleasure, and; (3) providing accurate information regarding psychological, biological, and social/relational factors influencing the client's sexual concerns.

Multiple findings of the assessment identify factors for treatment. Even when the primary finding is a medical cause, effective treatment will require individual and couple interventions to maximize cooperation, recovery from past negative experiences, and enhancement of sexual and relationship quality.

Strategies for Involving the Partner

There are significant advantages to using couple interventions to treat SDs, even though initially they involve one person's psychological and physical responses. If the client does not have a partner or the partner refuses to participate, assessment and treatment strategies are adaptable for the individual.

When conducting an initial phone interview, it is important to request that both partners attend the initial assessment session unless there are specific reasons not to. The client with SD commonly views the problem as an individual failure. The therapist can shift that perspective by emphasizing that a key goal of therapy is making the sexual relationship more enjoyable for both partners. The therapist guides the initial conversation to include a survey of multiple causes of SD and notes that therapy is best provided in a couple format so that the changes planned during sessions are implemented in the relationship. Initial resistance by the individual who sought treatment is common, due to self-blame as well as worry about the partner reacting negatively to a suggestion that he or she participates. The therapist explains the rationale that intimacy and sexuality is a couple issue, that SD has a distressing effect on both partners, that therapy is more efficient and successful when both partners address the SD, and that there is less relapse with couple therapy.

When the client reports that the partner will not attend therapy, the clinician should not assume that the partner is unavailable. Sometimes the client is reluctant to have the partner attend sessions, for a variety of reasons such as a desire to portray the partner as being at fault or not wanting the partner to have an opportunity to present an alternative view. The therapist can explore such barriers by asking the individual what she imagines might occur if her partner was included in the sessions.

The therapist pursues strategies to induce the partner to join the sessions. The therapist encourages the client to invite the reluctant partner and role-plays how that discussion could unfold. The therapist can write a letter to both partners, emphasizing the importance of both individuals' perspectives and inviting both to attend the initial session. Also, the therapist can ask the client's permission to call the partner to introduce himself and to describe the value of the partner's participation. These strategies encourage a hesitant partner to undertake conjoint therapy. This is important because: (1) the partner as well as the "identified patient" experiences distress regarding the SD; (2) the prevalence of comorbidity of sexual problems (e.g., female dyspareunia concomitant with male premature ejaculation) is high; (3) the SD often originated in the relationship and continues to occur in that context; (4) therapy is more effective when the partner is actively engaged in treatment; and (5) because relapse rates are much lower for couple than individual therapy.

It is common for an SD to become evident after a client has inquired about couple therapy for more generic presenting problems (e.g., "We have difficulty communicating"). Sometimes one or both partners bring up a sexual issue, but often it is only when the therapist asks about the couple's sexual relationship that the clients reveal a problem. Given the threats to self-esteem that commonly are involved in SD, it is important to spend the initial session exploring the history of the couple's relationship, including their strengths and positive shared experiences and any stresses that they have experienced (Epstein & Baucom, 2002). Establishing initial rapport with both partners is essential before addressing sexual problems.

The Clinician's Role and Responsibilities

CBCST requires the clinician to provide *clinical leadership*—to formulate constructive goals in collaboration with the clients, provide specific cognitive and behavioral tools, and promote individual and relationship satisfaction. CBCST introduces *realistic optimism* and hope for couples that are distressed, pessimistic, and fearful about facing their problems. Optimism develops as the couple learns new cognitive, emotion regulation, and behavioral skills. The therapist begins by focusing the clients' attention on producing small but meaningful changes, which increase a sense of self-efficacy and counteract their pessimism. Confidence that they can recover and grow is important, because couples who seek therapy commonly have reached the point where they believe there is little or no hope and that their relationship is doomed (Epstein & Baucom, 2002; Loudon, 1998). The therapist presents the approach as a collaborative one in which clients' preferences and goals are prominent. Client investment in change is greater when the couple believe they and the therapist are working as a team.

Coordinating the Client's Care with Other Professionals

Many clients with SD are evaluated or receive treatment from other health care professionals. However, medical evaluations of clients with SD by general practitioners and specialists such as gynecologists and urologists are limited in scope and fail to include psychosocial factors such as relationship conflict, affairs, individual psychopathology, and life stresses (Wincze & Weissberg, 2015). Sex therapists need to be aware of the information that has been collected in a medical evaluation (e.g., cardiovascular and endocrine function). Ideally, the clinicians communicate to ensure that assessment and treatment are coordinated and that treatments are working in synchrony (Leiblum, 2007). Pharmacotherapies are most effective when integrated with CBCST that addresses individual psychological factors and relationship dynamics (Althof, Rosen, Rubio-Aurioles, Earle, & Chevret-Measson, 2006).

Providing Education Regarding Sexual Function and SDs

Focused sex education is essential, as unrealistic assumptions and standards regarding sex are a perennial feature of SD. Education about sexual function can relieve anxiety and distress, as it normalizes variation in responses and provides optimism for developing satisfying, pressure-free sexuality. Educational tools such as books, pamphlets, worksheets, and trusted web sites augment therapist interventions in CBCST. It is important for the therapist to provide accurate sex information; reasonable expectations of the body and sex function; and cognitive, emotional, and behavioral skills that will result in satisfying and reliable sexual function. Psychoeducation includes promotion of healthy behaviors; especially sleep hygiene, exercise, and eating patterns. Therapists should not make assumptions about the clients' health behaviors, so a survey of health behaviors is a standard component of a thorough assessment. An advantage of conducting part of the assessment conjointly is that partners can serve as reliability checks on the information that each other provides regarding health behaviors (e.g., how much each person truly is exercising and sleeping).

Core Principles in SD Assessment

The clinician's positive perspective and comprehensive outlook is crucial to motivating the clients and guiding them toward realistic goals. The following precepts serve to anchor the therapist and couple and guide the therapy toward sexual health (Metz & McCarthy, 2007).

1. Real-life problems rarely have a simple cause and a simple cure, in spite of clients' longing for "quick fixes." SDs have multiple causes, are multidimensional, are usually complex, and have multiple effects on the person, the partner, and the relationship.
2. Satisfaction with one's sexual life is grounded in realistic expectations regarding physical, psychological, and relationship functioning. Unrealistic expectations precipitate frustration, a sense of failure, and personal and relational distress.

3. The emphasis on perfect sexual performance is self-defeating and needs to be replaced with realistic appreciation of Good Enough Sex (GES), which involves acceptance of the inherent variability in couple sexuality.
4. Regardless of the cause(s) of an SD, sex is a relationship problem affecting the emotional life of the couple.
5. While CBCST employs a number of standard interventions, treatment needs to be individualized for each couple, to match their characteristics and needs.
6. Effective treatment integrates medical, pharmacological, psychological, and relationship factors and includes an individualized relapse prevention plan. Be aware that problems may not be eliminated entirely, and improvement involves coping with chronic issues such as bodily changes associated with aging.

Comprehensive Evaluation

Comprehensive evaluation is crucial to identify all of the factors contributing to an SD and design an effective treatment. The clinician assumes that the client's initial self-diagnosis is usually incomplete. In the past (1970s and 1980s), clinicians assumed that 90% of SDs were psychologically caused, whereas currently physicians and drug companies have proposed that 90% have biomedical causes. Clinicians need to be alert to the range of biopsychosocial contributors to SDs. Assessment in CBCST addresses all sources of the SD as well as their impact on the individual and couple. This thorough assessment promotes use of all available resources—medical/pharmacologic, psychological, interpersonal, and social—to address the SD. A comprehensive biopsychosocial approach identifies and targets causes and effects specific to a particular SD, using comprehensive interventions rather than simply treating the symptom. This is easier said than done, because couples often want a simple remedy.

Clinical failures are due to professional myopia, only finding what we were looking for, forming an incomplete diagnosis, and providing limited treatment. The biopsychosocial model prevents this professional trap (Groopman, 2007; Halvorsen et al., 1988). Approximately one-third of couples seeking therapy for one SD have multiple psychological, relational, and sexual problems (Loudon, 2002). For example, female non-orgasmic response may also involve psychosexual ("lovemaking") skill deficits, or male erectile dysfunction (ED) can co-exist with a woman's dyspareunia. A detailed cognitive-emotional-behavioral assessment involving both partners helps sort out etiologies and effects to promote efficient, comprehensive CBCST.

Three Phases of Assessment

Three areas of assessment assist in developing a CBCST formulation of SD:

1. consideration of the biopsychosocial context and comprehensive *causes and effects*;
2. determination of the *severity* of the individual and couple levels of distress; and
3. formulation of cognitive, behavioral, and emotional *change goals*.

It is valuable to use multiple assessment methods that provide a comprehensive overview of presenting problems. Clinical checklists and other assessment tools are invaluable aids. The SD Diagnostic Decision tree and diagnostic Summary Sheet are valuable assessment guides (Metz & McCarthy, 2003).

The Importance of Detailed Cognitive-Behavioral Sexual Assessment

A detailed analysis of a couple's sexual interaction, including cognitive, emotional, and behavioral components, sheds light on the determinants of an SD. Information about origins (e.g., past physical abuse of the partner; an affair) and current features of couple conflict (e.g., frequent verbal aggression) can reveal specific processes that are contributing to an SD. Events in each partner's personal history (e.g., neglect, attachment issues, alcohol abuse) and current psychopathology (e.g., depression, personality disorders) are identified as complicating the sexual relationship. The assessment identifies unreasonable performance expectations ("I should always have an immediate erection") or psychosexual skill deficits (e.g., lack of awareness of one's own or the partner's arousal pattern) that need to be included in a treatment plan.

Some cognitions are expressed spontaneously or are tapped easily by a therapist's questions (e.g., "What do you think is causing your lack of sexual arousal when your partner touches you?"), whereas others are covert and only partially manifested during a clinical interview. It is important to inquire about "automatic thoughts" and emotions that each member of the couple experiences in response to the other's actions. For example, the therapist asks, "When your partner starts to hint about having sex, what goes through your mind? What emotions do you experience?" Questionnaires such as the Sexual Desire Inventory (Spector, Carey, & Steinberg, 1996); Golombok Rust Inventory of Sexual Satisfaction (GRISS; Rust & Golombok, 1985); and the Derogatis Sexual Function Inventory (DSFI; Derogatis & Mellisaratos, 1979) can be useful for obtaining greater detail about each partner's cognitions and emotional experiences, although they are susceptible to social desirability response bias (Davis, Yarber, Bauserman, Scherr, & Davis, 1998).

Assessment of cognitions has the goal of identifying each partner's assumptions, standards, perceptions, attributions, and expectancies related to the SD. For example, unrealistic, perfectionistic, and rigid performance standards contribute to SD (Nobre, 2009). The couple that "expects" a female to experience orgasm every time or a man to have vigorous intercourse for 20 minutes before ejaculating are setting standards that are very difficult to achieve in real life couple sexuality. Women who enjoy sex do not experience or even necessarily want orgasm every time. The average duration of intercourse varies from 3 to 7 minutes (Rowland & Cooper, 2011).

Similarly, negative expectancies produce self-fulfilling prophecies. Thus, an individual who holds an expectancy of "I'm going to lose my erection before satisfying my partner" is likely to be distracted from focusing on erotic stimulation and experience anxiety, resulting in losing his erection just as he fears. Identifying erroneous cognitions provides specific targets for cognitive intervention.

The behavioral *functional analysis* component of the assessment involves specific descriptions by each partner of the sequences of events occurring—the who, what, when, where, and how—during sexual interactions. Each person's behavioral responses are stimuli and consequences for the partner. Couples typically do not fully understand how much they influence each other's behavior, as such patterns typically unfold very quickly and such self-awareness is limited. Individuals tend to notice their partner's behavior more than their own. Therefore, conducting a behavioral functional analysis not only helps the clinician assess behaviors influencing an SD; the therapist's feedback about the couple's behavioral patterns expands perceptions and understanding of key actions that the clients can make conscious efforts to change (Epstein & Baucom, 2002).

Comprehensive assessment involves *establishing rapport* by creating an empathic, comfortable environment. This requires the therapist's comfort in discussing sexual feelings and behaviors. Typically, the client follows the clinician's emotional lead and openness. From the first interaction, the clinician models comfort addressing sex and respecting the values of the couple.

Building Clinical Rapport: Comfort and Structure for the Sexual History

Every culture has its areas of "taboo"—death, finances, and politics are common ones. The client's private sex life is a major taboo. We publicly and openly joke about others' sexual behavior but conceal the truth about our own sex life. This makes it difficult to address SD. Therapist comfort in addressing sexual issues is an essential clinical skill (Risen, 2010). Clients intuit our level of professional comfort about sex, and will disclose in accordance with that milieu. At the same time, it is important to appreciate that the therapist is a product of a culture that considers sex a taboo topic. It is difficult to talk with clients about their sex life without feeling at least somewhat awkward. It is important for clinicians to view inquiry regarding sex as a legitimate and essential area for clinical attention, and to affirm the value and importance of sex as a positive element and source of energy in our clients' lives. Conveying one's ease and the appropriateness of asking about sexual details increases the likelihood that clients will become comfortable disclosing.

Client Barriers to Comfort

Individuals and couples commonly under-report distress regarding SD (Metz & Seifert, 1993); some couples focus on SD as a diversion from other issues such as mental health problems, secrets (e.g., compulsive masturbation, paraphilia, sexual orientation, affairs, domestic violence, drug abuse), or unexpressed couple conflict. It is common for a couple to present for therapy saying, "We have a wonderful relationship—except for sex." Other couples state that sex has "ruined" their lives; they are sexually "incompatible" and on the verge of divorce. This variability in presentation indicates the complexity of meanings that individuals attach to SD. Navigating through initial clinical presentations is best approached with patience and thorough evaluation.

Few people are exempt from embarrassment and shame that clients feel when they experience SD; these distressing emotions can be expressed through bravado, tears, depression, or self-blame. Because SDs commonly make clients feel embarrassment or shame, it results in the clients keeping secrets about their problems. The therapist's skill at developing rapport and creating an atmosphere of safety is crucial to elicit the assessment information needed to develop an appropriate and effective treatment plan.

Common barriers to client self-disclosure involve mistrust of the clinician or partner, fear of exposing embarrassing personal information, anxiety that the problem is incurable, or fear of being judged for one's sexual lifestyle. In spite of reluctance to self-disclose, clients generally want and expect the professional to inquire about their sexual situation (Ende, Rockwell, & Glasgow, 1984; Metz & Seifert, 1993), and respectfully address sexual concerns. The therapist's role is to create a context in which clients can tell their sexual stories and feel understood and supported (Risen, 2010).

The clinician needs to be aware, comfortable, and clear about professional boundaries, as well as skilled at taking a sexual history as easily as any other clinical history. The clinician helps clients overcome fears by assuming a non-judgmental attitude. It is easier to elicit information if one's questions are open-ended and provide the client permission to disclose sensitive information. Letting the client know that now is a good time to address sexual concerns and calmly listening facilitates the person speaking freely. Adopting an empathic "matter-of-fact" stance conveys to clients that sexual problems are common and can be resolved.

Ameliorating Client Discomfort

The following are examples of how a therapist can reduce the emotional distress of clients who are experiencing SDs. The therapist listens for underlying emotions, cognitions, and behaviors experienced by a man suffering anxiety or sadness while attempting to act as if nothing is wrong except for his sexual performance. His anguish manifests in avoiding sexual contact with his partner to prevent another experience of "failure" and shame. In another case, the therapist taps into a woman's confusion, diminished self-esteem, and anxiety elicited by her problem with experiencing orgasm. The therapist notices that the woman projects her self-blame and sense of failure as anger toward her partner, who she perceives as critical and rejecting. In either of these cases, in order to gather more information that can help the clinician test initial hypotheses, the therapist needs to create an alliance with both partners. The members of the couple then sense that the therapist cares about their distress and can help them improve SD and feel better about themselves.

The clinician's providing information about his or her professional training and background in working with sexual problems can help demonstrate expertise and openness. In addition, discussing therapist-client confidentiality principles is not only an ethical requirement, but crucial in promoting client comfort and security. Most important is demonstrating one's comfort in talking about sexual issues with warmth and empathy. These are among the highest rated qualities that people seek in a sex therapy professional (Metz & Seifert, 1993) (Table 2.1).

Table 2.1 Qualities Clients Want in the Professional

98%	→	Empathy, warmth, comfort in talking
93%	→	Professional excellence, well-trained
91%	→	Confidentiality, trust, security
70%	→	Not embarrassed
48%	→	Rapport
46%	→	Humor
30%	→	Leadership, clinician brings up sexuality topics
22%	→	Seriousness

Source: Metz & Siefert (1993) Used with permission of Sex Information and Education Council of Canada (SIECCAN), publisher of The Canadian Journal of Human Sexuality.

Table 2.2 The Value of Straightforward Discussion of Sex

Interviewing which is positive and affirming:
* serves to ameliorate shame and embarrassment
* affirms and respects sexuality
* validates the importance of sex in one's life and relationship
* indicates openness to personal growth
* counters media "hype" and unrealistic expectations of sex

Source: Metz & Siefert (1993) Used with permission of Sex Information and Education Council of Canada (SIECCAN), publisher of The Canadian Journal of Human Sexuality.

These qualities invite honest discussion and serve to reduce client anxiety and hesitancy (Table 2.2).

Common Barriers to the Professional's Comfort

Few clinicians are comfortable addressing all sexual issues. Studies document the need for specific sex therapy training (Miller & Byers, 2009, 2010).

The most common barriers for clinician comfort (Giami, Chevret-Measson, & Bonierbale, 2009; Risen, 2010) are:

1. fears of being invasive and being misunderstood; violating professional boundaries;
2. personal self-consciousness and embarrassment;
3. fear of giving too much emphasis to sex or seeming "strange";
4. not knowing what to do with a sexual concern that may surface; looking foolish or unprofessional;
5. not having a schema for conducting the sexual history.

Fears of being invasive or misunderstood. Clinicians can conduct an inquiry to collect crucial information about SDs without being unnecessarily invasive to the client's privacy. This involves adopting warm and matter-of-fact inquiries focused on the SD and its accompanying cognitions, emotions, and couple behavioral interactions, to achieve a clear functional analysis. Clients bring their own notions of what to expect of sex therapy, often based on talk shows or movies. To protect against being misunderstood, a brief explanation of the purpose and process of conducting a functional analysis to understand factors influencing the SD is good practice.

The therapist needs to be aware of the possibility of a client having ulterior motives, such as a desire to win over the therapist in blaming the partner. It is important for the therapist to present a balanced approach to listening and talking with the clients, expressing empathy for both parties' experiences (Epstein & Baucom, 2002). It is helpful to explicitly tell the couple that the goal is for both clients to feel heard and comfortable, so they are motivated to participate in sessions and resolve the SD. Obtaining clinical supervision is a valuable resource for developing clarity and solid boundaries, as well as for discussing complex dynamics in therapist-couple alliances.

Many clinicians are not interested in providing sex therapy. However, because sexual concerns are so prevalent, whether explicitly identified or hiding beneath the surface of other presenting complaints, the clinician has a responsibility to provide professional attention to sexual problems. This will vary according to the clinician's expertise, interest, and values, but at a minimum it involves a careful assessment of sexual issues and implications for treatment referrals. The PLISSIT model (Annon, 1974) describes levels of professional involvement in dealing with sexual issues. Every clinician can provide basic sexual health care.

The PLISSIT model describes four levels of clinician involvement with aspects of clients' sexual lives. Virtually all professionals can provide acceptance, convey a positive value for sexuality, and offer permission for pleasure and sexual function. Such permission ("P") includes openness to addressing sexual concerns: "How do you feel about your sexual relationship" or "Some clients notice a change in orgasm after surgery. What is your experience?"

Therapists provide accurate sex information based on the best scientific evidence. Give limited information ("LI") such as "Yes, depression and anti-depressant medication can have detrimental effects on sexual function" or "Yes, intermittent SD is common". Specific suggestions ("SS") include "Sharing worries with your partner can help" and giving suggestions for bibliotherapy, psychosexual skill exercises, and medical interventions. Intensive Therapy ("IT") involves CBCST. With experience and supervision, professionals develop comfort with sexuality, expertise with sexual interventions, and ability to provide an affirming therapeutic climate (Figure 2.1).

With clients who are shy or apprehensive, a brief explanation of the purpose of the inquiry is helpful. For example:

> I would like to learn more about what you are thinking and feeling when you experience SD. What happens and what do you think and feel about this experience? This helps me understand you so we can design a helpful intervention.

The Learning-Attitude-Behavior (LAB) interview approach. Client comfort with the clinician's approach can be aided by the LAB approach, which provides a comfortable way to address delicate areas of sex history by proceeding from the past to the present, and from cognitive to behavioral dimensions. It is more comfortable to be asked, "What did you learn about masturbation as a child?" followed with "What is your attitude about masturbation now?" The clinician becomes comfortable asking "How often did you masturbate as an adolescent?" and

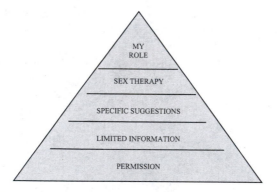

Figure 2.1 PLISSIT Model

Table 2.3 Sexual History Interviewing: Learnings, Attitudes, Behaviors

---

L → Learnings: "Who taught you about sex?" "What did you learn about touching...? Intercourse...? Oral sex...?"

A → Attitudes: "What did you think about...then?" "What do you think about...now?"

B → Behaviors: "How old were you when you first had intercourse?" "How often did you have intercourse?" "How often do you...now?" "How often would you like to have...?"

"How often do you masturbate now?" This level of comfort comes from repeated practice, beginning with role-plays in graduate courses or professional workshops.

The LAB Sex Interview moves from areas of less responsibility (what one was taught) to more personal responsibility (current attitudes and behaviors) (Table 2.3).

Clinician self-consciousness and embarrassment. The therapist can promote both her comfort and that of the clients by developing accurate sexual knowledge, realistic clinical expectations, and a framework for conducting the assessment and sexual history. This affirms the therapist's professional expertise and builds confidence in talking about sensitive topics. The therapist models comfort for the clients by affirming the value and importance of sexuality. An example of an introductory inquiry is: "An important aspect of a valued relationship is your sexual life. Does your sexual relationship contribute to positive feelings or is it an area of concern?" "How do you feel about your sexual relationship?" "How do life stresses affect your sexuality?" "When sex does not go well, what thoughts do you have?"

The therapist's comfort will be strengthened by rehearsing in front of a video camera or practicing taking a sex history with a professional peer. It is a process of desensitization. The following exercise helps identify the therapist's areas of discomfort and embarrassment regarding sexuality, with implications for how to set appropriate boundaries on what he discusses with clients.

Personal Exercise 2.1: Reflections for the Clinician

What I learned about sex growing up:

I learned about sex from:

- Parents.
- School.
- Siblings or peers.
- Society (TV, media, magazines).
- Religious community.

From these sources, I learned that sex is...

What I now think about sex (attitudes):

Sex is valuable, especially:

Sexual behaviors that I believe are not acceptable:

I am most comfortable sexually with:

I am most uncomfortable sexually with:

What I have experienced sexually (behaviors):

I feel most negative (uncomfortable, ashamed, unhappy, angry) with these sexual behaviors:

I feel most positive about these sexual behaviors:

My comfort focusing on sexual issues in therapy (clinical skills):

The feelings that present barriers to my discussing sex with clients are:

The things that I learned from my sexual life that are helpful to me as a clinician:

Another exercise that can promote the therapist's personal comfort with sexual issues is "Youthful Sexual Experiences":

Personal Exercise 2.2: "Youthful Sexual Experiences"

Experiences with peers are a common way to learn and grow sexually. Sexual experiences as a child, adolescent, and young adult help establish feelings about your body and sexuality. In retrospect, how do you feel about your childhood and adolescent/peer sexual experiences?

1. What sexual exploratory experiences did you have with peers—with children within 1 year of your age when you were 2–5 years old? Within 1–2 years when you were 6–12? Within 1–3 years when you were 13–18?
2. What were your sexual experiences with older or younger peers? How did you feel then about the experiences? How do you feel now? Was there a "power difference" involving intimidation or coercion?
3. How ready were you for different sexual experiences? How did this influence your feelings of comfort or anxiety regarding sex? How did you feel about the behavior at the time? Now?
4. What motivated you to engage in sexual exploration—Curiosity? Hostility? Rebelliousness? Fear of rejection? Loneliness? Peer pressure?
5. What are your feelings now about your youthful sexual experiences?
6. How do these feelings help/hinder your comfort as a therapist?
7. How do they influence your clinical objectivity in addressing clients' sexual issues?

Fear of giving too much emphasis to sex. Therapists sometimes fear that they are taking too much time, giving too much emphasis to sex, or seeming "strange" (unprofessional) to clients. They have grown up in a society in which people do not openly discuss sex, and the legitimacy of focusing on sexual topics *in one's professional role* is not clear. Given those societal taboos, the fear is that clients will view the therapist's focus on sex as inappropriate. This is part of a broader issue that all professionals who work with sensitive topics face—accepting that it is not only appropriate but essential to collect the information needed to understand client problems and design effective treatments. To avoid certain topics is to conduct an inadequate assessment. Thus, in exploring a man's history regarding ED, it is important to obtain information about his experiences with other partners (e.g., fear of pregnancy, arguments, intimidation, alcohol misuse), in addition to information about how he interacts now sexually.

Not knowing how to deal with a sexual concern. Not knowing what to do with a sexual concern is a major reason why clinicians evade sexual inquiry. No one wants to look foolish, incompetent, or unprofessional. Clarifying one's role within the PLISSIT schema provides focus and clarifies boundaries. Give oneself permission not to know everything. Using an organized approach to assessment, developing a comprehensive biopsychosocial treatment plan, understanding the components of effective CBCST, using appropriate psycho-educational resources, and being aware of referral resources increase clinical confidence.

If a clinician has limited expertise regarding sexual function and dysfunction, consider making a referral to a respected sex therapist. Clients find this helpful and respect the professionalism conveyed by the message, "I'm pleased you shared this important concern with me. I want to be helpful, but this is a problem that I don't specialize in. I believe referring you to a competent clinician is best." Have a roster of respected professionals for referrals.

Two scenarios warrant referral. First, if the therapist's past personal sexual experiences and current feelings are a significant barrier to addressing certain sexual issues, it is wise to refer. Second, when clients present a specific clinical problem that challenges the therapist's confidence and objectivity, it is appropriate to refer. When we understand and respect our limits, we benefit our clients by referring them to a respected colleague. Scheduling a consultation with the potential referral to obtain his or her feedback can help the clinician decide about the referral. Remember that the couple's well-being is the priority, and referring out is an effective intervention.

Lack of a schema for conducting the sexual history. Sexual problems warranting therapeutic attention are commonly veiled behind descriptions of other concerns, such as depression, anxiety, and relationship conflict. Clients' failure to mention sexual issues might be an intentional avoidance, or because other concerns are more compelling. Conversely, when clients describe sexual problems it may signal the need to explore whether sex is a cover-up against acknowledging other issues that are more threatening. For example, when a client describes "sexual incompatibility" it may mask fear of having made a mistake in committing to the partner.

A therapist's discomfort with discussing sexual concerns may arise from lacking an organized format for conducting the assessment. The complexity and ambiguity of clients' presenting problems can be intimidating, so confidence that one knows how to conduct a systematic assessment will contribute to therapist comfort. It also provides the structure for the clinical formulation and treatment plan.

Even if the clients' initial presentation is unrelated to sex, assessment includes a question about the sexual relationship. When the couple responds, "We have no sexual concerns," the interview can move on. Later the therapist can follow up with an inquiry, "You mentioned you have no sexual concerns, but I am wondering how your sex life helps you adapt to the problem that you describe."

There are three levels of a sexual history:

1. the initial question
2. the brief sexual history
3. the extended sexual history

The initial question is an open-ended probe about the couple's sexual satisfaction. "Sexuality is an important dimension in a relationship. How do you feel about the quality of your sexual life?" This question opens sexuality for discussion. If the couple's response is avoidance, probe further, "Okay. Tell me what you most value about your sexual life." Alternatively, the therapist can make a note to revisit sexuality further down the clinical road.

When a sexual concern does emerge, the therapist uses a brief sexual history as the guide for investigation. Some clinicians use extensive pencil and paper assessment tools that make the interview more efficient.

Interviewing Issues

Whether the sex history is brief or extended, it is crucial that the therapist investigates and understands the *specifics* of the couple's sexual activity. Without specific descriptions there is a strong risk of misdiagnosis. For example when a woman says she has lost sexual desire, a detailed inquiry may reveal that loss of desire is rooted in secondary non-orgasmic response. A couple may initially present with ED, but the details they provide may indicate that the accurate diagnosis is severe PE— his fast ejaculation triggers distress for the couple with subsequent disengagement (Loudon, 1998). In these cases, therapy would fail because it does not address the characteristics of the core SD. Thus, the interviews must focus on sexual and interpersonal behaviors and the cognitions and emotions that accompany them.

The Brief Sexual History

The brief history (Ende et al., 1984) addresses the following topics:

1. What is the problem?
2. What is its onset and course?
3. Why does the client think it is a problem?
4. What attempts have been made at a solution?
5. What does the client want?

Illustration of the Brief Sexual History

The initial contact with Sean and Colleen identified ED as the couple's concern. During the initial session, the brief sex history interview progressed as follows:

(What is the problem?)

Therapist:"Please describe the problem you're having with erections."

Sean:"Well it seems that anytime we try to have intercourse I lose my erection."

Therapist: "So you usually get an erection, but when you try to penetrate, your erection goes down. What's your perspective, Colleen?"

Colleen: "Well, sometimes Sean has trouble getting erect and puts pressure on himself. Most of the time when he tries to go inside me he loses what erection he has and gets very frustrated. I don't even want to have sex then."

(Onset and course)

Therapist: "When did you first notice the problem?"

Sean: "Oh, I don't know; maybe 2 or 3 years ago."

Colleen: "Wait, Sean! It's more than 4 years, I remember trying to talk to you about it, but you clammed up and would get irritated if I brought it up. That's when you began to avoid being sexual with me."

Therapist: "Does that fit your memory Sean?"

Sean: "Close enough."

Therapist: "So once you began to have difficulty, describe the pattern that developed."

Sean: "At first it did not happen all the time and I didn't think much of it. After a couple of months however it happened more and more."

Therapist: "Is that how it seemed to you Colleen?"

Colleen: "Yes, and the more it happened the more frustrated Sean got and the less he would try. If I tried to bring it up he would be irritated and avoid me."

(Why the Client thinks it is a problem)

Therapist: "What do you think caused the problem? What are your theories?"

Sean: "I thought at first it was a medical problem because it got worse."

Colleen: "I didn't know what to think. I worried he didn't find me attractive anymore after two kids."

Sean: "I can tell you, that's not the problem."

Therapist: "Okay, so tell me how you remember thinking about the problem as it developed and what the problem means to you now."

Sean: "At first I didn't know what to think and worried that I had a medical problem like on the TV ads. I saw my physician about a year ago, and we ruled out a medical problem. He gave me Viagra, and it did work, but I didn't want to keep using it, as I'd get uncomfortable sinus pain."

Colleen: "Oh, I didn't know that, Sean..."

Sean: "I was too embarrassed. I was a failure and knew I couldn't sexually please you unless I took a pill. That sucked."

Colleen: "I wish I had known, Sean, so we could talk about it. I could have told you my disappointment was not about your erections but that you would get so frustrated and disconnect from me. I was worried for you, didn't know what to do, and thought it must be me. I felt really abandoned."

(Attempts at solutions)

Therapist: "It sounds like each of you felt very hurt, anxious, and alone. Tell me how you attempted to deal with the difficulty."

Sean: "I tried to tell myself just to perform, but it didn't work. It didn't make sense because I'd never had an erection problem before. I didn't know what to do; I tried to ignore it, hoping it would just get better. I felt like a real failure not being able to please her."

Colleen: "At first I tried to be supportive and do things that I thought would turn Sean on, but nothing seemed to help, and I thought it must be me, that he didn't find me attractive any more. I couldn't understand why he wouldn't want to talk about it, so we could figure out how to deal with it."

Sean: "But it's MY problem. And I just feel so frustrated and know you're incredibly disappointed in me sexually."

Colleen: "I wish you'd talked to me about it..."

(What the Client wants)

Therapist: "It is good you can begin to talk about it now. What are you learning?"

Colleen: "We've gotten to a bad place."

Sean: "Yep, we haven't been living in the same world, and it's entirely my fault! I don't know what to do, but I hope you can help me."

Therapist: "Well, I'd like to help you both get to a new and better place. Let's talk about what you want to accomplish."

Sean: "I just want to get back to always having erections."

Colleen: "I want that too, but I want to get frustrations out of our bedroom."

Therapist: "Well, I don't know that having erections "always" is a reasonable goal, Sean, but having reliable erections most of the time, knowing how to handle the times you don't, and working together as an intimate team to prevent frustration is reasonable. What do you think?"

Clinical Observations:

Using the brief sex history provides the therapist with a perspective, and begins to open the couple to working together as an intimate sexual team. Notice the detrimental cognitions that surface ("I'm a failure," "I worried you weren't attracted to me."), the behavioral deficits (avoidance), and painful emotions (frustration, embarrassment, loneliness). These are areas for therapeutic intervention. Inquiring about these important features reveals the specific processes occurring, provides understanding of each partner's distress, and paves the way for designing an effective treatment plan.

The Extended Sexual History

Investigating detailed sexual behaviors is particularly important for clinical understanding. A common practice is to conduct the brief sexual history in an initial session and to request that the partners complete pencil and paper sexual surveys to provide background for the extended history. This involves a specific description of the couple's sexual interactions. Each partner is asked to describe their lovemaking, including not only the behaviors, but also their internal cognitions and emotions. Specifically, the topics covered are:

1. Quality of sexual discussion outside bedroom.
2. Sexual frequency; regularity.
3. How each partner anticipates and prepares for sex: cognitive, emotional, and behavioral components.
4. Initiation roles.
5. Place and environment of lovemaking.
6. Who does what, when, how, where, why.
7. Style: mutual or taking turns.
8. Each partner's cognitive focus before, during, and after sexual encounter.
9. Duration of each phase of sexual interaction.
10. How the couple handles difficulties.
11. Where in the lovemaking process the SD occurs.
12. Partner congruence in their descriptions.

Partners often do not concur on even basic behavioral data such as frequency. The important dimension in CBCST is not the concurrence between the clients' reports, but rather each person's cognitive interpretations and meanings attached to behavior. Their emotional experiences also are especially important (Everaerd et al., 2006).

Simms and Byers (2009) reported that women over-estimated their partners' desired frequency of sex, whereas men were accurate in their perception of the females' frequency desires. The more frequently partners engaged in sexual activities and the more similar their ideal sexual frequency, the higher their couple sexual satisfaction. The therapist inquires about these parameters and helps the couple reach consensus on their goals.

Conducting Comprehensive Sex Dysfunction Assessment

Understanding the Complexity of SD

Clinicians tailor their assessment for efficiency. However, as we have noted, it is crucial that the assessment include specific descriptions of the couple's sexual behaviors, cognitions, and emotional responses.

Assessing those areas of the biopsychosocial model ensures that initial causes, concomitant problems, secondary and maintaining causes, and detrimental effects are captured. Clients value a thoughtful, careful assessment, not first impression assumptions. It is important that couples receive a thorough evaluation to identify (or rule out) medical or mental health conditions influencing SD. This typically requires that the therapist collaborate with other professionals.

Identification of Causal Factors

Assessment is intended to identify not only the current characteristics of a couple's sexual problem but also its sources (depression, unresolved relationship conflict, diabetes, performance pressure, PTSD) and effects (relationship alienation,

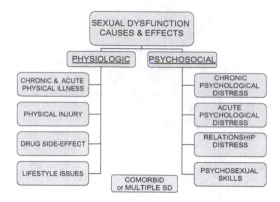

Figure 2.2 Potential Causes and Effects of Sex Dysfunctions

performance anxiety). Typically, there are several sources as well as maintaining factors in SD.

It is rare that an SD has a simple cause and a simple treatment. Rather, a number of elements co-occur and play contributing roles. While physiologically the pathogenesis may be a pharmacologic agent's impact on orgasm, the psychological and interpersonal factors that may interact with that biological cause are complex. The same element (for example, the cognition that one is "a failure") can have different effects. In one case, such negative cognitions reinforce a sense of powerlessness regarding loss of desire, whereas for another client the same negative cognitions inhibit orgasm. Why this occurs is not well understood.

The constellation of developmental experiences, current psychological health, specific cognitions and emotions, and interpersonal and relational factors presents a challenging but intriguing picture that calls for careful evaluation. To the extent that the clinician helps clients conceptualize their situation as a challenging mystery that they can work on solving as a team, the potential for a constructive assessment process increases (Figure 2.2).

The Comorbid or Multiple SD combination indicates that there is more than one SD in one-third of cases (e.g., Loudon, 1998).

Lifelong vs. Acquired SD

Determining the chronicity of SD—lifelong vs. acquired—provides useful clues to the etiology as well as implications for treatment planning. The inquiry regarding onset investigates when the problem began. The context refers to whether the SD occurs in all situations or only in a specific situation (e.g., with a partner vs. during masturbation). These differences provide "clues" that narrow the treatment focus. SDs that are lifelong and occur in all situations focus the clinician's attention on biological or significant psychological factors (Table 2.4).

Assessing Biophysiological Factors

Physical health is important for healthy sexuality. What is good for the body facilitates sexual desire, function, and satisfaction. SD can be caused by several biophysiological factors.

Table 2.4 Assessing Lifelong and Acquired SD

Assessing SD: Following the Diagnostic Clues: Onset & Context

	Onset & Context		Type or Source
1.	Lifelong & All	→	Neurological system or psychological system
2.	Lifelong & Variable	→	Psychological system or psychosexual skills
3.	Acquired & All	→	Biological: illness, injury, drug side effect
4.	Acquired & Variable	→	Psychological distress or relationship distress

Chronic and acute physical illness refers to medical illness that directly inhibits sexual response, such as hormonal deficits that inhibit desire, cardio-vascular illness that restricts arousal, and prostatitis induced PE. Illness characteristics that interfere with the neurologic, cardiovascular, or endocrinological systems impede sex function. SD frequently occurs with chronic and acute illnesses and injuries including heart disease, cancer, stroke, lower respiratory diseases, injuries from accidents, Alzheimer's disease, diabetes, pneumonia, kidney disease, blood poisoning, liver disease, hypertension, epilepsy, and Parkinson's disease (Enzlin, 2014). Virtually any illness, medication, or excessive lifestyle factor has the potential to contribute to SD. It is important to keep in mind that although an illness is associated with SD, the effect is not universal. Thus, diabetes is a common source of ED, but this occurs in less than half of type I diabetic clients, and is less frequent when the disease is well managed.

Physical injury assessment focuses on whether there has been trauma to the genitalia or neurologic system. Accidents resulting in physical trauma can have detrimental effects on sex function. There is usually an interactive element between the physical, psychological, and relationship dimensions. For example, injury to genitalia during military combat involves not just surgical interventions but the man accepting the "new normal" of his body and the acceptance and support of his partner.

Drug side effects in SD are very common, given the extensive use of prescription and over-the-counter (OTC) agents (Balon & Segreaves, 2005). Antihypertensive and antidepressant medications have detrimental sexual effects. Medications do not affect everyone the same—the role of cognitive expectations and dosage are crucial factors. For example, a man who began anti-depressant medication experienced PE, but when the dose was raised, he no longer had PE but developed ED, and when raised to a higher dosage, no SD. Some SSRIs are associated with low sex desire in women, and delayed ejaculation in men. Cold medications and antihistamines are often associated with desire and arousal problems. It is important that clinicians be aware of sexual side effects of medications, including OTC medications (Ashton, 2007; Wincze & Weisberg, 2015).

Lifestyle issues also are important factors that must be assessed. Lifestyle practices such as drinking and over-eating are associated with SD. Men who smoke have a higher risk for ED (Bach & Brannigan, 2016). Another important factor to consider in assessment is that health behavior habits typically are learned within the family and are affected by other family members' ongoing behaviors (Campbell, 2005). Consequently, clinical interventions may be needed at the couple and family level in order to have an impact on an individual's health behaviors affecting SD. The social factors include the couple's attitudes and behaviors regarding sexual health as well as the influence of the family and culture. When medical factors are suspected, it is wise to refer to a physician who is knowledgeable about SD (Tables 2.5 and 2.6).

Table 2.5 Guidelines for Referring to a Physician

It is good to have a primary care physician (family practice, internist) and to regularly schedule a physical examination. How regularly?
If the person is in good health and
• Younger than 30 years old, at least every 5 years
• 30–45 years old, at least every 4 years
• 45–60 years old, every 2 years
• 60 or older, every year

Refer for a medical evaluation if:
• The person is taking medication on a regular basis.
• Has a family history of diabetes, heart disease, endocrine disorders, or multiple sclerosis
• Genetic or lifestyle problems (e.g., sleep disorder, smoking, over-eating)

Table 2.6 Assessing for Physical Factors in SD

1. *Chronic & acute physical illness:* consider medical issues in the circulatory, neurologic, hormonal, or urologic systems. There are a number of illnesses that can cause SD:

Alcohol abuse	Diabetes
Sleep disorders	Peyronie's disease
Hypothyroidism	Polyneuropathy
Lipid abnormalities	Cancer
Systemic lupus	Arthritis
Parkinson's disease	Hypopituitarism
Multiple sclerosis	Epilepsy
Chronic renal failure	Hypogonadism
Cardiovascular disease	Sexually transmitted diseases
Toxemia	Urinary tract infections
Prostatitis	Cerebral tumor
Arteriosclerosis	Endocrine abnormalities
Chronic pain	Sleep apnea
Respiratory illness	Severe allergies

2. *Physical injury:* Pelvic surgery, prostate surgery, genital injuries, or neurologic trauma
3. *Pharmacological side effects:* A number of medications, OTC drugs, and illegal drugs. Has the client begun taking (or withdrawn from) an antihypertensive medication, mental health medication, or chemotherapy?
4. *Health habits:* Does the client have problematic health patterns such as smoking, poor cardiovascular conditioning, overtraining, sleep deprivation, drinking, overeating, or drug abuse?

Common medical factors associated with female arousal disorder and ED are alcohol abuse, diabetes, sleep disorders, cardiac disease, lupus, sexually transmitted infections, and pharmacology agents. Female non-orgasmic response and ejaculatory inhibition are associated with medical issues such as diabetes, sleep disorders, alcohol abuse, and side-effects of medications. Medical problems commonly associated with inhibited desire are hormonal disorders, thyroid problems, alcohol abuse, diabetes, and sleep disorders (Verschuren, Enzlin, Dijkstra, Gertzen, & Dekker, 2010).

Physiology Is the Foundation

It is essential that mental health oriented clinicians keep in mind that physiology is the foundation for sexual function, and for medically oriented clinicians to keep in mind the profoundly powerful psychological and relational factors. The body is the foundation on which psychological and relationship health is built. Negative effects on vascular, hormonal, and neurologic systems cause SD for both men and women. Accurate knowledge of how the body functions is the underpinning for realistic sexual expectations. Poor health habits, illness, medications, or unrealistic sexual expectations cause disappointment, frustration, and SD. With good physical, psychological, and relationship health, sexual function is lifelong, matures and grows, increasing in quality and satisfaction when couples accept normal aging processes (Dennerstein, 2010; Hillman, 2008; Kleinplatz, 2010).

Assessing Psychological and Relationship Factors

Psychosocial factors are common barriers to satisfying sexual function. Classic features of SD are performance anxiety and "spectatoring" (distraction from pleasure by monitoring one's sex response).

Chronic psychological distress refers to persistent psychological problems such as depression, bipolar disorder, generalized anxiety disorder, and obsessive-compulsive disorder. These require concomitant or prerequisite treatment. Sexual shame, sexual trauma, and body dysmorphic distress present barriers to sex function and satisfaction. It is crucial that the sex therapist assess for individual psychological difficulties. It is important to avoid singling out one client as the "identified patient" because that creates perceived inequity in the therapeutic alliance with the couple. When one member of a couple has a psychological disorder, the clinician needs to be sure to include ways in which the partner can make changes to improve the couple's relationship (Epstein & Baucom, 2002).

Acute psychological distress is a common cause of SD, especially adjustment disorders with depression and/or anxiety features (Laan & Both, 2011). The emotional distress that occurs when an individual experiences acute stressors (e.g., auto accident, job loss, death of a loved one, violence) is unsettling for the individual, and his attention is focused on negative cognitions about the stressors. Unfortunately, even when the acute emotional distress is resolved, sexual function does not automatically return, particularly if the individual has developed negative self-talk and expectancies of sexual failure. CBCST is necessary to treat the SD and regain sexual comfort and confidence.

Relationship distress involving disruptions in couple cohesion can precipitate SD. These include unresolved relationship conflict, alienation, and distrust—whether

Table 2.7 Psychological and Relational Factors in SD

1.	*Chronic psychological distress*: Does the client have a personality disorder or significant mental health problem?
2.	*Acute psychological distress*: Is the client dealing with current psychological stresses such as depression, anxiety, work stress, parenting, or loss?
3.	*Relationship distress*: Does the couple experience relationship distress such as emotional conflicts, alienation, loneliness?
4.	*Knowledge and skills deficits*: Do the members of the couple lack knowledge about their own and each other's body? Do they have deficits in their abilities to counteract detrimental cognitive, emotional, and behavioral features of SDs? When a client holds unreasonable expectations about sexual performance, is he able to evaluate and challenge them? What self-soothing skills does the client have for reducing emotional distress when experiencing SD? Do the clients lack sensual skills or interpersonal skills such as warmly talking of sex and cooperating to make sex comfortable?

overt or covert. The presence of disagreements is less problematic than the interaction patterns that couples engage in during conflict (Metz & Epstein, 2002). Conflicts become destructive when they involve behavior patterns such as one partner demanding and the other withdrawing, mutual avoidance, or escalation of verbal attacks, as well as negative cognitions (e.g., negative attributions about the partner's malicious intent) and unregulated negative emotion (anger, anxiety).

Psychosexual skills deficits are a common contributor to SD. Sex education focuses on anatomy, but rarely on sex function or psychosexual skills. Lovemaking is subverted by unrealistic fantasy sex portrayals in movies, pornography, soap operas, and romance novels. It is difficult for partners to obtain realistic information regarding sexual function. Psychosexual skill deficits are virtually universal with SD. Examples of psychosexual skills that commonly are relevant for particular SDs and need to be addressed (McCarthy & McCarthy, 2012) are:

- *Desire problems*—learn to create bridges to desire, enhancing attraction exercise, design preferred sexual scenario
- *Female non-orgasmic response*—identify and utilize "orgasm triggers", practice PM exercises, utilize multiple stimulation before and during intercourse
- *Female sexual pain*—dilator therapy, mindfulness exercises, guided intercourse intromission and coital thrusting
- *Premature ejaculation*—stop-start technique, circular thrusting, PM exercises
- *Erectile dysfunction*—wax and wane of erection exercise, multiple stimulation during intercourse, partner guided intromission at high levels of erotic flow
- *Ejaculatory inhibition*—enhance subjective arousal, transition to intercourse at high levels of erotic flow, use "orgasm triggers" (Table 2.7).

Identifying Comorbid or Multiple SDs

While many clients identify their SDs accurately, others do not, or focus on only one factor. For example, a couple presenting with PE on more thorough assessment identifies the comorbid difficulty of partner pain during intercourse. Or a couple may report ED when they do not know that it is normal for an erection to subside

Table 2.8 Comorbid and Complicating Features

- Physical/sexual abuse history
- Sexual identity disorder
- Sexual orientation secret
- Variant arousal
- Deviant arousal
- Issues of sexual fidelity
- Sexual compulsivity
- Preference for masturbation with pornography

after ejaculation. Or a female's low sex desire is a manifestation of a sexual trauma history that has not been treated effectively. Loudon (2004) found that one-third of couples presenting with SD experienced concomitant sex problems.

In addition to multiple co-occurring SDs, it is crucial to pay attention to other sexual concerns, especially secrets. Risen (2010) differentiates between sexual material that is *private* (information that does not directly affect the couple's sexual relationship but that the individual feels uncomfortable about sharing with the partner, such as occasional fantasies about an attractive neighbor) and *secrets* (material that does affect the couple's relationship, such as a paraphilia, affair, or unresolved sexual trauma history). It is important for the therapist to learn about secrets that are contributing to an SD and encourage the client to share this information so it can be dealt with therapeutically (Table 2.8).

Comprehensive Assessment: Cognitive, Emotional, Individual Behavioral, and Couple Interactional

The clinician addresses the complexity of male and female sexuality and relationship dynamics through assessment based on the biopsychosocial model. In addition to medical and mental health factors, sexual problems involve cognitive, emotional, and behavioral components (Epstein & Baucom, 2002).

The client is encouraged to keep written logs of cognitions, behaviors, and emotions, as well as record their impressions about the links among them. The Couple C-B-E Interactional Analysis Worksheet is helpful for this purpose. This assessment guides the clinician's understanding of factors contributing to a couple's SD and provides each partner a "look from the outside" to change their cognitive appraisals that have been negative, blaming of self or other, or pessimistic (Figure 2.3).

The clinician facilitates uncovering the couple's relevant cognitions, emotional responses and behavioral patterns. Eliciting descriptions of their sexual arguments produces important data. For example, a gay man discusses unrealistic sexual expectations (depending on his partner to ensure that he is sufficiently aroused), emotional sexualizing (misinterpreting emotions such as anxiety as sexual), behavioral deficits (rushing to oral sex or anal intercourse as soon as an initial erection occurs), and "spectatoring" (regarding the firmness of the erection). His partner interprets (makes an attribution about) the partial erection and quick loss of it as an indication that he is unable to arouse him and has a negative expectancy that their relationship is destined to deteriorate and end. The partner then behaves defensively and avoids sex, leaving the individual feeling lonely, rejected, and inadequate.

COUPLE C-B-E INTERACTIONAL ANALYSIS WORKSHEET
Michael E. Metz, Ph.D.

Name:_____   Name:_____

1 cognitions: # 4 cognitions:

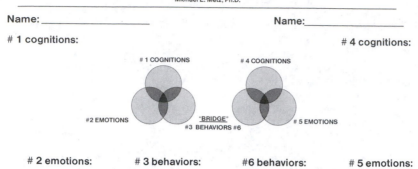

2 emotions: # 3 behaviors: #6 behaviors: # 5 emotions:

Figure 2.3 Couple C-B-E Interactional Analysis Worksheet

During the assessment, the clinician collects information about the cognitions, emotions, and behaviors, summarizing the pattern for the couple. The clinician then provides accurate information to the couple regarding sexual function (e.g., factors enhancing or detracting from arousal and erection) and teaches them strategies to alter, blend, and integrate new ways of thinking, feeling, and behaving.

Couple conflicts commonly are rooted in rigid scripted sexual standards, stereotypes of male and female sexuality, and a failure to integrate sexual thoughts, feelings, and behaviors. Cooperation to create positive and satisfying sexual interactions involves both partners paying attention to their cognitions, emotions, and behavioral responses. Resolving relationship conflict deepens intimacy (Metz & Epstein, 2002).

Relationship and Sexual Cognitions

Appreciating the complexity of couple dynamics is facilitated by awareness of relationship cognitions (Baucom, Epstein, Kirby, & LaTaillade, 2015). The members of the couple continuously process information, with many opportunities for cognitions to be distorted or unrealistic. Distinguishing the types of cognitions and the emotions and behaviors associated with them offers an empowering view into the complexity of sexual distress and strategies for therapeutic amelioration.

Awareness of the five kinds of relational cognitions (assumptions, standards, perceptions, attributions, expectancies) is an invaluable assessment schema for CBCST. Operating in both the relational and sexual domains, changes in cognitions can help alleviate SD and increase sexual satisfaction.

Partners hold *standards* about characteristics they believe sex and relationships should have, *assumptions* about healthy and unhealthy behaviors and how human sexual response works, employ *perceptual filters* (influenced by gender, socially constructed roles and past experiences) that lead them to notice only particular aspects of events, make *attributions* about causes of events, and hold *expectancies* about future events as well as their ability to alter these. Cognitions distinguish couples that have profound disruption over SD from couples who experience difficulties that do not escalate into distress. The same events take on different meanings, leading to different emotional responses and behaviors. Some couples with SD experience distress, whereas others who attach more benign meanings to the SD are sexually satisfied (Byers & Grenier, 2003).

Table 2.9 Detrimental Cognitions, Emotions, and Behaviors Associated with SD

Detrimental cognitions:

Standards:
- "Sex is immoral, bad."
- "I am unattractive, undesirable."
- "I am a failure, disappointment, poor lover."
- "We are incompatible sexually."
- "Her pleasure requires my full erection." "His erection requires me to be sexual."
- "The way a partner should show you that he finds you sexually attractive is ..."

Assumptions:
- "Most couples do not have sex problems."
- "Older people cannot enjoy sex."
- "Normal sex is automatic."
- "Sexual problems inevitably cause divorce."
- "Thinking about upsetting topics during sex will prevent PE."
- "If a man loses an erection, he's unlikely to get another one."

Selective Perceptions:
- "She is angry all the time."
- "He never acts like he's interested in me."
- "My partner always wants to avoid the problem."
- "I'm the only one trying to fix our sex."

Attributions:
- "We rarely have sex because my partner doesn't find me attractive."
- "My sadness about our sexual relationship means that I don't love my partner any more."
- "He is not erect. He doesn't love me."
- "She is not having orgasms; I am inadequate."

Expectancies:
- "No matter what I try, it will not be enough."
- "We'll never have a normal sexual relationship."
- "If we try to make love I won't perform, and we'll fight."
- "My partner will be upset and go to someone else. We'll get divorced."

Distressing emotions promoted by negative cognitions:
- Embarrassment and shame
- Anxiety, fear
- Loneliness
- Frustration, anger
- Sadness, depression
- Numbness, dullness, coldness

Destructive behaviors emanating from negative cognitions and emotions:
- Avoidance of sex
- Yelling, threats, blame and counter-blame, verbal aggression
- Defensiveness
- Apologizing, patronizing, hitting self or partner
- Withdrawal, shutting down, ignoring the partner, pouting

Negative cognitions elicit negative emotions. The standard "A man with ED is a failure" promotes depression. The cognitive expectancy, "If we try, I won't get it up" elicits anxiety (McCarthy, Bodnar, & Handel, 2004). Identifying cognitive-emotional-behavioral factors that accompany SD—the distorted cognitions, negative emotional responses, and behaviors such as avoidance—provides access to the rich complexity of experiences in their relationship. Without addressing the complexity of partners' inner lives, attention focuses solely on behavioral changes that are unlikely to occur as long as other factors operate as barriers.

Individual and Couple Satisfaction

Ultimately, relationship and sexual satisfaction is an *emotional* response (e.g., warm feelings of attachment). It is grounded in the individual's *cognitions* (e.g., accurate attributions, realistic expectations) regarding the partners' *behaviors* (e.g., sexual skill, cooperation) (Table 2.9).

Assessing Cognitive Components with SD

Self-reports offer the clinical opportunity to discuss and correct clients' unrealistic standards and assumptions, as well as erroneous perceptions, expectations, and attributions. The major self-report method to assess cognitions relevant to SD is through clinical interviews, as well as selective use of questionnaires. The clinician listens for clients' descriptions of cognitions as they talk about SD. For example, individuals voice their attributions for problems (e.g., "He doesn't get or keep erections when we make love because he isn't interested in me"). The clinician can ask specifically about particular types of cognitions (e.g., "What do you think has been causing your drop in sexual desire?"). When a client refers to his own or a partner's behavior with terms such as "always" or "never," it is a cue for the clinician to explore selective perceptions, as few behaviors always or never occur (Table 2.10).

Self-Reports Regarding Arousal/Eroticism Patterns

Assessing the client's arousal/eroticism pattern is crucial. Mosher's (1980) concept of three types of arousal/eroticism patterns includes: (1) *partner interaction* (focusing on the partner's body and their sexual interaction); (2) *self-entrancement* (focusing

Table 2.10 Clinical Worksheet: Assessing Sex Dysfunction Cognitions

	Partner A	Partner B
Assemble the distinctive cognitions that each partner expresses about the SD during clinical interviews and questionnaires/logs		
Assumptions		
Standards		
Perceptions		
Attributions		
Expectancies		

on one's physical sensations and feelings); and, (3) *role enactment* (use of external stimuli, fantasy role-play, sexual videos, or toys). For example, men with PE almost invariably use partner interaction arousal. He initiates and pursues sex with highly arousing activity ("sexual drag racing"); starts with oral-genital sex or immediate intercourse rather than relaxed kissing and massage, and does not connect with pleasurable physical sensations. The clinician needs to carefully interview the client about the sources of his eroticism experiences and sexual arousal. It helps to have the individual imagine himself beginning to have a sexual interaction, closing his eyes and visualizing it, and telling the therapist what is going on that is erotic and arousing. The therapist emphasizes that this level of detail is needed to understand conditions that are influencing the SD.

Assessing Emotional Components

An individual session with each client is important for understanding the emotional impact of the SD on the individual and relationship, as well as the role that emotional responses play in eliciting instances of SD. Emotional features are idiosyncratic; for some individuals the emotions are intense, but often feelings (e.g., sadness, anxiety) are mild and not noticed. For individuals who present strong emotions as the "lead" experience (what they notice first or most) tracking links between emotions and associated cognitions and behaviors is crucial. An example is a man's intense sexual anxiety traced to thoughts that his "failure" will lead to divorce. Consistent with traditional cognitive therapy procedures (Beck, 1993), the therapist coaches clients in noticing and keeping written logs of negative cognitions and associated emotions in specific sexual situations. Those logs can be evaluated for cognitive distortions and replaced by more reasonable interpretations. An advantage of conducting couple therapy is that the partner is a key source of data to challenge emotionally distressing cognitions. For example, the therapist can elicit partner reassurance to counter the client's negative expectancy (e.g., "Jim's thought that I'm going to leave him if he continues to have erection problems is wrong. I will be happier if sexuality improves, but I care about a lot more than erections. It's his caring for me that really matters."). Thus, the therapist listens for cues of sadness, anger, and anxiety; probes for associated cognitions; and guides the couple in evaluating those thoughts.

SDs are "triggers" for emotional distress. Once the distress occurs, it feeds back in distracting clients and counteracting desire and arousal. Consequently, a key target of CBCST is the reduction of emotional distress. Sensate focus/pleasuring exercises are an emotional-behavioral intervention that relieves distress.

Assessing the Severity of SD

Sexual disorders are not dichotomous; each is complex, multi-causal, and multi-dimensional. They also vary significantly in severity. Assessing problem severity is crucial because this determines treatment complexity and difficulty. Severe problems preoccupy the client and serve as stressors in the relationship. They are likely to elicit negative behavioral interactions between partners, such as verbal aggression or avoidance.

In understanding and assessing severity, life-long SD tends to be more severe, as is SD that occurs in all situations (e.g., across different partners) and in the context of a history of partner blaming and alienation. SDs involving both partners add to the severity, as does a history of failed change attempts. When SD involves lack of desire and pleasure, it has a more negative impact on the client and couple. Untreated SD becomes chronic and severe over time.

Comprehensive Treatment Formulation

Planning Treatment Based on Assessment of Factors and Severity

Determining the multiple causes, effects, and level of severity of an SD is crucial for an effective treatment plan. Incorporating information from the various components of biopsychosocial assessment and using a summary treatment form, the therapist identifies the physiologic and medical factors, individual psychological features, relationship dynamics, as well as cognition-behavior-emotion components that are areas for treatment. Thus, the multidimensional assessment leads to a treatment plan with specific interventions tailored to the relative contributions made to the SD by physical factors (e.g., chronic disease requiring medical intervention; psychopathology with biological aspects that may benefit from medication), cognitions about the self and relationship, emotional responses, and couple behavioral interaction patterns.

Treatment Design for the Individual and Couple

If a biological problem is suspected for either member of a couple, an early step is to refer for a medical evaluation. Each partner's dysfunctional cognitions and emotional responses also are identified, and a clinical decision must be made whether one or both partners' intra-psychic difficulties may need some individual therapy in addition to CBCST.

At the dyadic level, it is very important to identify detrimental couple interactions causing or maintaining an SD. In general, mental health professionals have considerably more training and experience identifying and intervening with individual problems than they do with tracking and intervening with dyadic processes. Consequently, it is most helpful when the sex therapist has background in both individual and couple functioning and can intervene at both levels (or make appropriate referrals).

Summarizing Assessment Findings to the Couple and Organizing Treatment

When the assessment has been concluded, the therapist reviews with the couple the biological, psychological, and relationship factors that have been identified as eliciting or maintaining their SD, or have become effects of the SD. This assessment feedback process approach is consistent with the overall collaborative nature of cognitive-behavioral therapies, a transparent stance by the therapist that is intended to foster a positive therapeutic alliance with clients and engage them as active

Table 2.11 Worksheet: Biopsychosocial Assessment Summary Sheet

Check specific cause(s) and detrimental impact/effect(s):
Check if suspected:

1. _____Chronic and/or acute physical illness SD
(What condition? _____)
2. _____Physical injury SD
(What injury? _____)
3. _____Pharmacological side-effect SD
(What medication or drug? _____)
4. _____Health and lifestyle habits SD
(What lifestyle condition? _____)
5. _____Chronic psychological distress SD
(What condition? _____)
6. _____Acute psychological distress SD
(What distress? _____)
7. _____Relationship distress SD
(Area(s) of distress (cognitive, behavioral, emotional) _____
_____)
8. _____Psychosexual skills SD
(Deficits in cognitive, behavioral, emotional and interactional features)

_____
_____
9. _____SD with another sexual dysfunction (mixed or multiple SD)
(What other dysfunction(s)?_____
_____

---

participants in their treatment. It also serves an educational purpose and promotes optimism and hope for change. Identifying, labeling, and offering reasonable sexual expectations and an overview of treatment give the couple a valuable perspective. This reduces distress and opens them to growth. Explaining the treatment plan enhances motivation for change.

The clinician's *Biopsychosocial Assessment Summary Sheet* offers a comprehensive checklist of areas to address. Based on SD etiology, personal and relationship impact, and severity, decisions are made about resources and strategies to resolve the SD. Identifying elements contributing to the SD and collaborating with the couple to decide treatment strategies bring confidence and optimism to counter distress (Table 2.11).

Initiating a Relapse Prevention Plan

CBCST is intended to develop clients' personal understanding of factors influencing SD and their skills for instituting and maintaining positive changes. Consequently, a plan for preventing relapse once improvement has been attained is a key component of the treatment plan. Comprehensive relapse prevention begins early in the therapeutic process, during the formulation and goal setting discussions. The couple discusses therapeutic goal(s), strategies and rationale, steps along the therapeutic way, potential problems, and the expectation that relapse prevention involves scheduled "check-ups." Concepts introduced in the assessment and treatment planning phase are incorporated into therapy, helping the couple adopt an overview of treatment and sense of empowerment that they are an intimate sexual team. Learning that treatment involves targeted areas, cooperation, change strategies, as well as follow-up meetings, provides them with relief, hope, and motivation. We provide a detailed description of how the therapist engages the couple in relapse prevention planning in Chapter 7.

Key Points:

1. Conduct a comprehensive biopsychosocial assessment to ensure effective therapy outcome.
2. Enhance the clinician's personal and professional confidence.
3. Build rapport with the individuals and couple, establishing a collaborative treatment team with them.
4. Assess individual and relationship aspects of SD.
5. Use comprehensive systematic assessment to design treatment.

Chapter 3

Overview of CBCST Strategies

As we have described in the first two chapters, SD is complex, with multiple initial and maintaining causes; including physiological, cognitive, behavioral, emotional, and relationship factors. CBCST emphasizes a biopsychosocial treatment approach that maximizes the potential for lasting gains. When there is a physiological component to an SD, medical and pharmacologic interventions are a crucial resource to integrate with the psychosocial aspects. Biomedical interventions can be useful even when the etiology is clearly psychological. An example is the use of Viagra to temporarily relieve performance anxiety. A man's more readily obtained erections counteract negative thinking and emotional distress that were contributing to ED. Due to its multidimensional conceptual and treatment model, CBCST is a powerful tool for helping couples deal with chronic physical illness (e.g., diabetes, multiple sclerosis), mental health difficulties (e.g., depression, generalized anxiety disorder, obsessive-compulsive disorder, PTSD), and relational problems.

Biological and Medical Factors in Sexual Dysfunction and CBCST Treatment Strategies

Clinicians must either rule out or address medical issues so they do not subvert therapeutic success. The fact that CBCST emphasizes individuals' psychological factors and couple problems by no means detracts from the importance attached to biological components of SD. The body is the foundation on which the psychological and relationship factors sit (Table 3.1).

Medical Illness and Disabilities

Chronic and acute medical illness, as well as physical disabilities, present obstacles to sexual function (Brotto & Kingsberg, 2010; Enzlin, 2014; Mona, Syme, & Cameron,

Table 3.1 Physical Factors that Contribute to SD

1. Medical illness and physical disabilities
2. Medication side-effects
3. Infertility
4. Menopause
5. Sexually transmitted infections
6. Behavioral health problems

2014; Verschuren, Enzlin, Dijkstra, Gertzen, & Dekker, 2010). Health problems may occur at any age, some precipitated by psychosocial stressors and others by bio-medical causes. CBCST uses all available biopsychosocial resources to help the person and couple. Furthermore, medical treatments for psychological disorders create biological side effects that must be taken into account. For example, a client struggling with severe anxiety may benefit from use of a short acting anxiety medication rather than an SSRI that can have detrimental sexual side effects.

The risk of physical illness and disabilities increases with age, especially after 50, and such illnesses and disabilities commonly result in sexual problems (Agronin & Robinson, 2014; Hillman, 2008). Whereas some illnesses and disabilities (e.g., stroke, spinal cord injury) have an acute onset, others (e.g., diabetes, arthritis) follow a trajectory of increasing severity. Some individuals and couples believe they are destined to have SD as a result of the condition and feel hopeless about maintaining a satisfying sexual relationship. In reality, available medical treatments together with psychological and interpersonal therapies can offer life-long sexual satisfaction, although not perfect sex performance. Kleinplatz (2010) interviewed couples who reported highly satisfying sexual relationships in spite of physical function difficulties. Their satisfaction resulted from flexible and accepting attitudes about what constitutes desirable sexual behavior; for example, accepting that a male needs more stimulation from his partner to get an erection, or that partners can experience a high level of satisfaction from oral or manual stimulation rather than depend on intercourse. With realistic expectations and flexibility, couples develop alternative sexual scenarios to adapt to whatever physical challenges exist. Sexual function and satisfaction—even if altered—is life-long.

An individual's sexual health is influenced by her partner's sexual health—physically, emotionally, and interpersonally. Stress researchers refer to this process as "spillover," in which the impact of a life stressor on one partner affects the other as well (Bodenmann, Atkins, Schar, & Poffet, 2010). When one partner has a health problem, it is essential to provide support so the couple can adapt together, developing their ability to engage in dyadic coping in which the partners work as a team to solve problems, rather than one partner trying to solve the other's problem. In this "we" approach to an illness, disability, or an SD, the couple addresses their shared stress and seeks solutions that enhance both individuals' well-being and their relationship (Bodenmann, 2005a, 2005b; Bodenmann, Pihet, & Kayser, 2006).

Even if a physical illness or disability does not cause SD, its symptoms and treatments may reverberate and contribute to SD for the partner. Thus, when a couple is adapting to multiple sclerosis, cancer, or arthritis, they need to develop flexible sexual scenarios that allow for satisfaction with forms of sexual interaction other than those that were familiar. Sex therapists play a key role in guiding and supporting couples in making a positive adjustment. In the CBCST approach, the therapist uses psychoeducation to increase awareness of the impact of illness and disability on individual and couple functioning (as well as alternative forms of sexual expression), combined with cognitive interventions to broaden partners' views of what is acceptable and satisfying sex, and to increase hope about achieving sexual satisfaction (Metz & McCarthy, 2012).

Medication Side Effects

A common physiological impediment to sexual function is the detrimental sexual side effects of medications. A guideline for clinicians is to suspect any agent—including over the counter medications such as antihistamines—when SD shadows

Table 3.2 Antidotes for Medication Side-Effects

Antidote	Dose	Sexual Dysfunction
Amantadine	100–600 mg/day in divided dose or prn	Anorgasmia; could be helpful for loss of desire or arousal
Bethanechol	prn 10–50 mg 1–2 hours before coitus	Dysfunction or arousal or orgasm
Bupropion (or bupropion SR)	prn 75–150 mg 1–2 hours before coitus, or daily 75–450 mg (mostly with SSRIs)	Dysfunction of desire, arousal, and orgasm
Buspirone	over 30 mg/day	Decreased desire; anorgasmia
Cyproheptadine*	prn 4–12 mg before coitus, or 4–16 mg/day	Anorgasmia
Dextroamphetamine	prn 5mg 1–2 hours before coitus, or 5mg or more/day	Dysfunction of desire, arousal, and orgasm
Methylphenidate	prn 5 mg or more, or 5–20 mg/day	Dysfunction of desire, arousal, and orgasm
Mirtazapine	15–45 mg/day	Impaired orgasm
Nefazodone	50 mg/day or more	Impaired orgasm
Neostigmine	prn 7.5–15 mg 1–2 hours before coitus, or 50–200 mg/day in divided doses	Dysfunction of arousal
Yohimbine**	prn 5.4–10.8 mg 1–2 hours before coitus, or 5.4 mg/day	Dysfunction of desire, arousal, and orgasm

* Cyproheptadine may cause severe sedation and possibly depression.
** Yohimbine may induce anxiety, especially in panic disorder patients (Segreaves & Balon, 2003).

medication usage. However, it is important not to automatically assume that a medication is a cause of SD. Side effects are neither automatic nor inevitable, as medications affect individuals differently. Clients can address possible medication side effects by working with the prescribing physician in trying alternative agents that are less detrimental, experimenting with compensation strategies (e.g., adjusting the time of dosage to be less proximate to sex activity), and introducing pharmacologic antidotes. Table 3.2 lists antidotes for a number of leading medications that commonly have sexual side effects.

Infertility

Infertility is a risk factor for SD (Leiblum, 1999; Milheiser et al., 2010; Shindel, Nelson, Naughton, Ohebshalom, & Milhall, 2008). It is not infertility itself that causes the SD, but the meanings that the partners attach to the infertility (e.g., "I am defective.") and their experience with the treatment protocol, especially intercourse on a rigid schedule (Leiblum, 1999). Infertility and its treatment are highly stressful for the individual, couple, and their sexual relationship (Daniluk & Frances-Fischer, 2009; Daniluk, Koert, & Breckon, 2014). Many clients perceive infertility as a fundamental failure to accomplish the biological function of sex. This is exacerbated when the couple experience pressure from family and friends who are "watching and waiting" for a pregnancy—a powerful form of "spectatoring." Traditionally, infertility was seen as a woman's problem. However, present estimates are that one-third of infertility factors involve a male cause, one-third a female cause, and one-third a combination of factors (Covington & Burns, 2006). Male sexual self-esteem is particularly vulnerable when there is a male infertility factor (Daniluk & Frances-Fischer, 2009).

Having intercourse on a rigid timetable—"sex on demand"—results in inhibited desire. Sex is no longer relaxed and fun. It becomes a task and a sense of failure when two weeks later the effort to get pregnant fails. Because the stresses of infertility affect both partners and their interaction (e.g., increasing the couple's tendency to avoid each other and engage in blaming), they are best addressed as a couple issue. The therapist can guide the couple in identifying infertility as a health issue, provide psychosexual skills to prevent the development of SD, reduce emotional distress through self-soothing skills, and promote cooperation in using couple approaches (Covington & Burns, 2006). CBCST is invaluable because it simultaneously addresses negative cognitions, emotional responses, and couple behavioral interactions.

Menopause

Menopausal symptoms are challenging for many women and their partners (Dennerstein, 2010). Menopause typically occurs between the ages of 45 and 55, but may occur as early as the 30s. The average age of last menstruation is 51 (Avis & McKinlay, 1995). With the decline of estrogen, the vulva and vagina experience less elasticity, lubrication, and changes in the vaginal walls. Although the physical changes associated with menopause can contribute to sexual difficulties, the psychological and interpersonal concomitants of menopause play important roles. The negative effects of changes in the vulva and vagina can be ameliorated when the woman and couple accept the physical changes as normal and use a vaginal lubricant and moisturizer. The quality of the couple's relationship contributes to good or poor adjustment to menopause. Menopause may bring mood fluctuations, sleep problems, difficulty concentrating, and anxiety (Liebman-Smith, 1987). When these are a consistent concern, it is wise to seek medical consultation. Couples can achieve a satisfying sexual relationship if they embrace menopause as a challenge that they actively adapt to rather than denying, minimizing, or catastrophizing.

Physiologically, there is not a "male menopause." Media claims about the existence of "male menopause" elicit anxiety and sell magazines, but are not based on scientific fact. Testosterone declines approximately 0.08% per year for men between the ages of 40 and 80 (McKinlay, Longcope, & Gray, 1989), which is not sufficient to cause SD. Physiologically, vascular and neurological systems remain functional but are less robust and efficient—"mellowing." For a man with abnormally low testosterone, consulting an endocrinologist with a sub-specialty in male sexual health to discuss testosterone replacement therapy (typically via gel) is advised.

Women and men commonly experience a "mid-life adjustment" that is primarily psychological. Rather than the crisis portrayed in the media, this process involves the realization that one's life is progressing, and the remaining time is limited. During this period, individuals typically reflect on life's meaning and purpose, and evaluate the quality of what they have achieved, including their intimate relationship. They use this as a time to re-evaluate. "What do I want to do with the rest of my life?" "What do I value about intimacy and sexuality?" This is a healthy search for meaning triggered by life events—job stagnation or success, children leaving home, deaths in the family. Mid-life involves a renewed "search for meaning" (Hill, 2008).

CBCST helps individuals and couples whose evaluations leave them distressed. The individual often applies unrealistic *standards* in judging the quality of his sexual relationship. When the client experiences SD, does he make distressing, biased *attributions* about the cause (e.g., "I am over the hill sexually.") and inaccurate *expectancies* or predictions (e.g., my partner will fall out of love due to my SD.")? Emotionally, does the client engage in excessive worrying that triggers anxiety, which distracts from sexual arousal? Does the individual's negative evaluation result in sexual avoidance or alcohol abuse? CBCST interventions can be used to counteract negative midlife evaluations, increase sexual acceptance, and engage the clients in constructive actions to enhance the sexual relationship and satisfaction.

Sexually Transmitted Infections (STIs)

Almost half of individuals will contract an STI in their lives (Fisher & Holtzapfel, 2014). The most common are chlamydia, herpes, and HPV (genital warts). The most feared STI is HIV/AIDS, which can be life threatening. Herpes, HPV, and HIV/AIDS cannot be cured but can be medically managed. The good news is that STIs are viewed as medical rather than moral problems. When the partner reacts to the STI (especially if contracted through an affair) in a moralistic, punishing manner the clinician needs to remain empathic and respectful, but confront the negative judgment and help them replace it with a positive emotional problem-solving approach. Given that STIs resulting from an affair typically create a crisis of betrayal in the couple's relationship, the CBCST therapist also needs to help the partners cope with the infidelity or refer the couple to another professional to do so. Gordon, Khaddoima, Baucom, and Snyder's (2015) largely CBT approach to the treatment of affairs is an empirically based approach that can be very helpful.

For couples where one or both partners have an STI, developing coping strategies is important. It is helpful to speak to a doctor and establish a medical understanding of a potential cause and its timing, as well as clear guidelines on how to deal with the STI. It may mean the couple uses condoms, avoids contact with infected areas, and do not have sexual contact when a herpes outbreak is beginning. A CBCST therapist also helps the partners cope with the emotional distress associated with the STI by guiding them in using emotion regulation strategies and challenging catastrophic thinking. Because STIs are a reality of sex in the twenty-first century, CBCST can help couples deal with them as a health issue so it does not control their sexuality.

Behavioral Health Problems: Substance Misuse/Smoking/Obesity

Traditionally, lifestyle issues were not thought to be powerful enough to undermine sexual function. This is a myth. Alcohol is a common cause of arousal problems (erection, lubrication, orgasm) before the age of 40 (George & Stoner, 2000). Drug misuse (including prescription and street drugs), smoking, and obesity have great potential to undermine sexual function. Medical consultation and treatment— as well as psychological interventions—are important and effective resources. Alcoholics Anonymous and alternative treatments (George & Stoner, 2000) are effective and present the opportunity to develop a new couple sexual style of desire,

Table 3.3 Individual Psychological Factors that Complicate SD

1.	Mental health challenges, including anxiety and depression
2.	Vicissitudes and responsibilities of daily life
3.	Emotional dysregulation: shame and anger
4.	Sexual dysregulation: misuse of pornography
5.	Self-esteem issues; body image and fears of aging
6.	Sexual secrets: paraphilia, sexual orientation issues, affairs, preference for masturbatory sex
7.	Unresolved history of sexual trauma
8.	Personal habits and preferences that interfere with intimacy

pleasure, eroticism, and satisfaction. It takes most clients six months to create a new sexual style as a sober couple.

The CBCST approach focuses on cognitive, emotional, and behavioral factors that influence substance use that interferes with sexual response. For example, psychoeducation can help dispel clients' myths about effects of alcohol on sexual performance. Similarly, many individuals use alcohol to reduce social anxiety and are unaware that benefits they perceive in their ability to form sexual relationships can be counteracted by the negative effects on sexual function. Interventions focused on reducing emotion dysregulation can contribute to the goal of reducing problematic drinking. CBCST interventions that improve couple communication and conflict resolution reduce stressors that trigger drinking episodes.

Individual Psychological and Life Stress Factors

A number of psychological features can complicate sexual function. Often, individual therapy and CBCST are conducted simultaneously, because the changes targeted in each therapy modality support those treated in the other (Table 3.3).

Mental Health Challenges

Psychological barriers to sexual functioning range in intensity, from distractions such as worries about looking foolish to profound social anxiety. A variety of psychological problems can interfere with sexual function, including depression, bipolar disorder, obsessive compulsive disorder, generalized anxiety, hygiene phobia, social phobia, post-traumatic stress disorder, panic disorder, and personality disorders. Among individuals with panic disorder, 75% experience SD, whereas 33% of social phobia patients experience SD (Figueira, Possidente, Marques, & Hayes, 2002). Consequently, individual psychotherapy and/or pharmacotherapy are valuable adjuncts to CBCST.

Individuals with panic disorder commonly fear sensations of physiological/emotional arousal because they associate these with risk of another panic attack (Barlow, 1988). Unfortunately, this fear extends to sensations of sexual arousal and sexual exertion (Sbrocco, Weisberg, Barlow, & Carter, 1997). Even when both partners understand intellectually that the anxiety disorder is unrelated to sexual attraction, the individual's inhibited sexual response based on avoidance of arousal contributes to relationship distress and conflict. In addition, low sexual desire is a common symptom of depression, as is social withdrawal. These symptoms detract significantly from sexual response and cause decreased relationship satisfaction. A "vicious cycle" develops in which depression leads to low sexual and relationship satisfaction, and low satisfaction and intimacy exacerbate the depression (Metz & Epstein, 2002).

CBCST can be helpful by addressing the cognitive, affective and behavioral links among psychological disorders, sexual problems, and relationship distress (Baucom, Epstein, Kirby & LaTaillade, 2015; Epstein & Baucom, 2002). Psychoeducation reduces the couple's distress by helping them set goals to cope with the partner's symptoms (dyadic coping). Cognitive interventions reduce negative attributions (e.g., re-attributing an individual's withdrawal as due to depression rather than a lack of love for the partner), negative expectancies (e.g., decreasing hopelessness about the couple's sexual relationship by focusing on incremental change steps), selective attention (e.g., keeping a log of the couple's positive sexual experiences to counteract global negative perceptions about their relationship), inaccurate assumptions (e.g., that the passage of time heals trauma symptoms), and unrealistic standards (e.g., that men should become sexually aroused automatically). CBCST includes interventions to increase emotion regulation for partners who experience anxiety and anger. Behaviorally, CBCST provides systematic procedures for improving communication and problem-solving skills, as well as intimacy-building patterns.

Vicissitudes and Responsibilities of Daily Life

Sexual function is affected by parental responsibilities; work-related burdens; financial pressures; caregiving for ill relatives; and engagement in various social, religious, family, and community activities. Major stressors such as sudden unemployment and life-threatening illnesses have impacts on psychological well-being. In addition, more minor events referred to as daily "hassles" have a cumulative effect (Helms, Walls, & Demo, 2010). Work-family conflicts are significantly related to degree of marital conflict (Fraenkel & Capstick, 2012). High workload and low workplace support are associated with affective distress, elevated blood pressure, and low well-being (Ilies, Dimotakis, & DePater, 2010). These complicate the couple's relational and sexual climate. Bodenmann et al. (2010) found that higher stress in daily life was substantially and significantly associated with lower levels of sexual activity and decrease in relationship satisfaction. Dyadic coping (but not individual coping) revealed a significant positive association with quality of sexual behavior, sexual satisfaction, and frequency of orgasm. Dyadic coping is associated with intimacy, confidence, and attachment (Bodenmann, 2005a, 2005b; Bodenmann et al., 2006; Cutrona, 1996).

Providing a couple the opportunity to identify life stresses and appreciate their impact on sexual feelings and behavior helps them cooperate and devise ways to balance their relationship with the life stressors that they face. The therapist guides the couple in making time for sexual homework assignments, including using time in session to schedule these.

Emotional Dysregulation: Expression of Negative Emotions

Individuals experiencing SD often feel entitled to express raw, negative emotions such as anger through criticism, blame, and hostile withdrawal. Such behavior is toxic to the relationship (Gottman, 1999; Kirby, Baucom, & Peterman, 2007). Each partner needs to develop the ability to self-regulate intense negative emotions and destructive behaviors.

Confronting unregulated emotions and destructive behavior is crucial in CBCST for SD. Identifying triggers to emotional responses and self-defeating behavior, providing cognitive-behavioral skills for conflict management, and guiding the couple in using psychosexual skill exercises can transform negative patterns into constructive solutions. Offering accurate information about sex (e.g., Laumann, Gagnon, Michael, & Michaels, 1994; McCarthy & Metz, 2008) provides perspective (e.g., that SD is more common than anxiety or depression). The therapist assists the couple in exploring meanings that they attach to SD (e.g., attributing them to failings of self or partner), regulating emotional expression, and cooperating as an intimate sexual team. Through this focus on self-regulation, each partner makes a positive contribution to their relationship. Specific strategies enhance partners' emotion regulation to reduce distress and work toward positive solutions.

Sexual Dysregulation

Sexual regulation is at the heart of sexual health and requires self-care similar to the physical regulation required for sleep and diet. This includes management of *emotions* such as anger, anxiety, loneliness, and sadness as well as *cognitions* regarding the meanings of interpersonal behaviors. The three components of sexual self-regulation are (1) acceptance and respect for the power of the body's "biological imperative" involving sex drive (Fisher, Aron, Masher, & Brown, 2002); (2) acceptance and regulation of males' common biological predisposition to focus on physical sex (Hamann, Herman, Nolan, & Wallen, 2004) and balancing biological drive with "personalizing" the couple's unique sexuality; and (3) achievement of a balance between eroticism and intimacy. For example, through therapy a man learns to appreciate the difference between emotional arousal and sexuality, reducing his tendency to misinterpret emotions such as loneliness, sadness, anxiety, and irritability as sexual feelings (Adams & Robinson, 2001). This area can be confusing because clients have had experiences in which sexual arousal and orgasm temporarily reduced distressing emotions—a form of "self-medicating." Sexual health involves developing sophistication in the experience and expression of feelings, differentiating between sexual arousal and emotional arousal.

Sexual regulation problems commonly include behavioral patterns such as compulsive use of Internet pornography, extreme frequency of masturbation, visiting prostitutes, frequenting "strip bars" over the objection of a partner (which can involve significant financial costs), and making rigid sexual demands of a partner rather than requests (Cooper & Marcus, 2003; Marcus, 2010). In contrast to these excesses of sexual behavior, sex inhibition or avoidance (more common among women but occurring in both sexes) is precipitated by negative moods such as sadness and anxiety. Although there are situations in which such moods are appropriate responses to conflict in the couple's relationship, and forcing oneself to engage in sex may constitute neglecting personal needs, sometimes individuals have an erroneous belief that they can never be sexually responsive/interested unless "the mood is right." Understanding that self-regulation involves self-care is empowering—an essential understanding for sexual health for both women and men.

Men (and women to a much lesser extent) exhibit various forms of compulsive sexual behavior (Marcus, 2010). The most common is pornography misuse—mislabeled "porn addiction." There are both individual and relationship aspects to the misuse of pornography. Some men secretly rely on porn to satisfy a variant arousal pattern (e.g., a fetish) while devaluing intimate couple sex. When the partner complains about their low sex frequency, the man denies that there is a problem and keeps his partner in the dark. This strategy usually backfires, as the partner perceives a lack of honesty and feels betrayed when the pornography use is uncovered. The rupture to trust becomes the primary source of conflict and distress in the relationship, overshadowing the need to deal with the factors motivating his use of porn and/or the variant arousal pattern. Often the compulsive sexual behavior is associated with undiagnosed psychological problems such as depression or attachment insecurity that require assessment and treatment (Marcus, 2010).

Sexual Dysregulation as an Individual Problem

When sexual response is not regulated, individuals develop blocks to sexual intimacy. How can the client recognize that he is at risk for obsessive or compulsive sexual behavior? (Table 3.4).

Clients who turn to sex as a panacea for their psychological pain are in a self-defeating compulsive pattern (Leedes, 2001). Compulsive sexual behavior commonly reflects unidentified and unacknowledged feelings. These clients live in a world that feels rejecting and unyielding, and they use sex to seek acceptance or a sense of control in a world that can feel overpowering (Cooper, Delmonico, & Burg, 2000). There is pain and suffering beneath the sexual acting out. The individual rationalizes unhealthy sexuality (e.g., "I use pornography because couple sex isn't exciting enough") but is not aware of a fundamental issue such as

Table 3.4 Recognizing Dysregulated Sexual Behavior

Compulsive sexual behavior involves detrimental and excessive preoccupation with particular forms of sexual thoughts, emotions and behavior:

Men:
- Preoccupation with erotic stimuli to the detriment of the couple relationship
- Extreme frequency of masturbation without the ability (e.g., no masturbation for 1 month) to cease
- Inability to limit Internet porn
- Going to prostitutes
- Frequenting strip bars
- Significant financial expenditures on sex
- Excessive or rigid sexual demands on the partner
- Extra-relationship affairs
- Sexual interest in other women at the expense of his partner

Women:
- Preoccupation with sexual/romantic fantasies (e.g., through "romance novels" or soap operas) to the detriment of relationship
- Preferring masturbation to partner sex
- Making demands on the partner for greater sex frequency or enacting a particular sexual scenario/script
- Extra-relationship affairs
- Excessive flirtatiousness or seductiveness
- Multiple surgeries for body enhancement

low self-esteem or feeling unloved. In a CBCST approach, the therapist carefully explores the psychological and relational functioning of the individual (cognitions, emotions, behavior) and helps the client understand the role that the compulsive sexual behavior serves.

Sexual Dysregulation as a Relationship Problem

Compulsive sexual behavior is detrimental for the individual and subverts an intimate relationship. Without acceptance of men and women's sexual nature, and without regulating sex drive and integrating them in a sex-positive relational climate, intense conflicts ensue. It is easy for a woman to interpret a man's interest in pornography as infidelity. This often is a misinterpretation; the man wants to be sexual with her and finds that pornography increases stimulation. This contrasts with cases of compulsive use of pornography that competes and detracts from the real-life couple relationship. The ultimate issue is whether a couple integrates eroticism into their relationship in a pro-intimate way—whatever *mutually* satisfying way that may take. Secret, compulsive eroticism subverts emotional intimacy.

When emotional and sexual intimacy are integrated, the individual weaves the partner into his life. Compulsive sexual behavior is anti-intimate. Sexually compulsive individuals have significant difficulty forming a close attachment, fear genuine intimacy, being "known," and losing emotional control. Sexual compulsivity hides sadness, anger, loneliness, and crushes loving feelings. In the CBCST approach, the therapist assesses for compulsive sexual behavior and identifies it as a target of treatment.

The Extent of Dysregulated Sexual Behavior

Compulsive sexual behavior is largely a male problem. The ratio of male to female occurrence is estimated as 4 to 1, and that 6 to 8% of men are "addicted" to sex (Kafka, 2014). More than two-thirds of people with sexual acting-out problems use the Internet as a venue. Twenty percent of "netizens" engage in online sexual activity, and over 15% of Internet pornography viewers have online behavior that is problematic (Marcus, 2000; Cooper, Griffin-Shelley, Delmonico, & Mathy, 2001). The Internet, smart phones, Facebook and other social media have power to elicit sexual compulsivity because of easy accessibility, unlimited variety of content, anonymity, the false promise of no real-life consequences, and confusion between sexuality that is virtual versus real.

Self-Esteem: Body Image and Aging

Sexual self-esteem is associated with the client's body image and worries about aging. Preoccupation with physical attractiveness ranges from mild (dissatisfaction with freckles) to severe (anorexia). Unfortunately, there is no argument persuasive enough to change the perfectionistic perceptions of some clients (Foley, Kope, & Sugrue, 2012). Plastic surgery, liposuction, breast implants, breast reduction surgery, penile enlargement surgery, and hair implants are examples of treatments individuals purchase in the pursuit of greater attractiveness. Although improved health behaviors (e.g., food choices, sleep patterns) are beneficial as is regular exercise and muscle conditioning, over-emphasis on physical attractiveness undermines self-esteem and sexuality. The detriment can be profound for individuals who identify with perfectionistic societal standards of attractiveness (Pascoal, Narcisco, & Pereira, 2012).

Body image distractions are common among individuals experiencing SD and are included in CBCST treatment targets (Wiederman & Sarin, 2014). These are addressed by guiding the individual's focus to sensations of touch and mindful attention to the physical feelings. This disciplined focus on touching or being touched stops "spectatoring" about physical appearance ("my fat stomach", "my small penis/breasts", "my surgical scar").

Body image concerns, including those associated with changes occurring with aging, are addressed in CBCST through cognitive interventions. The therapist explores the individual's personal standards for attractiveness and origins of those beliefs (e.g., messages from parents during childhood, media portrayals of beauty). Unrealistic standards and harsh self-evaluations are examined, with the therapist encouraging the client to challenge comparisons with perfect models. At the couple level, sensate focus/pleasuring exercises are used to enhance partners' mindful focus on pleasurable and erotic sensations. The focus is on enjoying the pleasure of one's body rather than judging it. CBCST provides the opportunity to experience affirmation in being a sexual person. Experiencing acceptance of oneself is healthy, rather than needing to perform and earn love.

Fears of aging involve fears of illness. As we age, illness becomes common and SD does as well. Men in "poor" or "fair" health are four times more likely to experience SD than men in "excellent" health (Hillman, 2008; Laumann et al., 1994; Wylie & Kenney, 2010).

Maintaining a healthy body at every age (25, 55, or 85) is important. The therapist can guide individuals who fear aging to focus their concerns specifically on physical and sexual health. Unrealistic fears of "inevitable" sexual decline set up a "self-fulfilling prophecy" in which negative expectancies cause SD. If the client predicts that he will "lose it," the resulting performance anxiety increases the likelihood that he will experience ED. CBCST emphasizes acceptance of bodily changes that accompany normal aging and taking a flexible approach to couple sexuality that provides a variety of satisfying forms of sexual expression (Kleinplatz, 2010; Metz and McCarthy, 2012).

Sexual Secrets

There is an important difference between *private* sexual thoughts and feelings and *sexual secrets* (Risen, 2010). Private thoughts and feelings (e.g., being attracted to a friend) need not constitute a problem. Sexual secrets are powerful because they do influence the relationship (e.g., an affair, a sexual orientation issue that is unknown to the partner) and are perceived by the partner as a betrayal when discovered. Sexual secrets undermine relational openness and cohesion. Addressing sexual secrets is integral to CBCST (Table 3.5).

Clients guard sexual secrets from everyone—partner, physician, best friend. Yet, secrets control their sexuality. The combination of high eroticism, high secrecy, and internalized shame are powerful forces driving the sexual secret. Any attempt by the partner to communicate about the secret is met by defensiveness and arguments.

Table 3.5 Types of Sexual Secrets

1.	Variant or deviant arousal
2.	Loyalty problems (extra-relationship affairs)
3.	A history of sexual trauma that has not been processed and has persistent effects
4.	Internal conflict regarding sexual orientation
5.	Preference for masturbatory sex over couple sex

The client who keeps a sexual secret perceives it as an impossible bind in which living a secret life is uncomfortable, but the prospect of honest disclosure seems fraught with danger.

Variant Arousal (Atypical Sexual Behavior)

Variant arousal patterns (benign paraphilias) have relatively low base rates but tend to be problematic for the couple relationships (Federoff, 2010). As many as 4% of men have a variant arousal pattern. Almost 1% of men have a deviant arousal pattern—a "noxious paraphilia" which is illegal and harmful to others. A paraphilia involves dependency on an impersonal object for sexual arousal. In mild cases, fantasy alone is sufficient to evoke arousal; in many cases, the individual needs the object (or imagery) to ensure sex arousal.

Variant arousal is distinguished by the focus that triggers arousal. Examples include fetishism (boot or foot), transvestism (cross dressing), sado-masochism (pain); and urophilia (urine). It is crucial to distinguish between personal preferences for body parts (chest, legs, hair, buttocks) that add to the individual's sexual pleasure and a paraphilia pattern that overrides the couple's sexual interaction. Eroticism enhances couple sexuality, whereas variant arousal undermines couple eroticism by interfering with sexual acceptance and connection. In CBCST, it is important to inquire about arousal patterns and explore the subjective meanings that the client attaches to these.

Deviant Arousal

Deviant arousal refers to sexual arousal associated with behaviors that harm others—exhibitionism, voyeurism, frotteurism, and the most harmful, pedophilia. Deviant arousal involves illegal sexual behavior and is highly damaging to the man and couple (Hanson & Morton-Bourgon, 2005, 2009). These patterns must be confronted and require professional intervention. Sadly, most men do not heed this advice, deny their deviant arousal pattern, and only address the problem after they are arrested or someone threatens to report them to the police.

Clients with a deviant paraphilia are not necessarily sex offenders; for example, if paraphilic content is limited to fantasy. They do not act on the sexual arousal pattern (he may fantasize about exhibiting himself but does not do so). In turn, not all sex offenders have a diagnosable paraphilia (e.g., the sexual acting out behavior is part of a sociopathic pattern or bipolar disorder) (Akerman & Beech, 2012; Hanson & Morton-Bourgon, 2005, 2009). However, most individuals who sexually offend are enacting a deviant paraphilia. It is crucial for the clinician to conduct a careful assessment of the client's arousal patterns.

1. How often is the content needed for excitement (desire / arousal / orgasm):

0	1	2	3	4	5	6	7	8	9	10

Never   Always

2. To what extent does your sexual arousal require focus on the paraphilac content:

0	1	2	3	4	5	6	7	8	9	10

Fantasy Only   Behavior Always

Sum the two ratings and enter below to indicate severity:

0	2	3	4	5	6	7	8	9	10	11	12	13	14	15	16	17	18	19	20

Mild   Moderate   Severe

Figure 3.1 Severity of Variant Arousal

Sexual Arousal Problems Vary in Severity

Sexual arousal problems vary in (a) level of the individual's dependency on atypical objects for arousal, and (b) degree to which the arousal is expressed via fantasy (benign paraphilias) vs. behavior (Federoff, 2010). A paraphilic behavior that is not necessary for achieving arousal and is never enacted is harmless (unless upsetting to the client or partner) (Figure 3.1).

Variant Arousal Is an Intimacy Challenge

A therapeutic way to understand a variant arousal pattern is as an intimacy disorder—the individual devalues intimate, interactive couple sex. The best way to approach these issues is for the individual to take responsibility for his sexuality and set realistic change goals. Because the client is accustomed to fulfilling sexual needs through the variant pattern, and efforts to change it are likely to be uncomfortable, motivating him to take personal responsibility for the problematic effects of his sexual behavior can be difficult. The CBCST approach involves identifying the specific positive and negative consequences of the variant arousal pattern. It is important not to minimize the positive consequences (e.g., rapid and reliable arousal) that the therapeutic intervention needs to counteract. Identifying negative consequences such as decreased intimacy is a prerequisite for building motivation for change.

Effective change efforts include involving the partner as an intimate sexual ally. If both partners accept a variant arousal pattern, then it is not problematic ("kink-friendly" therapy). However, most couples need to confront and change the variant arousal pattern because of negative consequences for their relationship. The more the partner combines firm conviction that change is necessary with empathy for the challenges that the man faces in developing a new arousal pattern, the better the chances that the couple can work as an intimate sexual team.

Loyalty Problems: Sexual and Emotional Affairs

Extra-relational affairs are one of the most complex and distressing issues in a relationship and warrant specialized understanding and intervention (Gordon et al., 2015). Affairs take on essential meaning to the traditional couple, violating basic assumptions regarding security and trust. Although consensual extra-relationship arrangements (open relationships or swinging) are not uncommon, infidelity is the most common reason reported for ending relationships (Gordon et al., 2015). An affair can be anything from paid sex, or a high opportunity/low involvement relationship, to a deeply emotional, long-standing love relationship. Although some individuals who engage in emotional affairs (intimate secret sharing of thoughts and emotions without sexual involvement) may deny that it constitutes an affair, the consensus among professionals and the public is that this is an affair (Glass, 2003). Among the common factors contributing to affairs are:

1. situations providing high opportunity;
2. emotional excitement, attraction, or physical pleasure;
3. experiences with a new person that allow the individual to discover or rediscover a lost part of the self;
4. when sex in the couple relationship has been dysfunctional, to see if one can be functional with another partner;
5. feeling unappreciated or lonely, and susceptible to feeling good from another's attention and affection;
6. a form of "self-medication" to reduce emotional distress associated with psychological problems such as depression and anxiety.

Approximately 18–24% of men engage in some type of affair and approximately 16–20% of women do (e.g., Mark, Janssen, & Milhausen, 2011). Contrary to popular mythology, the most common time for an affair is early in the relationship. Rather than one cause and one outcome, affairs are multi-causal, multi-dimensional, play out in different ways, and have different outcomes.

Affairs are usually highly disruptive for the primary relationship, as a discovered or disclosed affair throws both partners and the relationship into a crisis. The involved partner's investment in the affair detracts significantly from the connection with his or her spouse/partner. For example, when feeling stressed with the partner, the client escapes into the dramatic world of the affair. The injured partner commonly experiences post-traumatic stress symptoms, ruminates about the spouse's involvement with the affair partner, and pressures the involved partner to disclose details of the affair, which the involved partner attempts to avoid (Gordon et al., 2015; Snyder, Baucom, & Gordon, 2007). Although partners sometimes attempt to repair the rupture to their attachment bond by having sex, often the negative emotions (anger, anxiety, and depression) contribute to SD. The affair needs to be dealt with rather than denied or reacted to in a dramatic manner. A core issue is to understand the role of the affair from the perspective of both the involved partner and the injured partner, as well as how the affair affects the relationship, especially in the long term (Gordon et al., 2015; Snyder, Baucom, & Gordon, 2007).

Very few couples talk about their values and vulnerabilities to affairs. There is a mistaken assumption that since they love each other affairs could not occur; if the relationship is good, this protects from an affair; or if sex is good there is no reason for an affair. Because the majority of affairs are more complicated than simply sex, good intentions and positive feelings are not enough. Individual and couple therapy to address the meaning of an affair is part of comprehensive CBCST. The model developed by Gordon and colleagues (Snyder, Baucom, & Gordon, 2007), is highly applicable for integration with CBCST. The three-stage model of treatment includes (1) dealing with the negative impacts of the affair on the clients and their relationship (e.g., managing emotions in order to minimize destructive actions; coping with flashbacks), (2) identifying the meaning of the affair, in terms of factors that contributed to its occurrence, and (3) developing and implementing a plan for moving on that involves either disengaging and moving toward separate lives or strengthening the relationship and creating a new couple sexual style (McCarthy & Wald, 2013).

Sexual Orientation Conflict

Same-sex orientation is an emotional and erotic attraction and commitment to sex with a same-sex person. Orientation is not an "either-or" set of categories, with clear labels of heterosexual, homosexual, bisexual, and asexual. In contrast to earlier conceptualizations that pathologized individuals who were not heterosexual, current views emphasize naturally occurring variations and diversity in sexual orientation (Morrow, 2006a). Orientation is not a noun but an adjective, a normal human quality. Most men and women have had thoughts, feelings, fantasies, or experiences with people of the same sex. Individuals typically progress through a process of gender identity and sexual orientation development through awareness and exploration and eventually define their orientation (Morrow, 2006b). Sexual orientation, specifically for gay males, is to a large extent biologically grounded, and limited in change over time, although women's sexual orientation has been found to be more fluid (Diamond, 2013).

Individuals are complex in their sexuality, and there is a great deal of variation. Society tends to focus on defining an individual's sexual orientation according to whom the individual engages sexually. However, sexual orientation involves the person's level of attraction, self-identity, sexual fantasies, social preferences, and feelings of intimacy. Most people are complex in cognitions, feelings, and actions.

Some individuals who are primarily gay, lesbian, or bisexual choose not to express their orientation explicitly through behavior for a variety of reasons. They may (realistically) fear the oppression and discrimination that same-sex individuals commonly experience in society (Elze, 2006), and choose to pursue a heterosexual lifestyle, dating, marrying and raising children. Although this choice may avoid some sources of anxiety and result in significant sources of satisfaction, it creates distressing chronic turmoil as the person is unable to express his genuine sexual attraction. This internal conflict contributes to SD in the couple relationship. To the extent that the individual is successful in keeping the sexual orientation issue secret, this blocks efforts to address the SD. Yet, disclosure to the partner also carries significant complications for the quality and status of their relationship. When a sexual orientation issue emerges in a committed heterosexual relationship, specialized individual and couple therapy to address the distress is necessary.

EXERCISE: "Identifying Dimensions of Sexual Orientation"

Directions: For the dimensions below, consider the same-sex, opposite-sex, and both-sex preferences in terms of the client's past and present.

Orientation Dimension   Past→Present

- Sexual *attraction*.
- Sexual *identity*—homosexual, bisexual, heterosexual, asexual.
- Sexual *behavior(s)* with women, men, or both.
- Sexual *fantasies* of women, men, both, or neither.
- Emotional intimacy commitment with women, men, both, or neither.

Masturbation/Use of Pornography

A woman's concern about her partner's use of pornography/masturbation is a common issue that brings couples to therapy. Careful evaluation of the role and meaning of this sexual activity is important. Commonly a male's use of pornography is about fantasy, not a proclivity to seek sexual behavior with other partners, or a comparison between the people portrayed in video and his partner or the partner's value. It is important to assess whether the client is using the Internet to pursue extra-relationship sexual involvements. Whether the fantasy material serves as a bridge to desire for couple sex or is an impediment is a crucial determination. Some men are more comfortable and confident with masturbatory sex than couple sex. In this case, his sexual self-esteem and sexual skills will be important targets for treatment.

Trauma: Unprocessed History of Physical/Sexual Abuse or Neglect

Clients with a history of physical or sexual abuse or neglect find that the barriers to adult sexual health can be pronounced (McCarthy & Breetz, 2010). The essence of abuse is that the adult perpetrator's sexual wants are met at the expense of the child or adolescent's emotional needs. Although people commonly focus on the behavior involved in sexual abuse, the lasting effect is psychological—the betrayal of trust. Children expect that significant adults—father, mother, teacher, clergy, relative, neighbor—will protect them, not abuse them. The confusion and conflict between what is often experienced as physical pleasure combined with profound anxiety, shame, and bewilderment is traumatic and creates persistent detrimental effects. Therapy for abuse is more common for women than men. Men deal with victimization less well than women, considering it a shameful secret that represents an attack on their masculinity and blaming themselves for its occurrence (Turchik, 2012). Males abused by a male (by far the more common circumstance) often suffer from concerns that they were engaging in homosexual behavior and question their sexual orientation. Negative cognitions and emotional distress interfere with sexual function. Unresolved trauma is a factor to explore when clients exhibit resistance to CBCST for SD. When a history of abuse, trauma, or neglect surfaces, the individual needs to process the abuse, integrate this piece of history within the current relationship, and implement the mantra "living well is the best revenge" (Maltz, 2012; McCarthy & Breetz, 2010).

Personal Habits and Preferences that Interfere with Intimacy

A detailed assessment of specific characteristics of the two partners helps to identify barriers to sexual satisfaction that are based on personal habits and preferences. For example, a couple may sleep in separate rooms due to one or both partners' snoring or poor hygiene (infrequent showers, bad breath). Clients experience emotional and physical distancing when one person's behaviors (punctuality, insensitive comments) alienate the partner. Other sources of tension that reduce intimacy result from an individual's temperament and sensory sensitivities (e.g., easily upset by interruptions from children, phone calls, the partner making even low-level noise when getting up to use the bathroom at night) and affect the climate surrounding couple sexuality. These issues are significant when they reflect an individual's rigid beliefs or perfectionistic expectations regarding conditions for sex. A CBCST approach involves assisting the couple in creatively devising mutually satisfying solutions to differences in personal habits and preferences.

Relationship Factors in Sexual Dysfunction

Relationship problems play a powerful role in sexual dissatisfaction and SD (Metz & Epstein, 2002). Healthy relationships include strong identity as a couple, the ability to recognize and address differences and conflicts, and being able to communicate with and influence the partner. The therapist facilitates partners' acknowledging strengths as well as attention to their vulnerabilities, feelings of respect and love in spite of problems (empathy), resolution of chronic conflicts, and management of extra-relationship stressors (e.g., parenting, careers). Rather than dividing the couple, processing stresses and conflicts can bring them together as an intimate team (Table 3.6).

Inaccurate and Inappropriate Cognitions that Contribute to Low Empathy and Negative Response to Partner Behavior

A core contribution of cognitive-behavioral approaches to understanding and treating relationship problems, including SD, is a focus on the cognitions that partners experience about each other, themselves, and their relationship. Clients notice and interpret aspects of the partner's behavior, and the meanings that they attach to events in their relationship have strong effects on their emotional and behavioral responses to each other (Baucom & Epstein, 1990; Epstein & Baucom, 2002).

Table 3.6 Relationship Factors that Complicate SD

1.	Inaccurate and inappropriate cognitions that contribute to low empathy and negative response to partner behavior
2.	Deficits in communication and conflict resolution skills that undermine cooperation and being an intimate team
3.	Coercion and sex demands that poison relaxation and pleasure
4.	Lack of attention to the partner and relationship

As described earlier, the five major types of cognitions influencing relationships are: (a) *selective perceptions*—what one notices or overlooks during couple interactions (e.g., only noticing instances when the partner failed to pay attention); (b) *attributions*—inferences one makes about factors that have contributed to an observed event (e.g., attributing a partner's irritability to unhappiness about the relationship); (c) *expectancies*—inferences involving predictions about the likelihood of future events (e.g., predicting that if you ask the partner for a favor, he will not comply); (d) *assumptions*—beliefs about characteristics of people and relationships (e.g., an assumption that men automatically become sexually aroused by an attractive person); and (e) *standards*—beliefs about the characteristics that people and relationships "should" have (e.g., a standard about specific ways that the partner should express love). These cognitions have the potential to influence the quality of a couple's overall and sexual relationship, and can be risk factors for the development and maintenance of SDs. For example, perfectionistic sexual performance standards contribute to performance anxiety and ED. Similarly, attributing the partner's failure to comply with her request for a particular type of caress as due to a lack of sexual attraction detracts from eroticism. The process of "spectatoring" is a form of selective perception involving hyper-focus on sexual arousal and performance.

The distortions that occur in partners' "automatic thoughts" (Beck, 1993) create emotional distress and negative behavioral interactions rather than empathy and cooperation. Through distorted attributions, individuals believe they know their partner's underlying thoughts and emotions, but in fact their empathy for internal experiences is limited. CBCST focuses on assessing partners' cognitions, examining evidence regarding their validity, and maximizing empathy. Training in communication skills is an important vehicle for increasing accurate understanding between partners. Training in problem-solving skills enhances a sense of collaboration.

Deficits in Communication and Conflict Resolution Skills that Undermine Cooperation and Being an Intimate Team

Deficits in communication and problem-solving skills have long been identified as risk factors for relationship distress as well as SD (Epstein & Baucom, 2002; Metz & Epstein, 2002). Common patterns associated with SD are (a) one partner withdraws while the other pursues in a negative manner, (b) they engage in escalating exchanges of negative behavior, and (c) they avoid or withdraw from each other. In contrast, sexually healthy couples cooperate as an intimate team; they "have each other's back" and provide a "safe harbor" amidst the stresses of life. They have disagreements but are able to discuss them constructively, de-escalate negative exchanges before damage is done, and "repair" hurt feelings through constructive actions such as apologizing and proposing collaboration (Epstein & Baucom, 2002; Gottman & Gottman, 2015). Negative communication undermines sexual health. Negative verbal and nonverbal behavior is a sexual "turn-off," the antithesis of the environment for quality sexuality. The negative actions hurt, alienate, and push away. One client poignantly lamented, "No one wants to make love to a cactus." Relationship health requires an intentional decision to monitor and regulate negative thoughts, emotions, and behaviors. The clinician actively guides partners in expressing their thoughts and emotions constructively and engaging in empathic listening.

When partners understand each other's preferences but disagree, the clinician helps them apply positive problem-solving communication to make requests vs. complaints, generate mutually acceptable solutions, and implement potential solutions and evaluate their effectiveness (Baucom et al., 2015; Epstein & Baucom, 2002).

The communication skills approach used most in cognitive-behavioral couple therapies involves teaching couples expressive and listening skills (Baucom et al., 2015; Epstein & Baucom, 2002; Markman, Stanley & Blumberg, 2010). This approach holds both partners responsible for good communication and provides guidelines for expressing one's thoughts and emotions clearly (e.g., be brief and specific in describing thoughts and emotions) and listening well (e.g., focus on understanding the partner's thoughts and emotions so he can reflect them back to her). Empathic listening requires that the individual set aside his agenda while listening and do his best to "put himself in the other person's shoes" to imagine what the world looks like to her and what emotions she is experiencing. An empathic listener conveys understanding of the other's subjective experience by paraphrasing what the person expressed. The therapist provides psychoeducation about the goals and principles underlying the skills, models them, and coaches the couple as they practice them. Epstein and Baucom (2002) detail the procedures for therapists, and Markman et al. (2010) is an excellent lay person's guide to building communication skills.

The understanding and respect that are conveyed through empathic listening and feedback have a strong positive effect on the couple's relationship, as they provide affirmation of their bond. Empathy can be even more strongly experienced when it is accompanied by physical affection, although it is important that the partner receiving touch is receptive to it. Although most individuals long for greater closeness, others may be wary of touch and react with anxiety or anger. Establishing a new pattern of empathic listening that includes nonverbal cues of caring without physical contact (e.g., eye contact, soft tone, concerned facial expression) is a crucial prerequisite for initiating physical affection.

When the context feels safe, the body has "skin hunger"—a longing for hugs and comfort. Without physical touch, the person feels alienated, lonely, neglected. The exchange of touch can enhance self-esteem as well as relationship satisfaction. *Affectionate touch* refers to the day-to-day gestures of closeness—kissing, hugging, and holding hands—to reinforce feelings of intimacy and connection. Affectionate touch is non-sexual but provides acceptance and reassurance when the partner needs a "safe harbor." Where words fail, an embrace or gentle touch communicates concern, understanding, acceptance, and caring.

When SD occurs, all forms of touch commonly diminish and may even be absent. The avoidant behavior protects partners from fears of performance failure or unsatisfying sex. Reinforcing the role of touch is a powerful way to address avoidance and promote tangible emotional connection.

CBCST practitioners emphasize that skills for expression and listening lead to greater empathy but do not guarantee agreement between partners. Rather, it takes collaborative efforts to devise mutually acceptable solutions to a problem. Therapists guide couples in developing their ability to engage in constructive problem solving (Baucom et al., 2015; Epstein & Baucom, 2002). The steps include (a) defining a problem in observable behavioral terms (e.g., "We have trouble finding quiet, private times for making love."), (b) brainstorming a variety of possible solutions and listing the advantages and disadvantages of each possible solution, (c) selecting a solution or combination of solutions, making specific plans for implementing the solution (including who will do what), (d) having a trial period of implementing the selected solution, (e) evaluating the success of the solution, and (f) revising the solution if needed. This collaborative approach necessitates that partners identify cognitions (e.g., expecting one's partner to take greater responsibility) or emotions (e.g., residual anger from prior arguments) that interfere with the joint problem solving.

Throughout this process, the therapist establishes control over in-session interactions to promote empathy and minimize negative behavior. This climate encourages respectful, warm, and united feelings (vs. feeling bitter, resentful, or angry). It facilitates sexual energy and fires desire.

Case Example Highlighting Cognitions, Emotions, and Behavior In Negative Couple Interactions

The following case illustrates negative processes involving cognitions (C), behaviors (B), and emotions (E).

Mark's chronic lateness returning home from work (B) led Tracy to make attributions (C) that he was selfish, dismissive, and rejecting of her childcare stresses. She felt hurt (E) that he was dismissing her feelings. When he came home 35 minutes late, she said, "Where have you been?" (B), which Mark interpreted as "criticism" (C) and sharply responded, "At work!" (B). Tracy then expressed her frustration over having the kids underfoot while she was trying to prepare dinner, saying, "Mark, you are so inconsiderate!" (B). Mark attributed his lateness to benign causes, involving pressure at the office that delayed his departure (C). He also made a negative attribution (C) that Tracy lacked empathy for the burden he felt as the principal financial provider, as she worked part-time so she could stay home three days a week with their two small children. He felt deeply hurt (E), and thought he was not appreciated (C). Mark also perceived (C) that he "always" upset Tracy and believed that he was a failure (C) as a husband for not making his wife happy. He feared disappointing Tracy, making a negative prediction, "There will be hell to pay" (C). In his frustration and hurt (E), he avoided Tracy (B), which appeared to her (C) as hostile and insensitive to her needs, thereby reinforcing her hurt and anger (E).

Mark tried to deflect his attribution (C) that Tracy was criticizing him by "apologizing." Then he stopped the discussion and became quiet (B). He was ashamed to think that he disappointed his wife (C) and was angry with himself (E). When Tracy's criticism led him to feel overwhelming anxiety and anger (E), he would lash out and call her names (B).

Mark's actions (B) seemed to Tracy to be insensitive (C) and an indication that he was disregarding her efforts in the home and in their relationship (C), leading her to feel hurt and angry (E). Her hurt and frustration (E) were compounded by "knowing" (C) that Mark would not listen to her and would avoid her. Her hurt and anger (E) manifested as complaints and criticisms (B). Mark considered Tracy's behavior to be a betrayal, not the way a loyal partner should behave (C). He believed that in response to his hard work for the sake of their relationship Tracy should express appreciation and support (C).

Mark was irritated (E) and confused (C) about what to do (B). He predicted that it was completely hopeless to try to satisfy Tracy (C), felt sad and frustrated (E), and pulled away (B). He saw himself in a double-bind (C): "Stand up to her and it's a big fight; leave it alone and she acts worse." In turn, Tracy perceived that Mark consistently abandoned her (C), and she expressed anger about it rather than her underlying hurt (E). She made conflicting predictions (C) that created a double-bind for her: "If I say anything he gets mad or goes away, but if I say nothing, it won't get better." The cycle of negative cognitions, emotions, and behaviors took on a life of its own, resulting in Mark and Tracy perceiving that their positions were polarized, and that they were no longer intimate friends (C).

The following are questions that the reader can consider in understanding the process that occurred between the partners:

- In what ways did the partners' cognitions "fuel" their negative emotions and behaviors?
- How and where in this pattern could Tracy and Mark do something to interrupt and change their dysfunctional interactions?
- Track Tracy's cognitions/emotions/behaviors. Where are points for therapeutic intervention?
- Track Mark's cognitions/emotions/ behaviors. Where are points for therapeutic intervention?
- Given that they presented with a low frequency of sex, in what ways was their conflict pattern influencing their sexual relationship?
- What could Tracy and Mark do to heal from their conflict? How would this affect their sexual relationship?

The Paths between Conflict Resolution and Sexual Dysfunction

Conflicts in couple relationships are normal and inevitable, as they are based on differences in partners' needs, preferences, or personality styles (Epstein & Baucom, 2002; Markman et al., 2010). For example, when partners have different preferences for autonomy versus togetherness and lack problem-solving skills, these differences create significant distress (Epstein & Baucom, 2002) and can precipitate SD. Markman et al. (2010) emphasize that it is the process through which partners deal with their conflicts that determines the quality of the relationship, not the existence of the conflict itself. Couples who lack the ability to communicate and negotiate fail to resolve conflict.

A relationship characterized by chronic conflict involves struggles over *control and power*. When conflictual interactions dominate, it takes many positive interactions to balance them (Gottman, 1999). Conflictual behaviors are "vivid" negative stimuli that are emotionally upsetting, dominate the partners' perceptions, and elicit self-protective responses. When the couple responds with a pattern of *negative reciprocity* (exchanges of threats and put-downs), this escalates relationship distress. Negative behavioral reciprocity is maintained by negative attributions that distressed partners have about each other's feelings and intentions (Epstein & Baucom, 2002).

Relationship conflict is related to SD through three different processes: (1) relationship conflict and distress generated by SD, (2) relationship conflict and distress contributed to the emergence and maintenance of SD, or (3) relationship conflict is an opportunity for a couple to increase emotional and sexual intimacy by constructively dealing with their issues (Metz & Epstein, 2002). The conflict management skills taught within CBCST can have a significant impact on sexual and overall relationship functioning.

Conflict presents *opportunities* to deepen emotional and sexual intimacy (Metz & Epstein, 2002). With a respectful, affirming process of conflict resolution, partners develop self-esteem, reinforce respect and admiration, develop confidence that conflict can be resolved, and create sexual desire. The heightened enjoyment that couples report when they have sex after "making up" (resolving conflict affirmatively) illustrates the link between conflict resolution and sexual feelings.

Assessing Relationship Conflict in SD

Assessment of the role of relationship conflict in SD requires a focus on psychological, relational, and sexual factors. The couple benefit from describing the detailed features of their conflict pattern, as this helps them objectify (depersonalize) and understand the nature, dynamics, and meaning of their distress.

Clinical interview guides help couples see that there are choices in how to resolve differences in a cooperative manner. In the "Five Features of Relationship Conflict," the clinician assesses: (1) environment, (2) subject, (3) severity, (4) styles of interaction, and (5) the meaning of conflict to each partner (Metz, 1993) (Figure 3.2).

The environment of the conflict refers to the circumstances and situations in which conflict occurs—the "who," "when," and "where." Assessment includes how each partner's characteristics are expressed; for example, how an individual with obsessive-compulsive traits contributes to couple conflict by ruminating about and repeatedly discussing details regarding a conflict. Assessment also explores the context in which the couple's quarrels occur, such as locations, time of day, and involvements of other people. A couple may argue while in the car after visiting the husband's mother on Sunday afternoon or in the bedroom Saturday night after an adolescent's misbehavior when both have been drinking. Understanding that conflict occurs in one situation more than another helps the couple anticipate and regulate it.

The **subject of the conflict** refers to "what" the fight is about—family finances, household chores, parenting, sex, family relations, social life, religious beliefs, or

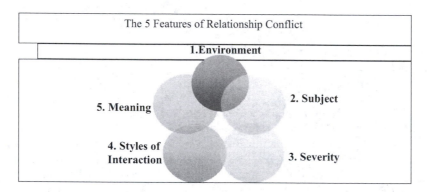

The 5 Features of Relationship Conflict

1.Environment

5. Meaning

2. Subject

4. Styles of Interaction

3. Severity

Figure 3.2 The 5 Features of Relationship Conflict

use of alcohol or drugs. Snyder's (1997) *Marital Satisfaction Inventory* (MSI); the *Dyadic Adjustment Scale* (DAS) (Spanier, 1976); and conflict topic inventories such as the *Relationship Issues Survey* (RIS; Epstein & Werlinich, 1999) ask partners to report degrees of conflict in areas of relationship functioning (e.g., sex, extended family, finances, children, goals in life). It is important to probe for underlying themes, because conflict over content issues can reflect deeper, broader meanings (e.g., conflict over finances may reflect an underlying pervasive power struggle).

The **severity of conflict** involves the frequency and intensity of behavioral interactions. This considers not only the intensity of negative behavior but also the amount of subjective distress that each partner experiences, whether expressed or concealed.

The **styles of conflict** refer to the forms of partner interactions during conflict—"how" they deal with conflict. Some styles have a constructive effect, whereas others have a destructive effect. The clinician can explore behavioral styles with questions such as, "How do you behave toward each other when you are having a disagreement?" Individuals who experience behavior patterns of aggression and withdrawal report detrimental sexual impacts. A model for understanding and assessing conflict-resolution styles focuses on two basic dimensions: (1) engaging vs. avoiding conflict styles and (2) constructive vs. destructive styles (Metz, 1993). These dimensions influence relational and sexual satisfaction. Styles that promote a constructive conflict resolution process are assertion, adaptation, and yielding/submission (in moderation). Styles that create a destructive process are aggression, denial, and withdrawal (Figure 3.3).

Assertion refers to constructive and cooperative responses conveyed in a clear, direct, non-coercive manner ("let's work this out" or calmly ask to "discuss the issue"). **Aggression** refers to destructive, threatening, punitive verbal or physical responses intended to compel compliance ("I'll get you back," throwing or breaking objects, criticizing, or pushing or slapping). **Adaptation** refers to positive efforts to adjust, modify, or circumvent a conflict through playfulness, hyperbole, or fatuous acknowledgment. Examples are humor, self-deprecation, teasing, or silliness. **Submission** includes yielding, obliging, acquiescing, or placating (prevent a problem from developing). **Denial** disowns, disavows, fails to acknowledge, or dissociates from conflict (refusing to talk). **Withdrawal** evades conflict through retreating or escaping (silence or staying away). Satisfied couples are characterized

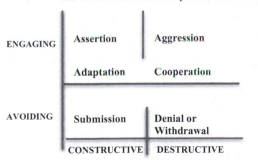

The Conflict Resolution Styles of the SCI Model

Figure 3.3 The Styles of Conflict

by high levels of assertion and adaptation, moderate levels of yielding/submission and denial, and low levels of aggression and withdrawal (Metz, 1993).

The **meaning of conflict** refers to the idiosyncratic importance that each partner attaches to the disagreement—"Why" is the couple struggling, and what does the disagreement mean to each person? What is each partner's cognitive appraisal of the conflict? The subjective meaning is determined by the person's assumptions and standards, attributions about causes of relational problems, expectancies about future interactions, and selective perception of events (Baucom et al., 2015; Epstein & Baucom, 2002). These cognitions influence the individual's emotional experience and its effect on sexual function.

Clients may not be aware of or express the meanings that conflicts have for them, so an important aspect of clinical assessment is to make these explicit. Common meanings underlying relationship discord include feeling devalued, abandoned, rejected, isolated, blocked in attempts to achieve personal goals, and controlled by the partner. The meaning ultimately determines whether the conflict serves to deepen understanding, acceptance, and love or is destructive to emotional and sexual intimacy. For example, a couple has frequent arguments when they are leaving the husband's parents' home, based on the wife being upset regarding the length of time they spent there. The topic is time, but these arguments reflect unstated concerns the wife has about the husband's loyalty to his parents rather than to her, and her desire to feel special to him. Identifying underlying meanings and understanding their importance helps the couple resolve core issues (Epstein & Baucom, 2002).

The attributions that individuals make regarding causes of relationship conflicts and problems can be tapped through clinical interviews and by means of self-report questionnaires. For example Pretzer, Epstein, and Fleming's (1991) *Marital Attitude Survey (MAS)* assesses the degree to which the client attributes relationship problems to his behavior and personality, the partner's behavior and personality, the partner's lack of love, or malicious intent. Individuals who make negative attributions about their partner subsequently communicate more negatively during problem-solving discussions (Bradbury & Fincham, 1992; Miller & Bradbury, 1995).

A measure that taps cognitions that are a source of couple conflict is the *Inventory of Specific Relationship Standards* (ISRS; Baucom, Epstein, Rankin, & Burnett, 1996). The ISRS assesses personal standards that an individual holds regarding the ways that partners should think and behave in an intimate relationship, along the major dimensions of degree of autonomy versus togetherness, distribution of power/control, and investment in the relationship. A comparison of partners' responses regarding their degree of adherence to each standard indicates degree of conflict between partners' standards. The less satisfied individuals are with the way in which their relationship standards are being met, the more distress and negative communication they exhibit (Baucom et al., 1996; Gordon, Baucom, Epstein, Burnett, & Rankin, 1999).

Assessing *the five features of relationship conflict* provides perspective regarding the role of conflict as a factor in SD. Investigating these—environmental circumstances, intensity of distress, the way in which the partners address sex, and the subjective meaning that the SD has for each partner—illuminates the features of conflict that warrant attention in CBCST.

Treating Relationship Conflict in CBCST

CBCST includes attention to the couple's conflict management patterns and skills. The clinician attends to the clients' relationship conflict history, current dynamics, and anticipation of conflict in the future. Whether the SD is caused by relationship conflict or the SD complicates one's ability to resolve disagreements, the conflict resolution pattern warrants therapeutic attention (Metz & Epstein, 2002).

CBCST focuses on strategies for (a) ameliorating the environmental precipitants to conflict, (b) exercising caution and good cognitive and behavioral skills when discussing conflict, and (c) decreasing the emotional intensity of disagreements. It is important to modify the couple's dysfunctional interaction style and facilitate empathic discussion of the meaning of the conflict.

Ameliorating environmental precipitants to conflict. Some aspects of a couple's physical and social environment tend to elicit conflicts or exacerbate the intensity of negative interactions (Epstein & Baucom, 2002). For example, some couples have arguments about differences in their parenting styles that are triggered by instances of child misbehavior. Conflictual discussions may be more likely to arise at the end of a day, or at bedtime when one person is ready for sleep and the other states, "We need to talk!" It is important for the therapist to inquire about the specific circumstances in which the couple experiences conflictual interactions. The partners are guided in compartmentalizing conflict by intentionally planning to set aside times and places for constructive discussions, and not engaging in conflict under poor conditions.

Exercising caution and good cognitive and behavioral skills. Therapy includes a goal of creating constructive communication, lessened avoidance, and less negative engagement. Although aggressive verbal behavior is more obvious than a partner's avoidance, the clinician maintains therapeutic balance with attention to both partners' contributions. A common pattern with SD couples is avoidance by the "identified" client, eliciting the partner's aggressive verbal behavior, which reinforces avoidant behavior and escalates intensity and negativity. The couple aggravates this negative engage/avoidance pattern to the point of extreme polarization.

These negative behavioral patterns become automatic, recurring quickly with minimal thought on the couple's part. It is important for the therapist to identify the specific sequence in the pattern, provide clear feedback about it, and engage the couple in a joint effort to prevent or interrupt it quickly. When environmental triggers are identified, the partners are coached to use caution. The therapist introduces constructive communication skills for expressing and listening, as well as problem-solving skills, and coaches the couple in practicing them.

Conflict interactions are influenced by one or both partners' cognitions about themselves, each other, and their relationship. Cognitive restructuring to address the meanings associated with the conflict is necessary. This includes softening unrealistic assumptions and standards about relationships (e.g., challenging the assumption that a caring partner should be able to mind-read her sexual needs). Discussion of the negative impact of clinging to the assumption and coaching about direct communication of each partner's needs helps the couple adopt a positive, realistic approach. CBCST facilitates the couple speaking about sexual thoughts, feelings, and beliefs in a positive milieu.

Partners are coached in developing their ability to assess the validity of their negative attributions, thereby creating a positive atmosphere for resolving conflicts. When an individual attributes a partner's SD to a global, stable trait (e.g., "He has very little interest in sex or me."), she attaches a hopeless meaning to the conflict, with an expectancy that the problem is unresolvable (Pretzer et al., 1991) and is likely to behave negatively during problem-solving discussions (Bradbury & Fincham, 1992; Miller & Bradbury, 1995). The CBCST clinician guides clients in noticing how each other's behavior varies across different situations, thus challenging the concept of an invariant negative trait. For example, the client who made the negative trait attribution regarding her partner's lack of interest in sex observed that he did approach her sexually on occasion. This led to a discussion about what conditions facilitated or inhibited sexual interest. The therapist helps the couple explore differences between those situations and devise ways of creating a sensual, erotic and safe environment.

The degree to which the therapist focuses on conflictual features of a couple's interactions varies according to the severity and meanings of the conflict. In addition to learning conflict resolution skills, they learn ways to experience and convey empathy—i.e., mutual acceptance and affirmation of important feelings (Christensen, Doss, & Jacobson, 2014). The goal is for each person to feel accepted, cared for, and positively regarded even when there is disagreement. Affirmation is central to the emotional "glue" in an intimate, sexually satisfying relationship.

CBCST provides a positive environment to experience cooperation to resolve the SD. The characteristics of CBCST—open communication, cooperation, and giving and receiving non-demand pleasuring—encourage empathy, equity, respect, appreciation of differences, and flexibility.

Decreasing the emotional intensity of disagreements. Conflicts that take place while one or both partners are highly emotionally aroused are unproductive. Consequently, in CBCST the clinician evaluates how intense the partners' emotions become during conflict discussions and teaches them emotion regulation skills. Epstein and Baucom (2002) detail procedures for increasing self-soothing and managing strong negative emotions based on the rationale that it is good to be aware of such emotions as an indication that an issue is of importance. Regulated expression of negative emotions maximizes the potential that she will understand that he is upset and can hear *why* that is so and *what* he would like her to do. Mindfulness exercises (Ameli, 2014; Gehart, 2012) develop clients' acceptance of problems and regulation of strong emotions.

Non-Compliance in CBCST

Resistance or noncompliance with homework assignments (e.g., passivity, "I didn't understand the assignment," "I forgot," "I was too busy") presents valuable therapeutic moments. The therapist needs to determine whether it is the client's anxiety, fear of failure, a hidden issue, or a deficit in the therapist's understanding (Kaplan, 1974). The term "resistance" has a negative connotation suggesting intentional opposition, whereas in many cases clients welcome interventions that would solve their problems but have negative expectancies about consequences of trying the interventions and creating change. Dysfunctional sex is unpleasant, but interventions to improve it can seem threatening. Resistance is a "process pointer" to emotional and sexual impediments. For example, a man's failure to follow through on homework that involved inserting his finger in her vagina in the "Partner Genital Exploration" exercise identified his emotional discomfort with touching her genitals, fear of sexual intimacy, or difficulty with giving pleasure due to concern that it would arouse her and increase pressure on him to perform sexually. Identifying such issues presents an opening to ameliorate barriers to sexual function.

Intimate Coercion and Sex Demands

Playful sex is all about enhancement, sharing, and special energy (Metz & Lutz, 1990). Performance demands, especially intimate coercion, poison desire. Demanding sex or insisting on a specific erotic scenario is antithetical to intimacy and pleasure. It is about trying to control one's partner and define what is acceptable, or to mask a fear of failure. Sexual coercion involves behavior that is either active (demanding) or passive (avoidant). Either approach detracts from the positive collaborative atmosphere needed for couple sexuality.

The CBCST clinician needs to identify forms of coercion and intervene to reduce them. Individuals who pressure their partner may rationalize their behavior by saying, "If I didn't make an issue of it, nothing sexual would happen!" Those who are avoidant justify their pattern by saying, "His way of showing he wants sex turns me off. I can't feel like doing anything with someone who behaves that way." In both cases the therapist sees a "grain of truth" in the person's rationale, but realizes that the client has adopted a rigid and controlling approach to the sexual relationship. The clinician needs to focus the couple on using constructive communication and problem-solving skills to achieve patterns of interacting regarding sex that are respectful and pleasure-oriented.

Sex after Conflict

Many couples use sex to "make up" after an argument. Touch and sexuality are excellent ways to connect and reconnect. Touching can be warm and sensual or passionate and driven. A healthy function of sexuality is to energize and motivate the couple to address and resolve conflict. A caveat regarding "make-up sex" is that couples may inadvertently develop a pattern of interpersonal aggression as "foreplay." Sex comes after verbal or physical aggression, which reinforces the pattern of interpersonal conflict. A key intervention is to set a hard-and-fast rule of no sexual contact of any type for at least 72 hours after an interpersonal violence incident. It is crucial that the therapist takes a strong stance against aggression and engages the couple in forming a clear agreement that aggression and coercion are totally unacceptable. This frees the couple to take emotional and sexual risks. Security provides the freedom to be playful and erotic. If intimate coercion persists, couple therapy for intimate partner aggression is needed, as long as the clinician determines that conjoint treatment is unlikely to create a risk for violence and injury (Epstein, Werlinich, & LaTaillade, 2015; Stith, McCollum, & Rosen, 2011).

Deficits in Eroticism

A false assumption is that a solid relationship guarantees sexual desire and that intimacy is the core of sex; the more intimacy the better. The counter-belief is that sex has nothing to do with intimacy. Like many traditional sex beliefs, these "convictions" are not only scientifically mistaken but harmful. Relationship and sexual health balances relational cohesion and individual autonomy. Too much intimacy can smother the spark of sexual desire if one or both partners feel constrained and even "smothered." On the other hand, sex without emotional intimacy depersonalizes a relationship. Both intimacy and eroticism are necessary for sexual desire, and one without the other is insufficient (Perel, 2006). Intimacy involves warm, loving, secure, predictable feelings, whereas eroticism involves mystery, creativity, vitality, unpredictability. These are different sensations/feelings, but not adversarial or incompatible (McCarthy & Wald, 2013).

Summary

A key therapeutic goal in CBCST is to elicit and reinforce pro-sex feelings. The role of sexuality is to energize the bond and enhance feelings of desire and desirability. Sexuality is an important buffer amidst the vicissitudes of a shared life. It includes intentionally valuing one's body and sex. The hallmark of sexually satisfied couples is the regular experience that each partner wants to please the other physically and emotionally without pressure to perform. The partners blend and integrate emotional intimacy, cooperation, pleasure, and eroticism in an ongoing process that enhances their life as a couple.

Chapter 4

Details of CBCST Treatment Strategies

The overall framework for CBCST includes step-by-step in-session interventions and homework assignments. Psychoeducation materials are crucial for facilitating the therapeutic process, as they broaden clients' understanding of sexual function and socialize them in the active roles that they play throughout treatment. Homework assignments are essential in transferring gains as the couple learns new skills for monitoring and changing negative cognitions, problematic emotions, and dysfunctional relational behaviors. Depending on the type and severity of SD, CBCST follows a progressive sequence of interventions to reduce dysfunction and enhance satisfying sexuality. Using a semi-structured protocol, treatment is individualized for each couple. The creative process of addressing the idiosyncratic components of a particular SD brings challenge and satisfaction for both the couple and therapist.

CBCST Trends in Sex Therapy Outcome Research

There is more than a 40-year history of sex therapy strategies and interventions that have gained wide acceptance among clinicians (e.g., Binik & Hall, 2014; Hawton, Catalan, Martin, & Fagg, 1986; Hertlein, Weeks & Gambecia, 2009; Killman, Boland, Norton, Davidson, & Caid, 1986; Metz & Weiss, 1992; Wincze & Weisberg, 2015), and from early in this history cognitive-behavioral approaches have had a prominent role (Perelman, 1980). Outcome evaluations of commonly used CBCST protocols report considerable variation in effectiveness (e.g., DeAmicus, Goldberg, LoPiccolo, Friedman, & Davidson, 1985; Hawton et al., 1986; Heiman & Meston, 1999; McCabe, 2016). There is a notable dearth of strictly controlled studies of effectiveness. McCabe (2001) reported effectiveness rates of 45% for female SDs and 53% for male SDs for brief structured sex therapy. Couples experienced lower levels of SD, more positive attitudes toward sex, increased perceptions that sex was enjoyable, positive contributions to their relationship, and lower perceptions of sexual failure. LoPiccolo and Lobitz (1972) found that CBCST improved orgasmic response in 50% of women treated for secondary orgasmic dysfunction, and that improvement rate was maintained at a 3-month follow-up. McCabe (2016) used brief CBCST for non-orgasmic women that included communication skills, sensate focus, and fantasy training, and found this program to be effective. Munjack et al., (1976) used a treatment for non-orgasmic women that included systematic desensitization, modified sensate focus homework assignments, and assertiveness training that emphasized communication about sexual preferences. They reported that 40% of the women achieved orgasm in 50% of their sexual interactions. Although those studies had encouraging findings, they were limited by designs that lacked control groups.

CBCST addressing female arousal and orgasm disorders has been found to be moderately effective. The sex therapy effectiveness data for male disorders suggests relatively good long-term outcome for ED but less treatment effectiveness for PE. Hawton et al. (1986) reported significant PE relapse (without a relapse prevention plan). Reynolds (1991) and Melnick, Soares, and Nasello (2008) reported evidence for effectiveness of a variety of psychotherapeutic approaches in treating ED.

Sexual desire is considered the most difficult SD to treat and has received little empirical investigation. Desire disorders have the least favorable prognosis compared with arousal and orgasmic SD. McCabe (2001) observed that both males and females who experience desire problems had a greater risk of relationship problems, especially lowered emotional intimacy. Research suggests there are multiple biological, psychological, and relationship factors that contribute to low desire, and that multidimensional approaches to treatment are more likely to produce successful outcome (Brotto & Luria, 2014; Meana & Steiner, 2014; Wincze & Weisberg, 2015). LoPiccolo and Friedman (1988) described treatment for low desire that incorporated sensate focus exercises, sexual fantasy, sensual awareness, sexual communication, and insight oriented therapy to help partners develop an understanding of the sources of the low desire, as well as cognitive restructuring and behavioral interventions to alter negative feelings and promote sexual pleasure. McCarthy, Ginsberg, and Fucito, (2006) described a cognitive-behavioral interpersonal treatment program and emphasized that therapy should prioritize sexual quality and satisfaction rather than the goal of intercourse frequency. Aroaz (1983) noted that detrimental cognitions lead to guilt and anxiety with subsequent loss of desire and described a cognitive approach utilizing hypnosis to correct negative sexual cognitions.

Treatment programs for SD frequently lack sufficient objective research methodology to allow an evaluation of effectiveness (O'Donohue, Dopke, & Swingen, 1997; O'Donohue, Swingen, Dopke, & Roger, 1999). Among the limitations are ambiguous operational definitions of SD (e.g., PE defined as ejaculation within 2 or 7 minutes vs. less than 15 intravaginal penile strokes) (Metz & Pryor, 2000), co-occurrence of multiple sex problems among 33% of clients (Loudon, 1998), ambiguity of treatment target variables and measures (McCabe, 2001), and absence of control groups. For example, Dekker and Everaerd (1983) conducted a follow-up study on 140 couples who received sex therapy with a cognitive-behavioral focus for a variety of SDs. At 5–8 weeks after therapy, couples reported improvements in sexual function and sexual satisfaction.

The limited evidence of treatment effectiveness from the existing studies suggests more positive results with couple therapy that includes communication and empathy training, cognitive strategies to ameliorate anxiety, interventions to reduce clients' focus on sexual performance, and development of psychosexual skills. Furthermore, combination treatments utilizing pharmaceutical and cognitive-behavioral interventions have been shown to be more effective than either approach used alone (Althof, 2003).

Why So Few Empirical Outcome Data?

There are several reasons for the limited empirical outcome data on CBCST. Early sex therapy publications (Masters & Johnson, 1970; Kaplan, 1974) described high success rates. The wave of enthusiasm for the treatments by those groundbreaking pioneers led many clinicians to use treatments without concern for empirical validation.

Early empirical research findings showing an association between SD and performance anxiety (Barlow, 1986, 1988) were consistent with the sex therapy techniques focused on relaxation training and sensate focus interventions. However, empirical questions of whether sensate focus exercises actually reduce clients' performance anxiety (both the negative cognitions and the anxious emotional states) and lead to reduced SD need to be examined. Controlled clinical trials using appropriate measures are required to answer these important questions, and are challenging and expensive projects.

For many years, the field of psychotherapy research focused on individual client characteristics. This tradition affected sex therapy outcome research, with the primary indices of success being rates of SD following treatment. However, SD has its roots in couple and interpersonal features, which both the interventions and outcome measures must take into account. The additional complexity of measuring couple dynamics (couple interactions, partner ratings) made controlled research complex and challenging. Recent developments in research design and dyadic statistical analysis, such as the actor-partner interdependence model approach (Kenny, Kashy, & Cook, 2006), offer the opportunity for more rigorous sex therapy process and outcome studies.

Research studies rely on external funding, and major funding agencies such as NIMH set priorities for the topics that they support. Few grants have been available for psychotherapy studies and even less for projects investigating sex therapy. The majority of funding for research related to sexuality has been for clinical trials of pharmacologic agents for sexual medicine (e.g., pro-erection medications; female desire agents; testosterone enhancement). More recently, and partly due to the disappointing real-life effectiveness of medication-only approaches (a low rate of patient prescription renewals), sexual medicine studies have expanded beyond studying effects on physical function to include relationship satisfaction measures (Perelman, 2009); Nevertheless, funding for psychosocial interventions for SD is negligible, in spite of evidence that SD has negative effects on individual and relationship well-being. Social priorities and funding have shifted away from SD to areas such as child sex abuse, sex offenses, sexual orientation, and STI/HIV issues.

Thus, CBCST outcome studies are few. There is a wealth of case studies, clinician presentations, and concomitant couple sex therapy data in pharmaceutical investigation. Evaluations of CBCST in conjunction with pharmacologic agents suggest that combination treatment is more effective than either component alone (Rosen, Miner, & Wincze, 2014). Such findings support the need to take into account interactive biopsychosocial realms of human experience.

Synopsis of Medical Treatments for SD

Although cognitive-behavioral interventions can have substantial effects, they cannot surmount a significant biological cause of SD. Grounding sexuality in the body does not dismiss the power of the mind. There is evidence that placebo effects account for approximately 20–25% of improvement in SD symptoms (Shamloul & Ghanem, 2013). Clinicians experience cases in which they formulated that a SD was caused by one factor (e.g., relationship conflict, an anxiety disorder) only to learn later that they had overlooked a biological cause (Halvorsen et al., 1998). Therefore, assessment of SD must include adequate attention to bio-medical factors. CBCST clinicians routinely collaborate with clients' physicians and make referrals for medical evaluations.

Medical Interventions

Areas of medical intervention include:

1. Management of medical problems that have detrimental sexual effects (e.g., hypertension and its medications, sleep apnea, diabetes, alcohol abuse);
2. Surgery (breast or prostate cancer, uterine adhesions);
3. Pro-sex medications including penile injections, PDE-5 inhibitors, and vaginal lubricants;
4. Sex devices such as EROS for women or a penile pump for ED;
5. Medical interventions for lifestyle issues include smoking cessation, cardiovascular conditioning, use of a machine for sleep apnea, or treatment of alcohol or drug abuse.

In the absence of a serious medical illness, CBCST considers medical interventions to be adjunctive therapies. A variety of medical conditions can interfere with sexual function indirectly by decreasing physical well-being and creating physical conditions that detract from the quality of life and compromise sexual function. The therapist needs to explore clients' subjective experiences of medical illness and disability. CBCST focuses on the importance of subjective well-being and sexual desire.

Medical Interventions Integrated into the Relationship

Medical treatments and pharmacologic interventions should not be used as "stand alone" remedies for SD. A core issue is whether the couple integrates these medical interventions into their style of intimacy, pleasure, and eroticism (McCarthy & Fucito, 2005). For example, pro-erection medications must take into account partners' cognitions about their sexual relationship, including attributions (e.g., "If he doesn't get an erection without a pill, he must not find me attractive") and standards (e.g., "Spontaneity is essential to an exciting sexual relationship"). Medications cannot counteract negative effects of relationship distress. Pharmacological agents are more effective when integrated with CBCST that addresses individual psychosexual functioning and the couple relationship.

Synopsis of Psychological Treatment

Client Education

Sexual anatomy and physiology education is a helpful component of CBCST. Although many clients have an understanding of sexual anatomy, they need more information about physiological function—how the sexual body works and what facilitates sexual arousal. Sex therapists see clients who are doctors, lawyers, or scientists and yet do not know the purpose of a pap smear, or men who think that they are "impotent" when their erection quickly subsides after ejaculation. The

CBCST approach provides opportunities for sexual education. For example, the Non-Demand Pleasuring exercises offer teaching moments about the importance of relaxation, touch quality, and taking time. "Partner Genital Exploration" provides an occasion to teach physiological differences between women and men, as well as the importance of relaxation as the foundation for sexual response.

Personal Accountability

Clients commonly hold unrealistic assumptions about sex being "natural," leading them to ignore the importance of creating conditions that produce emotional intimacy and sexual arousal. They cling to a standard that partners are responsible for causing each other's desire and orgasms. CBCST includes interventions that promote individual responsibility for sexuality while fostering the couple being an intimate sexual team. This involves education about the client's thinking (e.g., focusing in a mindful way on erotic cues) and behavior (removing distractions such as cell phones). It involves increasing "relational thinking" (Epstein & Baucom, 2002) to heighten awareness of dyadic processes (e.g., seductive talk) that enhance sexual experiences or detract from them (e.g., blaming). Psychoeducation is integrated with standard CBCST tasks such as sensate focus/pleasuring in which the person is encouraged to pay attention to the touch that she most enjoys, as well as touch that is unpleasant, and to communicate this. It is crucial for the therapist to help the client differentiate between taking personal responsibility and self-blame.

Addressing Individual and Relationship Factors that Interfere with Sexual Function

Sexual function is influenced by multiple factors. Individual and interpersonal barriers to sexuality need to be assessed and addressed. CBCST is well suited to provide an integrative treatment that targets individual and relational characteristics as well as bio-medical factors.

Identifying and modifying problematic individual characteristics. CBCST shares with psychodynamic models an understanding that earlier life experiences can have effects on current sexual function. CBCST includes the concept of cognitive *schema*, which acts as a template against which an individual's present experiences are interpreted and evaluated (Dattilio, 2010; Epstein & Baucom, 2002). Some negative schemas focus on the self (e.g., "I'm sexually unattractive"), some on significant others (e.g., "Men use women for sex"), and others on couple dynamics (e.g., "Relationships between gay men are doomed to failure."). The therapist conducts a systematic personal history, identifying prior life experiences associated with current positive and negative schemas. CBCST modifies schemas created within the context of couple therapy and new dynamic patterns. A referral for concurrent individual therapy might be needed for ingrained dysfunctional schemas.

A variety of psychological disorders pose barriers to sexual function and couple intimacy. Obsessive-compulsive disorder, post-traumatic stress disorder, generalized anxiety disorder, depression, and bipolar disorder are addressed in conjunction with CBCST. In cases where a client's psychological problem is a significant barrier to sex therapy, individual therapy and psychotropic medication is part of comprehensive treatment. Cognitive-behavioral couple therapy has been applied effectively in the treatment of individual psychopathology (e.g., Abramowitz et al., 2013; Bulik, Baucom, & Kirby, 2012; Monson & Fredman, 2012; Whisman & Beach, 2012). It is important that the CBCST therapist be skilled at individual diagnosis and make clinical decisions about treatment components and their sequencing.

The Importance of Ameliorating Couple Conflict

Unresolved couple conflict plays an important causative, as well as a maintaining role, for SD (Metz & Epstein, 2002). Conflict exists when partners have opposing preferences, needs, personal standards, or goals. It is the manner in which the partners respond to those discrepancies that influences the quality of their relationship (Epstein & Baucom, 2002; Kline, Pleasant, Whitton, & Markman, 2006). Therapy is enhanced when partners approach the problem with positive intentions to cooperate and use constructive problem solving to negotiate acceptable solutions. Unfortunately, partners who adopt an adversarial win-lose stance and engage in destructive behavioral patterns such as one partner demanding a change and the other withdrawing, reciprocating aggressive actions to coerce each other's compliance, or withdrawing subvert therapeutic change. These interactions and emotions detract from intimacy and sexual desire (Metz & Epstein, 2002).

A particular challenge occurs when a couple has covert conflict and hidden resentments that subvert homework tasks. A strength of CBCST is the therapist's ability to conduct an inquiry regarding cognitions and emotions associated with the failure to comply with homework tasks. For example, when a couple engages in homework only briefly, the therapist asks about each individual's thoughts and emotions before and during the exercise. One client describes an inability to relax during sensate focus because of persistent memories of the partner's criticism. The therapist explores the conflict between the partners' personal standards for how one "should" contribute to the relationship and works to substitute constructive problem-solving skills (Baucom, Epstein, Kirby & LaTaillade, 2015; Epstein & Baucom, 2002; Epstein, Dattilio, & Baucom, 2016). Addressing couple conflict is necessary in CBCST.

CBCST Strategies

The overarching conceptual model guiding CBCST treatment involves balancing three core experiential realms that promote sexual function:

Dimensions Contributing to Sexual Function

1. Psychological (cognitive and affective) excitement.
2. Physiological relaxation.
3. An intimate bond between erotic allies.

A variety of CBCST interventions foster psychological excitement, achieve a balance between physiological relaxation and sexual arousal, and increase couple intimacy and eroticism. Those interventions focus on (a) modifying partners' cognitions, (b) reducing aversive emotional states that interfere with relaxation and arousal, and (c) substituting constructive, collaborative, intimacy-enhancing interactions for negative patterns.

Cognitive interventions focus on *reinterpretation* (e.g., normalizing, positive reframing of negative attributions regarding motives), *validation* of the concept of self-interest (affirming that sexual "selfishness" is healthy for the person and relationship), *taking responsibility* for one's own pleasure, *thought stopping* techniques to reduce distracting cognitions, *mindfulness* to avoid "spectatoring," *challenging unrealistic standards* regarding sexual function, and *psychoeducation* (including bibliotherapy and video presentations) about sexual response. Erotic literature, pictures, and media as well as guided imagery and erotic fantasy are additional cognitive techniques to enhance excitement.

CBCST theorists and clinicians devote substantial attention to the role of emotion in human functioning (Thoma & McKay, 2015). Interventions that directly target aversive emotional states include relaxation training, coaching in stress-reduction self-talk (Meichenbaum, 1985), and training in mindfulness strategies (Germer, Siegel, & Fulton, 2013), as well as strategies for fostering acceptance of unpleasant emotional experiences (Hayes, Strosahl, & Wilson, 2011). CBCST strategies decrease emotional distress and increase positive emotional states.

Interventions that focus on modifying behavioral patterns influencing SD include graduated assignments to decrease performance anxiety and avoidance behavior, relaxation training for counteracting negative emotions, and relationship enhancing communication training. Behavioral interventions involve skill training, such as expressiveness, empathic listening, and problem-solving skills (Epstein & Baucom, 2002). Intimacy, compliments, and tender gestures promote an affirming and cooperative environment. CBCST provides training in expression of preferences and desires (direct but respectful) as well as increasing partners' comfort with sexual initiation and refusal skills. Sensate focus/pleasuring assignments include nonverbal and verbal guidance to encourage cooperation as well as sensual appreciation. CBCST provides oral or written *instructions* and *models* (personal demonstrations or video examples) of positive behaviors and coaching the couple in practicing them (Baucom et al., 2015; Epstein & Baucom, 2002).

The Core of CBCST: Psychosexual Skill Exercises

CBCST teaches psychosexual skills involving a series of pleasuring exercises. Multiple clinical approaches have been used to improve sexual function, including sex focused group therapy (Barbach, 1975; Metz & Weiss, 1992), body awareness workshops (Dobson, 1996), yoga and mindfulness (Brotto & Heiman, 2007), and comprehensive psychosexual skill exercises (McCarthy & McCarthy, 2012). CBCST involves collaboration with the couple and attends to each individual's unique cognitions, emotional responses, and behavioral patterns. Standard treatment components are tailored to each couple's characteristics, experiences, and values.

In-Session Interventions and Homework Assignments

The enhanced conceptualization of the human sexual response cycle—desire, arousal, plateau, orgasm, and satisfaction—informs the biopsychosocial model that

Table 4.1 Standard Sex Therapy Exercises

Tiered Stage	Cognitive-Behavioral Exercise/Assignment	Sex Response Cycle Phase
1.	Relaxation training—individual and couple relaxation training using "in-body" focused techniques	Desire phase
2.	Non-genital pleasuring—gentle massage designed for physical relaxation	Desire phase
3.	Genital exploration—relaxed exploration of genital touch	Desire/arousal phases
4.	Erotic pleasuring—the couple takes turns at sexual touch without orgasm	Arousal/plateau phases
5.	Relaxed intercourse—the couple learns to have intercourse with slow, pleasure-oriented thrusting	Plateau phase
6.	Progressive intercourse—the couple learns intercourse with arousal flexibility by using progressively more vigorous thrusting; removal of prohibition on orgasm; and sexual interaction flexibility training	Plateau/orgasm phases
7.	Maintenance plan-emphasis on afterplay—couple reflects on features that contribute to sexual function; develop a plan to preserve success as well as strategies to address a sexual lapse	Satisfaction

undergirds and guides CBCST. The physical and psychological progression during the sexual response process provides the schema for understanding (a) barriers to sexual response and (b) strategies to address these.

The sequence of exercises rehearses the stages of the sexual response cycle and helps the therapist and couple identify and correct impediments to pleasure, eroticism, and sexual function. The interventions are designed in a couple format for (a) increasing physical relaxation and non-demand pleasure to alleviate performance anxiety and barriers to sexual response, (b) facilitating psychosexual skills for pleasuring and eroticism, and (c) enhancing individual and relationship satisfaction. They provide the structure to identify where the couple has difficulties and the means for addressing them (Table 4.1).

The Sensate Focus/Pleasuring Framework

Sensate Focus/Pleasuring involves a set of psychosexual skill exercises assigned for couples to complete at home. The exercises direct awareness to pleasure, away from "spectatoring" (a distracting focus on sexual performance) and increase awareness of relaxation. Masters and Johnson (1970) believed that by removing the barriers to healthy sexual function (performance anxiety, shame, cognitive distraction, relationship conflict) and promoting physical, emotional, and interpersonal relaxation, clients would "naturally" function well sexually. Focusing on physical sensations provides a cognitive "blinder" to performance distractions, and circumvents relationship irritations and resentments to provide a pleasure-oriented experience without performance demands. Each partner is encouraged to focus on his own sensual experience. The evidence regarding the role of anxiety in SD (Barlow, 1988) underscores the need for physiological and psychological relaxation to ameliorate performance pressure and enhance pleasuring.

Sensate focus/pleasuring provides the behavioral structure for a wealth of clinical interventions and expansion of couple sexuality. The initial goal is sensual pleasure without sexual arousal. This provides the opportunity to restore natural sexual responsiveness through physical relaxation and enhanced sensory awareness. The focus on physical sensations serves to manage performance anxiety, negative expectancies, and distractions.

This format anchors treatment and provides the core on which the therapist identifies and intervenes with idiosyncratic cognitive, behavioral, emotional and relationship problems. CBCST employs semi-structured assignments in which the partners take turns giving and receiving sensual touch, which progressively transitions to interactive pleasuring and arousal. Exercises include body relaxation, non-genital pleasuring, genital pleasuring, self-exploration/ masturbation, bridges to sexual desire, arousal and eroticism, intercourse as a pleasuring experience, mapping the individuals' cognitive excitement continuum, and identifying and using special turn-ons. They are used to increase female arousal, eroticism and orgasm, to decrease sexual pain, to increase male arousal, erections, and ejaculatory control, to decrease ejaculatory inhibition, and to enhance the couple's ability to interact as an intimate sexual team (McCarthy & McCarthy, 2012).

It is especially important for the therapist to manage the psychosexual skill exercises when client anxiety and depression are involved. For example, a male's obsessive focus on his penis causes performance anxiety that contributes to ED. Self or partner pressure for a woman to experience orgasm results in performance anxiety that lowers pleasure and the likelihood of orgasm. The negative thinking commonly associated with depression (self-criticism, hopelessness) leads to inertia and withdrawal. Consequently, the therapist encourages the couple to focus on pleasure and away from sex performance. The client concentrates on the sensual pleasures of her skin and touching her partner—warmth, smoothness, texture, and shape. In cases of inhibited desire, the therapist focuses the couple on non-genital sensations, through exploration of relaxed touching, talking, hugging, kissing, tasting, and sounds. Partners are encouraged to share sensations and express emotions. This increases appreciation of sensual awareness, leading to reduced performance pressure. Subsequent psychosexual exercises incorporate arousal based on physical relaxation, use of pelvic muscles, attention to each partner's cognitive arousal continuum, and enhanced eroticism, as well as intercourse, orgasm, and satisfaction.

While using the semi-structured psychosexual skill exercises as the format for growth, it is crucial to individualize sex therapy. There is not "one right way to be sexual." It is important for the couple to develop their unique sexual style (McCarthy & McCarthy, 2009). Sex therapy helps identify partners' preferences and blend their differences. Do they prefer sex three times a week or three times a month? Mutual stimulation or taking turns? Do they prefer variety and spontaneity or predictable, scheduled sex? Is sex core to their relationship or a smaller part? Is sex primarily for intimacy, tension release, pleasure, or enhanced self-esteem? Is sex a way to feel emotionally attached or a way to maintain a mutually comfortable degree of intimacy? The sexual exercises provide a format to help the couple identify, accept, and blend multiple roles and meanings. The therapist explicitly raises these issues, as many couples have never discussed their preferences. This openness (and validation that variation in preferences is normal) is reassuring. These discussions are both educational and increase partners' understanding of each other.

Clinical Management of Sensate Focus/Pleasuring

CBCST provides experiences to alter and enhance the couple's intimate sexual relationship. The clinician is directive in therapy sessions and designs homework exercises. The level of clinical direction is guided by the severity of distress and the chronicity of the SD. Couple discussion is essential and invaluable, but without psychosexual skills change it will be insufficient. Therapist leadership to ensure homework compliance challenges partners' self-defeating cognitions and dysfunctional behaviors that cause or maintain the SD. Gentle guidance is required to provide experiences that promote sex function as well as satisfaction.

The therapist prescribes a progressive series of 6–12 homework assignments tailored to the particular couple, guiding the timing of the pleasure/eroticism process. Haphazard assignments that are not sequenced to approximate the sexual response stages undermine effectiveness and risk failure. In the early steps, the partners take turns touching each other's body excluding breasts and genitals, with one partner being the "giver" and the other the "receiver". During the psychosexual skill exercises, couples are instructed to have little verbal interaction, particularly in the initial stage. The focus is on touching and becoming aware of each other's body, and to appreciate the sensations. A "ban" on intercourse is imposed to facilitate the cognitive shift to pleasure rather than performance. The giver concentrates on touching her partner in ways that she finds interesting and enjoyable, not based on what she assumes he is thinking or will arouse him.

Subsequent step-by-step exercises increase touch options. The partner receiving the touching focuses on sensations and gathering information about her body. The receiver uses a technique of placing her hand over the giver's hand in order to show what touching is pleasurable in terms of pace and pressure. Communication continues to be primarily nonverbal. The giver learns to appreciate the partner's body and feelings. Subsequent exercises include the introduction of genital touch, progressive arousal and eroticism, and intercourse and orgasm.

Benefits of Detailed Cognitive-Behavioral Steps

The sensate focus/pleasuring exercises provide the clinician a framework to promote sexual pleasure and function. This framework has a number of benefits.

Structure for change. The pleasuring exercises provide a structure for behavioral change and enlist the couple's cooperation. CBCST is based on collaboration. The couple pursues psychological and physical relaxation, focusing on pleasure to block distracting cognitive "spectatoring," promoting cooperation as an intimate sexual team, and focusing on sensual/sexual sensations. The therapist often prohibits sexual activity beyond the homework (to refocus from performance to pleasure and eliminate pressure for intercourse). An alternative approach with a less distressed couple requires a 4-hour "ban" on sexual activity after a pleasuring date.

The structure of the psychosexual skill exercises provides the therapist the opportunity to set realistic expectations for the couple regarding sensual and sexual experiences. It is helpful for the couple to understand the difference between partner interaction arousal (focusing on arousing aspects of both touching and being touched by one's partner giving and receiving pleasure) and self-entrancement arousal (focusing on physical and psychological stimulation that enhances one's own arousal). The man who fears loss of desire or ED learns that his body requires relaxation for sexual function. He learns the value of relaxation as the physical foundation for easy and reliable erection. "Working" at and worrying about getting an erection backfires. The sensate focus/pleasuring exercises offer the clinician the opportunity to teach realistic expectations and specific psychosexual skills that promote sexual function and satisfaction.

Ongoing assessment tool. The sensate focus/pleasuring steps provide ongoing assessment. Careful attention to the details of each partner's experiences identifies key areas that are targets for change. The therapist becomes aware of clients' anxieties and inhibitions. A man with ED who has difficulty focusing on physical sensations alerts the therapist to help him cognitively concentrate on physical sensations. When a partner is not compliant with a homework assignment, the therapist conducts an inquiry about his thoughts and emotions. A client who reports being "too busy" to engage in the homework assignments opens the door for a discussion of the stresses in her life, priorities in the relationship, or disguised fears of what would happen if there was increased sexual intimacy. CBCST is an experiential approach in which the therapist guides the couple in exploring subjective thoughts and emotions associated with sex, and designs interventions to reduce barriers to sexual enjoyment.

Step-by-step tool for cognitive-behavioral intervention. The in-session processing of homework assignments provides an efficient path to identify and reduce cognitive and emotional barriers to change. The therapist is supportive but holds each partner accountable for behavioral compliance at each step. Although couples hope for a "quick fix", the therapist is alert for difficulties to identify detrimental cognitions, emotions, and behaviors that contribute to SD and impede treatment. Some barriers are internal (e.g., a fear that improved sexual function will lead to increased pressure for frequent sex), whereas others involve negative interpersonal processes. For example, the therapist learns that a husband was irritated when his partner "pestered" him to do homework, which triggered his longstanding anger that she "tries to control me," which led him to engage in passive resistance. The CBCST therapist works with the couple to shift their "power struggle" pattern (e.g., encouraging him to take responsibility for his behavior). This detailed focus on relationship process is a hallmark of CBCST.

The questions typical in processing psychosexual skill exercises include:

Homework Processing Probes

1. Tell me how the exercise went.
2. How did you schedule your homework?
3. How many times did you engage in the exercises?
4. Who initiated the exercise? How did you decide?
5. What was pleasurable and in what ways?
6. Describe discomfort, distractions, or irritations you experienced during the exercises.
7. How easy was it to focus on sensual pleasure?
8. What did you most like when you were the receiver?
9. What did you most like when you were the giver?
10. Did you talk during the exercise?
11. How did you guide your partner if something was uncomfortable or you wanted a different type of touch?

---

12. Did you feel turned on during the exercise and, if so, when?
13. What percentage of the time were you distracted, and what distracted you?
14. How did you handle any negative thoughts that occurred?
15. How did you bring your attention back to the sensual pleasure?
16. How well do you think you did on this stage of the homework?

Such probes provide direction for intervention. The question "How did you schedule your homework" might yield, "I asked that we do it, but she had to talk on the phone with her friend" can help address a cooperation issue, the importance of role leadership, and scheduling homework times during sessions so each partner knows when and where. If the couple does not follow-up, this requires identifying the barriers and assisting the couple with problem solving to increase homework compliance. The probes encourage each individual to self-disclose thoughts and emotions (e.g., "I feel ashamed when I don't get an erection."), increasing each partner's understanding of the other's inner experience. This increases empathy and intimacy.

Psycho-Education in CBCST

A strong collaborative relationship between the therapist and clients is at the foundation of CBCST. The clinician provides the couple with a crucial cognitive framework regarding the therapeutic process. Although therapy "assignments" can seem mechanical, explaining their rationale provides reassurance and motivation. CBCST principles may be judiciously incorporated as psycho-educational "mini-lectures," illustrated during "teaching moments" or through creative assignments (Metz & McCarthy, 2004). For example, when the man rushes to intercourse just as he is becoming erect, the therapist encourages the couple to let the woman lead the transition to intercourse when he is in erotic flow and guide intromission. This psycho-education approach increases the couple's understanding of factors that cause and maintain SD.

Principles of CBCST

The following are core principles of CBCST that underlie therapeutic interventions:

1. Therapy is based on a foundation of *relationship cooperation and intimacy*. The ultimate goal is sexual satisfaction.
2. Healthy sexuality involves acceptance and a *positive value* for the body and sex.
3. Sex therapy goals are based on realistic expectations of individual and couple functioning.
4. Each partner takes *personal responsibility* for her sexual self—she is responsible for her desire, arousal, and orgasm.

5. Sex therapy includes accurate and realistic information about *sexual anatomy and physiology*.
6. Therapy teaches the importance of *relaxation* (vs. performance anxiety and spectatoring) as the foundation for sexual function.
7. Satisfying sexuality involves focusing on pleasure as well as sexual function.
8. Therapy is designed to build *cooperation* as an intimate sexual team and to assist each partner to express sensual and sexual wishes while increasing awareness of the other's wants and desires.
9. Therapy facilitates partners' flexible attitudes, adaptation to changes, and openness to alternative sexual scenarios.
10. Therapy helps a couple build positive, realistic expectations. Sex is integrated into their real life and real life is integrated into sex.
11. Therapy supports relationship "glue" through sexual playfulness.
12. Therapy assists the couple in developing a relapse prevention plan to promote long-term sexual satisfaction.

Therapy Is Based on a Foundation of Relationship Cooperation and Intimacy

While people seek simple cures to what appears to be a simple problem with a simple cause, SD is multi-causal and multidimensional. CBCST emphasizes that emotional and sexual satisfaction is the ultimate objective. The couple is an intimate sexual team that integrates individual needs and relational cohesion, including integrating eroticism with emotional intimacy. Men and women commonly want and crave both eroticism and the emotional connection involved in intimacy (Boul, 2007). CBCST is based on an assumption that couple relationships work best when both partners value, nurture, and pursue an integration of eroticism and intimacy (Lobitz & Lobitz, 1996).

Healthy Sexuality Involves Acceptance and a Positive Value for the Body and Sex

CBCST values sex as inherently good. Sex provides positive energy in life, an invaluable part of an individual's and couple's long-term comfort, confidence, closeness, and pleasure. Partners who denigrate each other elicit shame, a common factor in SD. Clients who develop SD usually do not value their sexual body, lack sexual confidence, underestimate the power of their sex drive, and minimize their desire for emotional intimacy (Cooper & Marcus, 2003). Negative cognitions (Boul, 2007; Fichten, Spector, & Libman, 1988) link sex with embarrassment or shame, and compartmentalize sex from real life. Sex-positive therapy (Kleinplatz, 2012) facilitates acceptance of sexuality and honors sex as a means to use one's body for fun, pleasure, affirmation, and attachment. Developing sexual self-esteem—the antithesis of shame—requires accepting and affirming sexuality, respecting honest sexual feelings, regulating sexual behaviors, and promoting healthy sexuality. Sexual self-esteem requires understanding, acceptance, and respect for each other's body and emotional and sexual desires.

Satisfying sex involves embracing the sexual body and appreciating the innate sex-drive imperative and its role in sexual satisfaction (Fisher, Aron, Masher, & Brown, 2002). Fear, disgust and shame-related notions of sex are serious barriers to sexual health and satisfaction. Sexual shame is a risk factor in chemical dependency (O'Farrell, Choquettem, Cutter, & Birchler, 1997). Sexually satisfied couples challenge negative ideas involving their bodies and value sex as inherently good.

CBCST is designed to promote sex as a source of positive relationship energy and invite clients to change. Accepting and affirming one's sexuality is a foundation for sexual self-esteem, a key aspect of overall self-worth. Therapy encourages partners to recognize and support the partner's sexual self-esteem, valuing each other's body and the joys of sexual pleasure. This fuels sexual confidence, comfort, pleasure, eroticism, and satisfaction.

Sex Therapy Goals are Based on Realistic Expectations of Individual and Couple Functioning

Unrealistic standards for both sexual function and relationship satisfaction set the stage for disappointment, sadness, and anger (Epstein & Baucom, 2002). They contribute to negative behavioral interactions such as criticizing or withdrawing. CBCST helps the couple based on accurate information about physiological, relational, and psychological function. Psycho-education about sex is a foundation for satisfaction, as is setting reasonable standards for the self and partner.

Each Partner Takes Personal Responsibility for His or Her Sexual Self

Passivity of either partner limits the promise of a positive therapeutic outcome. Each partner must be accountable for her sexual thoughts, emotions, and behaviors and take responsibility for ameliorating barriers or deficits. She is responsible for her desire, arousal, and orgasm. Rather than being a burden, taking responsibility empowers the individual to create the conditions that will lead to sexual satisfaction.

Sex Therapy Includes Accurate and Realistic Information about Sexual Anatomy and Physiology

Realistic, age-appropriate sexual expectations are essential for sexual health and satisfaction. Good physical health and healthy behavioral habits are vital for sexual health. These are grounded *in knowledge* about biological, psychological, and relationship factors in sexual response. Unrealistic expectations are based on inaccurate information that precipitates frustration, distress, and a sense of failure. CBCST includes a strong sex education component. The therapist provides psychoeducational explanations regarding sex during sessions and gives the members of the couple concise sex education readings for homework.

Importance of Relaxation for Sexual Function

Physiological, psychological, and interpersonal relaxation is the basis for sexual function; this is increasingly important after age 40 (Pfaus, 1999). In the absence of performance anxiety, cognitive distraction, shame, and negative couple interactions, the body naturally responds sexually. Although it might seem that physiological relaxation is inconsistent with sexual arousal, in fact adequate physiological relaxation is essential for sexual function. Anxiety contributes to SD (Barlow, 1986). CBCST techniques target both the cognitive and physiological components of anxiety. CBCST is a combination of interventions for (a) identifying and modifying anxiety-eliciting cognitions (e.g., "I'm going to fail to have an erection again." "My partner will find someone else if I'm not more sexual with him."), (b) physical relaxation training, (c) structured homework assignments focusing on pleasurable sensations, and (d) coaching the couple to soothe each other as well as themselves during sexual interactions. Mindful touch, non-demand pleasuring, and a prohibition on intercourse provide the opportunity for relaxed, progressive arousal.

Cognitive focus on the sensual feelings of gentle touch is the mechanism for relaxation as the foundation for sexual response. In youth, even high levels of anxiety can be overcome by sexual excitement. Establishing a solid foundation for sexual function in physical relaxation is a core principle of adult sexuality. The sensate focus/pleasuring approach provides the experience of progressing from comfort to pleasure, arousal, erotic flow, intercourse, and orgasm.

The physiological mechanism of the PDE-5 medications (e.g., Viagra and Cialis) is to *relax* the musculature surrounding the arteries in the penis to enable blood flow and erection. Barlow (1988) emphasized the need for physiological and psychological relaxation to ameliorate performance pressure and anxiety. Physical relaxation facilitates reliable sexual arousal. CBCST guides clients in building relaxation methods into their daily lives. The therapist monitors instances of non-compliance and engages clients in addressing barriers to using relaxation strategies (e.g., cognitions such as "I'm too busy to fit in time for that"). Clients who have a pattern of inattention to pleasant environmental stimuli benefit from coaching in mindfulness and pleasuring exercises (Ameli, 2014).

CBCST identifies and modifies couple interactions that contribute to tension. The therapist collects information from self-reports and observing the couple's behavioral process during sessions (Epstein & Baucom, 2002). The therapist gives feedback about counterproductive patterns (e.g., a demand–withdraw pattern fueled by anger and anxiety) and encourages them to adopt supportive and soothing interactions, such as empathic listening. CBCST is a holistic approach to SD. It takes into account multiple causes of SD and uses integrative interventions tailored to the characteristics of each couple.

Focusing on Pleasure as Well as Sexual Function

Comfort and enjoyment of touch is essential. Pleasure is the foundation for sexual arousal and heightened eroticism. Although sexual function, including intercourse and orgasm, is very important, it is best understood through the focus on desire, pleasure, eroticism, and satisfaction.

The psychosexual skill exercises provide structure to enhance couple experiences and guide cognitive awareness of the role of touch in pleasure and eroticism. The goal is to help couples appreciate the value of touch and the progression from sensual to erotic experience. Affectionate touch is crucial to bringing pleasure to the bedroom and serves as the platform for sexual response. Educating clients about the essential link with touch counters unrealistic beliefs that sexual arousal is an automatic response and occurs even if partners are emotionally distant or alienated. Through experiencing the developmental sequence of exercises, the partners are learning healthy couple sexuality. Awareness and attention to the five dimensions of touch (affection, sensual, pleasure, erotic, and intercourse) enhances couple sexuality (McCarthy & Metz, 2008).

Emotional intimacy is essential to a vibrant sex life, but this does not automatically ensure eroticism. In fact, an over-emphasis on intimacy can suffocate eroticism (Perel, 2006). Emotional intimacy provides the context for eroticism but is not sufficient to produce it.

Non-demand pleasuring. Non-demand pleasuring involves valuing sensual and playful touch. Sharing pleasure is a core aspect of quality couple sexuality. Each partner develops preferences for types of *affectionate touch* (kissing, hugging, holding hands); *sensual touch* (non-genital cuddling and massage, feeling close and safe, touching before going to sleep or on awakening, back or head rubs); and *playful touch* (mixing genital and non-genital touch, a shower or bath together, romantic or erotic dancing, whole body massage, valuing pleasuring for itself-not as "foreplay"). Few couples have the same preferences for non-demand pleasuring. This is not only normal, but is preferable. Differences add spice and promote a variable, flexible sexual repertoire. Important psychosexual skills include establishing preference patterns of multiple *vs.* single stimulation; mutual pleasuring *vs.* taking turns; times and places to be sexual; and communicating choices of staying with a level of pleasure or using it as a bridge to intercourse. The most crucial factor is attitudinal—valuing the enjoyment of pleasure *vs.* pressure to achieve sex performance.

Building Cooperation as an Intimate Sexual Team

In CBCST, individual and gender differences are respectfully valued and similarities mutually accepted. The exercises identify and integrate partner differences. Therapy assists each client to express sensual and sexual wishes while increasing awareness of the partner's wants and desires. The format of the assignments ensures "equal time" pleasuring. Any gender differences are viewed not as opposites but promoted as compatible and worthy of mutual support. It is counterproductive to view the partner's preferences as right or wrong, better or worse, rather as normal variations that the couple can creatively support. This skill for balancing needs is crucial for CBCST (Epstein & Baucom, 2002).

Facilitate Flexibility, Adaptation, and Alternative Sexual Scenarios

Flexibility is a core quality that serves as an antithesis to burden and one-dimensional sex controlled by performance anxiety, spectatoring, and obsessive focus on the partner's responsiveness. Valuing variable, flexible sexual experiences (Good Enough Sex—GES; Metz & McCarthy, 2012) and abandoning the "need" for perfect performance inoculates the couple against distress from SD by overcoming tensions, fear of failure, and rejection. The normal range of human sexual response includes SD symptoms, such as occasional lack of desire, sexual pain, or non-orgasmic response. Satisfied couples experience a variety of sources of satisfaction in their lovemaking. Flexibility is promoted by appreciation of five purposes for sex and three arousal styles.

Five Purposes for Sex

Research as well as clinical experience identifies five fundamental reasons for sex (Meston & Buss, 2009; Metz & McCarthy, 2010, 2011:

1. reproduction;
2. tension and anxiety reduction;
3. sensual enjoyment and pleasure;
4. self-esteem and confidence;
5. relationship closeness and satisfaction. Sexually satisfied couples integrate the five purposes for sex.

Reproduction is a "natural" biological function, although conception is best viewed as a choice, not a mandate. Tension reduction is a common psychophysiological purpose of sex, reducing life stresses. Sensual enjoyment and pleasure is a core function of sex in a long term, satisfying relationship. Individuals seek enhancement of self-esteem through sex, including pride in being a sexual person. Sex serves to increase feelings of intimacy, love, and emotional support. In dysfunctional relationships, the purposes of sex may be negative, such as manipulation, control, proving something, or enacting revenge.

Individuals often pursue different sexual goals at different times, including different goals during a sexual encounter. For example, on a particular day one partner may seek tension release prompted by workday pressures, while the other may seek emotional closeness (Basson, 2007; Meana, 2010). Most individuals pursue each of these five purposes for sex at some time in their lives. Often, multiple purposes are pursued simultaneously. In fact, when the focus becomes too singular, such as becoming pregnant at all costs during infertility treatment, sex becomes stressful and eventually dysfunctional.

The potential for conflict exists as the partners become aware that they have different agendas. The CBCST clinician helps couples minimize distress by encouraging acceptance that partners pursue sex for multiple and fluctuating purposes and clear communication regarding each person's sexual agenda, as well as negotiation of an acceptable agenda.

Appreciating *different sexual arousal styles* (e.g. Metz & McCarthy, 2004; McCarthy & McCarthy, 2009) can help couples with this adaptation. Mosher (1980) distinguished three arousal styles based on whether one's arousal is focused on stimuli associated with the partner, one's own pleasure, or sexual role-play (Table 4.2).

"*Partner Interaction*" arousal focuses on the partner. The person is active, eyes open, looking at the partner, talkative (romantic or erotic talk), and energetic. This is the sexual style portrayed on TV and in the movies—passionate and impulsive sex.

Table 4.2 The Three Styles of Sexual Arousal

1.	Partner interaction arousal	→ focus on the partner's body, responses, and the romantic-erotic interaction
2.	Self-entrancement arousal	→ focus on one's own body, physical sensations, being receptive and responsive to touch, sensual pleasure and erotic flow
3.	Role enactment arousal	→ focus on external stimuli such as sex toys or pornography, role playing, imagination, unpredictability, or acting out fantasies

"*Self-entrancement*" arousal has the individual facilitating her own arousal by closing eyes, going within, becoming quiet and mindful while focusing on sensations. Routine and stylized touch helps the person become aroused, and this arousal is arousing for the partner.

"*Role enactment*" arousal focuses on role-play, fantasy, variety, and experimentation. This includes dressing in sexy clothing, role-playing being "tough" or "hard to get," acting out a scene from a movie or fantasy, having sex in new places, or using "toys" (vibrator, erotic video) to enhance erotic playfulness.

The partner interaction arousal style is the traditional male focus, whereas self-entrancement is more common among women. Men and women are capable of blending arousal/eroticism styles for increased enjoyment and variety. Such blending is an important feature in flexibility and adaptation to life's stressors, as well as inoculation against SD.

Clients who accept differences in arousal styles can avoid the common fear that "over-familiarity" (boredom) will subvert sexual function. The familiarity issue is ineffectually addressed with demands for excessive sexual variety or increased use of pornography. Because male sex drive is more specific and "object focused" (Buss, 1995; Fisher et al., 2002; Hamann, Herman, Nolan, & Wallen, 2004), the man has a responsibility to regulate and manage his sex drive wisely. He learns to balance self-entrancement and partner interaction styles to promote increased pleasure and function. Many couples accept arousal based on external stimuli (Hamann et al., 2004) while expanding their use and enjoyment of the other styles of arousal. The man learns sexual arousal is more reliable with "easy erections" based on self-entrancement arousal. He also learns that role-enactment style brings variety. This reduces concerns about boredom and dysfunction (Metz & McCarthy, 2004). Men are surprised to learn that sexual function is more reliable using self-entrancement arousal. The sensate focus/pleasuring assignments demonstrate the reliability of self-entrancement sexual response as well as partner interaction scenarios.

Helping the Couple Build Scenarios where Sex Is Integrated into Their Real Life and Real Life Is Integrated into Sex

Real life couples integrate the events of daily life into their sex life to create a realistic, distinctively personalized, and enriched sexual style. Sex serves as an escape from the vicissitudes of daily life. Regular frequency of sex with different roles and meanings insures that life and sex are integrated. CBCST provides psychoeducation about the importance of integrating sex into a busy life, to reciprocally improve life, and to experience sexuality that is enriched as integral to the couple's identity. CBCST facilitates this integration by expanding and enhancing a couple's repertoire of eroticism and intimacy.

Supporting Relationship "Glue" with Sexual Playfulness

Satisfying sex is personalized—occasionally playful, special, and spiritual. Playfulness is characterized by acceptance, trust, and pleasure. It is based on both people knowing that they are free to be playful without concern that the partner will judge or reject them. At times sex is tender, at other times lustful. The couple promotes, rehearses, and energetically embraces lust, passion and eroticism without shame. CBCST fosters playfulness by examining each partner's sexual assumptions and standards, challenging signs of inflexibility, helping partners remember the joys of playfulness, and stressing the rewards of sexuality. For many couples this addresses a broader difficulty that adults have developed with being playful while still viewing themselves as mature and responsible.

Assisting the Couple to Develop a Relapse Prevention Plan to Promote Long-Term Sexual Satisfaction

Relapse prevention is a core component of therapy in general (Witkiewitz & Marlatt, 2007). The in-session processing of homework assignments provides the couple detailed learning and identifies risk factors that could subvert gains. The barriers that have been identified and processed during therapy (e.g., intrusions of life stressors, pessimistic cognitions) can recur after treatment ends. The therapist and couple collaborate in designing an individualized relapse prevention plan that ensures that gains will be maintained and that they not interpret lapses as being "back to square one."

Cognitive Restructuring

There are specific cognitions associated with a specific SD (e.g., "I'm not a man if I can't get an erection") as well as generic ones ("My sex life is over"). By reducing the frequency and strength of these cognitions, CBCST can ameliorate emotional distress and negative couple interactions (Meisler & Carey, 1991; Mitchell, DiBartolo, Brown, & Barlow, 1988; Nobre & Pinto-Gouvelia, 2006).

Working with Cascading Negative Thoughts

The client's negative cognition that initially surfaces typically is one piece of a cascading sequence of detrimental cognitions. An important cognitive therapy assessment procedure is the "downward arrow" (Burns, 1980; Dattilio & Padesky, 1990; Epstein & Baucom, 2002). The therapist asks the client a series of questions that "dig deeper" to uncover underlying cognitions that are linked to emotional distress and negative behavior. For example, a woman who had been experiencing strong anxiety symptoms first expressed, "I feel anxious when my husband tells me he's not interested in sex." When the therapist inquired, "What does that mean to you?" she replied, "It makes me think I'm not attractive anymore." When the therapist asked, "When you think you aren't attractive, what else do you think?" She replied, "I start thinking he must be looking at other women and thinking about having sex with them." When the therapist asked, "When you think about him looking at other women, what goes through your mind?" she began to cry and said, "I'm scared to death that he's going to have an affair and leave me." This "downward arrow" assessment uncovered a core negative cognition at the root of the chain of thoughts triggering her anxiety. CBCST therapists use this approach to explore both partners' cognitions. Failure to identify underlying cognitions limits the effectiveness of cognitive restructuring.

Example of a Woman's Cognitive Negative Cascade

- "Why is orgasm so difficult for me?"
- "Why don't I get easily turned on?"
- "There's something sexually wrong with me."
- "I'm not a normal woman, and I never have been."
- "I'm doomed to a life without sexual pleasure."

Example of a Man's Cognitive Negative Cascade

- "I lost my erection again."
- "What is going on? I don't know what to do."
- "Erections should be automatic."
- "Without an erection I can't please my partner."
- "If we don't have intercourse and she doesn't have an orgasm she'll be angry…"
- "She says it's okay but I know she's just being nice."
- "She's disappointed and frustrated."
- "If my ED continues she'll find a lover and leave me."

Given the strong influence that negative cognitions have on the individual's emotional well-being (e.g., anxiety, depression) and behavior (e.g., excessive reassurance seeking, withdrawal from the partner), assessing and modifying them is an important component of CBCST. Cognitive restructuring involves helping the couple to:

1. Identify negative cognitions.
2. Appreciate their powerful role in spectatoring and performance anxiety.
3. Examine evidence from logic and sex education regarding their accuracy and reasonableness (e.g., almost all men have episodic bouts of erectile problems).
4. Test them by inviting feedback from the partner regarding his thoughts and emotions about SD.
5. Confront adverse thoughts ("I must perform…") with constructive and optimistic thoughts such as "Our couple goal is to experience pleasure, and there are many ways to do that."
6. Educate the couple about strategies that result in "easy erections" based on physical relaxation.
7. Set up "behavioral experiments" in which the couple uses sensate focus/pleasuring assignments to learn about sexual response (e.g., that erections are not automatic but wax and wane and wax again).

Table 4.3 illustrates an exercise in which the therapist guides the members of the couple in identifying the specific content of their negative cognitions regarding their sexual functioning and in replacing them with more constructive thoughts.

Table 4.3 Exercise: "Identifying and Restructuring Negative Sexual Cognitions"

The therapist assists the couple by discussing dysfunctional cognitions that arose in the assessment, and invites them to discuss and revise these. This bridges the partners' discrepant cognitions about the SD and provides positive anchors for the partners' thought processes during homework exercises

Her detrimental cognition	Her constructive replacement cognition	His detrimental cognition	His constructive replacement cognition
Example: "His decreased interest in sex with me means he doesn't find me attractive any more."	Example: "He still seems to like spending time with me and tells me he loves me. He seems so down on himself that it's hard for him to think about sex."	Example: "My career is going nowhere, I'm out of shape physically, and now I don't even feel interested in sex. I'm really going downhill!"	Example: "I've been experiencing a lot of stress from my job, I haven't had time to exercise. It's not surprising that I'm not interested in sex these days. I need to talk to my wife so she doesn't take it personally."
1.	1.	1.	1.
2.	2.	2.	2.
3.	3.	3.	3.

Table 4.4 Progressive Phases in CBCST

Phase 1	Developing comfort, relaxation, and cooperation
Phase 2	Promoting desire, pleasure, and arousal
Phase 3	Enhancing arousal and eroticism
Phase 4	Enjoying eroticism and flexible types of highly arousing sexual behavior
Phase 5	Couple satisfaction and relapse prevention

Step-By-Step CBCST Phases

Progressive Phases in CBCST

The therapist organizes progressive interventions to promote specific psychosexual skills. These exercises are designed to enhance the five core phases of CBCST that address the psychophysiological human sexual response cycle (Table 4.4).

Phase 1 promotes comfort talking about sex, embracing a positive body image, and psychophysiological relaxation, including a focus on one's own sensations. The therapist provides a model of comfortable and non-judgmental discussion of sexual topics and encourages members of the couple to explore ideas regarding what would be satisfying for them. Frequent use of terms such as "working as a collaborative sexual team" helps convey this positive mindset.

Phase 2 promotes desire, pleasure, and arousal. Important features are enhancing pleasure and playfulness, managing the cognitive arousal map ("arousal continuum"), and appreciating the dimensions of touch.

Phase 3 assignments are intended to enhance arousal and eroticism. The "Erotic Pleasuring" and "Partner Genital Exploration" exercises promote understanding of each other's sexual bodies and provide a forum for learning ways to achieve cognitive and physiological pleasure, arousal, and erotic flow.

Phase 4 focuses on enjoying arousal and eroticism, including flexible types of sexual behavior together. Developing alternative scenarios to intercourse is an important feature.

Phase 5 involves maintaining gains and inoculating against future SD using an individualized relapse prevention plan.

These phases provide a framework in which the therapist can creatively design interventions. Interventions teach psychosexual skills that are specific to the particular SD and foster couple cooperation. For example, with female non-orgasmic response, attention is devoted to relaxation and working cooperatively to increase pleasure, arousal, fantasy, and erotic flow (subjective arousal in the 8–9 point range on a 10-point scale). Table 4.5 lists psychosexual skill exercises used in each phase of CBCST.

Table 4.5 Psychosexual Skill Exercises

Phase	CBCST Exercise
1. Developing couple comfort, relaxation, cooperation	Couple: Talking about sexual feelings
	Individual: Identifying and restructuring sexual cognitions
	Couple: Partner spooning
	Individual: Positive body image
	Individual: Deep breathing relaxation
	Individual: Physical relaxation
	Individual: Pelvic muscle training
2. Promoting desire, pleasure, and arousal	
	Couple: Relaxed pleasuring
	Couple: Valuing pleasure and touch
	Individual & couple: Valuing touch
	Couple: Partner genital exploration
	Couple: Playful nicknames
	Individual: Mapping your erotic flow
3. Enhancing arousal and eroticism	
	Couple: Easy and confident arousal
	Couple: Erotic pleasuring
4. Enjoying eroticism and flexible types of highly arousing sexual behavior	
	Couple: Initiating intercourse and other forms of arousing sexual behavior
	Couple: Enjoying flexible intercourse
	Couple: Developing flexible sexual scenarios
	Couple: Sexual playfulness
5. Couple satisfaction and relapse prevention	
	Couple: Mutual Admiration Society
	Individual & couple: Reviewing the features of satisfying couple sex
	Couple: Relapse prevention and maintaining satisfaction

Couples complete each phase before proceeding to the next. Some assignments can be undertaken at the same time (e.g., pelvic muscle training and couple relaxed pleasuring).

Implementation of CBCST Exercises

The therapist shares information with the couple about the purposes of the exercises and the reasons for introducing them in this order. Clinical judgment directs how much time is devoted to each exercise. Couples vary in their readiness to move from one stage to the next. Interventions are designed to (1) provide the behavioral *structure* that increases physical and emotional comfort, acceptance, and security, (2) guide the couple through *incremental steps* that challenge the status quo by exposing them to experiences that broaden the meanings and emotions attached to sex, (3) use *controlled repetition* (desensitization) that results in increased comfort and confidence within the "cocoon" of homework assignments, and (4) identify and modify partners' cognitions that have contributed to negative emotions and dysfunctional behavior.

Phase 1: Developing Sexual Comfort

Step 1: Developing Couple Sexual Comfort

The goal in this initial step is to develop comfort and a sense of security for the members of the couple. Couples with SD usually enter therapy emotionally distressed and wary about being vulnerable as they deal with sexuality. It is crucial that the therapist establishes rapport and assists the couple in scheduling homework times. Couples are expected to reserve time for two to four homework sessions of approximately 30–60 minutes between therapy sessions. The therapist's role is as an active collaborator who consistently checks on their homework experiences and helps them identify and deal with barriers that may arise.

Clear and specific directions are particularly important at the beginning of treatment, especially brief didactic explanations about sexual avoidance. The therapist explains that *relaxed physical touch* facilitates comfort and *openness*, relaxation facilitates *pleasure*, pleasure enriches *sensuality*, sensuality provides the foundation for sexual *arousal,* and arousal develops into *eroticism.* This increases the couple's confidence as well as drawing their attention away from negatives to skills for enhancement. The goal of therapy is to reduce sex performance demands and increase pleasure. The therapist discusses the five dimensions of touch, expanding the clients' perspective that sexuality is more than intercourse and orgasm. The initial couple exercise is "Talking about Sexual Feelings." The therapist gives the couple a handout with a set of questions to discuss to learn about past experiences that have influenced each partner's current thoughts and feelings about sex. The therapist discusses "ground rules" the couple can follow during their discussions, with an emphasis on listening empathically and avoiding judging or criticizing one's partner. This sets a positive tone for the therapy. The questions are modified based on whether it is a same-sex or an opposite-sex couple.

COUPLE EXERCISE: "Talking About Sexual Feelings"

- What did you learn about sexuality as a child and adolescent?
- What did you learn about masturbation, petting, intercourse, oral sex, and orgasm?

- Who taught you?
- What did it mean to you at the time? Now?
- What are your attitudes and beliefs about sexuality?
- What is okay and what is not okay during lovemaking?
- What do you believe is okay but not feel is okay?
- What do you now believe about intercourse, masturbation, sexual experimentation, stimulating yourself with your partner present, orgasm, and how a man and woman are supposed to act during sex?
- Tell your partner what you sexually like and want to try.
- Discuss your sexual concerns, remembering to speak empathically, warmly, and respectfully.

Step 2: Training the Mind and Body for Relaxation

It is important to provide couples with "tools" to help them relax while engaging in homework assignments. In this stage, the couple learns that physical relaxation is the foundation for pleasure and eroticism.

Relaxed breathing promotes body relaxation. The couple is taught relaxed breathing, including spooning in which partners match their breathing. They lay down, one partner's back to the other's chest. The person who is behind is instructed to place a hand gently on the abdomen of the partner and quietly match his or her breathing for three minutes. They are then to trade places and match breathing for another three minutes. This promotes comfort, relaxation, and cooperation.

The therapist introduces progressive muscle relaxation. The partners are instructed to lie down comfortably and begin by tightening each foot for three seconds, then release the tension and enjoy sensations of relaxation. The client systematically tenses and relaxes sets of muscles, including those in calves, legs, buttocks, abdomen, hands, biceps, shoulders, and the face. By practicing cognitive focus on sensations, the client is learning to decrease tension and increase pleasure. Relaxation training is particularly helpful for couples who have difficulty concentrating on physical sensations.

Step 3: Pelvic Muscle Management

Learning pelvic muscle (PM) management is a very useful psychosexual skill in addressing SDs, particularly PE and non-orgasmic response. The goal is to identify and learn conscious control of the PM. The PM extends from the pubis (the bony prominence on the front of the pelvis) to the coccyx (the end of the spine). For men, the easiest way to identify their PM is to squeeze off urination. For women, squeezing her legs together helps identify the PM.

EXERCISE: "Pelvic Muscle (PM) Training"

This exercise is intended (1) to improve conscious awareness of the sensations of the PM and (2) to strengthen the PM.

Each day, practice the PM exercise for one minute. While concentrating on the physical sensations: (1) contract (tighten) the PM and hold for 3 seconds; (2) then relax the PM for 3 seconds while consciously focusing on the sensations. *Do this 10 times—tightening for 3 seconds, relaxing for 3 seconds—*for a total of 60 seconds.

Do this exercise *3 times.* At first it may be difficult to hold the muscle for 3 seconds, but over time the PM is strengthened.

EXERCISE: "Creating the PM 'Continuum'"

This exercise is intended to increase conscious awareness and control with the PM. The PM can be tightened to varying degrees. Imagine a continuum from 1 to 10, with "1" (relaxed), "5" (medium), and "10" (tight). *Practice moving from one level to another level to another, holding the PM at that level for 3 seconds and then relaxing.* Use zero as "home base" and return to it after each contraction. For example, tighten the PM to "10" and hold for 3 seconds, then relax to "0", then tighten to "5" and hold for 3 seconds, and then relax to "0" and stay that way for 3 seconds.

Once the client has learned to tense and relax the PM at three points on the continuum, *extend the continuum* from 3 stopping points to 5 stopping points "1", "3", "5", "7", & "10", always using "0" for home base. Tighten the PM to a level of 10 and hold for 3 seconds, then "0", then 7, then '0' and so forth. Move down to 7, 5, 3, and relax at 0. Then move back up the scale. Then move randomly from one point to another.

The PM training provides the individual awareness of the level of relaxation. This awareness offers an efficient measure of total body relaxation because the rest of the body follows the lead of the PM. PM relaxation is important for ameliorating SD and aids sexual function. There are two physical requirements for sexual function: relaxation and stimulation. The more physically relaxed the person is, the less physical stimulation is required. The more tense or anxious, the more stimulation is needed. Reasonable sexual expectations include awareness of balanced sexual function. Youthful sexual experiences, especially for males, lead clients to assume that arousal comes easily. It is difficult to recognize the important role that relaxation plays in facilitating arousal.

CBCST protocols for treating female and male arousal problems utilize the PM. Maintaining control over the PM enhances pleasure and arousal, and rhythmically contracting the PM ("ratcheting up") is an effective technique for enhancing erotic flow and orgasm. In PE, the PM is used to help delay ejaculation by maintaining focused relaxation. The PM is involved in orgasm/ejaculation, so PM strategies help manage the onset and pleasure of orgasm.

Use of muscle relaxation and deep breathing, couple "spooning", and PM training promote the objectives of phase 1. With the focus on relaxation and cooperation, the couple has begun the step-by-step process to recover sexual function and enhance satisfaction.

Phase 2: Nurturing Desire, Pleasure, and Arousal

This treatment phase promotes pleasure and arousal. The flow moves from physical relaxation to calm touch, sensual pleasure, and relaxed arousal (without urgency for orgasm).

Step 1: Relaxed Couple Pleasuring

This couple exercise encourages sensual pleasure and sexual desire based on relaxation. Educating partners about the dimensions of touch is a core aspect of enhanced pleasure and sexual function (Figure 4.1).

1. *Affectionate touch* refers to non-sexual touch that occurs in day-to-day closeness and indicates caring. It includes warm embraces, holding hands, kissing, and hugging. Affectionate touch anchors the couple's milieu of attachment and comfort in which sensual and sexual feelings thrive.
2. *Sensual touch* includes non-genital holding, stroking, cuddling, and massage. Sensual touch involves receptivity and responsiveness to pleasure and is integral to the sexual process. On a 10-point scale of subjective arousal, sensuality is 1–3.
3. *Playful touch* intermixes non-genital and genital touch and can include whole body massage, romantic or erotic dancing, showering or bathing together, fun or seductive touch, and sexual playfulness like strip poker or Twister. On the arousal scale, playful touch is 4–5.
4. *Erotic, non-intercourse (or comparable high-intensity) touch* involves manual, oral, rubbing, or vibrator stimulation and taking sexual risks ("stretching"). Levels of pleasure can be from 6–10 (orgasm). Some couples enjoy erotic flow to orgasm, while others prefer being orgasmic during intercourse. Erotic non-intercourse touch is especially applicable to lesbian and gay couples.
5. *Intercourse (or comparable high-intensity) touch* is the fifth touch dimension. Both conceptually and in terms of technique, intercourse is best understood as a natural continuation of the pleasure/erotic flow process. Clients create problems when they set intercourse as a pass-fail test apart from the pleasuring process. Young heterosexual couples learn to switch to intercourse as soon as they can (at levels 4–5 of subjective arousal), based on whether a man has an erection and a woman is lubricated. A very important psychosexual skill is to learn to transition to intercourse at high levels of subjective arousal, 7 or 8 on the 10-point scale.

Each dimension of touch has value as a way to experience pleasure. Couples fall into the trap of intercourse or nothing. In other words, if touching involves more than affection, the demand is to continue to intercourse. As a result, a partner who is not interested in intercourse avoids sensual and playful touch, and certainly erotic touch. This sets the couple up for a struggle in which one partner avoids touch while the other pursues sex and resents low intercourse frequency. The partner who is avoiding

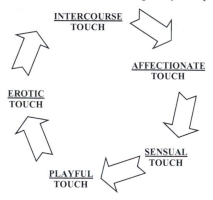

Figure 4.1 The Five Sensual-Sexual Dimensions of Touch

contact feels that his or her need for intimacy and touch has been subverted by the focus on intercourse. This polarized impasse is both unnecessary and alienating. Valuing each type of touch for itself, stemming from an awareness of choices for pleasurable connection, is a solid base for quality couple intimacy, pleasure, and eroticism.

Awareness, touch, pleasure, and subjective arousal are emphasized along with physiological arousal. The therapist encourages partners to appreciate that sexual desire, pleasure, and eroticism are easy and tangible when touch is valued and enjoyed. The cognitive concept is to value the five dimensions of touch—affection, sensual, playful, erotic, and intercourse. This expands the couple's thinking, providing a broader focus than performance and intercourse. Many clients experience discomfort about one or more forms of touch; for example, some people find it difficult to "let their hair down" to engage in playful scenarios (Metz & Lutz, 1990). They fall into self-conscious spectatoring in which they evaluate playful interactions as silly and embarrassing. Those negative cognitions must be addressed to facilitate touch and experience pleasure.

Each type of touch is valuable for itself. The couple takes advantage of opportunities to foster pleasure and sexual response. The focus is on sharing pleasure rather than "foreplay" for "real sex" (intercourse). Without a pleasure orientation, quality couple sexuality suffers. Each form of touch has value as a way to experience pleasure. This counters the trap of dichotomous thinking of intercourse or nothing. When a partner is not interested in intercourse, the couple still has many options for sharing pleasure and intimacy (Table 4.6).

EXERCISE: "Valuing Types of Touch"

The purpose of this exercise is to identify the types of touch that each partner likes and how often each type of touch actually occurs. Each partner completes the form individually, and then they share their perspective and preferences. What are the present percentages of affectionate, sensual, playful, erotic, and intercourse touch? It is important that each person is honest and forthcoming, so the therapist has a clear picture of how the partners experience touch. The second part of the exercise is even more important. What is the percentage of touch that each person wants? This increases awareness of needs, feelings, and preferences so the partners can understand and satisfy each other.

Table 4.6 Valuing Types of Touch

Touch type	Current percent of touch	Percent of touch you want
1. Affectionate touch		
2. Sensual touch		
3. Playful touch		
4. Erotic touch		
5. Intercourse touch		

The therapist guides the discussion with questions such as, "What has this exercise taught you about yourself, your partner, and the role and meaning of pleasurable touch in your sexual relationship? To finish this exercise, each partner can make one request to enhance touch in their sexual repertoire. The therapist emphasizes the difference between a request and a demand, noting the negative effects that occur when one person tries to coerce the other.

In making a request, what is the partner willing to try in order to facilitate the new pattern of touching? Ideally, the couple adopts a variable, flexible sexual repertoire

An essential homework exercise is "Relaxed Couple Pleasuring." The focus of this assignment is enjoyment of sensual touch. With relaxation, sensuality can flourish, allowing the person to soak up physical pleasure. This is not as easy as it sounds. Pressure for sexual performance ("sex on demand") is a common and toxic feature of SD and distressed sexuality.

This homework assignment is built on the traditional sensate focus/pleasuring exercises. The couple is instructed to set aside an hour, meet in a comfortable private setting while nude and without external distractions. They begin by using soothing physical touch. One partner lies on the bed, face down, and receives gentle, slow pleasuring to the entire back of the body for 15 minutes. Then the partner receives soothing touch for 15 minutes to the front side of the body, with the "giver" not touching breasts and genitals. Then the roles are reversed and the other partner receives pleasurable touch to the back and front of the body, again avoiding sexual stimulation. If either partner feels anxiety about nudity, the therapist designs alternatives such as pleasuring while wearing underwear or with lights dimmed. Negative cognitions associated with nudity are explored. The therapist balances relaxation with a gentle challenge to remain open to touch and pleasure. Each partner is instructed to focus on physical sensations of pleasure, not try to perform for the other.

Typically, the couple is assigned three pleasuring exercises before the next therapy session. Having a minimum of two exercises facilitates relaxation by instilling cognitive discipline to focus on physical sensations. During subsequent therapy sessions, the couple describes the behavioral experience as well as what each person was thinking and feeling during the exercise. Common concerns are being distracted from focusing on sensations as well as difficulty in not pursuing sexual arousal. The therapist normalizes the difficulties and encourages partners to accept the challenge and practice narrowing their attention to the sensations of physical touch.

Processing the homework during the subsequent therapy session presents teachable moments in which the therapist coaches the couple in cognitive focusing. If either partner reports sexual arousal, the therapist acknowledges that this can occur but that it signals the need to practice focusing on relaxing physical sensations. This presents an opportunity to educate the clients about the three styles of arousal, indicating that if the person experiences arousal he has rushed ahead to partner interaction arousal instead of staying "in the moment" of sensual pleasure.

Step 2: Partner Genital Exploration and Comfort

The goal for this step is to for each individual to learn about his or her own and the partner's genital sensations while enjoying physical relaxation. Similar to desensitization techniques, the couple is instructed to intentionally experience relaxation in what otherwise is an erotic situation—touching genitals. The individual "explains" her feelings as she leads the partner in exploring her genitals. The discussion helps maintain focus and relaxation. This exercise confronts clients' fear that the focus on relaxation and pleasure could cause a decline in sexual arousal. The focus on relaxation is part of the shift to expand the potential for sexual desire from partner interaction to self-entrancement arousal. Later, the vibrant excitement of partner interaction is reincorporated into their sexual repertoire.

The couple is instructed to practice this exercise a minimum of three times so they reach a level of comfort with genital exploration. This can be supplemented by creating playful nicknames for genitals.

PARTNER EXERCISE: "Genital Exploration"

Sexual activity is enhanced when partners are able to share awareness of sensations with touching. This assignment is designed to provide an opportunity for learning about each other's body and how to enhance sensual pleasure. It is not designed to sexually arouse the partner, but to invite him or her to enjoy relaxed pleasuring that explores genitals in a sensuous, playful manner. Approach this with an attitude of openness. Allow thoughts about genital touch to focus on of openness and exploration. Some have termed this assignment "Show and Tell."

With a heterosexual couple, the woman receives touching first. She begins by lying on her stomach, with her partner gently and sensuously pleasuring the entire back of her body for 7–8 minutes. This touching is meant to be relaxing, soothing, comforting, and gentle. She then rolls over and lies on her back while he pleasures the front of her body for another 7–8 minutes. The focus is relaxed, sensuous, comforting touch. She keeps her attention on her body and sensations. Distractions come and go—these are natural—but gently and patiently she brings her attention back to her body and what she is experiencing. She is free to guide her partner by giving verbal directions or taking his hand, showing how she wants to be touched, or simply explore how various types of touch feel. Next, the woman pleasures the man—first the entire back of his body for 7–8 minutes, then the front for 7–8 minutes. The focus is on relaxing and enjoying the pleasure of touch. When they relax with pleasure, neither will feel sexually aroused. They then continue relaxed pleasuring until both feel comfortable with genital touch.

After finishing total body pleasuring (approximately 30 minutes), she comfortably positions herself in a reclining position, propped up on her back with pillows. He positions himself alongside, facing her. For the next 15 minutes, she leads him in an exploration of the sensuous parts of her body. Then he will lead her in a sensuous exploration of his body, again for 15 minutes. The person whose body is being explored is in control and takes the lead.

The couple begins by slowly exploring the sensations in the woman's breasts and nipples. They discuss sensations, what she prefers, and what is uncomfortable. He asks questions to learn what she feels. To help the communication, couples are encouraged to use a graduated number system (from 0 to 5) to report the level of sensual pleasure.

Discussing and talking as they proceed with the body exploration, the partners use the following "map to guide the touching:"

Body Exploration Guided by the Woman:

- breast and nipple sensations
- stomach and abdomen
- hips and upper thighs
- inner thighs
- outer lips of vagina and perineum (the area between vagina and anus)
- interior of the vagina

She leads the exploration. Some women have uncomfortable associations with gynecological examinations, so be sure that she is in control of the exploration. She can take his hand and direct him in touching. She might have him form a "y" sign with his index and middle finger, then take his hand and gently show him how to pleasure the outer lips of her vagina with his two fingers. The partners talk, describe, and discuss this shared experience.

When the woman is ready to explore sensations inside her vagina, she asks him to sit alongside her legs, and guides his inserting one finger as she directs him in slowly massaging the skin inside her vagina at specific spots.

Many women notice that they feel very little beyond 3/4 to 1 inch inside their vagina. The couple is asked to imagine her vagina as the face of a clock with the top as 12 o'clock. She teaches him about her body and sensations. They work cooperatively to learn, confirm, and enjoy, taking 15 minutes to explore her erotic body.

Then it is the man's turn to lead the exploration of his body. The sequence is the same.

Body Exploration Guided by the Man:

- breast and nipple sensations
- stomach and abdomen
- hips and upper thighs
- inner thighs
- testicles and perineum (the area between testicles and anus)
- penis—shaft, head

The man takes the lead and is in control of the exploration of his body, especially his testicles ("balls") and penis. Many men have uncomfortable associations with urological examinations, so be sure he is in control of the exploration. He takes her hand and directs her in the touching. She can "cup" each or both testicles and describe the sensations. He shows her how to pleasure his genitals. Women hear that men's testicles are very delicate. He teaches her so she does not over- or underestimate testicular sensitivity. The couple moves on to exploring the sensations in his penis. She places his penis onto his abdomen, gently lying it down. He asks her to take her index finger, and beginning at the base of the penis, very slowly explore the sensations on the shaft of the penis. He gives her feedback about what he is feeling. She can ask questions. He shows her the responsive parts of his penis. Again, it is crucial to talk, describe, and discuss the experience as they take 15 minutes to explore the man's erotic body.

Most of the information that we receive about another's body comes from the "grope method." We discover by silently trying this or that ("groping in the dark") and listen for a reaction to see whether "it felt good." Rarely do couples actually talk about their bodies and what is pleasing. This exercise offers that opportunity. Some couples prefer to "start all over" by pretending that they know nothing. They learn together, exploring their bodies in a relaxed way. The anus and rectum is a pleasurable part of the body for most individuals. The couple explores and discusses sensations from anal touching. They are instructed to be sure to wash their hands with soap after anal contact to prevent transfer of E-coli bacteria (friendly to the intestines) to the vagina or penis (unfriendly to the urinary tract). Some couples use a lubricant like K-Y jelly or a sensual lotion (be sure it is hypoallergenic). The therapist encourages the couple to improvise.

The Sensuous Genital Exploration takes approximately 1 hour.

COUPLE EXERCISE: "Sexual Nicknames"

The problem with formal "clinical" sexual language is that it is long, Latin, and cold. There is nothing playful or inviting about words like "fellatio," "cunnilingus," or "coitus." The slang terms "blow job," "go down on," and "fucking" have a negative, almost derogatory connotation. Encourage couples to make up nicknames and language such as "play with the family jewels," "come into my wonderful vaginal world," "climb the Grand Tetons," "admire Big Ben," "really know me," "share my wetness," "take me inside you," "let me be with you," "my beautiful parlor," "big whopper," and "share my body." As long as both partners like the terms, this adds to sexual playfulness.

This provides an opportunity to be creative. Think of one or two favorite words/phrases for erotic body parts - penis, vagina, breasts, buttocks, and testicles. Add favorite words/phrases for intercourse, oral sex, manual sex, and erotic scenarios. Be sure that the language is inviting. Combine this with playfulness, touching, and teasing to create special experiences.

Phase 3: Enhancing Arousal and Eroticism

This third phase builds on relaxation and sensual pleasure to increase understanding of arousal, eroticism, and erotic flow. The "map for erotic flow" is a cognitive tool for developing sexual desire, managing arousal, and enhancing eroticism. The mind is a powerful sexual tool.

Step 1: Your Cognitive Map for Erotic Flow

This step focuses on developing awareness of the range of sexual arousal. A helpful psychosexual skill guideline involves the concept of "erotic flow". Desire involves pleasure, arousal, and high levels of eroticism. Coaching couples involves messages such as "go with the flow; you can't force it." An analogy that couples find helpful is canoeing; they need to go with the flow of the water, not paddle against it. This cognitive awareness is combined with practicing skills to pace sexual arousal and build erotic flow.

EXERCISE: "The Sexual Arousal Continuum"

Individual and interpersonal sexuality is enhanced by one's ability to manage arousal and erotic flow, and to cooperate in giving and receiving pleasure. Each partner has arousal patterns, techniques, or desired sequences that blend reality and imagination to facilitate sexual arousal. By understanding the influences that specific images, feelings, and behaviors have, the partner can alter these to slow down, steady, or intensify arousal. The person: (1) develops a sense of how calming or stimulating a specific image, feeling, or behavior is; (2) learns to modify the arousal pattern; and (3) embraces the image, feeling, or behavior to enhance erotic flow. Begin the process of "mapping" the sexual arousal continuum by identifying images, feelings, and behaviors, and assigning a personal arousal level to each (Table 4.7).

Table 4.7 The Sexual Arousal Continuum

Phase	Focus/activity	Arousal level
D	physical exercise—individual recreation with partner—e.g.,	*Between 1 and 20*
E	walk, shopping, movie…	
S	emotional discussion	
I	romantic eye contact	
R	embrace—cuddle	
E	verbal compliments	
A	kiss—mouth closed	*Between 21 and 50*
R	undressing self in lover's presence	
O	smile from partner	
U	sexual embrace	
S	being undressed by lover	
A	fantasy of body pleasure	
L	fondling of chest/breast	
P	kissing and fondling genitals	*Between 51 and 80*
	continuing embrace, feeling bodies	
L	together	
A	gentle and loving kissing	
	oral sex to partner's legs, relaxed	
T	and gentle	
	oral sex to partner's genitals,	
E	relaxed and gentle	
A	memory of sexual time on beach	
	intercourse initiated with slow	
E	movements	
	sharing sexual feelings and gentle	
U	intercourse	
	erotic talk and teasing role-play of	
O	insistence/resistance	
R	increasing speed for intercourse	
	fantasy of group sex with orgy	
G	environment	
	grasping of erotic parts of partner	
A	(e.g., penis, butt, breasts…)	

Phase	Focus/activity	Arousal level
A	-------------------- fast and deep thrusting/gyrating intercourse	Between 81 and 100
S	-------------------- imaging/remembering partner's excitement with orgasm	
M	-------------------- own orgasm	
R	-------------------- silent embracing and cuddling	Between 75 and 100
E	-------------------- talking of pleasure and affection	
S	-------------------- gentle pleasuring of partner's back	
O	-------------------- thanking lover for being sexual	
	-------------------- recall of partner's sounds during	
L	lovemaking	
U	-------------------- slow, playful, relaxing	
T	-------------------- sharing intimate feelings	
	-------------------- sharing good feelings about the day/	
I	week, work, kids	
O	-------------------- talking of schedule tomorrow	
N	-------------------- resting…	

Step 2: Couple Erotic Pleasuring

The focus of erotic pleasuring is to learn to enjoy heightened arousal without going to orgasm. This facilitates exploring relaxation and pleasure, leading to sexual arousal and eroticism. Women who experience orgasm difficulty enjoy the freedom to explore parameters of excitement without pressure and with the support of her partner. For men with ED, this exercise provides confidence in gaining erections and letting his erection subside, then comfortably regaining it. This is the "wax and wane" of erection exercise. He obtains an erection with maximum relaxation and openness to touch, which provides renewed confidence in his sexual function. In treating PE, the stop-start procedure is used for learning ejaculatory control. These psychosexual skill exercises are powerful therapeutic interventions to regain sexual confidence. His renewed sexual confidence enhances her desire and arousal.

COUPLE EXERCISE: "Couple Erotic Pleasuring"

Couple Erotic Pleasuring provides an experience to promote excitement, then reduce it, and resume arousal without orgasm. This "Intentional Teasing" experience is useful for enhancing and managing erotic flow and rebuilding sexual confidence.

The man comfortably positions himself in bed with his back propped up by the headboard or wall. His partner sits between his legs with her back resting against his chest. This allows him to reach his hands around her torso and for her to take his hands and guide pleasuring. She can become as aroused as she wishes (but not to orgasm). She guides him in the quality of touch that erotically pleases her. Go slowly, letting arousal flow at its own pace.

After 15 minutes, it is his turn. He gets into a reclining position, and she sits between his legs facing him. She has access to his chest and genitals. She places a pillow under her, and slides her legs under his thighs to use the weight of his legs to stabilize her so there is no back strain. He uses his hand over hers to erotically pleasure his body—chest, stomach, testicles, and penis. He becomes as sexually aroused as he wishes (but not to orgasm). He guides her hands, demonstrating the quality of touch that erotically pleases him. The couple is to go slowly, letting arousal flow.

Enhancing and managing erotic flow helps the giver appreciate the quality of touch the partner finds wonderful, builds cooperation, and enhances the ability to manage pleasure and arousal.

The most common problem encountered with this exercise is difficulty in becoming aroused—the couple is "spectatoring" and "can't get into it." The antidote is to slow down, concentrate on relaxing one's body, and consciously focusing on the sensations. The partners practice the basic requirements for arousal—relaxation, focusing on sensations and couple cooperation. The other common difficulty is one partner—usually the male—proceeding to orgasm. This indicates the need for regulated arousal, an invitation for cognitive and behavioral "pacing"—slowing the stimulation well before the point of ejaculatory inevitability. When the couple has enjoyed this exercise three times, they are ready to move on to intercourse.

Phase 4: Enjoying Erotic and Flexible Intercourse

Step 1: Initiating Relaxed Intercourse

When the couple has expanded comfort with their bodies, learned relaxation, experienced self-entrancement arousal, and increased confidence with variations in sexual arousal, they are ready to learn to have intercourse with self-assurance and flexibility. Few couples attempt relaxed intercourse on their own initiative. However, when they experience the penis being in the vagina without moving to orgasm, they find it intimate and pleasurable. Performance anxiety can block this experience, especially fear of dyspareunia, ED, or PE. However, the step-by-step exercises prepare the couple for intercourse. For many couples, intercourse is the pass-fail test where everything sexual is supposed to come together naturally. Before assigning this exercise, the therapist should inquire about any negative cognitions that either partner has involving performance pressure.

The goal of this step is to integrate the couple's sexual skills so they become confident with initiating intercourse and enjoying relaxation during intercourse. The relaxed intercourse exercise is adaptable for dyspareunia, female or male inhibited orgasmic response, ED, or PE. Relaxed intercourse is a natural continuation of the pleasuring/eroticism process.

COUPLE EXERCISE: "Initiating Intercourse"

The traditional view was "sex equals intercourse," with other sensual and sexual scenarios considered "foreplay." The CBCST view is that pleasuring, eroticism, and intercourse are all parts of a continuous, flowing process. The best way to think about intercourse is as *a special pleasuring experience*.

The couple is to begin with the Couple Relaxed Pleasuring exercise. Then the male lies on his back and invites his partner to straddle him and pleasure his penis to bring about an easy erection. It is her initiative to take his penis and insert it into her vagina. He relaxes and focuses on the pleasure. She comfortably moves up and down. The therapist emphasizes that they should not proceed to orgasm. Their focus is on enjoying close and pleasurable intercourse for 10 to 15 minutes, then gradually slow down and stop, enjoying cuddling as a way to end the experience. They are to complete this exercise a minimum of two times. In subsequent exercises, they may allow intercourse to promote an erotic flow, which naturally culminates in orgasm.

What if the Man Has Trouble with Intercourse?

The most common point at which men have trouble with the graduated steps is at the moment of initiating intercourse. Performance anxiety peaks, especially if he adheres to the belief that "sex equals intercourse" and views intercourse as the "moment of truth." The therapist challenges this self-defeating belief by reminding the man that he knows how to get and keep an erection; he has learned that relaxing his body and focusing on pleasure is the key. He allows her to manage intercourse initiation. He is to remember that she is his intimate sexual friend who wants him to experience pleasure and satisfaction. If he continues to have difficulty with erections, an option to consider is using a pro-erection medication (Cialis or Viagra) as an additional resource to "get over the hump." When he is comfortable with intercourse, he gradually phases out the medication (except in cases where a physical condition significantly interferes with erectile function).

After the couple completes the Initiating Intercourse exercise three times, they learn the "stuff-it method" as an additional enjoyable technique. This supports enjoying performance-free intercourse. Although some couples experience stuffing the penis into the vagina as "strange", most report this intercourse experience to be relaxed, sensual, and intimate.

Step 2: Intimate and Flexible Intercourse and Other Forms of Arousing Sexual Behavior

In this step, the couple enjoys intercourse (or other comparable forms of arousing sexual behavior), encourages partner pleasure, and develops alternative sexual scenarios.

COUPLE EXERCISE: "Enjoying Intercourse"

Begin with Couple Relaxed Pleasuring. The partners share mutual pleasuring, including manual and oral stimulation, blending self-entrancement with partner interaction arousal. It is important that the pleasuring be slow, tender, caring, and rhythmic.

The couple allows arousal to be at least a level 7 or 8 before transitioning to intercourse. The transition to intercourse is unhurried and flowing, with the woman guiding intromission. She utilizes the type of thrusting that she finds most arousing—slow up-and-down, circular, or rhythmic in-and-out. He enjoys the freedom to caress, stroke, fondle, and kiss her body throughout intercourse. Multiple types of stimulation during intercourse facilitate arousal for both partners. This includes clitoral stimulation, whether by his hands, her hands, or indirect stimulation from coital movement. The couple focuses on what is most arousing and creates erotic flow. They experiment, cooperate, and give feedback to establish mutually enjoyable intercourse. They enjoy intercourse for 3–9 minutes.

The couple experiments with variations of man-on-top intercourse. If they enjoyed multiple types of stimulation during the pleasuring/eroticism phase, they should continue this during intercourse. The key is to enjoy building eroticism throughout intercourse. They kiss, he fondles her breasts, she stimulates his testicles, and they scratch each other's back or stroke the other's thighs.

Throughout, each partner takes care to balance sensual self-entrancement arousal with partner interaction arousal and not rush to orgasm. Balancing arousal styles is especially important if they have struggled with low desire, ED, limited responsiveness and lubrication, PE, ejaculatory inhibition, or non-orgasmic response. The therapist reminds the couple about the value of fantasies and suggests using fantasy to enhance erotic flow. Behaviorally, the couple experiments with position variations, her legs fully elevated and resting on his shoulders, putting a pillow under her buttocks to adjust the vaginal angle, locking her legs around his body. The goal is to enjoy the entire pleasuring, eroticism, and intercourse process. Couples engage in this exercise a minimum of three times.

Flexible Lovemaking

Sensate focus/pleasuring techniques involve being receptive and responsive to giving and receiving sensual, playful, erotic, and intercourse stimulation rather than rigid, totally predictable, goal-oriented intercourse. As with other exercises, the therapist explores any cognitions that may interfere with partners' flexibility in trying new sexual behaviors.

COUPLE EXERCISE: "Developing Flexible Scenarios"

The therapist provides psychoeducation regarding flexible sexual scenarios and gives the couple an assignment to design alternative sexual scenarios. Enjoying flexible, variable couple sexuality includes intimate intercourse as well as erotic, non-intercourse and sensual, cuddly scenarios. The GES approach involves pleasuring that flows to intercourse in 85% of encounters (whether using enhanced psychosexual skills or a pro-erection drug). Pleasuring/eroticism develops into an erotic flow (including response to partner arousal) that transitions to intercourse at high levels of arousal.

Partners learn to accept that not every sexual experience needs to end in intercourse. Flexibility and variability enhance sexual desire rather than inhibiting it. Manual, oral, and rubbing stimulation are excellent ways to experience high arousal and orgasm for one or both partners. The therapist stresses not switching to intercourse as soon as they become aroused. The majority of women find it easier to be orgasmic with manual and oral stimulation than in intercourse (Graham, 2014). Orgasm reached through erotic, non-intercourse stimulation is satisfying for both partners.

A key to intimate sexuality is awareness that there are a number of ways to give and receive pleasure rather than feeling anxious, panicking, and treating intercourse as a pass-fail test. The therapist confronts sources of anxiety, especially the cognitions that contribute to unrealistic, narrow standards for sex. Performance anxiety is reduced when partners stay actively involved in a sexual give-and-take. She can request oral stimulation to enhance erotic flow, while he can ask for mutual stimulation and they piggyback on each other's arousal. The couple is free to pause intercourse, relaxing and talking, then increasing arousal, rebuilding erotic flow, and returning to intercourse.

Sometimes an encounter does not involve erotic response or intercourse. Rather than feeling frustrated and withdrawing, either partner can say that this will not be a sexual night, but transition to a warm, caring, sensual scenario. Ending the encounter in a genuine positive and close manner reinforces sensuality and intimacy. It motivates them to look forward to a sexual encounter when they have the time and energy for an experience that integrates intimacy, pleasuring, and eroticism.

The couple is asked to create three sexual scenarios. The therapist encourages them to be creative and flexible by allowing only one of the three to include intercourse. The partners take turns initiating scenarios. The therapist emphasizes the need to not "judge" each other's (or their own) scenarios, instead focusing on enjoying thinking about and implementing variable, flexible couple sexuality.

Step 3: Sexual Playfulness

With the goals of the CBCST protocol nearing realization, the next focus is to create sexual fun and enjoyment. Sexual playfulness is one of the hallmarks of a satisfying couple sex life. A common pattern among couples experiencing SD is loss of flexibility and playfulness (Metz & Lutz, 1990). The therapist promotes humor, playfulness, fun, and delight with sex. This facilitates feelings of "specialness."

Sexually satisfied couples value adult playfulness, whether sexual humor, light-heartedness, teasing, or use of "nicknames." Mature couple playfulness has a deeper side, including sharing memories of unique times, traditions, special moments, private meanings, spirituality. Playing together is part of the process of creating intimacy and brings unique and special meaning to their relationship. For some couples, play was never a part of their relationship, and they feel awkward when the therapist encourages these interactions. The therapist can devise a hierarchy of playful interactions. Other couples report that playfulness existed early in their relationship but was abandoned as they became busy with life responsibilities. The therapist's goal is to help those couples acknowledge the positive effects of playfulness in the past and identify ways to be playful now.

Sex itself is a form of healthy, adult playfulness when unburdened from performance anxiety. For sex to be playful, the couple behaves with (1) kindness and caring, (2) respect and acceptance, (3) safety and security, and (4) enjoyable silliness. Teasing oneself is fine, but teasing the partner can be risky. A man might refer to his slow-to-erect penis as his "wet noodle," but his partner must be sure that she signals (by voice inflection, warm twinkling smile, gentle gesture) kindness and acceptance when she says "...So-o-o, can I cuddle and kiss our little wet noodle?"

Intimacy deepens when partners know each other well enough to understand the sexual scenarios they are open to experimenting with. Playfulness signals that feelings of closeness are important and their relationship is special. The focus of play brings them full circle to the primary goal – relationship intimacy and satisfaction.

COUPLE EXERCISE: "Sexual Playfulness and Alternative Scenarios"

Sexual comfort is increased by developing an innovative scenario. This exercise involves the couple deciding on an activity to cultivate and ensuring trust in that scenario. It requires that partners talk about what each person will do in the scenario, and decide on a signal to pause or stop should the activity stretch one partner's comfort level too far.

The couple discusses scenarios from the following list to incorporate into their lovemaking – or they can create their own. There are no right or wrong desires, only individual preferences. Neither partner presents a preference as a demand. Be sensitive to the fact that everyone has areas of shyness and discomfort, so one's partner has a right to say "no" or modify a proposed scenario.

The therapist asks the partners to indicate each person's level of interest and comfort with each scenario. They are to rate each from 10 (very high) to 1 (very low). Each person should evaluate his or her comfort in terms of three criteria for intimate play—caring, respect, and security. The couple is to reach consensus on what they will try (Table 4.8).

Table 4.8 Partner Preferences for Playful Sexual Scenarios

Playful Scenario	Level of Interest: HIS	HERS	Level of Comfort: HIS	HERS
Playing "strong" or aggressive; shy or "hard to get"				
Wearing sexy lingerie or briefs				
Talking "dirty" during sex				
Playful bondage (e.g., hands tied with crepe paper)				
Sex in special places (e.g., in front of the fireplace; car; beach)				

Playful Scenario	Level of Interest:		Level of Comfort:	
	HIS	*HERS*	*HIS*	*HERS*
Holding hands while having intercourse				
Acting "naughty" or "wild"				
Using sexual "aids" or "toys"—dildo, feathers, or vibrator				
Pretending you are virgins having sex for the first time				
Taking turns performing a strip tease				
Having phone sex				
Taking turns with "her night" and "his night"; requesting a special erotic scenario				
Watching an "X" rated video as the entrée to lovemaking				
Gazing into each other's eyes during intercourse				

Use this exercise as an opportunity to think boldly of oneself as being a sexual person who has the right to pleasure, eroticism, and joy. For example, Troy and Rebecca discussed a number of scenarios and discovered that they both were interested in wearing sexy lingerie and briefs—Troy rated a desire level of "7"; Rebecca a "6." Troy wanted Rebecca to dance for him wearing the lingerie, in which she was less interested, feeling shy. Rebecca wanted Troy to wear silk briefs and hold his crotch and invite her to explore what was there. They agreed to try this. During the first exploration, Rebecca would dance for thirty seconds, and then Troy would stand before her and invite her to explore his crotch for 30 seconds. If either verbalized, "I want to stop for now," they would immediately stop and hug, no questions asked, and later share how they felt. This agreement provided the safety needed to try new sexual activities.

Rebecca enjoyed being seductive, feeling proud that Troy was aroused. Troy revealed that he felt embarrassed. They agreed to repeat the exploration, Rebecca dancing for a full minute and Troy wanting to keep his crotch exploration invitation to the same thirty seconds. With repetition, each experienced increased comfort and expressed feelings of sexual self-esteem and enjoyment of couple eroticism. They decided to incorporate this new scenario into their lovemaking several times a year.

Step 4: Mutual Admiration Society

The value of positive affirmation is well documented. "Positive psychology" and relationship cooperation research verifies this (Peterson, 2006). As the couple approaches completion of therapy, they mindfully offer compliments before sleep—or sex. This involves variations of the "mutual admiration society" (Metz & McCarthy, 2010, 2011).

COUPLE EXERCISE: "Mutual Admiration Society"

This exercise involves the couple talking for a minute (literally) as they go to bed. They are to take turns giving each other a "short list" of things about the other person that they noticed and appreciated that day. This list should be three things that were valued. For example, "You handled that issue with our son very well" or "Thank you for calling to let me know that you'd be late for dinner." This is a positive way to provide closure to the day; no discussion is required.

Phase 5: Couple Relapse Prevention

Maintaining gains and relapse prevention are essential components in comprehensive CBCST. Individuals and couples are at risk of relapse without an agreement to continue the attitudes and behaviors that have helped expand positive feelings and healthy couple sexuality. The following procedures help to ensure maintenance of gains and lower the risk of relapse.

Step 1: Maintaining Gains

This finishing step in CBCST, maintaining gains, is an intervention that enlists the couple to design the cognitive, behavioral, and emotional features that they intentionally continue to ensure progress. Their goal is to maintain pleasure and inoculate against future SD.

COUPLE EXERCISE: "Reviewing the Features of Satisfying Couple Sexuality"

This exercise asks each partner to list 3–5 features of couple sexuality that are particularly valuable. We suggest doing this separately and then sharing the list. Often, there is overlap; for example, listing the importance of psychological and physical relaxation or the importance of giving and receiving pleasure-oriented touch. It is particularly important to be aware of unique features to increase the partner's awareness of what promotes desire, pleasure, eroticism, and satisfaction. The partners need to remain committed to a satisfying intimate sexual relationship, both individually and as a couple.

COUPLE EXERCISE: "Relapse Prevention"

From the following list of "Relapse Prevention Strategies and Guidelines," each partner chooses two that are personally relevant. Thus, in the individualized relapse prevention plan the couple has 2–4 guidelines to implement. Couple sexuality cannot be treated with benign neglect. The therapist stresses that the couple needs to remember to put time, energy, and communication into enduring desire, pleasure, eroticism, and satisfaction.

Relapse Prevention Strategies and Guidelines

- Set aside quality couple time and discuss what you need to do individually and as a couple to maintain a satisfying and secure sexual relationship.
- Every 6 months have a formal follow-up meeting either by yourselves or with a therapist to ensure that you remain aware and do not slip back into unhealthy sexual attitudes, behaviors, or feelings. Set a new couple goal for the next 6 months.
- Every 4 to 8 weeks, plan a non-demand pleasuring, playful, or erotic date when there is a prohibition on intercourse. This allows you to experiment with new sensual stimuli (alternative pleasuring position, body lotion, or new setting) or a playful, erotic scenario (being sexual in the shower, a different oral sex position or sequence, or engaging in an asynchronous scenario rather than mutual sex). This reminds you of the value of sharing pleasure and developing a broad-based, flexible sexual relationship rather than intercourse as an individual pass-fail performance test.
- Maintaining positive, realistic expectations about couple sexuality is a major therapeutic resource. 5 to 15% of sexual experiences are dissatisfying or dysfunctional. That is normal, not a reason to panic or feel like a failure. Therefore, whenever you have a sexual experience with which you are dissatisfied, talk about it as a couple in an encouraging way, remembering positive sexual experiences you have had together and taking a realistic perspective regarding normal fluctuations in sexual quality.
- Accept occasional lapses, but do not allow a lapse to become a relapse. Laugh or shrug off the experience and make a date in the next few days when you have the time and energy for an intimate, pleasurable, erotic experience. A relapse means giving up and reverting to the cycle of anticipatory anxiety; pass-fail intercourse performance; and frustration, embarrassment, and avoidance. Turn the experience into a lapse by immediately planning another positive experience.
- The importance of setting aside quality couple time—especially intimacy dates and a weekend without children—cannot be overemphasized. Intimate couple time is a priority, even if only for an afternoon. Therefore, make a specific schedule for a period of couple time each week, if only for an hour or so. Stick to the plan as seriously as you would any other important scheduled event. If you are concerned that scheduled dates will not feel romantic or special, talk together about honoring the importance of your relationship, and remember past intimate couples times you have enjoyed.

Creative Alternatives and Supplemental "Tools" for CBCST Intervention and Relapse Prevention

The step-by-step outline of structured interventions provides a progressive framework for the therapist to adapt, supplement, and create interventions targeted to the treatment and relapse prevention needs of the particular couple. A valuable feature of CBCST is the strategy of using all available tools. Therapists bring creativity in tailoring CBCST interventions to the characteristics of each couple, adapting clinical expertise with multiple, adjunctive therapeutic strategies. Some clinicians incorporate hypnosis, guided imagery, mindfulness, self-pleasuring, homeopathic methods, sexual devices (e.g., vibrator, EROS), sensual bodywork, spirituality and prayer, body exploration, yoga, journaling, etc.

A valuable resource for treatment effectiveness and relapse prevention is bibliotherapy. The therapist incorporates books and other written materials to supplement in-session work. Audio-visual materials (e.g., the video *Becoming Orgasmic* that accompanies Heiman and LoPiccolo's (1988) self-help book) which are compatible with the couple's comfort level can be invaluable. Written and audio-visual materials that the couple has available at home for regular reference and review serve as reminders of progress they have made in the past and cues to continue to engage in relationship enhancing activities together.

Enhancing Compliance with CBCST Treatment and Relapse Prevention Strategies

CBCST relies heavily on clients' active participation with interventions, especially with homework exercises that are designed to alter counterproductive patterns and enhance the couple's collaboration as a sexual team. Similarly, relapse prevention strategies require that couples remain actively engaged with positive interventions. Problems with treatment adherence can result from a variety of factors (misunderstanding the therapist's directions, avoidance driven by anxiety, logistical barriers, cultural values that are inconsistent with therapeutic interventions, covert relational problems). Short-term intensification of anxiety presented by homework exercises requires adapting assignments. The therapist explores the clients' experiences with the tasks "like a detective," assessing and acknowledging barriers to treatment adherence and working collaboratively with the couple to minimize these. Enlisting the partners' thoughts to facilitate compliance is critical. Adopting a stance that encourages clients to articulate their fears and providing a realistic notion of what to expect at different points in treatment is cognitively and emotionally valuable. When partners are coached in noticing and valuing signs of progress and when positive responses to treatment are identified, couples are unlikely to become discouraged. Clients are encouraged to contact the therapist by phone if they have concerns or questions so these can be addressed and lead to treatment adherence. Chapter 7 describes strategies for further relapse prevention.

Summary

Contemporary CBCST uses all biopsychosocial resources appropriate to the clinical presentation and formulation. Comprehensive assessment and treatment are based on an understanding of sexual physiology and the importance of relaxation for reliable sexual function. Addressing common relationship features involved in SD is crucial because sexual function is grounded in the couple relationship, with interactive causes and effects. Cognitive, behavioral, and emotional strategies are employed to create the milieu for partners to learn psychosexual skills, realistic expectations, and cooperative "team work" for sex function and satisfaction.

Chapter 5

Treatment Strategies for Female Sexual Dysfunction

The most common female SDs are inhibited sexual desire, inhibited arousal, non-orgasmic response, and sexual pain. In addition, a notable number of clients seek assistance because of conflicts over a discrepancy between partners' preferred frequencies of sex. CBCST addresses the biopsychosocial causes and effects of SD through accurate and reasonable understanding of the female body, sexual response, subjective and objective arousal, and interpersonal dynamics affecting the sexual relationship. Comprehensive treatment requires appreciation of the biological, psychological, interpersonal, and social factors that negatively affect the woman and her sexual relationship.

Female Anatomical and Physiological Factors in Sexual Function

The body is the foundation for sexual function; the "hardware," whereas the individual's psychological functioning and relationship interactions are the "software." Clients' (as well as therapists') accurate knowledge about sexual anatomy and physiology is essential for sexual function and sexual self-esteem. Sexual function is grounded in good physical health, so it is important to assess the health of the woman and her partner, and to address ongoing problems in their health behaviors. CBCST confronts health habits that compromise sexual functioning, such as alcohol or drug abuse, over-training, smoking, sleep disorders, obesity, and cardiovascular problems. CBCST takes a holistic approach to understanding and treating SD.

Body Knowledge and Acceptance

Sex for procreation is "natural," and the client is well aware of the most basic physiology involved, but satisfying lovemaking is a complex process requiring sophisticated knowledge of each other's body. In addition, satisfying sexuality is dependent on self-confidence, comfort, awareness, sensitivity, imagination, communication, and psychosexual skills. A core axiom of CBCST is to transform performance-oriented sex to pleasure-oriented sex. Performance-oriented sex is based on lack of knowledge about psychological, interpersonal, and physical health influences on desire, arousal, and orgasm. Consequently, CBCST includes an important component of educating females and males about their sexual bodies and a holistic approach to enhancing pleasure and function.

Responsive Sexual Desire: A New Model of Female Sexuality

Women and men experience a similar physiological arousal sequence, although psychological and relational factors are somewhat different. Basson (2001) found that in committed, long-term relationships, women's sexual desire becomes more integrated into their psychological processes than is true for men. In a new relationship, romantic love and sexual passion lead to easy sexual response. However, over the course of a long-term life partnership increased distractions and fatigue lead to a different sexual desire pattern (Fisher, 2004; Perel, 2006).

In the Basson model of female desire and arousal, women have a lower biological urge for the release of sexual tension than men do. Orgasm is not necessary for satisfaction and does not need to occur at each sexual encounter (Basson, 2001, 2007). A woman's desire is *responsive* rather than a spontaneous event, greatly influenced by subjective experiences such as positive feelings and sexual attraction to her partner (Baumeister, Catanes, & Vohs, 2001; Fisher, Aron, Masher, & Brown, 2002; Regan & Berscheid, 1995). Whereas a man's sexual desire is energized more by physical drive, a woman's sexual desire is more likely to develop from receptivity to sensual and playful touching. Sexual desire is responsive to physical contact and emotional receptivity.

Female sexual response often begins in sexual neutrality, but sensing an *opportunity* to be sexual, the partner's desire, and an awareness of *potential benefits* to her and their relationship (emotional closeness, bonding, love, affection, healing, acceptance, commitment), she becomes aware *at that time* of desire to continue the experience for *sexual* reasons and experiences arousal, which may or may not include orgasm. This brings a sense of physical well-being with added benefits of emotional closeness, love, and acceptance. In this model, sexual desire for women is more psychologically and relationally driven, with eroticism valued within the context of interactive couple sexuality.

Physiological Differentiation of the Sexes

Understanding causes of female SD requires consideration of physiological similarities and differences between women and men. Sex differentiation occurs before birth; every embryo begins as female, but androgens triggered by sex chromosomes lead to the development of males.

Realizing the common anatomical structures of men and women helps in understanding similarities and differences in sexual pleasure and response. The sensitivity of the clitoris corresponds to the sensitivity of the head of the penis. Vigorous, direct stimulation to the clitoris is irritating, even painful. After ejaculation, stimulation to the head of the penis is "too much." Women's ovaries and men's testicles come from the same gonadal tissues. Her gonads developed into ovaries and remained inside her torso; his gonads became testicles and descended into the scrotal sac. Breasts and nipples of women and men are frequently erotic. At times, her breasts may be more sensitive, depending on hormonal fluctuations. Understanding and accommodating each other's bodies is a perennial feature of satisfied couples.

Embracing Gender Differences in Sexual Response

Human sexual response is a dynamic combination of cognitive, emotional and physiological processes. Women's minds and genitals respond differently to sexual arousal than men's (Palace, 1999). Chivers, Seto, Lalumiere, Lann, and Grimbos (2010) studied the degree to which the experience of arousal mirrors physiological genital activity. They reviewed 134 studies (based on 2,500 women and 1,900 men) that measured the degree of agreement between subjective and objective arousal. Researchers measured physiological response using changes in erection for men and genital blood flow for women. Men's subjective and physiological measures of arousal showed a greater degree of congruence than women's. The lower correlation between women's physiological and subjective arousal indicates that other factors are influencing the link and must be considered. Consequently, it is important for a sexually knowledgeable physician or nurse practitioner to assess physiological factors in cases of female SD.

Hormones. Hormonal influences are one of the factors making the link between women's physiological and subjective arousal complex. Higher levels of estrogen produce sexual benefits including vaginal lubrication, greater elasticity, reduced pain and paresthesia, and improved pelvic blood flow, which promote easier, more intense orgasm. Conversely, reductions in estrogen, as during menopause (Dennerstein, 2010), commonly inhibit sexual response. The physician who is most competent in assessment and treatment of hormonal factors, including testosterone, is an endocrinologist.

Illness and accidents. Acute or chronic medical conditions, ranging from life-threatening illness to diabetes to poor health habits to injuries and surgeries, can cause SD. Because the body is the foundation for sexual function, medical assessment is important, especially as clients age. The first physician to consult for a medical assessment is an internist or family practitioner.

Chemical agents. With the number of pharmacologic agents used in our society, and their detrimental effect on sexual mood and function, it is crucial to determine what prescription(s) and over the counter agents a client is taking, as well as recreational drugs. When clients are not responding favorably to CBCST, a review of physiological factors, chemical agents, and comorbid disorders is a wise course. Any drug can have a detrimental effect on sexual function (especially antihypertensives and SSRIs). The most common detrimental agent is alcohol, which depresses the central nervous system. An internist is the best physician to consult about the impacts of medications to treat the client and her illness. Negative side effects of medications, both prescription and over-the-counter medications, are the major bio-medical factor causing SD.

Pregnancy and parenting of newborns. A common concern among expectant mothers is how pregnancy will affect their sexual relationship. As the woman's body changes both in pregnancy and during the postpartum period, sexual feelings also change. Even the most loving and intimate relationship will be affected by the decrease in available time, energy, and privacy once the baby is on the scene, as well as by hormonal changes.

After a vaginal delivery, intercourse should not be attempted until it is physically comfortable. This usually requires 6 weeks (or longer), especially if an episiotomy was done. A common pregnancy complication is short-term dyspareunia. Bertozzi, Londero, Fruscalzo, Driul, and Marchesoni (2010) found that dyspareunia significantly compromised a woman's sexual health, including reoccurring urogenital infections. Although almost all women resume sexual activity within 1 year of delivery, 16% reported dyspareunia that continued to compromise intercourse significantly. Those couples can develop satisfying alternative sexual scenarios involving non-intercourse erotic stimulation. Couples often present with distress about negative effects that pregnancy and parenting of newborns have on their sexual relationship. Consequently, an important component of CBCST is educating couples about such common effects, challenging negative cognitions that they experience about sexual symptoms (e.g., an unrealistic belief that sex should "bounce back" quickly), encouraging them to seek medical assessment, and coaching them in problem solving to develop solutions to challenges of maintaining a positive level of couple closeness while caring for a newborn.

Myths about female sexual function. It is important to determine whether the woman or her partner holds myths that affect their sexual relationship. For example, some couples believe that there is a relationship between penis size and sexual desire or function for the woman (or man). It is not the size of the penis, but how the couple cooperates for sex and emotional connection. A related myth is that a large penis increases the likelihood of the woman being orgasmic during intercourse. This is based on the mistaken belief that the vagina is the woman's major sex organ. In truth, the woman's most sensitive genital organ is her clitoris, which has a multitude of nerve endings (like the glans of the penis only concentrated in a much smaller area) and is the focal point of sexual pleasure. Some men are aware of the importance of the clitoris but are unaware that women commonly prefer indirect clitoral stimulation, whether with his hand, tongue, or penis.

During intercourse, the clitoris is stimulated by pulling and rubbing action caused by pelvic thrusting-stimulation, which is independent of penis size. The vagina has few nerve endings, most of which are in the outer third. The vagina is an active rather than a passive organ, which means that the vagina swells and expands with arousal to engage the penis and adjust to whatever size it is. Typically, 10 to 20 minutes of pleasuring (foreplay) allows the vagina to expand fully. If a couple rushes intercourse, they mistakenly think the penis is "too small" as intercourse does not feel snug. The remedy is enjoying pleasurable touch and genital stimulation before intercourse to allow her vagina to reach full arousal (vasocongestion). Sexual incompatibility based on the couple's genitals is, with extremely rare exceptions, a myth. The educational component of CBCST is important for dispelling such counterproductive beliefs.

Menopause. Approximately 20% of women experience SD during menopause. Lower estrogen can cause decreased desire, irritability, sleep disturbance, and lessened lubrication (Dennerstein, 2010; Hillman, 2008). Vaginal lubricants are the most common adaptation couples use to reduce painful intercourse. Some women find support on their own or utilize tips for coping at menopause information sites, women's support groups, and educational media. Others are unaware of such resources and benefit from a therapist's referrals and sex education. It is helpful to educate her partner, who can be supportive of her and collaborate in strategies to have a satisfying sexual relationship.

Psychological Factors in Female Sexual Dysfunction

CBCST recognizes the strong effects that an individual's psychological functioning can have on her sexual desire, arousal, and orgasmic response. There are several areas to consider:

1. Low self-esteem, poor body image, low sexual self-confidence, and performance anxiety (Wilhelm, Buhlmann, Hayward, Greenber, & Dimaite, 2010), especially fears about not being attractive/arousing.
2. Self and partner monitoring ("spectatoring").
3. Inaccurate and unrealistic sexual cognitions—selective attention, inaccurate negative attributions, and inaccurate expectancies, as well as unrealistic or inappropriate assumptions and standards (Baucom, Epstein, Kirby, & LaTaillade, 2015; Epstein & Baucom, 2002).
4. A tendency to be easily distracted and preoccupied.
5. Inadequate strategies for managing life stresses.
6. Inadequate knowledge and skills for physical and emotional relaxation.
7. Poor body awareness.
8. Sexual inexperience.
9. A history of physical and sexual abuse (and chronic PTSD symptoms).
10. Emotional discomfort with "selfish" physical pleasure, and other cognitive-emotional conflicts (Barbach, 1975; Foley, Kope, & Sugrue, 2012; Nelson, 2008).
11. Lack of self-pleasuring skills and negative beliefs about masturbation.

Low Self-Esteem, Poor Body Image, Low Sexual Self-Confidence, and Performance Anxiety

Our society cultivates a young woman's dissatisfaction with her body and places a high premium on changing the body she has (Foley et al., 2012). Body image, sexuality, and self-esteem are interwoven and subject to fear of not being "good enough." Fear of sexual decline with aging creates an impossible dilemma. One only has to survey women's magazines with their emphasis on an idealized body and the demand to be attractive and sexy.

Body perfection promotes alienation when a woman's body does not meet rigid standards. This precipitates performance anxiety as well as distraction from pleasure. Many women have been taught as they were growing up that nakedness and sex are bad, even shameful.

Self and Partner Monitoring

Spectatoring during sexual touch needs to be addressed to promote relaxation and pleasure. Spectatoring creates performance anxiety. The woman with SD falls into the trap of over-concern for the partner, which is exacerbated if her partner has SD (Brotto & Luria, 2014).

Spectatoring in SD focuses on three areas:

1. Over-focus on *the partner*:

   - "Does he find me sexy?"
   - "Is he angry with me?"

- "Does he like my breasts?"
- "Does he think I'm too fat?"
- "Is he getting an erection?"
- "Will he be disappointed if I don't have an orgasm?"

2. Hypersensitive cognitive focus on herself:

- "Am I lubricating yet?"
- "Why am I not responding?"
- "Will I reach orgasm?"
- "Is my stomach too pudgy?"
- "Are my breasts too small/big?"

3. Cognitions about *the relationship*:

- "What's wrong with us?"
- "Our relationship is in danger."
- "We don't love each other anymore."

The negative cognitions involved in spectatoring commonly produce a cascade of other negative cognitions, as well as negative emotional and behavioral responses. For example, a woman may begin with a concern that her partner will not find her body attractive, then have an expectancy that her partner will be "turned off," leading her to monitor his nonverbal behavior and make negative attributions about any "signs" that he is not enjoying their sexual interactions, leading to anxiety and a loss of arousal. Such cognitive cascades are common, and override her focus on physical pleasure and the joy of sexual interaction. They disconnect her from her body, its pleasurable sensations, and de-eroticize the interaction.

Inaccurate and Unrealistic Sexual Cognitions

Spectatoring involves selective perceptions, in which the individual focuses on specific negative aspects of a sexual situation (e.g., parts of her body that she dislikes) and overlooks positive aspects (e.g., that her partner showed interest in her by initiating sex). There are several other types of negative cognitions commonly associated with SD that require modification. In the above example, the woman had a negative *expectancy* (prediction) that her partner would be turned off by her body. As is true of automatic thoughts in general, this expectancy becomes her "reality" as she imagines her partner becoming upset as he looks at and touches her. This leads her to lose any arousal that she had begun to experience and to stop touching her partner, which in turn produces a self-fulfilling prophecy in which her partner does lose interest in the sexual interaction.

Similarly, if a woman makes negative attributions about causes of a partner's actions, these cognitions are likely to interfere with sexual desire, arousal, and orgasm. For example, she might notice that her partner did not have an erection as soon as they removed their clothes, as he did in the past, and attributes it to a loss of sexual interest in her, resulting in her lack of arousal. Individuals typically believe the negative attributions that they make, leading them to behave negatively with their partners (Epstein & Baucom, 2002).

Women are socialized to hold high standards for their own physical and sexual attractiveness. Such rigid beliefs are highly resistant to disconfirmation from positive feedback. Thus, a woman who fails to meet her personal standards for beauty wishes that her partner would find her sexy but doubts it, no matter what he tells her. She enters a sexual encounter thinking negatively, which undermines her sexual responsiveness. Women with SD evidence significant failure cognitions (Nobre & Pinto-Gouveia, 2006), which are associated with sadness, resentment, disillusionment, self-blame, frustration, behavioral disengagement, arguing, and low relationship satisfaction.

Given the power of cognitions in influencing individuals' well-being in general, and specifically in the sexual realm, CBCST emphasizes assessment and intervention with negative sexual cognitions. The conjoint nature of CBCST offers opportunities for partners to contribute to each other's "cognitive restructuring." For example, when a woman makes a negative attribution that her partner's lack of interest in having sex is due to his decreased attraction to her, his response that it actually is a result of his being stressed and distracted by his job can be helpful in shifting her negative inference.

Tendencies to Be Distracted and Preoccupied

Modern life proceeds at a rapid pace, with pressures to carry out multiple roles. A particularly burdensome phenomenon is the need for cognitive and behavioral "multi-tasking." Some clients not only expect to multi-task, but take pride that they can do so. However, cognitive capacity is limited. Simultaneously trying to focus on comfort and pleasure, a partner's sexual reaction, one's children down the hall, and various career and household tasks detracts from the pleasure of sensual and sexual touch.

Furthermore, there are individual differences in the ability to maintain focus on one topic and selectively ignore competing stimuli. Whereas some clients qualify for a diagnosis of Attention Deficit Disorder, many others have sub-clinical tendencies toward being easily distracted. Distraction can affect many areas of a person's life, and contributes to SD by interfering with attention to sensual and erotic cues.

Similarly, there are differences in clients' tendencies to become preoccupied. This can involve a diagnosis of Obsessive-Compulsive Disorder, but many individuals experience subclinical levels of preoccupation, especially regarding vivid memories of past upsetting life events. For example, a woman who was strongly criticized about her body by a former lover may be preoccupied with thoughts of rejection in subsequent relationships.

CBCST clinicians explore distracted, preoccupied thinking that can interfere with sensual and erotic experiences. When a woman's history reveals upsetting sexual experiences, it is crucial to inquire about persistent distraction and preoccupation associated with them.

Inadequate Stress Management

Stress and its negative effects on well-being are commonly unrecognized or underestimated in social and family life. Compared to 30 years ago, clients have 30% less leisure time, more work demands, and reduced opportunities for self-care (Shifren, Monz, Russo, Segretti, & Johannis, 2009). This adds performance anxiety to daily living. Stress lowers sexual activity as well as relationship satisfaction (Schar & Poffet, 2010). Role strain is a common contributor to daily stress levels as individuals, especially women, attempt to balance responsibilities from their jobs, couple relationship, parenting, and caretaking roles with ill or disabled aging parents. It is difficult to value and integrate emotional intimacy and sexuality when investing great time and effort in competing roles. Women commonly describe a challenge of integrating being a mother, employee, caretaker with a sense of self as a sexual person. Although men's lives also are stressful in today's competitive world, research indicates that in couples in which both partners work full-time, women spend more time than men engaged in childcare and household tasks, producing an especially high level of role strain (Enns, Rice, & Nutt, 2015).

Individuals in today's world increasingly also are inundated with anxiety-provoking news stories about terrorism, concerns for community violence, and global economic problems. These stresses can have less obvious but pervasive negative effects on individuals and their intimate relationships. Given the multiple sources of stress in women's lives ranging from proximal family roles to workplace demands to societal stressors, it is important that CBCST clinicians identify the various stressors in each client's life and assist her and her partner in developing strategies for managing them.

Inadequate Knowledge and Skills for Relaxation

Relaxation is a core aspect of mental health and positive sexual function. Forms of relaxation training have long been considered a crucial component of cognitive-behavioral therapies. Relaxing one's body counteracts a variety of distressing emotions, such as anxiety, anger, and depression. Many individuals lack adequate knowledge about the value of relaxation and techniques that foster relaxed states. Based on societal standards that value initiative, hard work and achievement, many clients have developed a belief that relaxation is laziness and wasteful. Consequently, their approach to most any problem (including SD) is to increase effort rather than relax. In CBCST, we identify and work to weaken such counterproductive beliefs, teaching women the positive effects of relaxation, which ironically can lead to greater achievement of their goals, including satisfying couple sexuality.

Poor Body Awareness

Although many women are dissatisfied with aspects of their bodies and engage in spectatoring regarding them, this hyper-focus often co-exists with (and contributes to) inattention to positive aspects of their body and physical sensations. Sexual desire, arousal, and orgasm depend in part on noticing sensual and erotic stimulation; moving beyond distracting preoccupation to "in the moment" awareness and appreciation of sensory experience. Women who have poor body awareness rarely realize that this is the case. The therapist needs to assess the woman's level of body awareness, increase understanding of how important attending to positive sensations is, and facilitate use of techniques to increase body awareness.

Sexual Inexperience

The absence of self-directed, curious (non-abusive) sexual exploration in childhood is a predictor of SD in young adulthood (Reynolds, Herbenick, & Bancroft, 2003). A lack of sexual experience produces doubts, anxiety, and low self-confidence among women who have not had developmentally appropriate sexual experiences guided by their curiosity and comfort. Unfortunately, this leads to an avoidance of sexual experiences (thinking about them as well as engaging in them), perpetuating and exacerbating the problem. Consequently, CBCST addresses both the woman's need for sex education and her need to reduce her cognitive and behavioral avoidance pattern.

History of Physical and Sexual Abuse

There is considerable evidence that women who experienced physical and sexual abuse commonly develop SD, as their prior traumas undermine the sense of safety, trust, autonomy, mutual respect, and caring that are essential for sexual pleasure and satisfaction (McCarthy & Breetz, 2010). The woman often does not tell her partner about her prior abuse, based on shame or concern that the partner would reject her. Consequently, the partner may be unaware of reasons why the woman exhibits negative responses to sex and take it personally. Some partners who are told about her abuse history may have unrealistic assumptions and standards about it, expecting that "time heals all wounds" and failing to understand why the negative effects persist.

CBCST clinicians conduct an inquiry about past abuse or neglect experiences as part of the standard sex history. The clinician provides education for the couple regarding long-term effects of abuse and neglect and strategies to help the person heal and grow.

Internal Conflicts Regarding Sex

Although many individuals with SD commonly have internal ambivalence and conflict regarding sex and themselves as sexual beings, it occurs more often for women than men. For example, they may have learned from parents and others that sexual feelings and behavior (including masturbation) are inappropriate outside procreation, and thus they are uncomfortable with strong physical and emotional arousal or losing control, as well as fearful of the intimacy that comes with sexual involvement. If they have had physically or emotionally painful experiences in past relationships, they have difficulty taking a risk that their partner will be caring and supportive.

Some clients are aware of their internal conflicts and reveal them readily during initial interviews, but others lack either self-insight or are wary of disclosing their conflicts, fearing that the clinician will view them as pathological. It is important that clinicians inquire about the individual's thoughts and emotions regarding sex in an empathic and supportive manner.

Lack of Self-Pleasuring

Exploration of genitals as a young girl is normal and healthy (Herbenick et al., 2010; Reynolds et al., 2003). Although masturbation rates are lower than for men, 60–65% of women between the ages of 18 and 60 masturbated in the past year (Herbenick et al., 2010) and more than a third of women over 70 masturbate (Reinisch, 1991).

Self-pleasuring provides tension release, as well as a way to manage partner differences in desire. It is normal and healthy, although embarrassment and shame are common feelings (Laumann, Gagnon, Michael, & Michaels, 1994). For some women with SD, internal conflict and avoidance of masturbation contribute to a lack of body awareness and comfort with sexual arousal. Because masturbation exercises are a core component of treatment for female SD (Dodson, 1996; Heiman & LoPiccolo, 1987), it is important for sex therapists to identify and intervene with a woman's negative feelings about masturbation.

CBCST Strategies to Address Female Sexual Dysfunction

McCarthy, Bodnar, and Handal (2004) describe three principles for treating female SD. First, the traditional view of female sexuality emphasized intimacy and pleasuring and deemphasized eroticism, but integrative CBCST promotes intimacy, pleasure, *and* eroticism. A common myth is that emotional intimacy assures a vibrant sex life. Sexuality, especially desire, is smothered when there is a lack of balance between intimacy and eroticism (Perel, 2006). The second principle is that through therapy a woman develops her "sexual voice;" she becomes comfortable assertively making requests to promote receptivity and responsiveness. The third principle involves acceptance of individual differences in sexual experiences. It is crucial to help a couple accept variability in orgasmic response. Only one in six women follow the male pattern of orgasm through intercourse thrusting alone. It is difficult for men to appreciate the variability of orgasmic response and that the woman's satisfaction is more flexible than solely based on orgasm (McCarthy & Wald, 2016).

The therapist uses the structure of sensate focus/pleasuring exercises as a foundation for addressing detrimental cognitions, emotional responses, and behaviors, as well as to promote psychosexual skills that facilitate female and couple sexual function and satisfaction (O'Donohue, Dopke, & Swingen, 1997). These traditional sex therapy procedures are enhanced with a variety of cognitive-behavioral interventions, including mindfulness techniques (Brotto & Woo, 2010).

Enhancing Self-Esteem, Body Image, and Sexual Self-Confidence

Cognitively challenging the myth of "a perfect body, a perfect life" and the commercialism that promotes cosmetics, fashion, and thinness can assist the client to maintain balance. As is true for challenging longstanding personal standards (Epstein & Baucom, 2002), it is important that the therapist not suggest that the individual's belief has no merit. The woman is encouraged to pursue feeling attractive and confident, but without the perfectionism that can never be satisfied (Kleinplatz, McCarrey, & Kateb, 1992). Sexual self-esteem is the "reputation" she has of herself, her body, and her attractiveness. The therapist guides the woman in freeing herself of the trap of buying into commercially propagated standards, instead valuing her own characteristics. Sexual self-confidence is a powerful aphrodisiac.

Therapeutic interventions include cognitive restructuring with the individual, women's body awareness groups, and bibliotherapy (e.g., Dodson, 1996; Foley et al., 2012). CBCST promotes acceptance of her body and confidence in her attractiveness. This involves the therapist directing her partner to cease detrimental comments about her body ("you're getting fat...") and shifting his focus to what he enjoys about her body, touch, and sexuality. Be aware that a male partner may have hidden concerns and performance anxiety regarding his arousal (erection). The therapist helps the woman feel less responsible for his arousal, freeing her from the belief that she needs to "turn him on." The therapist can provide psychoeducation that men are more easily aroused when they are relaxed, and that men are not automatically aroused by the presence of an attractive partner. By reducing performance pressure on herself, the woman can contribute to a relaxed sexual atmosphere.

Reducing Spectatoring

As we described previously, spectatoring is a form of selective perception driven by an individual's concerns and negative expectancies (e.g., that she will not become aroused or that her partner will not be attracted to her body). In CBCST, the therapist emphasizes that sex is much more enjoyable and natural when people are not self-conscious. The therapist can draw an analogy between negative effects of sexual spectatoring and another experience that is familiar to the client. For example, a skilled athlete who becomes self-conscious about her tennis swing experiences deterioration in performance. Worrying about her sexual response or a partner's reaction is decidedly "un-sexy," whereas focusing on what she enjoys about being with her partner is arousing. The therapist introduces a variety of strategies for intentionally shifting her attention away from spectatoring to positive sensual and erotic experiences. Sensate focus exercises are a major means for such re-focusing. For individuals who have difficulty concentrating on positive sensory input, mindfulness exercises are very valuable.

Cognitive Restructuring to Reduce Inaccurate and Unrealistic Sexual Cognitions

While there are not distinctive, unique cognitions associated with each SD, detrimental cognitions are commonly associated with sexual problems and need to be addressed. As described earlier, the five major types of cognitions that influence a woman's SD include (1) selective perceptions (e.g., "I don't do anything sexually well any more"), (2) inaccurate attributions (e.g., "He turned me down for sex because he's not attracted to me"), (3) expectancies (e.g., "I'm not going to enjoy this."), (4) inaccurate or inappropriate assumptions (e.g., "I'm a mom (grandmother) now so I can't be a sex kitten"), and (5) unrealistic standards (e.g., "He's supposed to initiate and seduce me."). Such negative thoughts are detrimental for sexual desire, arousal, and orgasm (Nobre, 2009). They are associated with sadness, depressed mood, disillusionment, guilt, anger, as well as lack of pleasure and satisfaction (Meisler & Carey, 1991; Nobre & Pinto-Gouveia, 2006).

Confronting negative cognitions, testing their accuracy, and reframing them are important therapeutic strategies. Although sometimes clients are aware of and readily report their cognitions, often therapists need to probe for them. Some clients initially are only aware of distressed emotions, but when the therapist inquires about "automatic thoughts" popping into the person's mind when they are feeling upset, clients are able to describe their cognitions. Because many of the negative cognitions regarding sex occur during the client's life outside the therapist's office, it is helpful to ask clients to keep a written log of upsetting situations, the emotions experienced, and the associated automatic thoughts. Such "dysfunctional thought records" are a standard component of cognitive therapy (A. Beck, 1993; J. Beck, 2011; Leahy, 2003).

Once the individual's relevant negative sexual cognitions have been identified, a variety of cognitive therapy interventions can be used to modify them. Examples include: (1) providing accurate sexual information to establish realistic, reasonable assumptions and standards; (2) guiding the client in challenging negative attributions by thinking of alternative causes for a sexual event; (3) challenging negative expectancies by guiding the client in remembering instances in which the negative sequence did not occur, and by setting up "behavioral experiments" in which the client tests whether the prediction will come true; (4) prescribing experiences in sensate focus/pleasuring exercises that provide experiential opportunities to restructure cognitions; (5) coaching the client to list advantages and disadvantages of trying to live according to a perfectionistic sexual standard, and then devising a toned-down version of the standard that is consistent with the client's values but is more realistic; and (6) affirmation from participating in a women's sexual health support group that the client's sexual self is normal.

Given that partners influence each other's thinking as well as their behavior, changing the partner's cognitions is also important in CBCST. It would be very difficult to modify her perfectionistic sexual standards if her partner held the same beliefs. It is possible to work with both partners' cognitions simultaneously in conjoint sessions (with each person providing input to challenge the other's negative thoughts). However, if an individual has rigid ideas and reacts defensively when challenged in front of their partner, an individual session or two may be needed. Because conducting interventions to modify clients' cognitions often involves use of subtle clinical skills, we highly recommend that sex therapists consult detailed descriptions of cognitive therapy in texts and training videos.

Reducing Tendencies to Be Distracted and Preoccupied

Mindfulness training offers powerful interventions to reduce cognitive distractions and preoccupations (Brotto & Heiman, 2007). Mindfulness is particularly helpful for women who tend to be distracted easily and whose minds drift to distressing negative thoughts during sexual activity. By learning to be fully present in the moment, accepting her sexual feelings, and appreciating that thoughts are simply thoughts and not accurate portrayals of reality, an individual can reduce her distractions and self-critical notions. Brotto and Woo (2010) use mindfulness strategies to develop a woman's "presence" with her sexual thoughts and feelings.

Mindfulness exercises are practiced in the session as well as daily practice at home. With repeated practice of calm breathing and guidance from the therapist in relaxing her body, a woman can become aware of the high level of her distractibility and how this is overcome by a mindful focus. Mindfulness exercises involve immersing oneself in focusing on sensations (sight, touch, taste, smell, sounds), in a variety of life situations as well as sex. For example, a therapist may encourage a woman to take a mindful walk in a park, looking at the plants, listening to the birds, and smelling the flowers. In order to increase positive body awareness, the therapist suggests taking a bath or shower and focusing on the sensations of her skin as she blocks distracting judgments and other thoughts. It is helpful for the client to keep a journal of her mindfulness experiences. During sexuality exercises she is encouraged to utilize fantasy, erotic scenarios, and/or a vibrator to boost sexual pleasure and arousal. She identifies physical sensations by doing a "body scan," paying attention to sensations in each part of her body.

Stress Management Strategies and Relaxation Training

For couples that are overwhelmed with personal, professional, and family responsibilities, strategies for stress management are necessary. They address the context and environment that blocks relaxed sexual interaction. A large body of research has examined two major types of strategies for coping with stress (Folkman & Lazarus, 1988): *emotion-focused coping* and *problem-focused coping*. Both types are relevant for helping clients cope with stressors that interfere with satisfying sex.

Emotion-focused coping strategies deal with reducing the emotional arousal that occurs when individuals are responding to life stressors, regardless of whether the actual stressors are resolved. A variety of activities have potential to reduce negative emotions. Again, mindfulness exercises (e.g., mindful walking, focusing on pleasant tastes and textures as one eats an orange, mindful deep breathing) can be helpful in shifting one's thinking away from stressors to pleasant and relaxing sensory stimuli. Training couples in progressive muscle relaxation (Bernstein, Borkovec, & Hazlett-Stevens, 2000) is a common therapeutic strategy used to reduce physical and emotional symptoms of stress. Physical activities such as light exercise, playing with a loved pet, taking a soothing shower, or dancing to music can shift attention away from stressors and relax her body. It is important to minimize the use of alcohol and other substances, even though they can temporarily reduce negative emotion. Addressing sleep deprivation is advisable, although excessive use of sleep to avoid stressors can backfire. Finally, cognitive reappraisal or acceptance of a stressor (e.g., "It's not so bad.") can reduce emotional distress as long as that appraisal is realistic (Gross & John, 2003).

Problem-focused coping involves strategies for directly reducing or eliminating the presence of life stressors. In CBCST, couples are taught systematic problem-solving skills (Epstein & Baucom, 2002), which include the steps of (1) defining a problem in terms of observable behaviors (e.g., the couple has great difficulty getting their young children to sleep at night, resulting in no time for couple intimacy), (2) brainstorming and creating a list of potential solutions (and specifying each partner's role in carrying out the solution) without evaluating them, (3) listing advantages and disadvantages of each potential solution, (4) selecting a solution from the list to be tried, based on its relative advantages and disadvantages, and making a plan to carry it out during the coming week, and (5) observing the degree to which the solution was successful in reducing the stressor. If the solution was adequate, the couple can continue it or enhance their efforts with other solutions from their list; if not, they select a new solution. In addition to teaching the couple problem-solving skills, the therapist can help them reduce stressors by identifying additional resources that they can use, such as their social support network and community resources.

Stress researchers (Bodenmann, 2005a, 2005b; Falconier, Randall, & Bodenmann, 2016; Revenson, Kayser, & Bodenmann, 2005) have studied the importance of *dyadic coping* for reducing negative effects of stressors. Because partners may have different preferred ways of coping, there is a danger that approaches will be incompatible. Coping works well when partners collaborate on a coping approach or support each other's coping style. The therapist assesses and works to enhance couples' dyadic coping with stressors affecting their individual and couple sexual functioning.

Increasing Body Awareness

There are a number of body-focused exercises. Among these are:

Pelvic muscle (PM) exercises. Therapists can instruct female clients in the use of the PM as an important source of sexual pleasure as well as a core psychosexual skill for promoting orgasm. Sexual sensations are enhanced by consciously tensing and relaxing the PM. The PM is easily identified when she stops the flow of urine. It is felt in the perineum (the area between the vaginal opening and anus). To enhance awareness, the woman moistens a finger with saliva or a water-soluble lubricant and inserts it in her vagina. With her finger inside, she tightens the PM and notices the muscular contractions.

To strengthen the PM, the woman is instructed to use the exercises previously described in Chapter 4. The PM exercise enhances sexual pleasure by building erotic flow to orgasm.

EXERCISE: "Genital Appreciation"

Positive body image at any age requires comfort with one's genitals. Feeling proud and eager to be seen and touched is an elusive feeling for many women. Women commonly are conditioned to have negative feelings about their genitals and erotic responses. This exercise invites self-acceptance and pride in her body.

The therapist describes the steps of the exercise and asks the woman to carry it out as homework. She is to get naked and make herself comfortable on a bed or sofa. She props pillows behind her back so she can lean against the headboard, comfortably spread her legs, and have a small mirror to study her genitals. Next, she identifies the outer lips (labia) surrounding her vagina, propping the mirror so she then sees her labia. She then spreads her labia, identifying the urethra by the opening to her vagina. It is important that she take her time, paying attention to the texture of the skin and whether her vagina is moist or dry, then gently sliding back the skin covering her clitoris. She moistens a finger with saliva or a water-soluble lubricant and inserts it into her vagina to explore its interior, noticing the texture of the skin, its wetness, the warmth inside, and gently presses the upper wall. In a mindful way, she explores the sensations around her vagina and notices that at about 2 inches inside the sensation tapers off. She is aware of sensations in different areas of the vagina, feeling free to explore it before lying back, relaxing, and reflecting. This might be the first time she has touched and explored her genitalia. If she becomes anxious during the exercise, she does deep breathing and reminds herself that touching is normal and healthy. She is learning important information about her body.

The therapist encourages her to entertain cognitions such as, "This is my body;" "My genitals are beautiful;" and "My genitals are a source for pleasure for me and my partner."

The woman repeats this exercise 2–3 times (or as many times as needed) in order to promote comfort and self-esteem. Throughout the process, she is mindful of her thoughts, feelings, and physical sensations. The therapist inquires about her cognitions regarding the exercise, using cognitive restructuring to reinforce positive, constructive thoughts about her sexual body and person.

Self-pleasuring (masturbation) exercises. Treatment for SD, especially non-orgasmic response, utilizes self-pleasuring exercises (Dodson, 1996; Heiman & LoPiccolo, 1988). Masturbation involves (1) permission for pleasure; (2) increased awareness of sensual and erotic sensations; (3) increased confidence with her body's sexual responsivity; (4) self-knowledge to assertively guide her partner; (5) provision of an alternate scenario for sexual pleasure. Self-pleasuring/masturbation psychosexual skill exercises involve a series of skills beginning with body awareness/acceptance, non-genital body exploration, genital exploration, erotic stimulation, using erotic fantasies, multiple stimulation (including vibrator stimulation), using "orgasm triggers" (e.g., letting one's head hang off the side of the bed), and letting go and allowing pleasuring/eroticism to naturally flow to orgasm (McCarthy & McCarthy, 2012).

Remediation for sexual inexperience. The therapist provides sex education that is helpful in remediating gaps in a woman's sexual experience, as do the set of body awareness exercises. Referral to a female sexual health support group can be invaluable. Another very good source of information is bibliotherapy (Foley et al., 2012). The sequence of sensate focus exercises also provides the woman experiences with her own and her partner's body and sexual response.

Interventions for Relationship Factors in Sex Dysfunction

As we have emphasized throughout this book, individuals' sexual problems exist in a relational context, and there is substantial evidence that overall relationship conflict and distress are associated with SD (Metz & Epstein, 2002). The causal direction between relationship problems and sexual problems appears to be bi-directional, with conflict contributing to sexual problems and SD being a significant stressor affecting partners' feelings about each other and their relationship. Consequently, CBCST pays considerable attention to relationship dynamics, to establish a positive context for a couple's sexual interactions and for addressing SD.

Effective treatment of female SD requires that her partner acknowledges and affirms her distressed emotions and conveys empathy and support. It is crucial to engage the partner in the therapy so that the couple cooperates as an intimate sexual team. This includes increasing the woman's assertiveness, sexual self-esteem, and self-efficacy. Developing couple collaboration with progressive psychosexual skill exercises is empowering.

The treatment of choice for female SD is CBCST because the relational environment is paramount. The woman's progress is supported by enhanced communication, non-demand pleasuring, and mutually satisfying couple conflict resolution.

Common Couple Interventions

1. Enhancing couple psychosexual skills and cooperation.
2. Healing deficits in emotional intimacy (empathy).
3. Resolving relationship conflicts.
4. Enhancing eroticism.
5. Increasing freedom to engage sexually vs. the poison of sex on demand.
6. Establishing regularity as the catalyst for realistic, satisfying sex.
7. Creating satisfying alternative sexual scenarios.

Enhancing Couple Psychosexual Skills and Cooperation

A major advantage of CBCST is the opportunity to enhance psychosexual skills. Sexual function is not simply the result of good intentions; CBCST's strong suit is behavioral change. The sensate focus/pleasuring protocol—and its many adjunctive exercises—provides experiential learning opportunities for increasing sexual skills. Key interventions include cognitive focus on physical sensations (self-entrancement arousal style), cognitive and physical relaxation training, "partner genital exploration," use of PM exercises, cognitive tools such as "arousal continuum," and relaxed intercourse and intercourse "acclimation." Individualized exercises enhance couple skill and pleasure with kissing, touch, receiving and giving oral sex, anal pleasuring, seductive dancing, fantasy role-play, and sexual playfulness.

Shyness and embarrassment are rooted in self-doubt. Discussions in a women's group, in couple therapy, sexual education audiovisuals, and bibliotherapy enhance her confidence. Psychosexual skills such as how to pleasure his penis, comfort giving and receiving oral stimulation, and use of her PM are important. Behavioral proficiency is promoted by individual cognitive "rehearsals," as well as training in couple psychosexual skills via verbal instructions, bibliotherapy, and video examples. Exercises provide a behavioral foundation for the couple adopting non–demand pleasuring, erotic scenarios and techniques, and relaxed intercourse.

Women experiencing SD are often hesitant to express themselves regarding sexual thoughts and feelings, fearing that their partner will be disappointed or judge them. Consequently, a core psychosexual skill is developing her "sexual voice" (McCarthy & Wald, 2016). Her partner uses the information that she conveys to expand his understanding and acceptance rather than be limited by societal stereotypes about women's sexuality. CBCST provides the milieu to facilitate the woman's comfort with her sexual voice and promotes cooperation as an intimate sexual team.

Healing Deficits in Emotional Intimacy

A positive relationship environment in which the woman feels valued as a person, not a "sex object," is crucial. Receiving empathy for her thoughts and emotions is a largely unrecognized sexual aphrodisiac for women (Johnson, 2008; Love & Stosny, 2008; Meana, 2010). Code words for empathy are "romance," "connection," "intimacy," "soul mate," "listened to," "understood," "accept me for who I am," and "I want to feel special." CBCST facilitates mutual expression of empathy by coaching partners in expressive and empathic listening skills. The therapist provides psychoeducation about the power of these skills to enhance intimacy in couple relationships, models the skills, and coaches the couple as they repeatedly practice the expressive and empathic listener roles.

CBCST educates couples about pathways to intimacy in addition to empathic communication. The therapist describes how partners can feel closer when they work on and accomplish tasks together, share leisure activities such as taking a walk, discuss a common interest such as art, and share their dreams for the future. The therapist can guide a couple in brainstorming possible (feasible and mutually interesting) intimacy-building activities and assign them homework of selecting and carrying out an activity from their list.

Mutually Resolving Relationship Conflict: Cooperation

Unresolved relationship conflict, especially if the disagreements are intense, detracts from sexual receptivity and desire (Metz & Epstein, 2002). Anger and resentment are "poisons." Is it acceptable to use sex as a way to make up after an argument? Absolutely. Touch and sexuality are excellent ways to connect and reconnect. Touching can be warm and sensual or passionate and erotic. A healthy function of sexuality is to energize and motivate the couple to address and resolve emotional and practical conflicts.

A caveat about make-up sex is that some couples fall into a destructive pattern of psychological and physical aggression serving as "foreplay." In other words, make-up sex comes after aggression. This reinforces fighting, and the negative residue of the aggression is likely to persist and significantly detract from intimacy and mutual trust. People do not forget the aversive things that their partner has said or done. A useful intervention is to set a hard-and-fast rule of no touching of any type for at least 72 hours after an aggressive incident (psychological or physical). In order to carry out this intervention, the therapist must first have a detailed discussion with the couple about forms of psychological and physical aggression, so the criteria are clear (Epstein, Werlinich, & LaTaillade, 2015). Some couples are surprised to hear criteria for psychological aggression (e.g., breaking an object in anger, without touching one's partner), so the therapist may need to spend time discussing why such actions can hurt a relationship.

A major CBCST intervention to enhance couples' conflict resolution is training in problem solving. Problem solving is by nature a collaborative process rather than a continuation of competition and conflict.

Enhancing Eroticism

One of the strongest held myths is that a relationship with strong emotional intimacy automatically results in vibrant sex. As we have noted, the challenge is to balance intimacy and eroticism (Perel, 2006). Although emotional intimacy is crucial, intimacy can smother eroticism just as eroticism without emotional intimacy can smother cooperation. Intimacy and eroticism are different, but not adversarial or incompatible (McCarthy & McCarthy, 2009).

Couple Exercise: "Positive Feedback"

Communication is particularly important to enhance each partner's self-esteem. Partners take turns sharing affirming thoughts. Because many men are uncomfortable

with emotional communication, this anxiety manifests as lightheartedness and teasing rather than thoughtful and serious feedback. Coaching by the therapist is crucial
to enhance genuine communication.

Communication Prompts:

1.   The thing I most admire about you is…
2.   The sexiest thing about you is…
3.   You make me feel special when…
4.   The thing you do that turns me on is…
5.   What enhances eroticism for me is…
6.   I feel embarrassed to tell you but I think I would enjoy…
7.   The mood that promotes sexual vitality for me is…

Increasing Freedom to Engage Sexually vs. the Poison of "Sex on Demand"

A basic principle in CBCST is "If you don't have the power to say no to sex, you
don't feel the freedom to say yes to sex." Performance demands, especially intimate
coercion, poison sex. Demanding sex to be carried out just one way or insisting
on a rigid erotic scenario negates intimacy and sharing. Demands involve coercing
one's partner to prove something or to mask one's fear of failure. Rather than enhancing couple sexuality, it intimidates the partner and destabilizes the relationship.
At the other extreme, a partner who avoids sex is practicing "covert coercion"
(passive-aggressiveness). When either polarizing position becomes a pattern, it undermines the intimate sexual team. Consequently, it is important for the therapist
to inquire how sex is initiated and by whom, and the freedom each partner feels
to request variation.

With freedom to engage in sexuality focused on mutual pleasure, couple sexuality develops a reliable and regular frequency. When the therapist initiates an agreement that coercion is totally unacceptable, it frees the partners to take emotional
and sexual risks. The danger is the couple settles into a routine and over-values
safety. This leads to de-eroticizing the relationship. Security that derives from lack
of coercion provides the freedom to be playful and erotic.

Establishing Regularity as the Catalyst for Realistic, Satisfying Sex

A hallmark of a satisfying relationship is that sex occurs on a regular basis. Couples
who have sex three times one week and then no sex for six weeks are at risk of
alienation. Regular sexual frequency (whether 3 times a week, once a week, or
2 times a month) provides a sustaining and satisfying benefit. Regular sex provides
"emotional synchrony," inoculates against "sex on demand" (especially if it is the
woman who ensures regularity), indicates respect for gender differences, and recognizes physiological (contact hunger and sex drive) and emotional needs.

When a man realizes that sex will occur regularly and he does not have to "beg,"
he recognizes that his partner accepts and understands his sex drive and wants to

please him. Regular sex provides the woman with more comfort and less pressure, which promotes relaxation and pleasuring. Their lovemaking style promotes her desire and arousal. Similarly, when a man's stressful work life results in his being interested in sex less often than his partner, the partner's recognition of that preference and cooperation in establishing a regular frequency of sex over time will result in a more relaxed relationship and likely greater desire. Thus, regular sex (which includes valuing sensual, playful, and erotic sexuality) is a win-win for the couple, reducing struggles over intercourse frequency.

The important feature is both partners' acceptance of their couple sexual pattern. When this "schedule" is known, partners take turns initiating, which promotes feeling desire and desirable. Seeing one's partner as engaged and involved is an aphrodisiac. Identifying "what's in it for me, my partner, and us" clarifies the value and rewards of couple sexuality and promotes integration of life's moods and realities.

Creating Satisfying Alternative Sexual Scenarios

Alternative sexual scenarios provide flexibility. They serve as an antidote to the myth that sex should be spontaneous, perfect, and always involve intercourse. Alternative scenarios are sexually satisfying experiences that do not require sexual function or intercourse. Realizing that sexually satisfying experiences are possible even when there are difficulties with desire, lubrication, erection, intercourse, or orgasm facilitates long-term satisfying couple sex. Alternative scenarios provide creative solutions when there is a discrepancy in sexual desire or an experience when erection or orgasm is not present. For sexually satisfied couples, rain checks and alternative scenarios are common. Because of younger men's higher biological sex drive and gender expectations, accepting alternative sexual scenarios can be more challenging for them. For couples with SD, developing alternative scenarios is an empowering strategy.

Case Example: Mandy and Steve

After several painful arguments about sexual frequency, Mandy and Steve discussed how to reach agreement when they had different sexual agendas. Their expectation had been that intercourse was required for a satisfying sexual experience. However, using the criterion of mutual satisfaction without perfection that they learned in therapy, they discussed alternative sexual scenarios that were affirming. This is an illustration of an alternative scenario that kept sexuality "regular" and satisfying.

- Mandy turned off the light and asked, "Tired?" "Yeah, it's been a bear of a day."
- "Too drained to make love?" she asked.
- After a long pause Steve responded, "To be honest, I am so tired that making love would feel more like work than fun."
- "I'm really awake. Would you mind helping me?"
- Slowly rolling over, Steve replied, "Here I am," and gently placed her head on his shoulder. Mandy cuddled against Steve and lightly began to touch her genitals with one hand and cradled Steve's testicles in the other while Steve stroked her hair and

kissed the top of her head. After a few minutes, Mandy felt her vulva begin to swell and cupping Steve's testicles, she felt moisture in the lips of her vagina.

- Aware of Steve holding her, she began to rock against his body while slipping her finger along the shaft of her clitoris with progressively rapid strokes. As her breathing and excitement quickened she felt fullness in her pelvis and could sense orgasm coming. She altered the pace of caressing her clitoris to long and steady strokes. She felt the rhythmic muscular contractions of orgasm, and when these subsided, she clutched Steve in an affirming, connecting embrace.
- After several minutes, Steve kissed her, said "wonderful" and rolled over to fall asleep. Mandy reflected how relaxed and invigorated she felt, how generous Steve had been, and how good it felt to have this alternative scenario. This was not a "win-lose" or "either-or." Each felt their sex life fit real-life as a committed couple. Relationship and sexual satisfaction was their priority.

Treatment for Specific Sex Dysfunctions

For each female SD, we describe the prevalence and distinguishing features, core CBCST interventions, and a case illustration. The CBCST interventions for addressing biological, psychological, and relational factors are applied for each SD as needed.

Unless there are extenuating circumstances, the treatment of choice for SD is CBCST. This is especially appropriate because of the ubiquitous emotional component and relationship cooperation features of female desire, arousal, and orgasm. The partner's participation is ideal whether relationship dynamics have served as a barrier to function or there is partner encouragement. Individual therapy can be concomitant with couple work. The sensate focus/pleasuring structure provides a safe and affirming therapeutic format. For women without a current partner, strategies and exercises can be adapted for masturbation and fantasy rehearsal.

The Framework for CBCST Interventions

The classic sensate focus/pleasuring format provides a step-by-step framework to promote relaxation, pleasure, arousal, erotic flow, and orgasm. With reliable pleasure and ongoing satisfaction, women are motivated for regular sex for herself as well as couple satisfaction.

Sexual Desire Issues

While inhibited desire (Female Sexual Interest/Arousal Disorder) is the most common SD, it is important to remember the frequent comorbidity of SDs. Because of the circularity of sexual and relationship functioning, it is rare that one difficulty does not interact with another. CBCST does not depend on a linear cause and effect model. Intervening at a particular point in the circular process of cognitive, behavioral, and emotional distress serves not only to address barriers to sexual function but also to explore complex psychological and relational characteristics. By the time clients seek assistance, the various physical, psychological, and interpersonal factors influencing their sexual relationship are highly intertwined. Rather than trying to figure out what came first, it is best to identify intervention points that are most likely to improve the clients' well-being. Typically, CBCST simultaneously targets a number of factors that the assessment has indicated are contributing to an SD.

Sexual Interest/Arousal Disorder (FSIAD)

The DSM-5 term for female desire problems is Sexual Interest/Arousal Disorder (FSIAD). Desire may be physically impaired through hormone imbalance, a side effect of medications, illness, or surgery (Segraves & Woodard, 2006). Psychological factors such as stress, internal conflicts, anger, depression, low self-esteem, anxiety, and persistent symptoms from prior traumatic sexual experiences can inhibit desire. Sexual ignorance, religious prohibitions, disturbed communication, hostility between partners, destructive interaction patterns, excessive demands, and fatigue also are factors implicated in FSIAD. Regarding co-morbidity, loss of desire can result from deficits in sexual response—a woman who has difficulty with orgasm develops low desire as her motivation for sex decreases and she avoids sex to prevent further frustration (Basson, 2010; Kaplan, 1974). Inhibition accompanied by strong negative emotions and phobic reactions to anything sexual is labeled "sexual aversion." As a phobic response, aversion is treated using in vivo desensitization and/or medications, as well as cognitive interventions when the aversion is associated with past traumatic experiences.

Severe desire problems have the least favorable prognosis of all female SD. Therapy is lengthier and often requires individual work to address causes such as fear of pleasure, romantic success, intimacy, and PTSD. Relationship factors usually are involved, especially with secondary desire problems. Women experiencing sexual aversion may have had either insufficient touch or abusive touch during childhood (Zoldbrod, 2015).

Sexual desire is best conceptualized as a continuum involving physiological, psychological, and relational dimensions. Cases range from mild to complete absence of desire. Interestingly, once involved in sexual activity, some women who report low desire experience arousal and orgasm. Sometimes desire is low with a spouse but present with another partner. More commonly, low sexual desire exists in an otherwise caring, affectionate relationship. Conflict-ridden relationships are at significant risk for FSIAD.

It is important for the clinician to assess factors that affect any aspect of the woman's sexual function, such as the broader context of her life (her job, family relationships, and overall health) and the quality of the couple's sexual relationship. Are problems with desire the primary concern, or is it the result of non-orgasmic response, sexual pain, or chronic relationship dissatisfaction? As with other SD, it may be lifelong or acquired, generalized or situational, and due to psychosocial factors or combined medical and psychological factors.

Prevalence

FSIAD is the most common female SD, and desire problems cause the most couple distress (Weeks, 2004). The Global Study of Sexual Attitudes and Behaviors found a prevalence rate of 26–43% for lack of interest in sex among women aged 40–80 in 20 countries (Laumann et al., 2005). In the United States, surveys report 27–32% of women aged 18–59 reported lack of interest in sex.

There has been considerable discussion about the interpretation of these data. Researchers and clinicians suggest that the model of sexual response described by Masters and Johnson (1966) and Kaplan (1974) typifies male desire (Tiefer, 2004; Wood, Koch, & Mansfield, 2006) and overlooks important contextual factors for female desire such as social roles, a circular rather than linear flow of desire, and the relational context that encompasses sexual interactions. The complexity of sexual desire is illustrated by data indicating that women do not differentiate between desire and arousal (Basson, 2010; Graham, Sanders, Mulhausen, & McBride, 2004).

Clinical Presentations

Sexual desire problems present in a number of ways, including: "I used to enjoy sex, but now I don't care." "We have busy lives with family and careers, a pretty good marriage, but I could easily live without sex." "I like romantic movies and novels and feel warm and close with my partner, but I'm not interested in being sexual." "Sex is way down on my priority list."

Accurate Expectations: What Is Normal?

A controversial issue involves a comparison between female sex desire and male desire. Men and women commonly believe that men have a greater interest in sex (Baumeister, Catanes, & Vohs, 2001; Regan & Berscheid, 1995). Gender differences in sexual desire and arousal have led to professional reconceptualization of women's sexuality as responsive rather than internally generated (Basson, 2001; Diamond, 2008; Meana, 2010). Sexual desire overlaps with arousal; it is relationally focused, with emotional intimacy both a generator of desire and a reinforcer of satisfaction (Basson, 2007; Laan & Both, 2011).

Approaches to Treatment

At issue is the anchor used to determine desire. Some clinicians assume that if a woman is able to experience orgasm, sufficient desire is present. Sexologists suggest that the traditional criteria for desire that were developed from a male model are insufficient for understanding female desire. The core components of desire are positive anticipation and a sense of deserving pleasure. This involves openness to touch, the presence of romantic or erotic thoughts, emotional connection, and responsiveness to the partner's desire. Factors that facilitate desire include an inviting milieu such as a walk, a romantic evening, erotic fantasy, or couple activities.

Is the sole issue desire or is it the manifestation of inhibited orgasm, sexual pain, dissatisfaction with the partner's lovemaking skills, or his SD? Use of the sensate focus/pleasuring exercises provides diagnostic clarity as well as an intervention to ameliorate the negative feedback loop. This promotes physiological relaxation and cognitive clarification of the emotional and sexual barriers. When the therapist hears signs that a woman is resistant to sensual pleasure, further inquiry can explore whether this is based on a fear that her body will "not get into it" (arousal) or "I won't be able to get there" (orgasm). Alternatively, the woman may reveal negative feelings about the couple relationship that make her uninterested in intimacy with her partner. The data from sensate focus and other pleasuring exercises offer guidance to the clinician to address cognitive barriers as well as tailor intervention strategies.

Strategies and Interventions for Pleasure, Arousal, and Eroticism

Two fundamental principles anchor CBCST for female desire:

1. Establish the woman's emotional and sexual conditions for openness, receptivity, and responsiveness.
2. Encourage her sexual "voice," taking responsibility for her sexual desire, and "building bridges to sexual desire" (McCarthy & Wald, 2015).

Rather than the traditional concept that female desire depends on romantic love, attraction, a strong relationship, and her partner being a great lover, the guiding concept in CBCST is that the woman has a right to sexual pleasure and desire. Therapy promotes a sense of deserving pleasure—whether she is overweight, in a stressed relationship, has a history of sexual trauma, or is not orgasmic. CBCST facilitates feelings of personal validation, acceptance, and freedom. Her conditions for satisfying sex include freedom from fear of sexually transmitted infections, unwanted pregnancy, coercion, and threats of negative consequences.

An empowering concept is Basson's (2007) "responsive female desire" model rather than the male model of desire based on biological drive, erotic fantasies, spontaneous erection, and need for orgasm. The responsive desire model suggests that women's desire begins at neutral, but if she is open and responsive to touch and emotionally aware of her feelings as well as her partner's, she experiences pleasure and chooses whether to act on her desire. The responsive model is helpful to understand why a history of sexual trauma, emotional neglect, or unresolved relationship conflict is detrimental to women's desire and satisfaction (Lemieux & Byers, 2008; Nobre, 2009).

CBCST for female sexual desire illustrates the need to integrate accurate and reasonable age and situation-appropriate expectations with multiple therapeutic strategies (McCarthy & Thestrup, 2008a, 2008b). The 35-year-old couple who have two children and who expect her sexual desire to be the same as that of college students have unreasonable expectations. The couple is challenged to cooperate in a way that brings energy and satisfaction to their sexual relationship. Among the myths that set up unreasonable expectations are (1) the need for spontaneity, (2) great sex every time, (3) simultaneous orgasms, and (4) nonverbal, intense erotic scenarios. Such idealized notions are self-defeating and are corrected in CBCST.

Building Bridges to Sexual Desire

A strategy that is helpful for many couples is "building bridges to sexual desire" (McCarthy & McCarthy, 2014; McCarthy & Wald, 2015): The woman is responsible for her desire and satisfaction, including designing a sexual encounter that is personally inviting. The crucial feature is positive anticipation and believing that she deserves sexual pleasure. The desire psychosexual skill exercises are designed to increase comfort, attraction, trust, and freedom to create her preferred scenario (McCarthy & McCarthy, 2012). Rather than attempting to enact one right way to have sex, she initiates and scripts an encounter from pleasuring to afterplay. CBCST addresses desire-inhibiting features such as anger, depression, past negative experiences, ambivalence about her partner, a belief that sex is for the man, performance pressures, and resentments. The woman can recognize environmental factors, such as the need for privacy and an inviting physical milieu.

EXERCISE: "Designing Her Preferred Sexual Scenario"

Although many women follow their partner's sexual script, it is important to identify aspects of lovemaking that intensify her sexual experience. While appreciating that fantasy is not reality, expanding sexual desire with erotic fantasy is an important bridge to desire.

The therapist encourages her to develop a script with vivid detail. She imagines the setting and activities that lead to lovemaking, as well as the mood, dialogue, and physical interactions. She is like a movie scriptwriter developing an erotic scenario. Afterward, she reflects on the meaning of her sexual script. How similar or different is her ideal scenario, compared with their real-life sex? How does she explain the differences? What can she do to promote sexual experiences that are closer to her script in spirit and behavior? Reflecting on this exercise assists her in talking with her partner about cooperation for satisfying couple sexuality (McCarthy & Wald, 2015).

Empathic Communication

An essential therapeutic intervention is promoting open discussion of differences in sexual desire, including those associated with gender. The therapist offers permission and normalizes desire differences as well as provides information about the Basson model. Understanding the normal distribution of human sexual phenomenon helps partners appreciate the wide variation in sexuality. Acceptance of the desire issue helps a woman not feel second-class in a sex competition. She accepts and refines her "sexual voice." An important concept is if she is unable to say no to sexual activities that her partner desires without negative consequence, she will be inhibited from saying yes and confidently pursuing pleasure. Couples can avoid a yes-no power struggle by finding flexible ways of cooperating and developing alternative scenarios for pleasure that are not predicated on one-dimensional intercourse performance.

Appreciating Inherent Variability in Satisfying Sex

An important cognitive goal of CBCST is helping couples appreciate the normal variability of sexual quality within the relationship. Wanting great sex every time is unreasonable and leads to disappointment and dissatisfaction. The quality of sex varies, with approximately 35–45% of encounters rated as being very good, 20–25% very good for one partner (usually the male), 15–20% being okay or "get by" sex, and 5–15% experienced as dissatisfying or dysfunctional (Frank, Anderson, & Rubinstein, 1978; Laumann et al., 1994).

The best estimate is that 1 in 3 regularly orgasmic women never or only seldom experience orgasm during intercourse. These data suggest that one of the most common male complaints, that a partner cannot reach orgasm during intercourse, is not an SD but rather a normal variation of female response (Sugrue & Whipple, 2001). When orgasm is the sole indicator of sexual satisfaction, this results in sexual dissatisfaction.

Healthy female desire and response involves sexual anticipation, emotional benefits, and openness and receptivity to touch. Her responsive desire is based on intimacy, comfort, security, cooperation, pleasure, and variability/flexibility. It is important for clients to realize that desire ebbs and flows, without worrying that this constitutes an SD.

Psychosexual Skill Exercises

Grounded in helping the couple appreciate and accept the variability and flexibility of female sexuality, providing accurate scientific information, promoting realistic expectations, and supporting the criterion of couple sexual satisfaction, CBCST psychosexual skill exercises are used to evaluate sexual comfort and confidence. The sensate focus/pleasuring series is designed for relaxation, receptivity, and graduated pleasure. Their creative use provides the format to develop and initiate bridges to desire, with a woman's preferred ways to "set the stage" with mood, time, and milieu. These include her preferences for initiation (nonverbal gestures, verbal initiation), quality of tenderness, level of control, how and when to transition from sensual pleasure to erotic stimulation, and her preferred arousal/orgasm pattern whether before, during, or after intercourse. This includes preferences for mutual pleasuring versus taking turns, multiple stimulation versus single stimulation, giving and receiving oral pleasure, style and quality of manual stimulation, intercourse positions, multiple stimulation during intercourse, and preferences for arousal styles (partner interaction, self-entrancement, role enactment). It is important that she has the option to direct how and when the couple will transition to intercourse, depending on her preference for high versus moderate level of arousal, as well as who she would like to initiate the transition and guide intromission (McCarthy & Thestrup, 2008a, 2008b). It is important to establish satisfying after-play scenarios, such as the quality of touch for emotional connection, silence or intimate talk, and features that enhance satisfaction. Facilitating exploration of sexual preferences honors her sexual desire and offers balance to her partner's sexual preferences.

Autonomy and Cohesion: Her "Voice" and Partner Cooperation

A guiding principle for sexual desire is balancing individual autonomy and relationship cohesion. Perel (2006) describes the importance of blending eroticism and intimacy. Schnarch (1991) emphasizes individuation and challenges the use of sexual exercises, believing that they promote an other-centered need for sexual validation. Lobitz and Lobitz (1996) advocated integrating partners' desire and arousal, suggesting that an involved, aroused partner is a major aphrodisiac. Using sexual exercises in a mechanical manner is ineffective, whereas using exercises in a manner that confronts avoidance and inhibition while facilitating involvement is invaluable in promoting couple sexuality.

A useful clinical strategy, especially for women who do not feel deserving of pleasure or are afraid to claim their sexual voice, is a women's sexual health support group (Barbach, 1975; Heiman & LoPiccolo, 1988). Female SD groups, originally designed to teach women to be orgasmic, have expanded to help with desire, pleasure, pain, eroticism, and other sexual concerns. Group discussion and homework assignments (e.g., journaling, writing a letter to her genitals, reflecting on her desires) are empowering. When the barriers for desire are severe, individual therapy can be important. Judicious use of pharmacotherapy, especially for depression, panic disorder, or generalized anxiety can be helpful.

An important cognitive strategy is to help the woman shift to *inviting* pleasure and desire rather than *reaching* for them. Couple assignments that promote desire include relaxation training, building comfort with nudity, body image work, taking turns initiating, identifying characteristics of the partner that she finds attractive, making requests for change that increase attraction, identifying turnoffs and confronting these without fear of hurting the partner's feelings, establishing trust and vulnerability, promoting playfulness, initiating erotic scenarios, and using her right to say "no" in order to progressively say "yes."

Interventions to build desire include (Leiblum, 2010):

- Warming up to physical pleasure through graduated forms of touch.
- Promoting comfort, safety, and patience.
- Being aware of distractions in daily life and reordering priorities. Relaxed and pleasurable sex is inviting.
- Establishing good sleep rituals and planning ahead to reserve physical energy.
- Addressing ways to improve partner attractiveness (shower, mouth rinse, compliments).
- Acknowledging and addressing emotional resentments.
- Addressing psychosexual skill problems.
    - Reducing performance anxiety (the demand for sex, doubting her sexual value).
    - Overcoming cognitive, emotional, and behavioral difficulties.
    - Promoting positive thoughts and beliefs about the role of sex in her life.
    - Enhancing sexual self-esteem.
    - Promoting positive sexual feelings (things that sexually interest her—fantasies, music, movies, books, sexy clothes, playful interactions, compliments, flirting, or role-playing).

Structured Couple Exercises and the Intimate Sexual Team

Structured couple exercises provide the format to promote comfort and sensual pleasure that invite eroticism (McCarthy & Wald, 2015). Behavioral exercises are a step-wise progression from safe, patient, and soothing touch; to relaxed touch for pleasure; to inviting pleasure to evolve to eroticism that includes oral pleasuring, intercourse, and orgasm. Especially important for clients who disown sexuality is to engage in afterplay with intimacy, holding, discussing, and embracing so that integrated sexuality is valued by the woman. An essential element and guiding principle in CBCST is fostering the woman's belief that her partner is her intimate and erotic friend (Metz & McCarthy, 2010). She perceives him as being accepting of her needs and open to her requests (McCarthy & Thestrup, 2008a; 2008b).

Clinical Issues

There are several common individual and couple patterns that inhibit desire. A woman may have learned that her sexual role is to service her partner, based on the notion that sex is primarily for men. Another woman may believe that she does not deserve pleasure, or that experiencing pleasure is shameful. Another negative cognition is the narrow belief that the only purpose for sex is reproduction. The clinician interviews the woman in a sensitive manner, conveying lack of judgment about beliefs that she may hold.

A common *individual feature* in inhibited desire is deficits in psychosexual skills. A common *relationship feature* is resentment. For example, a woman may experience her partner as selfish and uninterested in her pleasure. When desire problems have developed after a period in which the woman was sexually functional, it is common that her partner expected her to easily feel desire. Basson's model of female sexual desire provides an understanding of changes in a woman's desire as well as an avenue for promoting realistic and reliable desire in a committed relationship.

Resentment results from chronic, unresolved relationship conflict that poisons the sexual environment. Amidst the busy activity of modern life, it is easy for partners to become overwhelmed with responsibilities, with each person failing to empathize with the other's stress. The emotional hurts that develop over weeks, months, and years precipitate an alienated or even hostile mood. This serves as a barrier to openness let alone eagerness for sexual connection.

In contrast to gradual erosion of sexual desire due to chronic conflict and disengagement, more acute and severe events such as infidelity, uncovered secrets such as gambling losses, and medical problems kept hidden from the partner can have major impacts on desire. Revealed secrets complicate sex therapy as they undermine trust and a sense of safety that form the foundation of an intimate relationship (Gordon, Khaddoima, Baucom, & Snyder, 2015). CBCST clinicians urge clients to disclose and process the secret with their partner, in session or at home. The Synder, Baucom, and Gordon (2007) model, which approaches infidelity as a traumatic experience and provides a three-stage treatment, is an excellent intervention for a variety of betrayals that seriously harm sexual desire.

Case Example: Patricia and Todd

Married for 14 years, sexual desire had been a problem for both partners since the birth of their third child. Both Patricia and Todd had physicals in the last year that ruled out medical problems. Psychologically, Patricia evidenced mild depression, work and parenting stresses, but no significant relationship conflict. She had chronic feelings of exhaustion and being overwhelmed. Sleep was inconsistent. Todd had similar feelings, as well as anxiety about ED. Each felt anxious that if their relationship remained non-sexual, it would doom the marriage.

Todd's verbal criticism about sexual frequency (less than 10 times a year) reflected his belief that the children were more important to Patricia than their relationship. Her continuing to allow the 3-year-old to sleep in their bed confused and frustrated him. When his resentment was particularly evident, she would "service" him sexually, which she grew to resent.

A set of CBCST interventions was instituted to shift the atmosphere in the couple's relationship:

1. Increasing "team" cooperation: coaching Todd and Patricia toward cooperating as a team (taking turns answering the phone, putting the kids to bed, and a brief meeting Sunday evening to discuss tasks for the week ahead).
2. Creating privacy in the bedroom: working together to help the 3-year-old to transition to his bed.
3. Restructuring their daily lives within the constraints they faced; providing "off duty" time for self-care.
4. Developing expectations that are more realistic: Learning about Basson's model of female sexual desire to help them accept that in a committed relationship female desire is predicated more than male desire on couple cooperation, openness to relaxed touch, willingness to engage in non-demand pleasuring, patience to allow relaxation, touch, and closeness.
5. Bridges to sexual desire: Facilitating emotional and sexual desire via adaptations of sensate focus/pleasuring exercises to promote anticipation and responsiveness.
6. Building structure in their schedule to produce regularity in sexual frequency.
7. Guiding the couple in devising appealing alternative sexual scenarios.

Couple Discrepancies in Sexual Desire

Couple and sex therapists commonly hear couples complain of conflict over how often they prefer to engage in sexual activities. Although a prevailing stereotype portrays men as wanting sex more often than women, we often see couples in which it is the female who desires sex more frequently. It is important for the therapist to conduct a careful assessment of both partners to determine whether either has a desire disorder. When it appears that both have levels of desire within a normal range, the core therapeutic goal becomes helping them bridge their difference, modify their negative cognitions about the meaning of the discrepancy, and facilitate reaching agreement that respects each person's sexual self and promotes emotional intimacy.

Case Example: Susan and Tom

Susan, 30, and Tom, 33, sought marital therapy for Susan's dissatisfaction about infrequent sex. Married for 3 years with one child, both partners reported major stresses in their careers. Susan managed a coffee shop, and Tom was a lawyer who soon would come up for partnership evaluation.

During their individual sexual histories, they reported conflict over sexual frequency. Tom reported that they had intercourse every few days except when he traveled for work. Susan reported that since the birth of their child intercourse occurred less than once a week, and she felt she was unsatisfied without sex that is more frequent. Tom said that he was attracted to Susan and enjoyed sex with her, but that he often felt tired and distracted by the responsibilities he had in life. Tom accused Susan of being a "sex junkie," and Susan accused Tom of making their relationship low priority. The more the couple argued about sexual frequency, the less sensual and erotic the atmosphere between them was. The therapist used CBCST to address several features of their relationship:

1. Couple communication skill training was used to assist them in calmly discussing their sexual dilemma using expressive and empathic listener skills. They recognized they had fallen into a self-defeating demand-withdraw conflict pattern. He noted that her desire "pushes me back," and his hesitation fueled her wanting more sex.

2. With careful reflection, Susan shared with Tom her worries about losing physical attractiveness since giving birth (stretch marks), feeling desexualized in her role as a mother, believing that Tom did not desire her, as well as fears of abandonment (her father left her mother when she was a girl). Tom revealed that sexual pressure from Susan added to the overall stress he felt, feeling overwhelmed by all of his responsibilities, which led him to feel performance anxiety and embarrassment at his periodic low interest in sex. For Susan the conflict had amplified her emotional and sexual drive, whereas for Tom it demoralized him and amplified his avoidance. Each was able to appreciate the other's feelings and communicate empathy.

3. Sensate focus/pleasuring exercises that emphasized relaxation and being a sexual team were instituted.

4. The therapist guided the couple in thinking of alternative sexual scenarios. Understanding the different meanings and purposes for sex, Susan and Tom were able to appreciate each other's desires and fears. Susan realized the pressure that Tom felt when she approached with "sex on demand," especially in the context of his feeling overwhelmed by work and other responsibilities. Tom appreciated Susan's worries about sexual attractiveness as well as wanting orgasm for tension release. This understanding helped them to develop alternative sexual scenarios. When Susan was stressed and Tom was exhausted, they would decide how to be sexual that did not require an erection or energized engagement. One scenario was for him to manually stimulate Susan to orgasm, and another was a mutual erotic scenario.

5. To prevent the continuation of their polarizing sexual interaction, they chose a "regular frequency" of intercourse twice a week. Tom would be the "bean counter" to ensure this regularity. A feature of their relapse prevention plan was to affirm Good Enough Sex.

Sexual Aversion

Sexual aversion is a phobic reaction that is often traced to trauma. Similar to other phobias, aversion to sex involves protective avoidance of stimuli that have become associated in the individual's mind with highly distressing experiences (Kaplan, 1987). The experiences need not have been sexual abuse or rape. Binik (2010) suggested comorbidity between sexual aversion and vaginismus, in which the association is between intercourse and fear of severe pain. Strong negative emotions are triggered by cues such as an erect penis, nudity, and even non-sexual hugging. Aversion can be triggered by cognitions (i.e., thoughts or images of conditions that the person associates with traumatic events) as well as actual life situations, and varies in severity, with extreme levels reaching panic, disgust, and revulsion (Foley et al., 2012). Aversion is not a choice; it is a strong emotional reaction that blocks pleasure and eroticism. Another manifestation of aversion is dissociative sex, in which the individual protects herself against engagement by distancing her consciousness from her body during sexual activity; i.e., her mind is elsewhere. Individuals often use alcohol or drugs to assist them in "going through the motions."

The prevalence of sexual aversion is difficult to establish because clients who avoid sex also avoid couple and sex therapy (unless pressured by the partner).

Treatment Considerations

Cognitive-behavioral strategies adapted from phobia treatment are the core interventions for sexual aversion. Strategies to promote feelings of safety, empowerment, self-assurance, as well as skills to manage unwanted emotions are important. Interventions that promote comfort and pleasure are crucial. Mindfulness techniques include cognitive training to be fully present in her body, awareness of sensations with an emphasis on how present sensations are being caused by positive sexual experiences rather than traumatic ones, self-soothing, and learning to notice and counteract triggers (e.g., shifting her attention to warm feelings associated with hugging her partner rather than memories of a former partner hurting her). Cognitive restructuring of the anxious associations with sex as well as behavioral strategies to modify aversive reactions using pleasant masturbation rehearsal and progressive desensitization are helpful. As in the treatment of phobias in general, graduated exposure to feared stimuli is a core intervention. The sequential steps of sensate focus exercises provide an excellent structure for such desensitization procedures.

Aversion also may signal fear of uncontrolled passion. Growing up amidst alcohol abuse, domestic violence, sexual abuse, or family of origin overprotection can create a fear of strong emotions, by oneself as well as by other people. Fear of her partner's sexual excitement ("he gets out of control...") or a belief that men cannot control sexual urges, is destabilizing. A woman suffering sexual aversion may experience a partner's lust as terroristic. The possibility that sexual activity including flirtatiousness, touch, and cuddling will escalate to uncontrolled behavior can produce panic, as the individual "catastrophizes" intimacy behaviors spinning out of control into sexual aggressiveness and even injury.

Cognitive, behavioral, and pharmacologic treatment options are helpful to reduce such aversive responses to sexual cues. Individual therapy can precede or accompany CBCST. Individual therapy provides the forum for the person to develop a new meaning for why her aversive response occurs, and what impact it has on her and her partner. This is a cognitive re-attribution process. The therapist guides the individual in identifying her negative expectancies (predictions about sex getting out of control) and either challenging them cognitively ("My partner is a kind, sensitive, and rational guy who would never hurt me.") or through behavioral experiments (e.g., homework to schedule sensual touching and to observe whether there is any evidence of either partner losing control). The members of the couple collaborate to engage in positive behavioral changes regarding affectionate and sexual expression, working as an intimate team to counteract conditioned trauma responses (Calhoun & Tedeschi, 2006).

Case Example: Tricia and Conrad

Tricia had grown up in an alcoholic family in which her parents would explode in rage, including occasions of physical violence and police involvement. She remembered feeling afraid, hiding in a closet, uncertain of what might happen. As an adult she was very apprehensive that any conflict situation could get out of control. Whenever marital emotions ran high or when Conrad would be sexually excited, Tricia wanted to withdraw because she feared an uncontrollable situation. Sexual frequency was very low unless she drank heavily. Even with alcohol, she found it distressing to have sex and experience her husband's passion.

Treatment involved a chemical dependency evaluation, couple therapy to establish relationship stability, and a female sexual health therapy group. CBCST involved identifying her fears (aversion) of passion and guiding her in challenging her catastrophic expectancies, in vivo exposure through psychosexual exercises with Conrad to build comfort and pleasure, and eventually integrated eroticism. It was particularly helpful for Conrad to talk with Tricia about passion and reassure her that he experienced very pleasurable feelings with her but was not "out of control" or at risk of doing something dangerous. He enjoyed acting wild, which built his excitement, but he could stop any time. Conrad wanted Tricia to "have fun sexually." Tricia began to feel trust and permission to release her hidden desire for pleasure and eroticism, especially after the couple planned several brief sexual interactions in which Conrad expressed his desire for Tricia and enjoyment of their mutual touching but intentionally stopped the interaction, demonstrating his self-control.

Inhibited Sexual Arousal

Inhibited arousal is not a separate DSM-5 diagnosis, as it has been replaced by the FSIAD diagnosis. It is important to reiterate that physiological arousal does not necessarily coincide with the woman's subjective experience (Graham et al., 2004); however, a woman becomes frustrated when she wants to feel aroused but cannot (Wylie & Hallam-Jones, 2005). One woman described this as "desire but no fire;" neither her body nor her mind became excited.

With arousal, there is an increase in blood flow through both vaginal and clitoral tissues. Increased blood flow through the middle wall of the vagina results in vaginal lubrication. Increasing blood flow to the clitoris leads to swelling and fullness (Wylie & Hallam-Jones, 2005). Women observe whether arousal is growing in their bodies. For one woman the signals are feelings in her nipples with swelling and hardness. She feels "desire to have them sucked." Another woman feels like rocking her pelvis, whereas another feels fullness in her genitals. For another her clitoris and labia feel swollen, responsive to stroking. Another woman observed that she becomes wet right away (Foley et al., 2012).

Women are less responsive to physical sensations and pleasure when they are preoccupied with their body image, sexual adequacy, or distracted by frustration. Preoccupation with attractiveness is a cognitive distraction. The message that it is the woman's responsibility to turn her partner on promotes performance anxiety, a powerful barrier to her arousal. When a woman seeks therapy with complaints of low desire, painful intercourse, or non-orgasmic response, careful assessment often reveals that a core problem is inhibited arousal.

Prevalence

Approximately 16% (Lewis et al., 2004; Nicolosi et al., 2004) to 19% (Laumann et al., 1994) of women experience lubrication difficulties. Because it is common for lubrication to wax and wane, the important clinical indicator is her subjective arousal and feelings of distress.

Treatment for Inhibited Arousal

The central theme in treatment is the woman's receptivity and responsiveness. In traditional heterosexual gender roles, the male controlled "foreplay" and stimulated the woman until he decided she was ready for intercourse. In contrast, in CBCST, *she* determines the type of stimulation and when to transition. She focuses on pleasuring scenarios and techniques, and the timing and sequencing of touch. She is encouraged to orchestrate her pleasure and not take care of her partner. This is designed to prevent performance anxiety and spectatoring. The focus is her full engagement in pleasure and eroticism.

Cognitive interventions address expectancies (e.g., "I'm never going to get aroused."), attributions (e.g., "There's something wrong with me physically."), and standards ("A normal woman gets aroused automatically when her lover touches her.") associated with inhibited arousal. Behavioral interventions focus on psycho-sexual skill exercises that teach relaxation and focus on physical sensations and pleasure. This reduces preoccupation with body image. Self-entrancement arousal, PM training, and developing her arousal continuum are empowering. Cognitive tools such as yoga, mindfulness, and fantasy enrichment also are helpful. A similar approach is used with same-sex couples.

Amplifying Eroticism

The sensate focus/pleasuring format provides a step-by-step structure to promote relaxation and pleasure that expands to playful touch and erotic response. Intercourse is part of the erotic flow process, but not the centerpiece. The woman experiments with preferences regarding single versus multiple stimulation, taking turns versus mutual pleasuring, enjoying manual, oral, or rubbing stimulation, and using a massage oil or lubricant. The perennial roadblock to arousal is reluctance to claim her sexual voice. She is distracted by anticipation and fear of her partner's impatience and frustration. Through experiences with sensate focus, she comes to accept a comfortable flow from relaxation to pleasure, arousal, and eroticism.

Non-Orgasmic Response

Traditionally sex therapists believed that the primary cause of non-orgasmic re-sponse was a woman's fear of being out of control, ranging in severity from em-barrassment to panic. This resulted in a sense of powerlessness, her arousal blocked by shame, spectatoring, worrying about partner disapproval, performance pressure, and fear of looking out of control. Although this may be the case for some women, there are a variety of other psychological and interpersonal factors that can reduce the likelihood of orgasm, including forms of psychopathology (depression, anxiety disorders), negative attitudes about being a sexual being that were developed during childhood socialization, as well as relationship factors such as couple conflict.

A third cause of non-orgasmic response is pharmacologic agents, in particular SSRIs. When serotonin is increased, the 5-HT receptors are stimulated, causing inhibited orgasm. Treatment for pharmacologically induced orgasm problems involves the woman consulting with the physician (ideally a conjoint session with her partner) to change her dosage regimen, seek an alternative medication with reduced sexual side effects, or add an antidote to ameliorate the negative effect.

Clinical Perspective

Differences in masturbation, frequency of orgasm, and subjective reports of overall sexual satisfaction show that orgasmic response and sexual satisfaction for women is more flexible than for men (McCabe, 2011). From an evolutionary point of view, men have a need to ejaculate for the purpose of procreation, whereas female orgasm is not necessary for conception.

Non-orgasmic response is a psychological problem when a woman or her partner believes that orgasm is necessary. A male partner may have an expectation (standard) that the female must have an orgasm every time. A woman may feel sexually satisfied but worries that her partner feels inadequate because he does not "bring her to orgasm" (especially during intercourse). Although it may be difficult for the man to understand that sex can be pleasurable and satisfying without orgasm, it is crucial that he accept that the choice is hers. If she is fine with her pattern of orgasm, it is important for him to appreciate that this is normal, not an SD. In fact, pressure from him for her to experience orgasm is a powerful barrier to female orgasm as well as couple satisfaction.

Prevalence

Whether an orgasm problem exists is subjective. Less than 8% of women have never experienced orgasm (Reinisch, 1991). The NHSL study (Laumann et al., 1994) reported that one in four women had orgasm difficulties for over 1 month in the past year. For some women the inability to orgasm exists regardless of circumstances—alone or with a partner, or by method of stimulation (intercourse, oral sex, manual sex, rubbing sex, or vibrator). Other women have orgasms under certain circumstances, such as masturbation, but not with their partner. It is important to appreciate that one in three women are never or almost never orgasmic during intercourse (Graham, 2014). For most women, orgasm during intercourse occurs when there are multiple sources of stimulation, especially clitoral stimulation.

Negative Cognitions and Emotions Involving Orgasmic Disorder

It is important to consider a medical or pharmacological cause for non-orgasmic response. These causes include diabetes, thyroid deficiency, alcoholic neuropathy, arterial disease, or vitamin deficiency (Foley et al., 2012). Medications that impede orgasm include antidepressants, anti-hypertensive drugs, and tranquilizers. Some clients are unaware that recreational drugs, notably alcohol, are problematic, even if they make the individual feel receptive to sex.

The outcome studies conducted for treatment of non-orgasmic response have lacked solid research methodology, making it difficult to evaluate effectiveness (O'Donohue et al., 1997; O'Donohue, Swingen, Dopke, & Roger, 1999). Factors that adversely influence outcome include longer duration of the SD, a greater extent to which the SD has been incorporated into the woman's self-esteem and poorer adaptation to the SD by the couple.

An important component of CBCST is patient education. Body image work and masturbation exercises have been found to be effective for women with primary non-orgasmic response (Heiman & Meston, 1999). This protocol includes providing information about ways to achieve orgasm, permission giving, self-exploration, and pleasuring exercises. The woman identifies what feels sensual, pleasurable, and erotic to her. Examining her genitals with a mirror, altering cognitions regarding masturbation, use of sexual fantasies to enhance sexual response, as well as therapist encouragement are features of the directed masturbation program (Heiman, 2007). Success rates have been reported to be between 80 and 90% for women with primary non-orgasmic response (LoPiccolo & Stock, 1986), with lower rates for women with secondary non-orgasmic response (Kilmann, Boland, Norton, Davidson, & Caid, 1986; Kuriansky, Sharp, & O'Connor, 1982).

As we have noted, for some women a barrier to orgasm is fear of losing emotional and behavioral control. Non-orgasmic response also can be caused by shyness or avoidance of sexual touch. Associated cognitions include, "Orgasm is not important for me," or "I'd look foolish." Rather than valuing sex for pleasure, tension release, self-esteem, and relationship intimacy, she places little personal value on orgasm. In such cases, interventions focus on the woman's cognitions about the value of sex, promoting sex-positive and pleasure-affirming cognitions, encouraging the belief that she deserves the pleasure of orgasm, and mental rehearsal of being orgasmic. An especially important feature is developing her "arousal continuum" of increasingly erotic physical, emotional, and contextual stimuli. Behavioral interventions include training in PM management, self-pleasuring, physical relaxation, genital stimulation, erotic fantasies, erotic flow, and imaginary rehearsal of orgasm.

The therapist encourages the woman to keep her PM relaxed while building sensual pleasure, until she experiences erotic feelings. She then contracts and holds the PM for several seconds, then releases it. As she continues to contract and release ("ratcheting up") her PM, it helps her reach the "tipping point" for orgasm. The key is to focus on pleasure, arousal, eroticism, and letting go.

Addressing the barriers the woman has experienced promotes her assertiveness in eliciting her partner's cooperation and support (Hurlbert, 1991). Some women learn to enhance orgasmic response working individually, whereas most do better with conjoint CBCST. Women report that participating in a sexual health group is invaluable. Psychoeducational reading materials and audiovisual materials (e.g., the video accompaniment to Heiman and LoPiccolo's *Becoming Orgasmic* text) offer excellent resources for learning to be orgasmic.

Couple Approach to Orgasmic Response

CBCST offers couples the opportunity to improve communication (Metz & Epstein, 2002) and cooperate for pleasure. Communication enhancement provides the "climate" for sexual growth. Sensate focus/pleasuring exercises promote couple cooperation, a greater focus on pleasure, development of arousal and erotic flow, and his support and cooperation under her leadership, which facilitates letting go and enjoying orgasm.

A therapeutic issue that often arises is the partner's unintended pressure that she achieves orgasm, whether out of his concern for her or his feeling of inadequacy. It is important that the therapist help him understand that most women do not reach orgasm each time, and that one-third do not have orgasm during intercourse. The therapist emphasizes that the woman can feel satisfied without orgasm, and that the important value of sex is pleasure and a sense of connection. The therapist educates the man further, noting that with his cooperation and support she will be able to focus on pleasure, provide leadership and control of the couple's sexual interaction to heighten her arousal, and feel the level of security that enables her to focus on erotic flow and orgasm.

CBCST employs a sensate focus/pleasuring format with guided exercises that promote the woman's "sexual voice," her freedom to enjoy erotic flow to orgasm, and the partner's support. The following are examples of these eroticism-enhancing exercises.

EXERCISE: "Acting Out Orgasm"

A woman can overcome self-consciousness and embarrassment by role-playing orgasms by herself. This involves lying back, relaxing, and creating a sexual mood by reading erotica or imagining a sexy scene from a romance novel. Some women prefer soft music while others find that high-energy dancing sets a sexual milieu. The therapist gives the woman homework to imagine and role-play the most dramatic, wild orgasm she can. She moves her hips, rocks upward, downward, side to side, and presses her thighs together. She quickens her breathing, makes sounds, and acts out a whirlpool of excitement. She is dramatic while grabbing the pillow, sheets, digging her fingernails into the mattress as she moans and yells in pretend ecstasy.

Some women laugh and feel ridiculous while thinking about or actually trying this exercise while alone at home. However, this is a reminder that sex needs to be physically energetic—a "letting go." Confronting self-consciousness is excellent practice for loosening internal controls over sexuality. After practicing role-play orgasms on her own, she can demonstrate her orgasm role-play with her partner. He is coached to be accepting and admiring. She develops comfort with letting go and appreciating that vibrant lovemaking is an aphrodisiac for her and their relationship.

EXERCISE: "Cooperating for Pleasure, Eroticism, and Orgasm"

Integrated into the sensate focus/pleasuring format, this 3-part homework has particular value in promoting sexual freedom, inviting orgasm, and ensuring cooperation. Many women find it easier to masturbate to orgasm and then integrate orgasm into partner sex. She focuses on herself, feels partner support, and explores her pleasure/eroticism response—touch, intercourse, manual stimulation (by self or partner), oral sex, rubbing stimulation, and/or a vibrator.

This exercise involves three stages focused on sexual pleasure, eroticism, and orgasm. Incorporating intercourse allows her to increase sensation with penetration, increase her ability to regulate pleasure and manage arousal; and each partner to be "in charge" of their own pleasure during intercourse.

Each session lasts 30–60 minutes. She repeats each exercise until she feels comfortable with pleasure, arousal, and eroticism.

Segment 1: Take time to relax, such as showering together and putting on music.

Begin pleasuring using massage, manual stimulation, self-stimulation, oral stimulation, or a combination of techniques that she finds enjoyable. Take time and allow this to be sensuous, pleasurable, and erotic for her.

After 10–15 minutes, he lies on his back and assumes a passive role. She sits astride him kneeling with one leg on each side. She inserts his penis inside her vagina while he relaxes his PM, remains passive as she takes charge. She takes his penis in one hand, with the other spreads the lips of her vagina, and inserts his penis using a stuffing motion. This might feel awkward at first, but she continues the process until the penis is inserted. An erection is not required in order to begin intercourse. After the penis, flaccid or erect, is inserted, neither partner moves. They remain still, enjoying and exploring the feelings of containment. She experiences her vagina around his penis.

The couple focuses on sensations for 3–5 minutes, and then she experiments by flexing her PM. She experiments with sensations and teases his penis. If he feels arousal toward ejaculation, he signals her, either nonverbally or verbally, and she ceases movement.

After enjoying these sensations for 5–12 minutes, she withdraws his penis, and they pleasure each other until both feel satisfied without an orgasm.

Segment 2: Begin with gentle pleasuring and then insert his penis. She experiments with pelvic movements while he is passive, allowing her to engage in whatever movement she desires. Begin with slow side to side and back to front pelvic movements, and then slow up-down thrusting. She stays attuned to her sensations, developing awareness of movements that produce pleasurable sensations within her vagina. She can be selfish, acting upon her feelings and not influenced by what she thinks he is feeling.

He can experiment with slow thrusting. If he feels the urge to ejaculate, the couple ceases movement. This process heightens arousal by the teasing effect it produces.

Segment 3: The therapist encourages partners to experiment with intercourse positions, including female on top; kneeling astride him with her back to his face and her face toward his feet; sitting face to face astride the male; side-to-side positions; male on top; and female kneeling with the man entering from behind. In whatever position, the couple continues to experiment with mutual thrusting or with one partner controlling the thrusting. It is important to be mindful and aware of positions and movements that produce pleasurable and erotic sensations.

She decides whether to continue intercourse to orgasm (with or without multiple stimulation), or she might wish to be orgasmic with manual, oral, or rubbing stimulation.

Sexual Pain Disorders

Sexual pain disorders include dyspareunia and vaginismus. Dyspareunia may be caused by vaginitis, Bartholin gland abscess, sexually transmitted diseases, uterine difficulties, pelvic inflammatory disease, endometriosis, vulvovestibulitis, or lack of lubrication. In vaginismus, the vaginal muscles constrict involuntarily, making entry painful or impossible.

Sexual pain occurs if a woman has intercourse after childbirth before an episiotomy has healed or while she has a vaginal infection. If breastfeeding, she usually has decreased vaginal secretions and is advised to use a lubricant. Bergeron, Rosen, and Pukall (2014) found that sexual pain is multi-causal and multifaceted, requiring diligence in diagnosis and treatment. The woman experiences burning, itching, rawness or stinging with intromission, thrusting, or deep penetration. Genital pain can be caused by allergic sensitivity to soaps, fabrics, topical ointments, and medications. Too often in the past, sexual pain was attributed to psychological causes ("it's in your head"), which stigmatized the woman. The pain is in her vulva, although cognitive and interpersonal factors are important in treatment.

Assessing and treating sexual pain in a comprehensive biopsychosocial manner is crucial. The first line of diagnostic investigation is a full and thorough medical examination with a gynecologist, internist, or nurse practitioner with a specialty in sexual pain. CBCST is integral to comprehensive treatment.

Prevalence

The NSLH (Laumann, Paik, & Rosen, 1999) reported that 8–21% of women experienced sexual pain. Only 60% sought treatment, and 40% of those did not receive a formal diagnosis and treatment (Harlow, Wise, & Stewart, 2001).

Treatment

Treatment for sexual pain is often complex and challenging. Some cases are easy to resolve using a vaginal lubricant, the woman guiding intromission at high levels of arousal, and controlling intercourse positions and movement. Bergeron et al. (2014) approach pain disorders from a biopsychosocial model with an integrated treatment team consisting of a physician (or nurse practitioner) with specialization in sexual pain, a female physical therapist with a specialty in pelvic musculature, as well as a CBCST clinician. Interventions involve the woman increasing awareness and comfort with her genitalia, learning PM management, and mindfulness. Empowering her to take control of her body and orchestrating physical contact is crucial. Her involvement and arousal are the antidotes to hypervigilance about pain or viewing intercourse as the man's domain (McCarthy & Thestrup, 2008b).

Interventions include pelvic floor physical therapy, biofeedback, pain management, PM training, and psychosexual skill exercises to increase desire and function (Glazer, Robke, Swencionis, Hertz, & Young, 1995). Studies have reported success with combination CBCST and behavioral pain management (ter Kuile et al., 2009). Treatment results in less pain and cognitive catastrophizing (Bergeron, Khalife, & Dupuis, 2008). Body therapies, including biofeedback, also have been effective (Danielsson, Torstensson, Broda-Jansen, & Bohm-Starke, 2006; McKay et al., 2001).

Bergeron et al. (2014) offer a number of suggestions for clinicians: be prepared to work hard, resist thinking of yourself as the client's savior, be humble, avoid attempts to attribute the pain to a single cause, educate yourself about what the other professional disciplines do that can contribute to treatment success, aim to treat multiple targets simultaneously, do not become disheartened if the client is not immediately enthusiastic about improvement, and expect treatment gains to come in small increments.

Treatment is intended to help the client recognize that she can manage pain and enjoy couple sexuality. The experience of pain is reduced by cognitive and psychosexual skill exercises. Genital self-exploration assignments help her localize the pain so she understands where it hurts and can show her partner. Sexual anatomy education is helpful. Relaxation training, especially the use of breathing, is an important feature. Understanding her predictive expectancy of pain helps her appreciate how this inhibits arousal and increases pain. Understanding that anticipation of pain contributes to an involuntary contraction of vaginal muscles helps her understand why penetration is painful. She is guided in focusing on breathing, relaxation, and mindfulness.

Physical Therapy

Specialized physical therapy is effective in treating sexual pain. A female physical therapist with a sub-specialty in pelvic floor musculature helps the woman identify her PM and teaches her to control her body. Learning muscular relaxation relieves chronic muscular tension. The physical therapist uses a tampon-like instrument to offer direct and immediate feedback about vaginal response. Another intervention is ultrasound (deep heat) treatment to increase blood flow and promote healing if there has been trauma to the tissue.

The PM and Dilator Therapy

Women commonly are unaware of how to exercise voluntary PM control. There are two main techniques: (1) PM training, and (2) dilator therapy. These desensitize vaginal musculature and train the vagina to allow penetration without contractions.

Dilator therapy is practiced under the guidance of a physical therapist who explains how to use the dilators and determines when to proceed to the next size. Vaginal dilators are rubber or plastic cylinders with rounded ends that come in sets ranging in size. The woman engages in dilator therapy in the privacy of her home, taking 10–20 minutes daily, 3–5 times a week to gently insert dilators until the vagina becomes comfortable with the repetition. She progressively increases the diameter of the dilator, allowing the vagina to adjust. If dilator therapy is not comfortable, the woman can insert her pinky finger. She can integrate the dilator therapy with her partner.

Couple Treatment

The sensate focus/pleasuring exercises provide a supportive environment for treatment of pain. The partner's understanding and support is crucial. Beliefs about genital pain, attributions of causality, predictive expectancies, and degree of openness to change are addressed. In addition, the emphasis on desire and satisfaction allows the couple to create alternative sexual scenarios. Discussion of the biopsychosocial causes of pain and how each factor can be addressed changes partners' negative outcome expectancies.

CBCST focuses on psychological and relationship factors that promote and facilitate comfort, pleasure, eroticism, and intercourse. This requires significant attitudinal, behavioral, and emotional growth for both partners. The woman viewing her partner as an intimate and sexual ally provides the underpinning for overcoming fear of pain. This opens the door to desire, pleasure, arousal, orgasm, and satisfaction.

Summary

CBCST addresses the components of a psychobiological model of sexual function to assess and treat women who are experiencing problems with sexual desire, arousal, orgasm and pain. Biological causes are considered primary, and sex therapists need to work closely with physicians to diagnose and treat physical conditions contributing to SD, whether they be chronic diseases, physical structural abnormalities, or unhealthy lifestyle behaviors. A responsive sexual desire model guides the clinician in understanding women's response patterns with their partners. Individual psychological factors addressed in CBCST include chronic problems such as depression, low sexual self-esteem, anxiety disorders, and difficulty managing and coping with distracting life stressors. Counterproductive negative beliefs about sex learned in childhood also are important foci of cognitive interventions, as are performance pressure and associated spectatoring. Individual and couple exercises focus on increasing positive body awareness, eroticism, and pleasure. CBCST also emphasizes the couple as an intimate sexual team who collaborate through effective communication, conflict resolution, and practice of psychosexual skills to create a positive sexual atmosphere within which a woman can learn about her body, develop sexual self-esteem, and fully enjoy her sexuality. The therapist serves as the woman's and couple's teacher and guide as they overcome barriers to sexual fulfillment.

Chapter 6

Treatment for Male Sexual Dysfunction

The SDs that men experience, in order of frequency are: (1) Premature Ejaculation, (2) Erectile Dysfunction, (3) Hypoactive Sexual Desire Disorder, (4) Ejaculatory Inhibition and (5) painful sex (Binik & Hall, 2014). CBCST is the treatment of choice for male SDs, because although physiological and sexual function factors are crucial, it is the psychological and relationship factors that determine why some men with SD experience sexual distress while others successfully adapt. Accurate understanding, realistic expectations, and couple cooperation are crucial. These form the milieu for the man and couple to learn psychosexual skills with a focus on sharing pleasure, sexual function, alternative sexual scenarios, and relationship satisfaction.

The sexual socialization of young men emphasizes that sex performance is natural, predictable, easy and automatic. The male learns that sexual response is autonomous; he needs nothing from his partner other than being sexually present. Although this scenario works for adolescents and young men, this performance standard becomes unrealistic as men age and becomes a risk factor for SD. A crucial feature of mature male sexuality is experiencing and affirming couple sexuality as variable, flexible, and pleasure-oriented. Sex is not an individual performance.

CBCST offers valuable broadening of the meanings that men and couples attach to sex, the development of psychosexual skills, the value of couple cooperation, understanding the interpersonal process of sexuality, the importance and rewards of emotional intimacy, and the acceptance of variable and flexible sex. It contributes to preventing relapse, as well as inoculating clients against risks for SD that can occur with aging (McCarthy & Threstrup, 2008b). This perspective allows CBCST to relieve distress associated with sexual difficulties and promote individual and couple satisfaction.

Public and professional awareness of male SD has increased with the marketing of pro-erection medications such as Viagra and Cialis for erectile dysfunction (ED). At the same time, clinical experience with ED shows that sex is rarely simple, in spite of people's longing for "quick fixes" and the messages promoted by drug company advertisements. Sexual medicine interventions (pro-erection medications, medications for ejaculatory control, testosterone enhancement) offer increased hope and options, but an imbalance has developed in treating male SD with an inordinate emphasis on a biomedical approach. The failure of biomedical approaches to benefit many couples (Brock et al., 2002) as well as evidence of a significant placebo effect (Hatzichristou et al., 2005), highlight the oversimplification of couple sexuality. Unfortunately, physicians who do not specialize in sexuality, such as those in family practice, only occasionally initiate discussion of sexual concerns with their patients (Aschka, Himmel, Ittner, & Kochen, 2001). In contrast, CBCST addresses both sexual response and the psychological and interpersonal factors that contribute to sexual satisfaction.

Thus, a male SD that on the surface appears to be an individual problem is inevitably a relationship problem, whether the relational dynamics are primarily a cause or an effect of physical dysfunction. Even for a man who is in individual therapy because he has no partner, refuses to involve his partner, or has a partner who is unwilling to participate, the SD inevitably involves relationship factors. He has a "virtual partner" in his mind—someone from the past, a current partner, or one imagined in the future. Understanding and working with the complexity of male SD requires an interactional, relational perspective. Some men resist this due to fear of experiencing loss of face in discussing sexual problems in front of their partner. The comprehensive couple approach is more likely to address all of the factors influencing an SD and reduce relapse (McCarthy & McCarthy, 2014).

Assessment Determines Treatment

Understanding the sources and current impact of the SD is based on taking a careful history, as well as systematically inquiring about current conditions. Typically, the *initial* cause(s) of SD has been replaced over time by *maintaining* cause(s), especially avoidance and couple distress. Overlooking an initial or maintaining cause, or a detrimental effect that an SD is having on the individual or couple, reduces the effectiveness of treatment.

Similar to assessment with female SDs, CBCST assessment with males focuses on physiological, psychological, relationship, and environmental context factors. The **physiological factors** include: (1) *sexual anatomy and physiology*; (2) *physical illness*; (3) *physical injury*; (4) *drug side effects*; and (5) *health behaviors and lifestyle issues*. The **psychological factors** include: (1) *personality traits and temperament*; (2) *psychopathology*; (3) *past traumatic experiences* that continue to have negative effects on individual well-being and sexual function, and (4) *psychosexual skill deficits*. **Interpersonal factors** include: (1) *differences between partners' temperaments, personalities and sexual desire*; (2) *relationship conflict* and deficits in conflict-resolution skills; (3) *lack of intimacy*; and (4) overall *relationship distress*. **Environmental context factors** include: (1) *family stressors* such as demands of childrearing; (2) *external relationship stressors* such as demands of caring for an elderly parent; (3) *job and financial stresses*; and (4) *broader societal stresses* such as economic problems and terrorism.

Assessment of SD also needs to take into account the common occurrence of "mixed" SDs, in which a primary SD co-occurs with another SD (e.g., ED with low desire or PE with partner dyspareunia), a situation that occurs about a third of the time (Loudon, 1998).

The following are descriptions of physiological, psychological, interpersonal and environmental factors affecting sexual function that clinicians need to be familiar with and include in their assessment of SD.

Physiological Factors

The importance of knowledge about sexual anatomy and physiology. Knowledge is powerful, as demonstrated by "false feedback" utilized during sexual performance studies (e.g., Bach, Brown, & Barlow, 1999; Palace, 1999). For example, men who viewed erotic films and were given false feedback that their arousal was below that of the average participant in the study had lower efficacy expectancies that they would be aroused when watching the next film as well as decreased physiological arousal as assessed with a penile strain gauge. There was a strong association between efficacy expectancies and physiological arousal, providing evidence of the role of cognitions on sexual response.

Realistic knowledge of sexual physiology: (1) helps the man's partner understand the reasons for using particular cognitive-behavioral interventions (relaxation training, pelvic muscle use, erotic flow); (2) helps the partner clarify his or her role and not take on blame for the SD; and (3) promotes couple cooperation as an intimate team. Men's (and women's) sexual function is an ability that changes over the course of a lifetime. It is helpful for both partners to understand that youthful male sexuality is physically driven, whereas with age psychological and relational factors have stronger influences that can increase or decrease the quality of the couple's sexual experience.

Many men have poor understanding of sexual anatomy, physiology, and the biological mechanisms of sexual function. For example, a "common sense" belief is that sexual arousal and erection should be very easy, that it occurs automatically in the presence of an attractive partner. A related counterproductive belief is that like many tasks in life one can overcome sexual problems by focusing greater effort on them. The reality is that arousal and erection occur easily *if* the man is physiologically and emotionally relaxed. There are a variety of psychological and relational factors that can interfere with a relaxed state. While the vitality of the body in adolescence and young adulthood can override the detrimental force of anxiety, distractions of life stresses, and relationship problems, those experiences eventually prevail, contributing to or exacerbating SD. Therefore, imparting accurate knowledge about his sexual body and how it responds to psychological and relational conditions is a crucial component of CBCST. Integrating physical relaxation with sexual stimulation within a supportive, cooperative relationship ensures satisfying male sexual function.

The physiology of erection. Erection is a natural physiological response. Even before birth the male fetus has spontaneous, reflexogenic erections. An erection typically occurs within minutes of birth. Every night during sleep, whether sexually active or not, the healthy man has a 10- to 20-minute erection every 60 to 90 minutes. These erections occur during rapid eye movement (REM) sleep. Physiologically, nighttime erections are the way the body oxygenates tissues of the penis to maintain healthy function. Laboratory studies with 90-year-old men in good health demonstrate ongoing erections.

Erection occurs when nerve impulses from the brain (psychogenic erection) and from genital stimulation (reflexogenic erection) combine to cause more blood flow into than out of the penis. The penis is a sophisticated hydraulic system. There are three sponge-like cylindrical bodies that run the length of the penis that are fed blood from small branches of the penile artery into the spongy tissue. The tubes swell with blood to cause an erection. These cylinders make up the shaft of the penis. An erection occurs as the microscopic muscles that surround the arteries relax, causing dilation. Blood rushes into the spongy tissues creating a "hydraulic" elevation of the penis. Simultaneously, muscles near the base of the penis constrict, preventing blood from leaving. When the erection subsides, those microscopic muscles constrict, and the veins carry the blood away. We have found that men (and women) are often surprised to learn that an erection occurs through *physiological relaxation*.

The chemistry of erection. Complex chemical processes are involved in erection. Erection occurs when nitric oxide acts on the smooth muscles surrounding the penile arteries, which relaxes the muscles. An enzyme called phosphodiesterase type 5 (PDE-5) blocks muscle relaxation. A pro-erection medication works by inhibiting PDE-5 so that it does not block muscle relaxation. It enhances (prolongs) the effect of relaxation, which encourages blood flow, producing an erection. It is *relaxation* (not performance efforts) that facilitates erection.

The neurologic system. Nervous system responses to both mental and physical stimulation lead to arousal, penile firmness, and orgasm. Neurological problems can result from diseases such as multiple sclerosis and diabetes, medication side effects, alcohol and drug abuse, and physical injuries. Psychological, relational, and environmental stressors also can inhibit neurological function.

The nervous system in the lower spine is connected to the penis via the pelvic nerve, which branches into the cavernous nerve that manages the three spongy cylinders of the penis. Damage often occurs to this nerve supply during prostate or rectal surgeries. An erection is a neurologic reflex involving the spinal cord and brain. The spinal reflex causes relaxation of the smooth muscles and dilation of the penile arteries, resulting in an erection. Higher central nervous system areas in the brain are involved in obtaining and maintaining erections, as well as triggering ejaculation and orgasm.

The vascular system. Vascular system problems are the most common physiological cause of ED. When a man is relaxed and open to psychological and physical stimulation, blood flow increases to his genitals. A number of physical, psychological, relational, and situational factors can interfere with this natural function. Common physical factors that reduce blood flow include high blood pressure, side effects of medications, vascular disease, high blood sugar (poorly controlled diabetes), smoking, and vascular injuries. Consequently, it is crucial that CBCST clinicians collaborate with clients' physicians in evaluating possible vascular causes of SDs.

The hormonal system. The hormonal system influences desire and erection chiefly through testosterone. Very low levels of testosterone disrupt sexual desire. Possible causes for low testosterone include a systemic hormonal problem (thyroid disease), fatigue and stress, alcohol and drug misuse, or a pituitary tumor. The popular notion of "male menopause" is not supported by empirical data (McKinlay, Longcope, & Gray, 1989; McKinlay & Feldman, 1994). Testosterone replacement therapy is warranted and helpful for men with T-levels far below the normal cutoff, but should not be used indiscriminately, as it may increase risks for health problems such as sleep apnea, cardiovascular disease (including blood clots), and prostate enlargement (Vigen et al., 2013).

The myth of penis size. There are widespread myths regarding the link between male sexual anatomy and the quality of lovemaking. A destructive myth that is the basis for an enormous amount of male anxiety concerns penis size. It is true that there are differences in the flaccid size of the penis, but men are unaware that such differences have little to do with sexual function in the erect state. The average penis is from two and a half to four inches in the flaccid state and from five and a half to six and a half inches when erect. The diameter is about one inch when flaccid and one and a half inches when erect. The key concept is that a normal penis (including almost all penises) is of proper size to function during intercourse. Interestingly, four of five men believe that their penis is smaller than average (Zilbergeld, 1999). This illustrates how the competitive performance model dominates male sexuality, leaving men feeling anxious and insecure. We encourage the man to see his internist or urologist for a penile exam and receive objective information and support. Sexual health is promoted by adopting a positive body image; including accepting his penis and understanding that penis size is unrelated to sexual function and satisfaction for the man and his partner.

A related myth is that a large penis results in a female partner being orgasmic during intercourse. This is based on the mistaken belief that the vagina is the woman's major sex organ, whereas in truth, the woman's most sensitive genital organ is her clitoris. As we noted in Chapter 5, most women prefer indirect clitoral stimulation whether from a partner's hand, tongue, or penis. During intercourse the clitoris is stimulated by pulling and rubbing action caused by pelvic thrusting— stimulation which is independent of penis size. The vagina swells to engage the penis, adjusting to any size penis. As described earlier, it takes 10 to 20 minutes of pleasuring for the vagina to fully expand, so if a couple rushes intercourse, the man may mistakenly think his penis is "too small." The remedy is enjoying pleasurable touch and genital stimulation before intercourse to allow the woman's vagina to reach full arousal. Sexual incompatibility based on the couple's genitals is, with extremely rare exceptions, a myth. Consequently, in CBCST we educate couples about genitals and the common myths about them.

The anatomy and physiology of ejaculation and orgasm. Knowledge about anatomy and neurophysiology helps men (and women) understand ejaculatory problems, as well as the rationale for treatment to teach the man relaxation, focusing on pleasure, PM relaxation, and vaginal "acclimation." Ejaculation involves several processes: erection, emission, ejaculation, and orgasm (Perelman, McMahon,& Barada, 2004). These processes are integrated by a complex set of interactions among the neurological, hormonal, and vascular systems. *Erection* refers to the processes in the central nervous system, peripheral nervous system, and vascular system leading to penile rigidity. *Emission* refers to the collection and transport of fluids that form the semen in preparation for ejaculation. Sperm from the testicles travel through the *vas deferens,* which joins in the *prostate gland* with the tube exiting the *bladder* to the *urethra.* The urethra runs through the chestnut-sized prostate, then out through the penis. With arousal, the neck (exit) of the bladder closes (that is why it is difficult to urinate when one has an erection), the testicles draw up against the body, and semen collects in the *verumontaum,* a balloon-like chamber inside the prostate gland. When the man is highly aroused and the verumontaum fills with semen, it enlarges to three times its normal size. When the man reaches the point of ejaculatory inevitability, orgasm is no longer a voluntary response.

Ejaculation is the process of pushing the seminal fluids out of the verumontanum through the urethra and penis. Ejaculation occurs when nerve input reaches the spinal cord and causes the reflexive ejaculatory response. The man's pelvic muscle (PM) is directly involved in ejaculation by rhythmically contracting to force the semen out. Teaching the man to identify and relax his PM is a core psychosexual skill used in treating PE and ejaculatory inhibition.

Orgasm refers to the subjective experience of pleasure associated with ejaculation. Orgasm is a natural, healthy extension of the pleasuring–arousal–eroticism process. Orgasm is primarily an experience in the brain, and although emission, ejaculation, and orgasm are integrated, synchronous events that seem simultaneous, technically erection is not required for ejaculation, and ejaculation is not required for orgasm.

Ejaculatory neurophysiology. While ejaculation is a biological reflex, the brain interprets sexual information that may augment ("turn on") or inhibit ("turn off") arousal. Signals from the brain to the lower spinal cord link with neurologic impulses to signal the ejaculatory system. This results in emission and activation of the PM, resulting in two to ten rhythmic contractions (ejaculation).

Awareness of how the body works can help the man and couple ground their sexual expectations on accurate and realistic knowledge. Expecting 15–20 minutes of vigorous intercourse without ejaculation is physiologically unreasonable. Understanding the role of the brain as an "interpreter," the role of relaxation, and the role of the PM aids management of ejaculation.

Health behaviors and lifestyle factors. Sexual response occurs within the broader context of the individual's physical well-being. A variety of health conditions can interfere with normal function, so it is important to include an inquiry about current health and the individual's health behaviors. We strongly advocate that clients have an exam by a physician, not only to identify sex-specific problems such as low testosterone, but also to evaluate the individual's overall health status. Any condition that detracts from the person's overall level of energy, vitality and physical comfort may contribute to an SD. For example, a man who has developed arthritis may be uncomfortable during sexual activity and distracted by anticipated pain. The therapist inquires about health behaviors including nutrition, exercise, substance use, and most important, sleep patterns. Many clients are unaware that these aspects of their general health may be contributing to the SD and that lifestyle changes are important components of treatment for SD.

Psychological Factors

Personality traits and temperament. Some characteristics of individuals that can contribute to SDs are not forms of psychopathology, but rather levels of normal human traits and temperament. Epstein and Baucom (2002) described a number of core personal needs and motives that influence individuals' well-being in their intimate relationships. Those include *communal needs* for closeness and connection, and agentic needs involving the individual's personal impact on his environment. The major communal needs include affiliation, intimacy, altruism and succorance, whereas the agentic needs include autonomy, power and achievement.

Assessment of clients' needs and motives is relevant for understanding SD. A prime example is when a man's high achievement motivation contributes to sexual performance anxiety as he views sex as an area of life in which he must excel. Differences between two partners' needs also can be a source of conflict in their relationship that plays out in their sexual relationship. For example, when partners differ in their levels of need for intimacy, they may develop a demand–withdraw pattern in which the individual with a greater need for intimacy feels neglected emotionally and sexually by the partner and pursues him or her, while the partner feels "smothered" and tends to withdraw. Therapists need to be aware of cues that individuals' personality traits may be contributing to the way they construe sexuality and the manner in which they cope with sexual problems. The therapist can get a sense of needs and motives by asking about each individual's goals and priorities in life.

Psychopathology. The assessment of client anxiety and depression presents an additional complication because many males are reluctant to report symptoms, due to perceived social stigma for men to not have "emotional weaknesses." Underreporting of problems occurs both during clinical interviews and on self-report questionnaires. Consequently, clinicians observe the client for signs that he may be experiencing symptoms, interview him individually so he is less concerned about losing face in front of his partner, and convey acceptance and respect for the man. Working to engage the man in a collaborative effort "to uncover any good leads for solving the sexual difficulties" appeals to clients who are motivated to take a practical approach to solving life problems. It is helpful to provide the individual and partner information about findings linking psychological symptoms to SDs, noting that this involves more than physical functioning.

Past traumatic experiences. Males who had traumatic experiences (physical abuse or neglect) earlier in life often continue to have negative effects on their overall psychological well-being and sexual function. When the individual sex history uncovers abuse experiences, it is important to integrate this into couple treatment as well as consider a referral for individual therapy. Males who were sexually victimized as children or adolescents by male abusers often developed self-esteem problems due to shame about being a male who was controlled by someone, as well as confusion about the implications for their sexual orientation (McCarthy & Breetz, 2010). They benefit from therapy to help them reduce confusion and self-condemnation. As with female clients, it is helpful for therapists to challenge the commonly held myth that "time heals all wounds," helping them understand that untreated trauma responses can persist indefinitely.

Psychosexual skill deficits. Many males and their partners are unaware of the importance of the range of psychological and physical pathways to arousal. Based on the myth that males are automatically aroused in the presence of an attractive partner, no matter how tired or distracted they may be, many men and couples use limited strategies for arousal. In turn, men who lack sufficient skills for arousing a partner detract from their own arousal and sexual satisfaction when they notice that the partner is not sexually responsive. The sex therapist should inquire about the couple's sexual behavior, providing a clear rationale for asking for a detailed description. It is crucial to assess sexual behavioral repertoires. This includes not only forms of sensual and erotic touch, but also the partners' skills for creating an erotic atmosphere. This assessment will reveal how much sexual skill education the couple needs.

Interpersonal Factors

Differences between partners' temperaments, personalities and sexual desire. The myth that "opposites attract," is pervasive. Nevertheless, research generally has indicated that relationship satisfaction is higher when partners share values, goals and desires. Differences in sexual desire are a common presenting complaint of distressed couples. As with other topics of disagreement, the implications for partners' relationship satisfaction depend less on whether there are conflicting preferences than on how the partners behave toward each other in managing their conflict (Kline, Pleasant, Whitton, & Markman, 2006; Metz & Epstein, 2002).

Deficits in conflict–resolution skills. Although people commonly think of the term "conflict" as connoting active aggression, theorists and researchers define it as the existence of a difference between two parties' preferences, values, or needs. The partners' awareness of differences creates discomfort as it may interfere with getting a man's needs met. However, the communication process through which couples define and discuss areas of conflict is the key to whether an issue takes a toll on the relationship or is resolved in a manner that is satisfactory to both partners. Cognitive-behavioral couple therapy (Baucom, Epstein, Kirby, & LaTaillade, 2015; Epstein & Baucom, 2002) includes a major emphasis on training couples in problem-solving skills. Many men and couples with SD lack sufficient skills to identify and carry out mutually satisfying solutions to sexual problems. Because men often are embarrassed by having an SD, they avoid open communication and problem-solving. Therapists must be sensitive to potential shame experiences (Epstein & Falconier, 2011) and appeal to the man's motivation to competently solve life problems.

Lack of intimacy. We have emphasized the importance of intimacy issues in SD. It is crucial to impress on the clients that sexual response is much more than physical bodily processes. Positive function is more likely to occur, especially in a long-term relationship, between partners who have a close emotional bond. Myths about male sexuality being automatic interfere with understanding psychological factors that contribute to desire, pleasure, eroticism, and satisfaction. Couples who lead busy lives spend little time sharing experiences that help them feel close and create a sexual milieu. CBCST educates couples about varied forms of intimacy beyond sexuality, assesses possible deficits in intimacy, and coaches the couple in increasing the range and frequency of their intimacy-building experiences.

Overall relationship distress. Weiss (1980) described the process of "sentiment override" in which individuals' global, long-term feelings about a partner and relationship act as a filter for experiencing the partner's current behavior. If a man is generally unhappy with his partner based on past experiences, even if the partner is behaving in a caring and sexually inviting way at present, he may experience little sexual interest and arousal with the partner. Yet, he is surprised and worried about his lack of response based on his limited understanding of male sexual function. CBCST provides education about the complex psychosocial factors that influence human sexual response. The treatment for an SD often involves interventions to improve the overall quality of the couple's relationship, including recovering from past hurts.

Environmental Context Factors

Internal family stressors. Males' focus on physical aspects of sex often causes them to overlook effects of life stressors on SDs. Many stressors occur within the family, such as demands of childrearing, household/yard maintenance, or his partner's illness or disability. Since clients commonly will not present information about life stressors, it is the therapist's role to inquire about them, introducing the idea that they can be distracting and detrimental. In CBCST, we interview the couple together and each partner individually to gather information about overall psychological functioning as well as life stressors.

External relationship stressors. Another common source of life stressors that clients overlook as contributors to SD is relationships outside the immediate couple and family. Clients learn that demands of caring for an elderly parent or trying to help an adult sibling who is having financial problems are stressful, and they can affect sexual function by causing cognitive distraction and emotional upset. The therapist inquires about external demands and how the client is coping with them.

Job and financial stresses. Demands of his job, experiences of job loss, and financial problems commonly affect the overall well-being of the man and couple. Howe, Levy, and Caplan (2004) found that such stressors "spill over" from one partner to the other and disrupt couple interactions. Clients underestimate the effects of these events on SDs, so the therapist's role is to assess these issues with the couple and educate them about their importance. CBCST involves an ecological view of factors influencing SDs.

Broader societal stresses. Males and their partners think even less of distal types of stress, such as national economic problems and terrorism, as relevant for understanding SDs. In some cases, these play a significant role as chronic distractions. Consequently, we suggest including questions about "any other concerns that have been on your mind."

Strategies to Address Male Sex Dysfunction

After conducting an assessment of the physical, psychological, relational, and environmental factors that may be influencing an SD, the therapist designs a treatment plan in collaboration with the couple. The following are core CBCST treatment strategies.

Promoting Accurate Knowledge and Reasonable Expectancies and Standards

A crucial feature in treating SD is providing the clients with accurate information about male sexual function and the role of couple cooperation for pleasure and satisfaction. CBCST provides a reality check amidst the hype and media depictions about sex. Information relieves sexual performance perfectionism and broadens the clients' views of factors that can contribute to an SD. Although this means that the interventions often are more varied than those the clients expected, the therapy is much more likely to be effective.

Modifying Cognitive Misattributions, Catastrophic Expectancies, and Unrealistic Assumptions and Standards

Cognitive restructuring is integrated throughout the CBCST process. Given that many men experience shame regarding their perception that they have failed in an important male role, it is important for the therapist to be supportive and not confrontational in challenging a man's negative thinking, especially with his partner present. Epstein and Falconier (2011) provide guidelines for addressing shame issues in couple therapy that can be applied to shame experiences regarding SD. These strategies include reducing partners' stringent standards for each other's intimate behavior, challenging negative attributions in which an individual's SD is ascribed to undesirable personality traits and intentions, and fostering acceptance of SD symptoms as natural while the couple plans ways to enhance their sexual relationship.

Increasing Self-Efficacy and Overcoming Avoidance

When SD occurs, men are confused and trapped in a perception of "failure." Having learned that sex function should be automatic, he feels inadequate. Having an expectancy of being powerless to "fix it," he avoids sex and withdraws in shame. He berates himself or blames his partner. Often, avoidance becomes a couple pattern. The partner tries to discuss the SD, but he resists ("What's the point of making me feel I'm a failure?") and withdraws. Alternately, both partners may avoid discussing the sensitive topic. In either case, failing to address the problem promotes paralysis, alienation, and resentment. In contrast, couples who develop constructive cognitions about an SD (e.g., not seeing it as anyone's fault or failure; viewing themselves as a mutually caring team that can work toward a satisfying sexual relationship) take a crucial step toward change. CBCST provides realistic optimism with the focus on rebuilding sexual confidence.

Reducing Performance Anxiety and Spectatoring

Performance anxiety based on unrealistic standards, as well as spectatoring or self-consciousness regarding performance, are core features of SD. Pleasuring exercises provide a format to reengage the man and ameliorate his performance anxiety. In CBCST, we consistently monitor the man's thinking about performance and guide him in shifting attention to pleasurable sensations.

Reducing Deficits in Psychosexual Skills

Young men experience sex as easy, automatic, and highly predictable. SD creates anxiety and confusion. One client said that he felt like a pilot trying to fly a plane without knowledge of instrumentation, panicking because he was about to crash. Core psychosexual skills include accurate knowledge of sexual anatomy and physiology, strategies to build bridges to sexual desire, balancing relaxation with desire, appreciation of one's cognitive arousal continuum, flexible use of his PM, use of sexual arousal pacing strategies, awareness of the multiple purposes for sex, using arousal styles (partner interaction, self-entrancement, role enactment), intercourse acclimating procedures, and afterplay and satisfaction strategies.

Sexual function occurs most reliably when the man and his partner integrate psychological/physical excitement, physiological relaxation, and a cooperative relationship. The clinician guides the couple one step at a time to re-establish sex function and confidence.

Enhancing Positive Couple Dynamics

CBCST places considerable emphasis on dyadic interventions. CBCST for male SD targets the following:

1. Promotion of partner communication about sex by developing the male's "authentic voice."
2. A focus on pleasure as well as sexual function.
3. Elimination of shame through sex-positive discussions and exercises.
4. Reduction of unrealistic sexual assumptions (e.g., that sex performance is automatic) and perfectionistic sexual standards (e.g., that sex should always be spontaneous and passionate).

5. Healing of deficits in emotional intimacy with cooperation, empathy, and conflict resolution.
6. Confrontation of fears of rejection and demands for sexual performance; promotion of freedom to engage sexually without the poison of sex on demand.
7. Teaching couple psychosexual skills.
8. Promotion of regular sex (the catalyst for realistic, satisfying sex) and the opportunity to develop alternative sexual scenarios.

Addressing performance anxiety, spectatoring, and unreasonable performance expectations are essential in treating Hypoactive Sexual Desire Disorder (HSDD), PE, ED, sexual pain, and ejaculatory inhibition.

It is important to target cognitive, emotional, and behavioral responses for each SD. Although all three components are very influential, fostering healthy cognitions is crucial in helping distressed couples successfully deal with sexual problems as an intimate team (Metz & McCarthy, 2010b).

Treatment of Hypoactive Sexual Desire Disorder (HSDD)

Clinical Perspective

Low sex desire and non-sexual relationships are very common in clinical practice (e.g., Aschka, Himmel, Ittner, & Kochen, 2001). Secondary HSDD most often results from a man's experience of an SD, especially ED. Desire problems are common outcomes for a variety of other psychological (depression, anxiety), medical (thyroid imbalance, side-effects of medication), relationship (anger, alienation), or physical SDs (ED, ejaculatory inhibition). Consequently, comprehensive treatment is necessary and challenging.

Prevalence

Low sexual desire is much more common for men than commonly believed. Approximately 20% of men are affected by low or absent desire (Laumann, Paik, & Rosen, 1999). A *general* lack of desire means the absence of sexual appetite under any circumstances, regardless of the situation or partner. More commonly low desire is *situational,* that is, specific to a partner or situation (e.g., anticipation of intercourse failure). Thus, a man may have desire when he masturbates but not during partner sex.

A striking fact is that when couple sex stops, in over 90% of the cases it is the man's decision—made unilaterally and conveyed non-verbally (Lindau et al., 2007). Not only does intercourse stop, but sensual, playful, and erotic touch also stops. The man avoids intimacy to not open the door to performance pressure. When the choice is "intercourse or nothing," it is nothing that ultimately wins.

The primary cause of HSDD is the man's loss of confidence with erection, intercourse, and orgasm. The man believes that he cannot please his partner, with the result that sex is a source of frustration and embarrassment, not pleasure. The essence of sexual desire is positive anticipation and the person's sense that he deserves sex for pleasure and connection. Instead, sex becomes a cycle of anticipatory anxiety, tense and performance-oriented intercourse, increasing frequency of failure, and eventually avoidance. A challenge for the clinician in identifying the causal process in HSDD is that the man will not disclose his lack of confidence because of embarrassment. The clinician is more likely to uncover the issue by interviewing the man individually and asking about it in a matter-of-fact manner (e.g., "Often, men lose desire for sex if they have been disappointed with their sexual performance, so it is just easier to avoid the whole thing. Have you had experiences like that?").

Other causes for HSDD include intra-psychic factors such as de-eroticizing the partner (often part of a cognitive shift in which the man no longer finds the partner attractive and interesting). The clinician is more likely to obtain open disclosure from the man if the inquiry is conducted without the partner present.

Secondary HSDD is much more common than primary HSDD. Usually a physical SD (ED or ejaculatory inhibition) is the primary cause. The pathogenesis involves suppression of desire in order to prevent his predictive expectancy of performance failure. The man blames himself and avoids sex because he is unable to achieve guaranteed sexual function (McCarthy, Ginsberg, & Fucito, 2006). In other cases, relationship conflict, stressful life experiences and other major distractions are uncovered as causes. A detailed sexual and relationship history can identify links between particular events (e.g., betrayal by his partner, loss of a job) and a decline in desire.

Individual Treatment

For a man reporting a complete lack of desire, a thorough medical examination including laboratory tests is essential to rule out physiological causes (e.g., disease processes, medication side effects). When physiological causes are identified, the therapist collaborates with the man's physician. If the man does not have a urologist who is well versed in treating SDs, the therapist provides appropriate referrals. When there is no evidence of physiological causes, the clinician assesses psychological, environmental, as well as relationship factors.

Strategies to treat the individually-based causes of HSDD include:

1. Acknowledging and addressing the man's negative cognitions (e.g., a sense of futility and pessimism). It is important that the clinician convey optimism that is based in sound science. When a man has developed a negative expectancy (e.g., that he will experience ED if he tries to have sex with a partner), it is important to help him understand the danger of a self-fulfilling prophecy in such situations and encourage him to engage in a sequence of erectile exercises that improve conditions for arousal.
2. Correcting unrealistic assumptions and standards, especially perfectionistic notions of sexual performance. Psychoeducation about normal sexual function is valuable for counteracting such unrealistic beliefs.
3. Instilling a sense of individual responsibility for his sexual drive and "sexual voice." This involves psychoeducation about the power of his thinking (e.g., imagining erotic scenarios) and behavior (e.g., that he deserves to ask his partner to touch him in ways that he finds arousing) in creating desire or detracting from it.
4. Exploring barriers to eroticism (shame, negative religiosity, sexual secrets, and depression) and encouraging the individual in developing positive beliefs regarding sex.

5. Educating the man and his partner about the goals and value of treatment strategies. Realizing that interventions are designed to enhance his sexual desire and satisfaction, which contributes to reducing his sense of helplessness about SD.
6. Addressing fears of vulnerability and emotional intimacy. Men commonly assume that sex is a physiological phenomenon, so CBCST educates them on how thoughts and emotions are powerful influences too. Psychological, relational, and sexual barriers such as fear of emotional intimacy (e.g., based on being abandoned by a parent or previous romantic partner), are identified, and the therapist helps the man "feel ready to let his guard down" with his partner.
7. Ameliorating resentment and anger.
8. Resolving relationship conflict.

Treatment as a Couple

How can the man (and couple) revitalize sexual desire? This requires attention to both the *presence* of negative relational characteristics and *absence or deficits* in positive relational factors. They are not just opposites of each other; they are quite separate aspects of a relationship, so improving one type may have little effect on the other; both need to change.

Reducing negative relationship characteristics. HSDD involves a cycle of anticipatory anxiety and helplessness based on expectancies (predictions) that sex will go poorly, which leads to tense, performance-oriented sex, which then increases negative expectancies and sexual avoidance (McCarthy et al., 2006). If in addition, the partners are experiencing conflict and are chronically upset with each other, the negative "sentiment override" and behavioral interactions create an anti-sexual atmosphere that breeds low desire.

Because negative anticipation easily becomes a mutual process (both partners remember past "failures" and predict more of the same), the therapist discusses the importance of rebuilding confidence that they can have pleasure-oriented, satisfying sex. The therapist educates them in creating positive anticipation through gradual steps toward sensual and erotic touch. This also involves cognitive restructuring to reduce negative thoughts such as "I can't please my partner" and "I've permanently turned my partner off."

Ongoing conflict can be addressed through communication skills and problem-solving skills training, emphasizing the positive effects of good will gestures and working as allies to overcome broader relationship problems, and interventions to reduce partners' negative cognitions (especially attributions that the partner has negative intent or a lack of love).

Increasing positive relational factors. It is important to reduce deficits in both sex-specific relational patterns and overall couple interactions. Keys for enhancing the sex-specific aspects of the relationship include rebuilding positive anticipation, valuing the partner as an intimate and erotic ally, socializing the couple in adopting the pleasure-oriented model of couple sexuality, and coaching them in blending self-entrancement arousal and partner interaction arousal. It also involves improving their health behaviors (e.g., sleep, physical conditioning, amount of alcohol intake), shifting their schemas about sex so they view intercourse as a natural continuation of the pleasuring/eroticism process rather than a pass-fail test, increasing flexibility with couple sexuality, temporarily using a pro-erection medication if the desire problem is caused by spectatoring or expectancy of ED, and maintaining a regular rhythm of sensual, playful, erotic, and intercourse touch.

Enhancement of the quality of the couple's overall relationship is a core aspect of CBCST. Reducing negative couple interactions does not automatically produce satisfying positive interactions (Epstein & Baucom, 2002). Intimacy-building interventions include generating a list of mutually enjoyable activities that a couple can share and engaging in them as homework each week; practicing expression of thoughts and emotions, as well as empathic listening; creating lists of brief actions that each person experiences as expressions of caring; and creating a shared vision of couple goals. The therapist harnesses couple creativity to build bridges for sexual desire (McCarthy & McCarthy, 2012).

Treating Erectile Dysfunction

Clinical Perspective

Since the introduction of Viagra in 1998, public and professional discourse about ED has shifted. To a great extent, professionals had viewed ED as caused by psychological factors, often ignoring physical/medical factors (Halvorsen et al., 1988). Unfortunately, the advent of pharmacological treatments has swung the pendulum in the other direction to the extent that the current distortion is that almost all ED is assumed to be physical and that Viagra, Cialis, or Levitra are the answer. The history of how ED has been conceptualized is a prime example of the need for and validity of a comprehensive, biopsychosocial approach for assessing and treating SD (Althof & Rosen, 2007). In the CBCST approach, the clinician evaluates the potential multiple causes of ED, as well as impacts on the couple, and designs a treatment approach that appropriately includes medical options, interventions for psychological causes such as performance anxiety, and couple therapy components for relationship features. Given that a couple may relapse by slipping back into old patterns when under stress, the therapist helps the couple develop an individualized relapse prevention plan.

Prevalence

Laumann, Gagnon, Michael, and Michaels (1994) reported that 16% of men experience ED, with the incidence increasing with age. Age-related development of illnesses and physical disabilities such as arthritis and vascular diseases, as well as side effects of medications such as antidepressants and antihypersentives, can negatively affect sexual function (Hillman, 2008; McKinlay & Feldman, 1994). Alcohol and drug abuse also contribute to ED.

Individual Treatment

Men without a partner can be treated for ED by adapting psychosexual skills training with masturbation and cognitive arousal training followed by fantasy rehearsals (Althof & Wieder, 2004; Sands, Fisher, Rosen, Heiman, & Eardley, 2008). Psychosexual skills include understanding that relaxation and sensuality comprise the foundation for sexual response and practicing the "wax and wane" of erection exercise during masturbation so the man does not panic when his erection subsides.

Couple Treatment

Given the significant effect that the relationship environment has on sexual response, including erections, couple treatment has major advantages. In addition to including the psychosexual skills of understanding how relaxation and sensuality are the foundation for sexual response and practicing the "wax and wane" of erection exercise, the man is coached in making requests of his partner for erotic stimulation; taught to "piggy-back" his arousal on his partner's arousal; instructed how to develop good timing for his sexual response (he does not attempt to transition to intercourse until he has reached erotic flow); encouraged to let his partner guide intromission; taught about engaging in multiple stimulation during intercourse; and when the couple chooses to have intercourse, emphasizing that the couple can shift to either an erotic scenario or a warm, sensual scenario. The most important concept is to accept the 85% Good Enough Sex (GES) approach rather than demand perfect intercourse performance. It is crucial that the man and his partner accept that his penis and couple sexuality are a variable, flexible, and human process. Performance with an erect penis is not essential to the man being a good lover or to couple sexual satisfaction.

Medical/Physiological Interventions for ED

Medical treatments (e.g., alternative antihypertensive medications or pro-erection medication) often can ameliorate ED. Medical treatments can restore erectile confidence, but they need to be integrated into the couple relationship, not a stand-alone intervention. Partner cooperation is essential for medical interventions to be helpful. There are cases in which a physician, without the involvement of the patient's partner, surgically implanted a penile prosthesis. Technically it was a success, but it was not integrated into couple sexuality and resulted in sexual avoidance. It is best for the therapist and physician to explore with the couple their thoughts and emotional reactions to potential interventions.

An incremental approach to medical treatments. In choosing a medical treatment appropriate for a specific SD, the guiding principle is to "gain the most for the least." Help the man and partner consider medical options incrementally. Our experience is that the outcome is best when the couple chooses a treatment that is the least physically intrusive, medically risky, and potentially detrimental (irreversible). To install a surgical implant when an oral medication will resolve the problem would be unwarranted. Involving the partner in the treatment decision is crucial because its effectiveness and the couple's satisfaction depend on their integrating the medical intervention into their couple sexual style of intimacy, pleasuring, and eroticism (Sidi, Reddy, & Chen, 1988).

- *Non-intrusive penile devices* include penile vacuum devices with manual or electrical "pumps" and the Rejoyn penile splint.
- *First line therapy: Mildly intrusive applications* include pro-erection medications (e.g., Cialis, Viagra, and Levitra) and the urethra insertion of alprostapil (MUSE).
- *Second line therapy: Moderately intrusive applications* involve penile injection therapy.

- *Third line therapy: Radically intrusive and irreversible surgery* is the treatment of last resort and includes a penile surgical implant with a rigid prosthesis, flexible rod prosthesis, or an inflatable prosthesis. Vascular reconstruction surgery is considered experimental, with low success rates.

Non-intrusive penile devices. *Vacuum constriction devices* draw blood into the penis, causing an erection, and trap the blood in order to maintain the erection for intercourse. This includes a plastic tube that fits over the penis in order to create an airtight cover. A vacuum is created around the penis by a small motor or manual pump. When erection occurs, a fitted rubber band is placed on the penis at the base. The erection lasts for approximately thirty minutes. These devices require a doctor's prescription. There is a high dropout rate due to awkwardness and lack of comfort for the man or woman. *Penile braces* are available without prescription at drug stores or on-line. The Rejoyn penile splint consists of a soft rubber brace that exposes the tip of the penis. Couples find that the device interferes with sexual comfort and enjoyment.

First line therapy. The pro-erection oral medications Cialis, Viagra, and Levitra help initiate and maintain erection by relaxing the smooth muscles in the penis. *Viagra* is the oldest of these drugs and stays active for up to 4 hours, as does Levitra. *Cialis* is marketed as the "weekender" for its longer-lasting results (30 minutes to 30 hours), and can be taken at a daily low dose. These medications enhance blood flow to the penis by blocking the PDE-5 enzyme, and can be used whether ED is caused by physical, psychological, or medication-related causes.

Studies assessing the strengths and weaknesses of the alternative pro-erection medications indicate that they are equal in efficacy. When a man takes the drug, he is likely to have an erection sufficient for intercourse in 65–85% of encounters. Cialis can be taken with food, but Viagra works best when taken on an empty stomach (Viagra's effect is slowed by high-fat foods). The blue vision or light sensitivity some men experience with Viagra does not occur with Cialis. Each medication has side effects for 5–15% of men, including headache, facial redness, upset stomach, and sinus congestion. Cialis blocks an enzyme found in smooth muscles, which explains why Cialis' most troublesome side effect (for 5–6% of men) is back pain. None of the medications can be taken with nitrates. The choice of medication will depend on the man and his doctor's preferences, as well as input of the partner, whose feelings are vital. Because medication effects vary from person to person, many men try one and adjust the dose or try another.

Weighing the costs and benefits of medical interventions is part of couple decision-making. Obtaining the desired effect is a matter of trial and error. New medical treatments for ED are being developed. Consultation with a knowledgeable physician about treatment options is crucial. Men are warned against self-medication with alcohol, recreational drugs, or over-the-counter remedies.

Some men are reluctant to use pro-erection medications because they view it as a sign of weakness. Medication can be a wise choice, as it is an important resource for regaining confidence with erection. Pharmacologic treatment as a stand-alone intervention is insufficient because it needs to be used consistently, does not automatically produce an erection, and complex psychological and relationship features need to be addressed. For example, if a man is unhappy with his partner, simply taking a PDE-5 inhibitor does not result in an erection. Consequently, CBCST may uncover psychological and relationship problems that the couple has been ignoring.

The Medicated Urethral System for Erection (MUSE) is a device used to insert an *alprostadil* suppository into the urethral opening. Eighty percent of the drug is absorbed after ten minutes. Reports of its effectiveness vary from 7 to 65% (Padma–Nathan et al., 1997). The most common adverse effects are penile pain, urethral burning, dizziness, and fainting. MUSE has a very high dropout rate.

ED is common with depression, but unfortunately, medications to treat depression may cause ED (or ejaculatory inhibition). With the physician's supervision, the man can choose an effective antidepressant with less likelihood of causing SD. This involves a trial and error process of trying different medications, dosages, and regimens of when to take the medication.

Anti-anxiety medicines can help when ED results from performance anxiety. Anti-anxiety medications can be taken PRN (as needed), one to four hours before sex. However, when individuals come to rely on medication to reduce anxiety, they do not develop self-confidence that they can tolerate anxiety or use skills to decrease symptoms. A good treatment choice is teaching the man and his partner anxiety management strategies, including relaxation techniques, mindfulness skills, and cognitive restructuring self-talk.

Second line therapy. Penile injection therapy involves the medication being applied directly to the penis by a tiny needle injection into the base of the penis a few minutes before sexual activity. The man is open to stimulation to build subjective arousal, and he can enjoy the pleasure of intercourse and orgasm. Injection therapy has a high dropout rate because men and their partners find it awkward and clinical. Men often rush to intercourse at low levels of subjective arousal because they fear losing their erection. For penile injection therapy to be beneficial, it needs to be integrated into a couple's sexual style of intimacy, pleasuring, and eroticism.

Third line therapy. Surgeries are the treatment of last resort. Implants involve rigid rod prosthesis, flexible rod prosthesis, or an inflatable prosthesis. Rigid or flexible rods are implanted into the penis to make it erect. There are inflatable models that allow for artificial engorging and deflating by means of a hydraulic system implanted in the penis and a fluid reservoir implanted in one of the testicular sacs (the testis is removed). Implants are irreversible.

When there is irreversible damage to the penile arteries and veins, *vascular reconstruction surgery* may be attempted. This surgery is experimental, with poor results, but its effectiveness may improve with increased knowledge and surgical experience.

Combination treatments. Physicians experiment with combination treatments that include medications and interventions designed to overcome physical (e.g., vascular, neurologic) and/or psychological (performance anxiety, depression) limitations. For example, PDE-5 agents are combined with testosterone enhancement or injection therapy. Combined medical and psychosexual treatments are the standard of care for SD after prostate cancer.

Limitations of bio-medical interventions. Although medical treatments are helpful, they have limitations and are rarely effective as stand-alone treatments. They succeed best when used along with the psychosexual skill exercises of CBCST and integrated into a flexible couple sexual style. The unrealistic 100% performance goal subverts couple sexuality. The 85% guideline of the GES approach in CBCST develops genuine confidence with sensual, erotic, and intercourse sexuality.

Psychological and Relationship Interventions for ED

Treatment of ED is best approached in the couple context. It includes both individual and couple psychosexual skill exercises (Metz & McCarthy, 2004). Psychosexual skill training in the context of the relationship helps overcome spectatoring, builds confidence, and balances the couple's sexual life.

It is important for the couple to openly talk about ED. The therapist gathering individual psychological/relational/sexual history information promotes both partners' engagement in treatment. Getting individuals' embarrassment in the open, offering sexual education, and outlining a therapeutic plan confronts the man's (and partner's) hopelessness. Identifying cognitive, behavioral and emotional aspects of sexual and relationship problems reveals the barriers to satisfying sexuality. Understanding the interconnections among ED, subjective cognitions and emotions, and their behavioral interaction patterns can identify a variety of intervention points. Table 6.1 illustrates common cognitions, emotions and behavioral responses in couples with ED. This broader perspective can be double-edged because it raises influences on ED of which one or both partners were unaware or they ignored. The couple may have entered treatment hoping for and expecting a simple bio-medical solution but now are faced with information about individual characteristics and couple dynamics that are "more than they bargained for." It is the therapist's role to introduce these factors in a supportive manner that avoids blaming and motivates the couple to engage in interventions that have a greater likelihood of success.

Providing information about erectile function. CBCST provides the couple a forum to discuss their understanding of sexual arousal and erection. To challenge unrealistic expectations, they discuss the *three requirements for erection*. The therapist provides the man and his partner optimism to transcend his naïve belief

---

Table 6.1 Common Cognitions, Emotions, and Behavioral Responses in Couples with SD

Man:

Cognitions:

"I am a failure. I can't please my partner. She is upset with me. I don't know what to do. What's wrong with me? Sex is supposed to be automatic, but I can't get an erection. This is hopeless!"

Emotions:

anxiety, shame, frustration, embarrassment, anger

Behavior:

repeatedly apologizing to partner, avoidance, silence, defensiveness, statements of blame toward self or partner

Woman:

Cognitions:

"I should turn him on. I am a failure. He's quiet so he must be angry. I have to talk to him or it will get worse. I don't know what to do. Sex will fail anyway. He feels terrible and it is my fault. I am not sexy. He doesn't love me anymore. I'm desperate because our relationship is falling apart!"

Emotions:

anxiety, irritation, loneliness, sadness

Behavior:

tries to soothe partner, criticism of self or partner, avoidance, silence

---

that erection should be automatic. The therapist validates the role of the partner in providing support and collaborating to create a mutually stimulating and enjoyable sexual milieu.

The sensate focus/pleasuring format used in CBCST incorporates strategies that promote erectile function. While not "automatic," erectile response is "easy" when the clients integrate three basic requirements: (1) sufficient *relaxation*, (2) sufficient genital *stimulation*, and (3) couple *cooperation*. Balancing physical relaxation with sensual touch is the foundation for erection. The more relaxed the man is the less physical stimulation is required. Table 6.2 summarizes how the psychosexual skill exercises detailed in Metz and McCarthy (2004) are applied to the treatment of ED. Styles of arousal and the PM are the building blocks of the "Easy Erection" exercise that is described in Table 6.3.

Table 6.2 Psychosexual Skill Exercises in the Treatment of ED

Progressive skills training comprises the set of CBCST core assignments used to treat ED. Depending on the skills deficits and couple dynamics, some or all are utilized. The therapist can incorporate standard exercises and create special assignments to address unique couple features

Phase One: Developing relaxation and comfort
Step 1: Increasing sexual comfort
    Goal: Develop comfort and assurance
    Couple exercise: Talking about sexual feelings
Step 2: Training his mind and body for relaxation
    Goal: Learn relaxation, the foundation for pleasure and eroticism
    Individual exercise: Deep breathing
    Individual exercise: Physical relaxation
Step 3: Learning PM control
    Goal: Identify and learn to consciously control his PM
    Individual exercise: PM training

Phase Two: Obtaining easy erections
Step 4: Partner genital exploration
    Goal: Learn about his and her responsiveness; enjoy relaxation with genital touch
    Couple exercise: Partner genital exploration
Step 5: Cognitive pacing with the sexual arousal continuum
    Goal: Broaden the range of sexual arousal
    Individual exercise: Developing his arousal continuum
    Couple exercises: Easy erections and buoyed confidence; Couple
    self-entrancement arousal
        1.   Soothing genital touch
        2.   Finding his calm erection
        3.   Choosing to wax and wane

Phase Three: Maintaining easy erections
Step 6: Couple erotic pleasuring
    Goal: Enjoy eroticism
    Couple exercise: Erotic pleasuring
Step 7: Couple pacing training
    Goal: Learn to enjoy arousal without proceeding to orgasm
    Couple exercise: Erotic pleasuring

Phase Four: Enjoying intercourse
Step 8: Initiating intimate intercourse
    Goal: Learn to adapt to intercourse
    Couple exercise: Cooperating for intercourse

Step 9: Pleasure-oriented intercourse
        Goal: Learn pleasurable intercourse
        Couple exercise: The "Stuff-It Method" for intercourse
Step 10: Progressive intercourse
        Goal: Integrate skills and increase confidence during intercourse
        Couple exercise: Progressive intercourse
Step 11: Playful intercourse
        Goal: Celebrate GES
        Couple exercise: Sexual nicknames
        Couple exercise: Humor and playfulness: Promote "specialness"

Phase Five: Couple style and relapse prevention
        Goal: Ensure maintenance of gains and enhance satisfaction
        Couple exercise: Relapse prevention and couple satisfaction

Source: (Metz & McCarthy, 2004).

Table 6.3 Couple Exercise: "Easy Erections and Buoyed Confidence"

Begin by engaging in couple relaxed pleasuring

Part 1. Soothing genital touch

    The man lies on his back and asks his partner to gently explore his genitals with slow touch for fifteen minutes. He is to concentrate on the quiet, calm sensations, consciously relaxing his PM. His partner provides feather-like touching and gently pleasures his penis. He focuses on the sensations. The couple do this exercise at least twice before moving on to part 2.

Part 2. Finding "Easy Erection." This includes developing confidence with obtaining erections, "wax and wane," and "welcoming erotic touch."

    Begin with couple pleasuring, gradually increasing fingering his penis. The couple is instructed to not work to obtain an erection, but rather to welcome an erection by his continued relaxation, keeping his PM relaxed, and focusing on the pleasure in his body and penis. The more relaxed and focused he is, the easier to become erect. He is most likely to get an erection with self-entrancement arousal—maximum body relaxation, minimal touch, and a focus on sensations.

    The partners are instructed to avoid pressure or the man will become distracted by spectatoring and lose relaxation. After calm touch, his partner increases stimulation, using slow stroking with her thumb and index finger. He identifies the *minimum* touch required to get an erection. His role is to keep his PM relaxed as he increases sensual touch, using both hands.

    If after engaging in this exercise three times he has not found his calm erection, he can add *mildly* arousing partner interaction fantasies from his arousal continuum. He is seeking the *mildest* physical (self-entrancement) and cognitive (partner interaction) arousal needed for an easy erection.

Part 3. Choosing to "wax and wane" and her "letting it flow":

    When he has an easy erection for 3–5 minutes, the couple choose to let it subside by stopping penile touch. As his erection subsides, he stays focused on his sensations. He signals her to resume touching him, to bring back a relaxed erection. He regains his erection easily when calm, mindful, and focused.

    Case example: Troy worked too hard during this exercise. He realized that he was trying to rush an erection rather than allowing it to occur. Rebecca invited him to be patient, maintain a relaxed PM, and let her provide the pleasure. It was difficult for Troy to be passive, because he believed that he did not deserve the sexual attention. As he was able to modify his sensual and sexual touch, the exercise resulted in easy erections.

    If arousal does not occur during the wax and wane exercise, the man is asked to practice wax and wane on his own. Then he practices with his partner.

Treating Premature Ejaculation

Clinical Perspective

Male ejaculatory dysfunction spans a continuum from ejaculation before intercourse to inability to ejaculate. PE is the inadvertent and unsatisfying speed of ejaculation. It is the most common male SD. PE involves three diagnostic criteria: (1) the onset of ejaculation with minimal sexual stimulation before, upon, or shortly after penetration and before the man wishes it; (2) marked interpersonal distress; and (3) not due to the effect of a substance. Diagnostic parameters include: (1) Duration: whether life-long or acquired and (2) Range: whether generalized or situational (Perelman, McMahon, & Barada, 2004).

There is no universally accepted definition for PE (Rowland & Slob, 1997). We describe PE as occurring when a man does not have the ability to choose when to ejaculate, and this creates distress in his intimate relationship. PE has been defined as duration of intercourse (e.g., less than 2 minutes); number of intravaginal thrusts (8 to 15 thrusts); or the capacity for voluntary control. Other approaches (e.g., Grenier & Byers, 2004) add the perspective of the man's partner, as well as the level of severity (Metz & Pryor, 2000). Assessment considers mediating factors such as the partner's preferences or frequency of sexual activity.

Althof, Abdo, Dean, Hackett, McCabe, McMahon, et al. (2010) conducted an extensive bio-medical review and recommended defining PE as the inability to last intravaginally longer than 1 minute. This criterion is an indicator of hypersensitive, neurologic etiology. Such cases (approximately 2–3% of PE) usually require pharmacologic agents. However, most PE involves psychological and relationship factors.

A common myth among men, couples, and professionals is that PE naturally improves with age. Some men experience a sexual "mellowing," but aging does not usually resolve PE.

Ejaculatory dysfunction often co-exists with another SD. For example, PE may occur when a man who worries about ED overcompensates by working at forcing his arousal. Consequently, assessment should include exploration of other SDs that the client did not mention.

The man's partner's emotional and sexual feelings are important in understanding PE and the goals of treatment. The goal of ejaculatory control is not to guarantee that a female partner has an orgasm during intercourse. The goal is to increase pleasure and eroticism for both partners. Her role is as an intimate, involved partner. He can pleasure her to arousal and orgasm with manual, oral, rubbing, or vibrator stimulation. Many women prefer orgasm before their partner ejaculates, but some prefer it afterward. It is important for the therapist to modify the belief that sex ends when he ejaculates. It is crucial that the man understands the importance of not "abandoning" his partner by ending the sexual activity when he experiences PE. The fundamental principle is that sexuality is about giving and receiving *pleasure*, not performing perfectly.

It is not only the causes of ejaculation problems that are complicated; so are their effects. This contributes to a vicious cycle, making the SD chronic and severe. The subtle intermingling of the partners' thoughts, emotions, and behaviors adds to the complexity. For example, a man who expects perfect ejaculatory control every time (cognition) becomes frustrated and angry (emotional distress) due to his unrealistic standard, and is irritable (interpersonal behavior), causing a female partner to feel anguish (emotional distress) and to leave the room (behavioral response), which he interprets as proof that she is dissatisfied with him as a lover (cognition), leading him to feel even more anxious about sex the next time (emotional distress). CBCST is designed to identify the complex processes surrounding the PE and intervene at multiple points to change such negative spirals.

Cognitions that the partners experience but do not express can increase distress. Thus, a man with PE thinks he is inadequate and feels ashamed, but on the outside he may be stoic. His partner can plainly see that he is unhappy but thinks there is nothing she can do and feels frustration, loneliness, and abandonment. If the man believes, "She is angry with me for ejaculating rapidly. I must change, or she'll go to a different man," or she believes, "He is utterly selfish and doesn't love me," the impact of the PE will be major. If instead the man and his partner think, "Let's enjoy touch, and find alternate scenarios for love-making," he can remain calm and suggest such a flexible approach. Unrealistic standards, negative attributions, and inaccurate expectancies generate emotional distress and interfere with partner cooperation and intimacy. Helping the couple identify and correct negative cognitions is important, as is improving their ability to communicate constructively about the problem. CBCST facilitates functional sexual behaviors, constructive cognitions, and positive emotions.

Prevalence

Estimates of the prevalence of PE vary from 3 to 75% depending on the sample and criteria used to define it. The best data suggest that PE affects 29% of men (Laumann et al., 1999). Severity of PE can be assessed with the *Premature Ejaculation Severity Index (PESI)*, a 10-item self-report questionnaire based on features such as the onset, percentage of PE events, the man and partner's emotional distress, chronicity, and presence of another SD (Metz & McCarthy, 2003).

The "do-it-yourself" treatment techniques recommended on the internet to reduce arousal (use two condoms, masturbate before intercourse, or distraction with anti-erotic cognitions about his mother-in-law) are ineffective. In addition, they cause loss of desire, ED, and relationship alienation. Because many men have already tried such techniques before reaching the therapist's or urologist's office, it is important to provide education about factors contributing to PE and empirically supported treatments for it. CBCST provides an integrated biopsychosocial approach to treatment.

Pharmacologic Agents for Ejaculation Problems

Medication is a resource, especially helpful with PE that is due to neurologic system function ("hardwired"). Some men elect to use medication on an ongoing basis, whereas others use it while practicing ejaculatory control exercises and then gradually phase out medication. Antidepressant medications (SSRIs) are prescribed "off label." It is the common side effect that SSRIs have for reducing sexual response that is helpful in counteracting PE. Currently, pharmacologic agents for PE are under study for FDA approval. It is likely that agents to facilitate orgasm for men with ejaculatory inhibition also will be available in the future.

An integrative approach to PE emphasizes the use of all available resources, including ejaculation-inhibiting medications. The medication must be integrated into the couple's sexual style. It is evident from clinical experience with the pro-erection medications that medication is rarely effective as a stand-alone treatment. The high dropout rate is due to a failure to integrate use of the medication as a couple (where both partners view it as helpful), failure of the medication to alleviate low sexual self-esteem, medication side effects, or disappointment that the drug was not the promised miracle cure.

Health food stores promote agents that claim to cure PE and ejaculatory inhibition, but without scientific evidence to support such claims. Medication is most helpful when used with the CBCST psychosexual skills program and integrated into the couple's sexual style of intimacy, pleasuring, and eroticism (McCarthy & Fucito, 2005). If a man depends on the medication to establish 100% ejaculatory control, he sets himself and the relationship up for failure. Striving for perfect sex performance subverts sexual function and satisfaction.

Outcome Effectiveness

Controlled studies examining the effectiveness of treatment for PE (DeAmicus, Goldberg, LoPiccolo, Friedman, & Davidson, 1985; Hawton, Catalan, Martin, & Fagg, 1986; Kilmann, Boland, Norton, Davidson, & Caid, 1986) indicate mediocre outcome, in contrast to the 95% success rate originally reported by Masters and Johnson (1970). The limited effectiveness may be due to the failure to determine and specifically treat the particular etiologic subtypes of PE. A review by Metz, Pryor, Abuzzahab, Nesvacil, & Kozner (1997) of outcome research suggested that cases of PE can be classified in terms of being primarily psychogenic versus due to a combination of neurophysiological problems, with primary or lifelong PE more likely to involve physiological causal factors. Because PE treatment programs have tended to be overly general, lacking detailed attention to the distinguishing features of the type of PE and failing to integrate multiple techniques, it is not surprising that they have had limited success (Table 6.4).

Table 6.4 Effectiveness of Behavioral Strategies to Reduce PE

Several techniques are associated with delaying ejaculation including:

	Correlation with ejaculatory latency
Using a different intercourse position	.57
Thrusting in a circular motion	.58
Talking during intercourse	.35
Using oral sex as a "warm-up"	.30

Source: (Grenier & Byers, 1997).

* Grenier, G., & Byers, E. (1997). The relationships among ejaculatory control, ejaculatory latency, and attempts to prolong heterosexual intercourse. *Archives of Sexual Behavior, 26,* 27–42. With permission of Springer.

Individual Treatment

The man can learn psychosexual skills to use on his own, which involve masturbation. Goals include developing realistic expectations of his body, identifying physical sensations that indicate he is approaching the point of ejaculatory inevitability, developing his "arousal continuum," learning sensual self-entrancement arousal, practicing the stop-start technique, practicing PM relaxation, using his PM before and during intercourse, and rehearsing "acclimating" to sensations of intercourse (Metz & McCarthy, 2003; Perelman et al., 2004).

Key concepts in ejaculatory control. The man is taught a set of basic principles for ejaculatory control that challenge common sense notions:

1. Realistic expectations based on the physiology of sexual function. He cannot "rush to orgasm."
2. Do-it-yourself techniques to reduce arousal (e.g., using two condoms, distracting oneself with upsetting thoughts) do not help, and in fact lead to ED and relationship alienation.
3. The strategy for ejaculatory control is counterintuitive. Rather than decreasing pleasure, his goal is to increase comfort, awareness, and pleasure.
4. Ejaculatory control requires him to identify the point of ejaculatory inevitability, maintain awareness at moderate levels of arousal and adjust his behavior (e.g., slow intercourse thrusting) to stay within that range.

Sensations of orgasm begin at the point of ejaculatory inevitability. Once he reaches the point of inevitability, there is no turning back. Whether he arrives there prematurely or voluntarily, it is important that he enjoy the feelings and sensations, rather than being frustrated and angry. Criticizing himself does not facilitate ejaculatory control, and it increases tension within the couple. It is not his partner's role to calm him, as he is responsible for developing a positive attitude about further experience of PE. The focus is on enjoying and sharing the entire experience of intimacy, pleasure, arousal, eroticism, intercourse, orgasm, and afterplay.

Couple Treatment for PE

Comprehensive couple treatment of PE requires that the man and his partner learn psychosexual skills based on traditional and newer cognitive-behavioral techniques (Metz & McCarthy, 2003; Zilbergeld, 1999). Contrary to the couple's wish for simple cures, no one psychosexual skill is enough to overcome PE. Rather, these skills are integrated within the context of couple sexuality. The skills include:

1. Developing couple openness and comfort so they work as an intimate team.
2. Pursuing the principle of "pleasure before performance."
3. Learning physical relaxation during lovemaking.
4. Identifying the point of ejaculatory inevitability.
5. Learning self-entrancement arousal and blending this with partner interaction arousal.
6. Learning to use the PM as a monitor of relaxation and as an arousal/ejaculation management technique.

7. Moderating his arousal using cognitive pacing techniques.
8. Managing arousal using behavioral pacing techniques and the "stop-start" procedure.
9. Learning penile "acclimation" during intercourse.
10. Developing an individualized relapse prevention program, based on acceptance that future instances of PE occur and do not signify a serious problem.

Cognitive-Behavioral Psychosexual Steps with PE

In *Coping with Premature Ejaculation*, Metz and McCarthy (2003) describe 11 sequenced steps for couples for effective treatment of severe PE. For milder cases, judicious selection of fewer steps is effective. Each exercise requires 30–60 minutes, completed at home between therapy sessions.

In Phase One, *Comfort and Relaxation*, the exercises promote positive valuing of sex, comfort with sexuality, and relaxation. In Step 1, *Increasing Couple Sexual Comfort*, the partners are coached in talking to each other about sexual feelings in an open, positive manner, using behavioral expression and empathic listening skills. Step 2, "*Training Your Mind and Body for Relaxation*," establishes the foundation for ejaculatory control and pleasure with relaxation. It includes mindful attention to bodily sensations and use of progressive muscle relaxation. Relaxation is facilitated by learning *PM Control* (Step 3).

Cognitive strategies involve consciously managing sexual arousal. In Step 4, "*Cognitive Pacing with the Sexual Arousal Continuum*," the man develops awareness of his unique arousal continuum. He maps out different activities and images according to the level of subjective arousal that he feels, on a continuum of 0–100. He is instructed to begin lovemaking with relaxed arousal, the point of Step 5, "*Self-Entrancement Arousal*." Rather than focusing on his partner's body, he focuses on his own physical sensations. He finds his "calm erection" (especially helpful for the man whose PE is based on overcompensation for fears of ED).

In Phase Two, *Pleasure Toleration*, the couple functions as an intimate team to maintain relaxation during genital pleasuring. He learns to welcome more—not less—pleasure, the focus of Step 6, "*Relaxed Couple Pleasuring.*" Step 7, "*Partner Genital Exploration*," establishes calm, relaxed genital touch.

In Steps 8 and 9, "*Stop-Start Pacing*," the couple develops comfort and confidence in arousal and ejaculation management. He learns to integrate self-entrancement arousal with partner-interaction arousal. Blending of cognitive and behavioral "pacing" is a powerful strategy.

In Phase Three, "*Pleasure Saturation*," the couple learns to enjoy extended intercourse. This involves integrating cognitive and behavioral skills and cooperating as an intimate team. In Steps 10 and 11, "*Intimate Intercourse*," the couple increases the amount of time in intercourse and adapts to prolonged intercourse. In the exercise, "*Initiating and Acclimating to Intercourse*," he relaxes his PM while she initiates intromission with minimal movement. They wait for his penis to "acclimate" to her vagina. Acclimation may take as long as 5 minutes, but once reached, they enjoy active movement without ejaculation. When they are ready for ejaculation, he tenses the PM and increases movement. In "*Progressive Intercourse*," the partners cooperate to integrate these skills, are open to spontaneity, and focus on pleasure and eroticism.

Phase Four, *Long-Term Satisfaction*, melds the cognitive-behavioral psychosexual skills into the partners' couple sexual style. They integrate positive changes into their pattern of sexual interaction and maximize long-term satisfaction with an individualized relapse prevention plan. Without this, couples are vulnerable to relapse by perceiving any reminders of past problems as catastrophic and returning to their former counterproductive ways of coping, especially sexual avoidance.

In the following case example, we label cognitions (C), behaviors (B), and emotions (E) to identify the C-B-E components.

Case Example: Sherry and Alex

Alex's chronic PE led Sherry to make attributions (C) that he was selfish, dismissive, and rejecting of her desires, leading her to feel hurt (E). Alex did not intend (C) to be selfish. Rather, he was deeply perplexed and judged himself to be a "failure" (C) at his sexual performance (B), and predicted (C) that he was disappointing Sherry. Based on his negative thoughts (C) and upset feelings (E) after ejaculating, he quickly disengaged from Sherry (B), which she interpreted as selfish (C). Alex appeared to Sherry (C) to be sexually satisfied, and when he stopped pleasuring (B) Sherry ("he rolls over and goes to sleep"), she attributed (C) that to his not caring about her sexual satisfaction. Alex focused on his failure (C), apologized and stopped lovemaking, became quiet and withdrawn, and even left the bed (B) as he felt ashamed and frustrated (E). Sherry concluded (C), "It's all about Alex!" They did not discuss this distressing pattern, so their negative interpretations, emotional responses, and behavioral pattern persisted.

For several years, Sherry had experienced Alex's PE and observed that (C) he failed to seek professional help (B). His actions violated her personal standard (C) about ways in which an individual should be sensitive and responsive to their partner's needs, which she perceived as abandonment (C) and hurt her deeply (E). She expressed her hurt feelings (E) through complaints, criticisms, and expressions of anger, even rage at times (B).

In turn, Alex interpreted Sherry's behavior as a lack of empathy for his distress (C). He viewed her behavior as violating his standard (C) about how she should support a partner who is experiencing a problem. When he criticized her as being unsupportive (C), she criticized him in return (B) for avoiding her and only caring about himself.

Alex was confused (C) about what to do to control his ejaculation, as everything he tried such as distracting himself (C) and masturbating before lovemaking (B) were not helpful. He viewed the situation as hopeless (C), labeled himself inadequate (C), and avoided Sherry not only sexually but also by being less affectionate (B). Over time, Sherry's anger and frustration with Alex led her to avoid him as well.

Alex and Sherry's story shows how interacting detrimental cognitions, emotions and behaviors cause, maintain, and exacerbate PE. During CBCST, the clinician helped them stop these patterns and establish reasonable cognitions, regulate their negative emotional responses, and engage in constructive communication and cooperative behaviors to improve their sexual relationship.

The therapist's assessment indicated that there were several factors contributing to or maintaining Alex's PE: neurologic reactivity, psychosexual skills deficits, psychological distress involving negative cognitions and associated anxiety and anger (toward himself and Sherry), and relationship conflict. His PESI score was 54, indicating moderate severity.

The multiple negative cognitions by both partners (negative attributions such as Sherry inferring that Alex was sexually selfish or Alex attributing Sherry's criticism as a lack of caring) were addressed through cognitive restructuring interventions during therapy sessions and through homework exercises.

The most helpful psychosexual skill exercises were "Relaxation Training," "PM Training," "Cognitive Pacing Arousal Continuum," "Self-Entrancement Arousal," "Stop-Start," and "Intercourse Acclimation." The couple learned to enjoy varied lengths and intensity of intercourse. Pleasure and intimacy became their focus, rather than sex performance. They created a relapse prevention plan that included engaging in the Couple Pleasuring exercise once a month, as well "check-in" conversations in which each partner was able to voice any worries about their relationship, receive empathic understanding, and engage in problem solving. This was particularly valuable for Alex to maintain a variable, flexible approach to couple sexuality.

Treatment of Ejaculatory Inhibition

Ejaculatory inhibition (delayed ejaculation) is the most misunderstood SD. It involves initiating intercourse, not being able to ejaculate, and giving up. There are many possible causes of ejaculatory inhibition, from depression to side effects of medications to fatigue (Perelman et al., 2004). Other common psychological factors include difficulty with losing control, intimacy issues, fear of pregnancy, internalization of negative messages from parents regarding sex, and lack of mindfulness regarding sensual and erotic stimuli. The most common cause is not valuing couple sex, often because the individual has developed a pattern of masturbation that includes fantasies and physical stimulation techniques that are more arousing than partner sex (Perelman, 2014). The man and his partner fall into a mechanical intercourse routine that is no longer erotic or that he experiences as considerably less exciting than masturbation. Typically, the man transitions to intercourse when he can (just beginning to get an erection with a subjective arousal level of "5") and approaches intercourse as simply a matter of thrusting, ignoring how important eroticism is to high arousal and orgasm. When he does not reach orgasm, he gives up in frustration and loses his erection.

This SD may be overlooked because the couple presents with ED. However, in contrast to ED, the man loses his erection from fatigue and frustration with prolonged effort to ejaculate. He "runs out of energy." It is important to assess for bio-medical factors such as side effects of medication, poor cardio-vascular conditioning, and medical illnesses such as neuropathy. It also is important to identify possible relationship factors, in which the man does not view her as his intimate, erotic partner. Ejaculatory inhibition can cause infertility, block sexual pleasure, and significantly disrupt relationship intimacy.

The discarded traditional labels "retarded ejaculation" and "ejaculatory incompetence" added to the sense of stigma about this disorder. In assessing ejaculatory inhibition, it is important to carefully examine both objective arousal (e.g., intensity of stimulation, time to ejaculation, masturbation pattern) and subjective arousal (e.g., level of distress, focus of attention, subjective feeling). The clinician approaches ejaculatory inhibition as a couple issue, using the CBCST biopsychosocial model of assessment, treatment, and relapse prevention.

Prevalence

Primary ejaculatory inhibition refers to the man who has never or rarely ejaculated during intercourse. Most men are able to ejaculate with masturbation and manual or oral stimulation, although some are totally unable to ejaculate during partner sex. The estimate is that 1–2% of young men experience primary ejaculatory inhibition. For those who never ejaculate, a careful medical evaluation is necessary.

In contrast, secondary ejaculatory inhibition (occurring in some situations but not others) increases with age and affects an estimated 7–15% of men over age 50 (Hartmann & Waldinger, 2007; Perelman, 2016). This pattern can be misdiagnosed as ED because the man eventually loses his erection. He loses the erection because he is unable to establish an erotic flow that culminates in orgasm. Traditionally, intercourse thrusting alone was enough for him to orgasm. As men age, there are more similarities than differences between male and female sexual response, including the need for partner stimulation to enhance erotic flow and orgasmic response. Men who are unaware of these normal changes or who become sexually self-conscious are vulnerable to ejaculatory inhibition (Metz & Miner, 1998).

Determining the Severity of Ejaculatory Inhibition

The clinician explores under what circumstances the man is easily orgasmic and under what circumstances he is unable to reach orgasm. The man who is orgasmic with an idiosyncratic masturbation pattern, but never with his partner, poses a very different therapeutic challenge than the man who is readily orgasmic with partner manual and/or oral stimulation but not during intercourse.

It is important to inquire about the amount and types of erotic fantasies the man uses during self and partner stimulation, and whether these serve as a bridge to arousal or as a distraction from erotic response (when he feels guilty about erotic fantasies). The clinician needs to ask him whether he feels subjectively aroused or whether he is struggling at low levels of subjective arousal during partner sex. In terms of situational factors, what types of stimulation, fantasy, situation, and partner activities facilitate high arousal and orgasm, and what factors inhibit his arousal and orgasm. Because this important information may be embarrassing for the man, and he likely has not shared it with his partner, the clinician needs to interview him individually and convey the rationale for asking him for personal disclosure.

Treatment Strategies

Treatment strategies include using multiple stimulation during pleasuring and intercourse; "piggy-backing" his arousal on the partner's; transitioning to intercourse at subjective arousal of "8"; using erotic fantasies to heighten his subjective arousal; using "orgasm triggers" (i.e., the cues/resources he uses during masturbation that allow him to let go and "come"); making requests for erotic stimulation; taking personal and sexual "risks" of trying new ways of becoming aroused (e.g., self-stimulation mixed with partner stimulation to enhance erotic flow); and pacing himself with erotic flow rather than trying to force orgasm.

Comprehensive CBCST includes an individualized approach featuring biomedical, pharmacologic, psychological, relational, and contextual components. For example, if ejaculatory inhibition results from an excessive masturbatory pattern (e.g., a 45-year-old man masturbating daily to internet pornography, but being unable to ejaculate intravaginally), treatment needs to address psychological and relationship factors in addition to the man's conditioned arousal to idealized erotic scenarios. Psychological issues may include low sexual self-esteem that leads him to avoid sex with the partner and relationship issues such as a lack of intimacy, diminished attraction to the partner, and chronic conflict in the relationship. Some men punish their partner by withholding affection and sex (Perelman, 2009, 2014). Careful assessment of the various risk factors for ejaculatory inhibition is necessary in order to tailor the treatment to the needs of each couple.

Motivation for Change

Assessing the motivation of the man and his partner is crucial. Among young men a common motivation not to ejaculate is the desire to avoid pregnancy (whether based on the woman's desire or his own). Commonly, a man has adapted to ejaculatory inhibition and does not view it as a problem. As a single man he may have developed a reputation as a "stud" in which he viewed intercourse as primarily serving the woman by bringing her to orgasm, with himself being orgasmic either with her stimulation or his own afterward. Often, his partner is more motivated to address the SD than he.

As with other SDs, ejaculatory inhibition is best conceptualized and treated as a couple problem. It is crucial to assess the partner's motivation. In the best-case scenario, she is his intimate sexual friend. In the worst-case scenario, she views the ejaculatory inhibition as a rejection of her sexual desirability and ejaculation as a pass-fail test of their relationship. Where there is couple alienation she threatens to tell others and humiliate the man.

Often this type of SD is part of a complex relationship power struggle. It is important to assess whether ejaculatory inhibition represents a hidden sexual agenda (a variant arousal pattern, a sexual orientation conflict, a preference for masturbation over couple sex, a self-punitive reaction to a past traumatic sexual experience, a means for punishing the partner). In addition to understanding the cause(s) and function of the SD, it is crucial to assess both partners' motivation for change. Is the emphasis on sharing pleasure or on sexual performance? The performance approach of forcing ejaculation to prove something to himself or his partner is likely to fail, and ultimately cause inhibited desire and avoidance. A healthy motivation involves the man anticipating couple sex, believing that he deserves sexual pleasure, enjoying receiving erotic stimulation, getting into an erotic flow, using orgasm triggers, and allowing high arousal to naturally flow to orgasm. Healthy motivation for the partner involves positive anticipation of the sexual experience and viewing herself as his intimate and erotic ally. Each person's arousal enhances the other's. When the assessment reveals motivation barriers on either person's part, those become the primary focus of intervention. Sexual skill exercises need to explicitly address the underlying motivation problems. For example, the therapist can guide the couple in setting a goal of increasing "teamwork" and collaboration and have them commit to using multiple stimulation methods and orgasm triggers explicitly tailored to enhance *both* partners' preferences.

Psychosexual Skills for Treating Ejaculatory Inhibition

Ejaculatory inhibition is the inverse problem to PE. Rather than helping the man "pace arousal" in order to delay ejaculation, the clinician helps the man and couple "pace arousal" to promote erotic flow and orgasm. The goal is to develop a relaxed, cooperative style that respects the man's physiological and psychological conditions that create high arousal and orgasm. The most common couple interventions are to encourage transitioning to intercourse when subjective arousal is high, to use multiple stimulation during intercourse (manual, kissing, fantasy), and to identify and use the man's "orgasm triggers" (Metz & McCarthy, 2007).

Cognitive-behavioral skills that facilitate orgasm include:

1. Physiological relaxation to create the non-demand foundation for sexual receptivity and responsiveness.
2. Using the man's cognitive arousal continuum. This includes reserving thoughts and behaviors that are highly erotic until he is turned-on and moving toward orgasm.
3. Relaxing the PM until shortly before he wants to ejaculate. Then he tightens, relaxes, and tightens to activate ejaculation.
4. Avoiding prolonged intercourse. Intercourse is reserved for high levels of arousal. The couple transition to intercourse when both are highly aroused and he piggy-backs his arousal on her arousal.
5. Using mutual excitement to build erotic flow.

The following case example (a composite rather than an actual individual case) illustrates the use of CBCST in the treatment of inhibited ejaculation.

Case Example: Brian and Alisha

Brian was 28 and had never ejaculated inside a woman's vagina. He had been married to 29-year-old Alisha for 8 months. Alisha has a 4-year-old daughter from a prior marriage, and they are eager to have a child of their own. During her pregnancy Alisha's first husband admitted to being gay. Alisha felt doubly stigmatized by being a single mother and having a gay ex-spouse. When she met Brian she felt reassured by his sexual interest, long-lasting erections, commitment to being an active stepfather, and desire for a baby. She assumed that his ejaculation problem would be cured by his becoming more relaxed and their commitment to getting married.

Brian had viewed ejaculatory inhibition as a sign of masculinity ever since adolescence. He had no difficulty ejaculating by himself during masturbation once or twice a day. The women he had been with were impressed by his sexual prowess, and friends were envious of the number of partners he had. Brian thought of himself as an unselfish lover, viewing foreplay and intercourse as focused on achieving the woman's orgasm. When women would manually or orally stimulate him, Brian did not find it erotic; in fact, he was put off.

Early in the relationship, Brian found Alisha's desire and sexual responsiveness very satisfying. However, a problem arose over their concern that they would not conceive if Brian failed to ejaculate. This quickly turned into a major stressor in their marriage. A "friend" of Alisha expressed concern about her choices of men, as she had first married a gay man and then a man who could not get her pregnant. During one of the couple's arguments, Alisha disclosed her friend's comment, and Brian responded defensively. He consulted the Internet, finding that it was easy to become pregnant by using his sperm through a basting tube to impregnate Alisha. Alisha was repulsed by the coldness of the technique; she wanted to become pregnant "naturally." The couple then consulted a fertility specialist, who fell into the trap of supporting Brian in the power struggle, based on the idea that whatever technique led to pregnancy was a success. They then consulted a minister, who also fell into the power struggle trap, this time supporting Alisha and stating that it was Brian's responsibility to resolve his ejaculatory problem so the couple could have children.

By the time Brian and Alisha consulted a psychologist with a specialty in CBCST, they felt alienated and had no sexual contact for over 3 months. In the first session, the clinician assessed the state of the marriage generally and the sexual relationship in particular. In the joint interview, the clinician asked each person's goals for their relationship, fears and concerns, and whether they were still consulting the fertility specialist, minister, or anyone else. The clinician emphasized that Alisha and Brian would need to commit to giving up the power struggle and work as an intimate team to develop a couple sexual style. Individual psychological/relational/sexual histories were scheduled to understand each person's emotional and sexual development and explore sensitive or secret issues. The most important thing to explore with Brian was what inhibited (interfered with) arousal/orgasm during couple sex, and to establish positive motivation for change based on being Alisha's sexual friend and wanting to have a child. The most important thing to explore with Alisha was her willingness to be Brian's intimate friend in resolving the SD, not just her desire to be pregnant. Her desire, pleasure, eroticism, and satisfaction enhanced Brian's appreciation for couple sexuality.

In the couple feedback session, Brian and Alisha developed a new narrative (understanding) about sexuality based on the therapist's input regarding factors influencing desire, arousal and orgasm. The therapist discussed how for years Brian's ejaculatory inhibition had positive effects in sexual relationships and contributed to his sexual self-esteem. However, now in their marital relationship it was interfering with his and Alisha's sexual enjoyment as well as their shared goal of having a child. Brian's rationalizing that his SD was not a big deal had to be confronted in an empathic and constructive manner.

As Brian focused on the advantages of being able to ejaculate during intercourse, the therapist guided the couple in setting up CBCST psychosexual skills exercises to engage in at home between therapy sessions. The key for Brian was to be aware of his subjective arousal, enhance pleasurable and erotic feelings, and transition to intercourse when there was an erotic flow. During the pleasuring exercises, Brian felt more aroused when he touched Alisha rather than being passive. For Brian, partner interaction arousal was more pleasurable than self-entrancement arousal. Brian was an active sexual participant during the exercises, and Alisha valued his "being present."

The therapist provided sex education regarding the importance of Brian focusing on stimuli that contributed to his arousal. The therapist asked him to be aware of orgasm triggers and use them during couple sex. Brian learned to create an erotic flow, and rather than trying to force orgasm, use his orgasm triggers to naturally extend his arousal, let go, and be orgasmic. He did this with Alisha's manual stimulation—using his trigger of a highly erotic fantasy, rhythmically moving his pelvis, and verbalizing how turned on he felt. In transferring this to intercourse, the key was not to transition to intercourse until his arousal was at an "8" level, to engage in multiple stimulation during intercourse, and to utilize his orgasm triggers. Alisha's arousal enhanced Brian's rather than the previous pattern of his distancing himself by "servicing" her. He learned to "piggy-back" his arousal on hers, which enhanced both partners' sexual satisfaction.

Intermittent Ejaculatory Inhibition

Intermittent ejaculatory inhibition (delayed ejaculation) is much more common than the primary form and increases with aging. The man finds subjective arousal waning, leading to increasing difficulty in reaching orgasm. He is confused about what is happening sexually, as it is a change from what he had previously experienced. This is compounded by the fact that because he does not ejaculate he eventually loses his erection. He becomes afraid that he is developing ED. As with other SDs, this can become a self-fulfilling prophecy. Sexual problems seldom remain static; unless addressed they become severe and chronic.

The sooner the man and couple confront intermittent ejaculatory inhibition the better. As with any SD, it is crucial to do a careful individual and couple assessment. Given that this is a secondary disorder, a careful inquiry about conditions that have changed is needed. There are two common causes. First, the man has developed a pattern (typically without realizing it) of approaching sex in a habitual manner, so he no longer experiences sufficient pleasure and arousal. Second, he has become increasingly distant from his partner (i.e., couple intimacy has decreased over time, often without the partners being aware of a slow erosion process) and obsessed with sex performance. Because the lack of intimacy and associated eroticism has manifested in insufficient arousal for consistent orgasms, he pushes harder to perform. This pressure, of course, backfires. The therapeutic intervention is to increase intimate, interactive sexuality, specifically making sexual requests. Another intervention is transitioning to intercourse at high levels of arousal and engaging in multiple types of stimulation during intercourse. CBCST addresses this through an integrated approach involving changing counterproductive cognitions, psychoeducation about sexual response, and psychosexual skills exercises. The following composite case example illustrates this approach.

Case Example: Grady and Susan

Grady began experiencing intermittent ejaculatory inhibition 4 years ago, when he was 53. He discussed the problem with his physician, who prescribed Viagra, which has become the all-purpose intervention for male SD. Grady found that Viagra improved his erectile confidence but had a negligible effect on orgasmic response. Susan was confused by Grady's inability to ejaculate and worried that he no longer found her sexually appealing. In an effort to reduce pressure on him, Susan purposely cut back her sexual interest and responsiveness. Although well intentioned, this compounded the problem. Both partners were experiencing inhibited desire, arousal, orgasm, and satisfaction by the time they sought help.

Ejaculatory inhibition is not discussed in the media or in medical or therapy journals. It was helpful when they consulted a CBCST clinician who correctly diagnosed the SD and its impact. He told Grady and Susan that if they built a new couple sexual style it could inoculate them against developing sexual problems as they aged. The therapist provided psychoeducation about ejaculatory inhibition and explained why Viagra was missing the mark. He commended Susan for trying to help, but suggested a different approach would have greater potential for success.

Rather than Grady treating ejaculatory inhibition as his problem alone, Susan was glad to step up to enhance their sexual relationship. Susan's sexual interest and responsiveness was an aphrodisiac for Grady. The therapist guided Grady in catching himself in counterproductive cognitions in which he held himself responsible for both partners' sexual satisfaction. It was a relief to Grady to be given permission to focus on conditions that aroused him. He "piggy-backed" his arousal on Susan's, a new sexual scenario for them. In addition, Grady requested both partner interaction and role enactment arousal. Playing out new sexual scenarios such as erotic dancing (striptease) and explicit sexual talk increased Grady's subjective arousal. The couple shifted to using multiple forms of stimulation: Grady manually stimulating Susan's clitoris; rubbing his penis between her breasts; and using erotic fantasies as a bridge to enhance erotic flow and Susan stimulating the head of his penis and testicles.

Grady was responsive to multiple stimulation during erotic sex, so it was natural that he also responded to multiple stimulation during intercourse. Grady had to challenge the standard that a "real man" only needs intercourse thrusting to be sufficiently aroused for orgasm. He learned that as men age they need partner stimulation, and Susan (whose orgasmic response was consistent when she received manual and oral stimulation) enjoyed intercourse more when she realized that Grady wanted and enjoyed her stimulation. This included kissing during intercourse, his stimulating her breasts and her stimulating his buttocks, his using erotic fantasies and her verbalizing how sexy she felt, and switching intercourse positions. Rather than expecting sex to be perfect, Grady and Susan transitioned to the GES criterion that Grady was orgasmic 85% of the time. When he was not, they still enjoyed the encounter. Most important, they felt satisfied as an intimate sexual team.

Treating Male Sexual Pain

When a man experiences painful ejaculation (e.g., pain in the tip of the penis during ejaculation, post-ejaculation headache), "dry" ejaculation (orgasm without ejaculation), or ejaculation without orgasm, a medical evaluation is warranted. This can be a symptom of an acute medical illness. For example, pain in the tip of the penis could indicate a prostate infection. From an integrative, biopsychosocial perspective, it is wise to consider physiological as well as psychological and relational factors. Including a physical therapist with a specialty in male pelvic musculature as part of the treatment team can be very helpful. The assessment and treatment of male sexual pain is in its infancy with the hope for more research and clinical insights.

Treating Male Hypersexual Behavior

Clinical Perspective

Hypersexual problems can involve a variety of behaviors such as compulsive masturbation that interferes with the sexual relationship, serial pornography use, and visiting prostitutes. There is considerable debate about whether this constitutes "sex addiction" and is a distinct dysfunction or is a feature of impulsive/compulsive behavior, obsessive-compulsive disorder, or a manic state. Although approaching deficits in sex behavior regulation with an "addiction" (12-step) model is helpful for some couples, we recommend addressing hypersexuality from an impulsive/compulsive perspective, with relationship features that include the individual's difficulty with intimacy and fear of vulnerability (Marcus, 2010). It is identified as a clinically significant problem if it interferes with the client's social, recreational, or occupational responsibilities; the individual's attempts to reduce or stop it have been unsuccessful; increasing time and resources are being spent on sex; more of the activity is needed to reach the same level of arousal; and the person is keeping the activities a secret from his partner (Braun-Harvey & Vigorito, 2015).

Men who turn to sex as a panacea for coping with stressful life experiences and emotional pain are in a self-defeating compulsive pattern (Leedes, 2001). Their sexual behavior is a symptom of unspoken, usually unrealized and unacknowledged, feelings. Sexually compulsive men pursue fulfillment of their emotional needs in a world that seems unyielding; seeking acceptance in a world that they experience as harsh, as well as control in a world that can be overpowering (Cooper & Marcus, 2003). The clinician looks for psychological pain and suffering beneath the man's sexual acting out. Men often use a "macho" rationale to justify their compulsive behavior (e.g., "Sex is part of being a real man" or "It's expected in my career to take clients to strip bars."). In addition, compulsive sexual behavior has been found to have co-morbidity with substance abuse, affective, anxiety, and attention deficit disorders, as well as a childhood history of attachment injuries and trauma (Marcus, 2010).

Prevalence

Compulsive sexual behavior is almost exclusively a male problem. About two-thirds of people with sexual acting-out problems use the Internet as a venue (Marcus, 2010). The types of online behavior vary, ranging from viewing photos and videos to sexual chat, to masturbating while sharing fantasies online, to arranging meetings for sex. Twenty percent of "netizens" engage in online sexual activity, and over fifteen percent of Internet pornography viewers have online problems (Cooper, Griffin-Shelley, Delmonico, & Mathy, 2001). The Internet has exceptional "power" to elicit sexual compulsivity because of easy accessibility, unlimited sexual variety, anonymity, and its "invitational" nature with the false promise of no real-life consequences.

Sexual Compulsivity as a Relationship Problem

Compulsive sexual behavior is detrimental for the man, as it can take up considerable time and undermine his behavior in many life roles, potentially compromise his health if he engages in risky sexual behavior, and subvert his intimate relationship. A male's pornography abuse and compulsive behavior that treats women as "sex objects" can distance him emotionally as well as physically from his partner. It is easy for a female partner to interpret the man's interest in pornography as infidelity. Without both partners understanding how he is using Internet sex to avoid the emotional vulnerability of a real intimate human relationship, the hypersexual behavior can take a major toll on the relationship (Marcus, 2010). A significant challenge for treatment involves the need to integrate eroticism into the couple relationship in a pro-intimate manner and increase his acceptance of genuine emotions within that relationship.

As important as working on intimacy in the relationship is, the conjoint therapy is unlikely to be sufficient to change the man's compulsive sexual behavior, as the physical and emotional arousal and orgasms provide strong reinforcement. Consequently, it is important for him to be involved in concurrent individual or group therapy, focusing on both the compulsive behavioral pattern (and his use of it to regulate emotional distress) and the underlying difficulty he has with intimacy. Men who engage in compulsive sexual behavior are in denial about its negative effects on them and their relationship. It is crucial for the clinician to guide the man in examining evidence of the harm that is caused. It will be more difficult for the man to deny negative effects if in joint sessions his partner expresses the pain she experiences and the therapist guides him in using empathic listening and reflection of her feelings. The man's willingness to engage in therapy provides reassurance for his partner that he finally is taking personal responsibility for his sexual behavior. It shifts his partner's negative attributions about his hypersexual behavior from it reflecting selfishness and a lack of caring to it being an expression of his inner vulnerability and turmoil. This does not mean that she needs to forgive him for his actions, but her increased empathy for his inner struggles increases her openness to collaborating with him in weaving her and their relationship into his life. This also reduces his experience of shame, opening him further to taking risks with emotional connection.

Assessment and Treatment

Marcus (2010) notes that individuals who engage in sexually compulsive behavior frequently experience shame regarding their actions and avoid disclosing it. Consequently, the clinician needs to be thorough but sensitive in inquiring about the frequency and types of compulsive behavior. Often it was the partner's discovery of the compulsive behavior that led the couple to seek therapy. Unfortunately, the man is likely to under-report the frequency and severity of his behavior, resulting in his taking limited responsibility for working on the problem. Increasing his motivation to acknowledge the scope of his compulsive behavior and address it is essential.

The therapist needs to establish rapport with both partners. It is important that the therapist demonstrate that he empathizes with the partner's distress regarding the man's sexual behavior and understands the impact that it has on the relationship, but at the same time is not condemning the man. The therapist conveys the goal of helping the couple understand the problem and the factors contributing to it, as well as guiding them in setting goals and cooperating to work toward those goals.

In an individual session with the man, the therapist needs to emphasize that if the man's goal is to change his sexual patterns in order to improve the relationship, the more the therapist learns about the scope of the compulsive sexual behavior the better. A caveat involves the ethical issue in couple therapy regarding handling of secrets disclosed by one partner. If the man discloses to the therapist that he is having an affair and engaging in risky sexual behavior, a therapist who holds such a secret is colluding with the man and unbalancing the couple therapy. Given ethical issues regarding confidentiality, therapists commonly deal with such complications by either stating to a couple during the initial consent procedure that they will not keep a secret *or* telling the couple that the clinician will keep a secret temporarily while assisting the person in preparing to disclose it to their partner.

Once the therapist understands the type and frequency of the individual's compulsive sexual behavior, he can discuss therapy goals with the couple. Some goals will involve the individual working on reducing effects of past traumatic relationship experiences and associated fears of intimacy and vulnerability. Those goals can be addressed in both individual therapy and couple therapy sessions. Other goals focus on building intimacy and shared erotic experiences.

Summary

Male SDs are multi-causal and multi-dimensional, with biological, psychological, relational, environmental, and cultural influences. Using a bio-medical intervention as a stand-alone treatment is limiting and often counterproductive. The biopsychosocial model of assessment, treatment, and relapse prevention is superior, because it simultaneously takes multiple causes into account. The man and his SD are addressed in an empathic, respectful manner, and his partner is invited to be his intimate and erotic ally in creating meaningful and enduring change.

Chapter 7

Relapse Prevention
Maintaining Gains and Enhancing Intimate Sexuality

Relapse prevention (RP) is an indispensable component of CBCST and has been applied extensively in the CBT field to maintain gains in treatment of diverse problems, such as substance abuse, smoking cessation, eating disorders, and sexually risky behaviors (Bowen, Chawla, & Marlatt, 2010; Marlatt & Donovan, 2005). It focuses on behavioral self-control strategies to teach individuals to maintain control over the behaviors by anticipating and managing potential relapse. Without an RP program, relapse rates are notoriously high for SD (Hawton, Catalan, Martin, & Fagg, 1986). Marlatt and Gordon (1985) identified risk factors for relapse including low self-efficacy, negative emotional states, interpersonal conflict, and anxiety.

RP and SD

Realistic expectations are the cognitive anchor for RP. To expect that the couple will never have another dysfunctional experience in which a man ejaculates rapidly or loses his erection or a woman experiences low desire or does not reach orgasm is unrealistic. Perfectionistic notions set the couple up for failure, sexual avoidance, and the blame-counter-blame cycle. The key to RP is to establish positive, realistic expectations, including that desire, pleasure, eroticism, and satisfaction are inherently variable. Whether once every ten times, once a month, or once a year, problems with sexual function will reoccur with almost all individuals and couples. Even when a couple has successfully resolved an SD, it is reasonable to expect that with the responsibilities of daily life (parenting, career, and household duties) the couple will experience variable sex. Without designing realistic, specific, measurable strategies to block this tendency to regress, disillusionment can easily occur.

The ultimate therapeutic goal is building a vital, resilient, and regular rhythm of sexual pleasure and satisfaction. Relapse involves the couple's return to pretreatment SD conditions, involving difficulties with sexual function in the areas of desire, arousal and/or orgasm, negative cognitions, distressed emotions, and sexual dissatisfaction. Developing an individualized RP plan is crucial to enduring desire and satisfaction. Traditionally, sex therapists and their clients ignored RP (McCarthy, 1990). Even treatment that had been helpful and effective was at high risk of relapse. A major contributor to regression after CBCST is the failure to build maintenance strategies (Hawton et al., 1986).

Comprehensive RP begins during the initial treatment planning and permeates the treatment process. It involves guiding the couple in understanding the purpose of the therapy interventions, drawing their attention to what they are learning during psychosexual skill homework, and identifying the specific factors that are contributing to progress so they can return to them when signs of relapse begin to appear.

RP Strategies: Preservation and Long-Term Growth Goals

Comprehensive RP maintains therapy gains, inoculates the couple against future SD, and promotes life-long sexual satisfaction. It involves two stages: (1) maintenance—*preservation strategies*; and (2) promotion of lifelong *growth strategies*. The gains preservation aspect has a micro-level focus, whereas the growth promotion aspect has a macro-level vision for relationship and sexual satisfaction. For purposes of preserving therapeutic gains, the couple is guided in developing a maintenance agreement that involves understanding the cognitive, behavioral, and emotional factors that promote sexual function and satisfaction. Consistent with the overall collaborative approach of CBCST, the therapist explicitly emphasizes that the couple need to pay attention throughout the therapy and notice what changes in their thinking, emotional responses, and behavior have contributed to improvement. They are encouraged, as homework, to keep logs of their observations about helpful interventions and what they have learned about conditions that lead to a satisfying sexual relationship. The couple decides what is necessary to ensure continued healthy sexual function. These represent "minimum daily requirements" for relationship and sexual health, similar to requirements for physical health. The preservation aspect of the RP plan involves identification of the partners' psychological and relationship needs for emotional and sexual health. An RP plan provides the couple clarity about the components of change that need to continue.

Promotion of long-term growth, the second component of an RP plan, extends this to the macro-level. The cognitive "scripts" of the RP plan are designed to promote "lifelong growth goals" such as Good Enough Sex (GES). During CBCST, couples with SD who have unrealistic assumptions and standards about sexual function develop realistic and constructive schemas, a macro-level change that influences how they think about their sexual relationship and behave toward each other. Their adoption of the GES model inoculates them from future distress when they experience dissatisfying or dysfunctional encounters.

Why Is RP So Important?

RP is based on a core concept that change is an ongoing process that is achieved by shifting conditions that are conducive to healthy functioning. One cannot assume that those shifts will continue "on automatic pilot" without conscious effort. It is akin to assuming that once an individual gains insight into causes of a problem behavior, this "aha!" experience will immediately change that behavior and maintain the change. A key premise in CBCST is that problematic and positive behaviors are shaped by the conditions in people's lives, and it is easy to slip back into dysfunctional patterns (especially if those were ingrained habits) unless effective cognitions, behaviors, and emotions are maintained.

The therapist teaches the couple that change is not "magic" but results from couple cooperation and requires intentionality, dedication, discipline, and flexibility. The therapist describes how making changes related to SDs is similar to changing any habitual response, such as shifting from a sedentary lifestyle to incorporate a routine of regular exercise. People readily understand how the client makes a good beginning by exercising three times per week, but in the midst of a busy life the routine slips away and stops. The therapist notes that couples who experience SDs are happy when they see their efforts in sex therapy paying off, maintaining the positive changes is challenging, so devising an RP plan is necessary. CBCST is an approach in which the couple's active participation and development of skills is essential.

As part of psychoeducation, the therapist describes the skills involved in modifying cognitions, emotional responses, and behaviors that are contributing to an SD. Understanding the factors involved in sexual desire, arousal, and orgasm allows the couple to work with the therapist to design a treatment program that is tailored to their needs. This includes developing psychosexual skills that promote emotional and sexual satisfaction. Psychoeducation also promotes cooperation, with each person recognizing her role and potential for influencing the SD. As each partner embraces that role and the power that comes with it, this counteracts perceptions of powerlessness and hopelessness that existed before CBCST. Reinforcing the components of the change program increases sexual confidence. However, drifting away from carrying out the program leads to regression. Rather than losing confidence, the couple resumes the activities that were working. This promotion of long-term growth provides inoculation against future SD and dissatisfaction.

RP provides structure to maintain therapeutic gains. Following the completion of therapy, it is helpful to schedule periodic check-in sessions (ideally at 6 month intervals for 2 years) during which the therapist inquires about the cognitive, behavioral, emotional, and interpersonal factors that foster individual functioning and relationship quality. This approach does not lead to the clients' dependence on the therapist; rather, it reinforces the responsibility that each client attends to sexual health.

Regarding lifelong growth goals, as therapy draws to a close the therapist collaborates with the couple in identifying "unfinished business" that the partners can keep in mind for further work, either on their own or with a professional. Because SDs typically have multiple causes, it is likely that a course of CBCST did not thoroughly address all of them. For example, the assessment may have determined that a major environmental influence on a couple's tendency to be distracted from erotic cues and to feel overwhelmed involves major stresses from their jobs. CBCST sessions can help them develop skills for coping with external distractions and protecting times for intimacy, but it is likely that the work pressures will persist. The couple may need additional help with the role strain they are experiencing. Similarly, CBCST can address an individual's sexual self-esteem problem, but it is not a substitute for psychotherapy for pervasive low self-esteem.

Although the clients are aware of individual or relational issues that could benefit from further professional assistance, the RP stage of CBCST provides a significant degree of closure, an "end point" to their work. This is an opportunity to celebrate their growth as an intimate sexual team. Consequently, the therapist takes the lead on tracking the couple's progress, from the initial problems to their current function and satisfaction. The therapist asks the partners to describe the changes, to be sure that they "own" them. Therapy typically begins with clients feeling distressed and discouraged, so this spotlight on progress and well-deserved praise for hard work boosts the couple's confidence and sense of self-efficacy.

Constructing an Individualized RP Plan

Comprehensive RP begins early in the therapeutic process, during assessment, feedback, case formulation, and treatment goal setting, and permeates throughout therapy. The therapist and couple discuss goals, strategies, their rationale, and steps along the therapeutic way. They discuss problems that arise, not only to make adjustments during therapy, but also to prepare for coping with signs of relapse after therapy has ended. If a couple ended treatment with an assumption that "we have solved our sexual problem," and an expectancy that they would not experience any problems in the future, this would be a setup for disappointment, anxiety, and hopelessness when the inevitable lapses occur. Building sexual comfort, skill, and confidence depends on expecting "bumps in the road" and not being destabilized by them. Closure in CBCST involves RP and scheduled "check-ins" with the therapist for an agreed-upon period.

The couple who understand the rationale and purpose for change interventions will be successful. They work as a team during the course of CBCST to implement a step-by-step change program. This perspective is compatible with "positive psychology" (Seligman, Rashid, & Parks, 2006; Lyubomirsky, Sheldon, & Schkade, 2005) and invites the couple to expand their focus from a problem-centered view of SD to working toward positive goals. Treatment involves targeted changes, cooperation, clarity about elements in the change process, and a broad perspective with hope and motivation. The last two therapy sessions focus on the couple developing an individualized RP plan. This is facilitated with a handout.

RP Strategies and Guidelines

1. Set aside quality couple time and discuss what you need to do individually and as a couple to maintain a satisfying and secure sexual relationship.
2. Every 6 months have a formal follow-up meeting either by yourselves or with a therapist to ensure you remain aware and do not slip back into unhealthy sexual attitudes, behaviors, or feelings. Set a new couple goal for the next 6 months.
3. Every 4–8 weeks plan a non-demanding, pleasuring, playful, or erotic date where there is a prohibition on intercourse. This allows the couple to experiment with new sensual stimuli (alternative pleasuring position, body lotion, or new setting), a playful scenario (sex play in the shower), or an erotic scenario (a different oral sex position or engaging in an asynchronous scenario rather than mutual sex). This reminds you of the value of sharing pleasure and developing a broad-based, flexible sexual relationship rather than focusing on intercourse as an individual pass–fail performance test.
4. Five to fifteen percent of sexual experiences are mediocre, dissatisfying or dysfunctional. That is normal, not a reason to panic or feel like a failure. Therefore, strive to maintain positive, realistic expectations about couple sexuality; this is a major RP resource.
5. Accept occasional lapses, but do not allow a lapse to become a relapse. Treat a dysfunctional sexual experience as a normal variation that can provide an important learning. Remember, you are a sexual couple, not a perfectly functioning sex machine. Whether once every 10 times, once a month, or once a

year, you will have a lapse and find sex dysfunctional or dissatisfying. Laugh or shrug off the experience and make a date in the next 1–3 days when you have the time and energy for an intimate, pleasurable, erotic experience. A relapse means giving up and reverting to the cycle of anticipatory anxiety, pass-fail intercourse performance, and frustration, embarrassment, and avoidance.

6. The importance of setting aside quality couple time—especially intimacy dates and a weekend away without children—cannot be overemphasized. Couples report better sex on vacation, validating the importance of getting away; even if it is only for an afternoon.

7. There is not "one right way" to be sexual. Each couple develops a unique style of initiation, pleasuring, eroticism, intercourse, and afterplay. Rather than treating your couple sexual style with benign neglect, be open to modifying or adding something new or special each year.

8. GES has a range from disappointing to great. The single most important technique in RP is to accept and not overreact to experiences that are mediocre, dissatisfying, or dysfunctional. Take pride in being sexually accepting and having a resilient couple sexual style.

9. Develop a range of intimate, pleasurable, and erotic ways to connect, reconnect, and maintain connection. These include five gears (dimensions) of touch.

    - Affectionate touch (clothes on)—kissing, hand-holding, hugging.
    - Non-genital sensual touch (clothed, semi-clothed, or nude)—massage, cuddling on the couch, touching before going to sleep or on awakening.
    - Playful touch (semi-clothed or nude)—mixing non-genital and genital touch—romantic or erotic dancing, touching while showering or bathing, "making out" on the couch, whole body massage.
    - Erotic, non-intercourse touch—using manual, oral, rubbing, or vibrator stimulation for high arousal and/or orgasm for one or both partners.
    - Intercourse—viewing intercourse as a natural continuation of the pleasuring/ eroticism process, not a pass-fail individual performance test. Transition to intercourse at high levels of erotic flow and utilize multiple stimulation during intercourse.

10. Keep your sexual relationship vital. Continue to make sexual requests and be open to exploring erotic scenarios. It is vital to maintain a flexible sexual relationship that energizes your bond and facilitates desire and desirability. Couples who share intimacy, non-demand pleasuring, erotic scenarios, and planned as well as spontaneous sexual encounters have a vital sexual relationship. The more ways in which you maintain an intimate sexual connection, the easier it is to avoid relapse (McCarthy, 2015).

Summarize the lessons that the couple learned from both the sessions and their homework experiences. The couple and therapist collaborate to highlight features that are valuable for growth, a list of potential barriers to continued sexual function, and positive strategies to maintain change. The couple adopts a regular clinical "check-in" with the therapist (e.g., every 6 months for 2 years) to support and maintain gains. Check-ins keep them accountable to each other, the therapist, and sexual growth. The RP plan establishes specific goals to ensure maintenance and inoculation from SD.

Cognitive, Behavioral, and Emotional Components in the RP Plan

We recommend that the therapist guide the couple in linking the knowledge and skills that they learned during therapy to an explicit and systematic written RP plan that the partners are committed to implement in order to maintain gains. A major advantage of a written plan is that it serves as "stimulus control," an explicit observable cue that reminds clients to engage in desired responses. Clients easily relate to the concept of a "reminder" (notes to themselves) to increase the likelihood that they will remember to complete tasks.

Cognitive component of the RP plan. The cognitive component highlights changes that the couple achieved in understanding sexual function throughout the CBCST process. This is based on psychoeducation regarding factors influencing female and male sexual response, understanding the rationale for how each step in the therapeutic process is designed to improve the quality of the sexual experiences, and development of sex-positive cognitions about oneself and their intimate relationship. It involves developing positive expectancies for sexual function based on understanding *modifiable* conditions that influence sexual response, adopting realistic standards for GES, challenging negative attributions that partners make about each other when their sexual interactions do not go well, and realizing that sexual difficulties need not create relationship alienation and distress. The cognitive restructuring that occurs throughout CBCST is explicitly built into the RP plan. Without the input from the therapist, couples drift toward paying less attention to their cognitions in daily life. People typically do not monitor and challenge their negative automatic thoughts until a therapist conveys the importance of doing so and teaches them skills for being their own therapist. Even clients who enthusiastically embrace the CBCST model and take an active role in monitoring and testing their cognitions regarding sexuality commonly need continued structure in an RP plan to maintain their gains.

Cognitive shifts that are important to maintain as part of an RP plan include valuing a pleasure rather than a performance orientation; perceiving the partner as an intimate sexual friend; seeking eroticism through knowledge of what each partner finds enticing; and feeling genuinely satisfied with GES, rather than pressure for perfect sex performance. It is crucial that the RP plan include a specific cognitive component of accepting that it is normal on occasion to not feel sexual desire or arousal. These are normal variations, not cues for anticipatory or performance anxiety. The therapist emphasizes the difference between a *lapse* (a temporary partial return to problematic functioning, which can be reversed through application of strategies used successfully during therapy) and a relapse. In the RP plan the couple's strategy for responding to a lapse is to approach their next sexual encounter with positive anticipation, relaxation, self-entrancement arousal, and enjoyment of a pleasurable build-up, erotic flow, transition to intercourse at high levels of arousal, and multiple stimulation during intercourse. Intercourse is the natural continuation of the pleasuring/eroticism process, not a pass-fail test.

In order for the positive cognitive orientation to persist after therapy ends, it is helpful for the therapist to guide the couple in writing a positive narrative (sexual script) as part of their RP plan. For example, she writes that she thinks of him as her intimate friend whose pleasure and arousal feed hers rather than as a demanding critic for whom she must perform. She welcomes his arousal rather than feeling intimidated by his erection. She enjoys both her arousal and his, celebrates her orgasm as well as his, and accepts that orgasms do not occur in a perfect sequence. She feels genuinely satisfied with the flexible standard of GES rather than striving for "perfect sex." Similarly, he focuses on eroticism and pleasure rather than worrying how his body or hers will respond. If he finds his mind drifting toward spectatoring and performance concerns, he focuses on pleasurable sensations of touching her or being touched, as well as letting her know what feels good. If he does not have an erection sufficient for intercourse, he asks for other forms of stimulation that feel good. The focus is pleasurable, flexible, variable couple sexuality.

Behavioral component of the RP plan. The behavioral component is grounded in the clients' awareness of conditions that contribute to sexual response, step-by-step psychosexual skills, and cooperation. This involves lifestyle modifications that are broader than changes in sexual behavior, such as ensuring friendly and positive moments when they reunite after a day's work, scheduling brief moments to relax as a couple, and ensuring regular intimate connection.

Behavioral components of sexual interaction include maintaining a regular rhythm of sexual experiences, blending self-entrancement arousal and partner interaction arousal, pacing with use of the "arousal continuum," not transitioning to intercourse until high levels of arousal, allowing the penis to acclimate to the vagina, and treating an episode of fast ejaculation or low desire as a lapse alerting the individual and couple to manage conditions such as progressive arousal. Central to the couple's cooperation in applying the psychosexual skills is their continued use of expressive and empathic listening skills. The RP includes a plan for when and how the couple decides to use the communication skills. Similarly, the RP plan will include the use of problem-solving skills. Given the link between couple conflict and SDs, it is crucial that the couple have reminders for identifying the first signs of conflict and ready access to the steps involved in a problem-solving discussion.

The challenge for the behavioral component is to use the skills in real-life sex. If a couple experiences a lapse in sexual function, they return to using the psychosexual skills in a structured way. They engage sexually at a relaxed pace, enjoying the sexual experience physically, emotionally, and relationally, varying intercourse positions and movements, and actively participating in the after play phase. Enjoying alternative scenarios of erotic sex or a cuddly, close scenario contributes to a pleasure-oriented rather than performance-focused approach to sex and helps prevent relapse.

Emotional component of the RP plan. In the CBCST model, partners' positive and negative emotional responses are key aspects of sexual function. Positive feelings toward a partner and sexual arousal are powerful experiences that lead individuals to anticipate future pleasure and seek it out. On the negative side, anxiety about anticipated performance problems, as well as possible rejection by the partner, detracts significantly from sexual desire, and results in avoidance of sex. Other negative emotions such as anger toward the partner can elicit either aggressive behavior or avoidance. Shame regarding past sexual victimization or present performance failure blocks positive sexual response and enjoyment. The CBCST procedures for treating a variety of female and male SDs consistently include assessment and intervention to reduce negative emotional responses and increase positive ones. The RP plan continues those efforts.

The emotional components of RP include continuing to counteract negative emotions (anxiety, anger, depression, and shame) that interfere with couple intimacy and sexual function, and to enhance positive emotions associated with affection, sensuality, and eroticism. It is unrealistic to expect that the couple will never experience life stresses and conflicts. Rather, the key is acceptance of those feelings and use of strategies for keeping them within reasonable bounds. Experiences of positive and negative emotions are not simply opposite ends of a single continuum. Decreasing negative emotions will not necessarily lead to an increase in positive feelings (Nezlek & Kuppens, 2008).

The strategies that therapists teach couples for regulating negative emotions are equally valuable for RP. Whereas there is evidence that trying to suppress one's negative emotions is ineffective, strategies that involve systematic attention to one's negative cognitions that elicit negative emotions and reappraising them work well (Nezlek & Kuppens, 2008). Challenging the validity of negative attributions about causes of sexual problems (e.g., that a partner's lack of arousal is due to a lack of love), testing the validity of negative expectancies (e.g., that relaxing one's body will lead to poor sexual performance) through logical analysis or a "behavioral experiment," and evaluating the disadvantages of perfectionistic sexual standards are examples of cognitive interventions that are a core component of an RP plan.

Couples include mindfulness and physical relaxation exercises in their RP plan to maintain regulation of negative emotions. In designing the written RP plan, the therapist reviews with the couple the specific mindfulness exercises that they found useful during the course of therapy and gains their commitment to continuing them on a regular basis (not only when distressed). It is repeated practice that makes those exercises most effective.

To maintain and further enhance positive emotions associated with satisfying sexual response and relationship quality, sensate focus/pleasuring and other mindfulness-oriented exercises are important components of an RP plan. The couple brainstorm a list of shared leisure activities that they can engage in that increase emotional intimacy. It is important to build in regular use of the psychosexual skills that were learned during therapy. Throughout the course of CBCST, the couple received the core message that sexual function does not exist in a vacuum; rather, it derives from a combination of relaxation, anticipation of pleasure, a collaborative and mutually respectful relationship, psychosexual skills for enhancing eroticism, and realistic expectations. The therapist stresses the importance of remembering the key role of positive emotions in satisfying sexuality.

RP Plan for Coping with Lapses

A key to successful RP is an explicit strategy for the couple's coping with inevitable lapses in sexual function. Success depends on their cooperating as an intimate team, accepting an occasional episode of SD as normal. A lapse is a single event, which can be expected and is not significant. A lapse is unlikely to become a relapse (a *pattern* of repeated problems in sexual response that is perpetuated by anticipatory anxiety, tense sex performance, and avoidance) if the couple adheres to their RP plan.

A useful way to reframe a *lapse* is to describe it as a "test" of the couple's growth and confidence. Lapses provide an opportunity to apply their knowledge and skills, which can reassure them that they have learned a lot about sexuality and have developed a positive frame of mind and skills for enjoying a satisfying sexual relationship regardless of their physical sexual response. By regrouping and resisting the tendency to panic, the couple reaffirms their coping skills and cooperates as an intimate sexual team. In fact, a couple's *full* acceptance of lapses would even include accepting temporary catastrophic thoughts such as "we're back at square one," telling oneself and each other that such extreme thoughts are unrealistic and then focusing on steps needed to settle down.

If a man does not have an erection sufficient for intercourse, it is important that the couple not relapse to responding in their old dysfunctional way. They are prepared to handle an episode of erectile failure with the cognitive, behavioral, emotional, and relationship skills that they learned through CBCST. He can regain an erection by relaxing his PM, asking his partner for a massage to relax his body, and focusing on sharing pleasure. Without panicking or apologizing, the partners transition to a sensual or erotic alternative scenario.

The *stress inoculation* approach to cognitive restructuring (Meichenbaum, 1985) is highly relevant for preparing couples to cope with lapses. It involves each individual identifying positive self-statements that he or she can rehearse and use at each stage of coping: (a) preparing for the stressor (e.g., "Just think about what I can do about it."); (b) confronting and handling the stressor (e.g., "Don't think about my stress, just about what I have to do."); (c) coping with feelings of being overwhelmed (e.g., "Relax and slow things down."); and (d) evaluation of coping efforts and self-rewards (e.g., "I am pleased with the progress I'm making."). Because the couple's task is to cope effectively with lapses as a team, the stress inoculation cognitions include positive *dyadic coping* (e.g., "When we work as a team, we can handle this." "We can relax and cuddle; no need to do more than that to enjoy our time together.").

The couple accept that this disappointing encounter will not flow to intercourse or orgasm, adapt their lovemaking, and continue to pleasure, touch, and stay connected. Anticipating lapses provides the couple strategies to prevent relapse. With this balanced view of their relationship and sexuality, they let it be an "oops" event. Later they calmly discuss whether the dysfunction was simply a random event or whether there are adjustments to employ the next time they make love. These include taking time to emotionally and physically relax, enjoy pleasuring, using multiple forms of stimulation, or trying a new erotic scenario. In constructing the RP plan, the therapist encourages the couple to smile or shrug off the negative experience and make a date in the next 1 - 3 days when they have the time, are not distracted or fatigued, and bring energy for a sensual or erotic experience.

A common strategy is to "back up" one step in the sensate focus/pleasuring exercises. If she felt distracted by work stresses and experienced difficulty focusing on sexual pleasure, the couple back up to soothing sensual touching. If he lost his erection as they began intercourse, they agree to back up to relaxed body pleasuring, followed by self-entrancement focus for an easy erection. The important feature is that they practice positive thinking and cooperative behavioral strategies.

A *"relapse"* consists of a series of consecutive experiences in which sexual function and relationship cooperation collapse and the couple becomes trapped in the dynamics that initially caused and maintained their SD—spectatoring, performance anxiety, and alienation. The RP plan includes the criteria for defining a relapse and steps that the couple can take under those conditions. When they conclude that they have slipped into a relapse, they review CBCST steps that they completed successfully and spend time practicing them anew. If their efforts do not result in noticeable progress, they seek professional assistance. It is important that they challenge their negative cognitions about the relapse, as even this return to problematic functioning does not signify a lack of benefit from their prior treatment. The substantial sexual knowledge and skills that they developed will be highly useful in recovering from the relapse.

The following are types of agreements that couples commonly find helpful as components of their RP plans:

1: Holding Couple "Motivation Meetings"

Have regular times (every month) to discuss their relationship and make adjustments. These can be brief but emphasize specific ways to nourish their relationship and maintain a priority on partnership. Discussing relationship issues and using constructive skills is important for satisfaction. An advantage of CBCST is that it engages the partners in regularly having serious communication about their relationship. Motivational meetings in the RP plan orient the couple toward continuing to devote time and energy to nurturing and enhancing their intimate sexual relationship.

2: Having "Check-In" Meetings

Planning a 6-month follow-up (between the couple or ideally with a therapist) helps them remain committed and accountable to quality, satisfying sex. This increases the likelihood that the couple will not slip back into unhealthy sexual cognitions, behaviors, or emotional responses. The biggest trap for couples who make progress in therapy is drifting back into treating sexuality with benign neglect. If they do not pay attention, sex can regress to marginal quality, performance-orientation, and infrequency.

During a check-in meeting, the couple reviews their RP plan to (a) assess their degree of compliance with its details, (b) reinforce gains by explicitly praising themselves and each other for progress, and scheduling a reward such as a celebratory dinner out, and (c) reinforce feelings of individual and couple satisfaction.

3: Scheduling Couple Dates

The importance of scheduling and carrying out quality couple time, especially nurturing relational intimacy, cannot be emphasized enough. For couples with children, it is especially important to set aside quality couple time. Although this can involve special events such as a weekend getaway without the children once a year, it is even more important to schedule frequent activities such as a night out together each week or two. Couples often report better sex on vacations, validating the importance of getting away, even for an afternoon.

Couple time can include going for a walk, having a sexual date, going to dinner, having an intimate talk, or just being with each other for an hour or two. The RP plan includes a list of couple activities including a number that are inexpensive and easily carried out. The therapist coaches the couple in generating a diverse list of couple activities for couple time.

4: Scheduling Touch and Pleasuring Dates

Setting aside times for pleasuring sessions (with a prohibition on intercourse and orgasm) reinforces communication, sensuality, and playfulness, and is a vivid reminder that an intimate physical relationship is much more than intercourse. This allows the couple to enjoy sensuality and experiment with new scenarios: an alternative pleasuring position, body lotion, a new setting or milieu. Keep the focus on pleasure and flexibility, rather than performance, to combat relapse.

5: Scheduling "Regular Sex": Reserving Time and Energy for Sex

Maintaining a regular frequency of sex requires planning. Sex can become a low priority, set aside until the partners have tended to everything else in their lives—children, school, work, social lives, community and religious responsibilities, relatives, yard work, shopping, haircuts. Sex is easily displaced when the members of the couple are exhausted and thinking "our work is never done." When their daily life is filled with competing responsibilities and little respite, sex is unlikely to feel special or energizing.

In an RP plan, it is important to include a goal of looking for windows of opportunity for sex in the couple's busy, complicated lives. It means attaching positive value to engaging in sex during the week, no matter what joys and stresses have occurred during the day—an ill child, work stresses, a flat tire, bad weather, the house needs cleaning. It is crucial that the couple not allow sex to be undermined by the responsibilities and vicissitudes of life, emphasizing that intimacy and sexuality is "our time." However, harried couples become defensive if the therapist suggests that protecting time for sex should be easy. Although theoretically it is preferable to save personal energy and alertness for regularly scheduled sex, it is important that the first priority is to spend intimate time together, whether one is feeling wonderful or tired. Reasonable expectations are essential. Planning ahead can help partners reserve energy and anticipate pleasure.

In addition to the challenge of having *sufficient time and energy* for sex, the couple needs to address concerns that they have about *scheduling* sex. Spontaneous sex is widely valued, as its impulsiveness is viewed as "authentic" and "genuine." The passion associated with thoughts of "I'm wanted," "Take me," "I'm needed," "I have to have you," is powerful. However, given the realities of couples' hectic lives, it is not realistic to expect that such moments will be frequent. Premeditated scheduling is necessary to ensure regularly occurring sex. Some partners have difficulty accepting this, as they view scheduling as "unromantic." Consequently, therapists need to discuss partners' cognitions about including regular scheduling of sex. When a client replies that it seems unromantic, the therapist can discuss, conveying empathy, how it will not be romantic if the couple rarely has sex and relapses into their prior pattern of disengagement. The therapist conveys the special value in scheduling, as each partner *chooses* to be there and *wants* to please the other, even when the mood is not "right." It also is helpful to point out that the desire for spontaneity is a desire for "vacation sex," which, ironically, most couples have to schedule but enjoy because they made a special effort to set aside time for themselves.

Regular sex as the intimacy blender. A requirement for blending real-life events and sex is regular frequency and a repertoire of intimacy, pleasuring, and eroticism. Rather than being boring, lethargic, or perfunctory, sex in the context of a committed relationship is honest and genuine, adapted to the rhythm of life. Sex can be lustful, respectful, passionate, tender, playful, soothing, or experimental. Couples who permit life's stresses and irritations to override regular sex are at risk of demoralization and alienation. Sex produces enduring benefits such as comfort, diversion, relaxation, trust, pleasure, cooperation, and intimacy. Older couples describe sex as "rebellion" against the limitations of aging (e.g., arthritis, fatigue). Deep respect for sex and the human experience includes encounters that celebrate the meaning of life.

Regularly occurring sex is essential to the GES model. When sexual frequency is a steady "hell-or-high-water" reliable experience, it serves as an "intimacy blender" that integrates the partners' full range of feelings and meanings amid the challenges of real life. Committed couples do not keep their moods and stresses from their bedroom. Rather, these have a place in their lovemaking. For example, when an individual is feeling anxious due to life circumstances, the partner's serene focus on physical relaxation and pleasure brings tension release. When a partner is sad about a personal loss, large or small, the calmness of soothing touch brings reassurance of an enduring positive base in one's life. When partners are irritated with each other after an argument, the touch of reconciliation (conveying enduring love in spite of conflict) transforms the annoyance to contentment. When a couple does not allow anxiety, depression, or irritation to prevent regular sex, the GES model plays an important role in their coping well with life's challenges.

When the relationship is grounded in cooperation, regular sex can "seal the deal" and ensure closeness. "Bonding" hormones (e.g., oxytocin) are released during sex (Pfaus, 2009). In a positive feedback loop, partners who deeply care for each other have GES experiences, and the intimate experience reinforces their loving feelings.

Constructing Life-Long Growth Strategies

To preserve gains achieved during CBCST, couples understand the lapse versus relapse process, identify situations that pose a high risk for relapse, specify coping strategies, and implement behavioral procedures as an intimate team to adapt flexibly to occasional episodes of SD. For life-long growth, it is important for the couple to be aware of the factors that promote sexual desire and function, and to carry them out on a regular basis with conscious intent.

Reviewing the GES guidelines semi-annually promotes long-term sexual growth. Because there is not one right way to be sexual, each couple develops their unique style of initiation, pleasuring, eroticism, intercourse, and afterplay that meets both partners' needs, flexibly adapts to the changes in their lives, and energizes their relationship. The more flexible their couple sexual style and the more they accept the multiple functions of touching and sexuality, the greater resistance they have to relapse. Expectations include accepting that long-term sexual satisfaction varies. The challenge is to accept disappointing or dysfunctional experiences without panicking or blaming. Satisfied couples accept occasional mediocre or disappointing experiences and take pride in having a resilient sexual style.

Principles for Lifelong Sexual Satisfaction

An effective RP plan not only includes strategies for maintaining the gains achieved during CBCST; it also provides *principles and methods for future growth in their sexual relationship*. An excellent source of information for designing a growth-oriented approach is research conducted by Kleinplatz and Menard (2007), in which a sample of older couples was interviewed in detail about their long-term relationships and asked to reflect on their "great" sexual moments. Qualitative analyses of the participants' interview responses provided valuable insights into "building blocks" for satisfying sexuality across the lifespan (Kleinplatz, 2010). Rather than high intensity desire and orgasm based on superior sex skills, what made people great lovers was their adherence to a GES approach to sex and a deep appreciation for the emotional and interpersonal factors that contribute to it. The eight components of optimal sexuality that Kleinplatz and Menard (2007) identified were: (1) being completely present and immersed in the sexual experience; (2) being highly connected emotionally with one's partner to the extent of feeling merged; (3) experiencing deep erotic intimacy through mutual respect, caring, acceptance, and admiration; (4) developing extraordinary communication, mutual empathy, and sharing of themselves throughout their encounters; (5) being willing to take risks in exploring sexuality and expanding sexual boundaries together; (6) creating a safe place for both partners to be genuine, uninhibited, and totally oneself; (7) letting oneself be vulnerable and swept away by the sensual experience with the partner; and (8) reaching a level of transcendence, bliss and timelessness characteristic of a peak life experience. It is crucial to understand that many of the individuals who described these experiences were suffering from illnesses and physical disabilities, and the sexual behaviors often did not involve intercourse. These characteristics are quite consistent with CBCST and the GES model. They are based on a high level of acceptance and enjoyment of one's experiences *as they are*, rather than a focus on performance. They are founded on an intimate relationship in which partners deeply appreciate each other and are happy to share their lives. CBCST clinicians encourage couples to include this set of "lessons" as guidelines in the RP plan for future growth.

Kleinplatz and Menard (2007) focus on principles and processes that are especially relevant for older couples, but are equally relevant for preventing relapses among couples of all ages who want to not only maintain therapeutic gains but also continue their sexual growth. The lessons are summarized in Table 7.1.

Table 7.1 Lessons for Current Functioning and Long-term Optimal Sexuality

---

1. *Great lovers are made, not born.* Individuals are not naturally good lovers, but improve over time based on experience and a high level of motivation to enhance couple sexuality. It often involves unlearning ideas and approaches from earlier in life, especially limited sexual scripts. With maturity comes greater self-knowledge (e.g., knowing what one desires sexually), comfort and ability to communicate effectively.

2. *Optimal sexuality flourishes in the context of a relationship deepening with time.* Over time, as the partners develop an increasingly intimate, equitable, trusting, respectful relationship, they enjoy open, empathic communication. Forming a deep bond through shared life experiences creates intimate and highly satisfying sex.

(Continued)

3. *Less willing to settle.* This involves a clearer sense over time of what one wants in a partner in general and sexually in specific. This includes discarding traditional gender roles for equitable roles in their sexual relationship. It is counter to the stereotyped view of male sexuality and the double standard.

4. *Great sex takes a lot of time, devotion, and intentionality.* This guideline emphasizes prioritizing sex and setting aside time for it. Planning and preparation (creating a sensual atmosphere) is important. As couples age, they may have sex less often but spend more time together when they do. This lack of spontaneity does not detract from the quality of the sex; rather, the intentional focus on being together and anticipation of pleasure increase satisfaction.

5. *Both exploration and familiarity have value.* Although popular media emphasize the excitement of trying new things sexually (e.g., new intercourse scenarios and positions), there are more subtle discoveries as partners do familiar things but reveal more of their subjective feelings and desires. The pressure to be innovative is counterproductive. Familiarity can create trust and comfort so that when a transient sexual problem occurs the couple will not be distracted and upset. Within that atmosphere of trust and safety, partners learn more about each other as sexual beings and enjoy those discoveries.

6. *Aging, chronic illness, and disability are not necessarily obstacles to optimal sexuality.* Individuals' perceptions of their mature skills as lovers, as well as being sexual in spite of illnesses and physical disabilities, are more important in sexual satisfaction than health conditions. When people shift their definitions of sexiness beyond traditional youth and physical attractiveness standards, they feel positive about themselves as sexual beings (Kleinplatz, 2010).

Structuring the RP Plan

CBCST is based on learning principles, and one of the key concepts (*stimulus control*) relevant to RP is that desired behaviors are more likely to occur when there are cues to remind the individuals of the time and place for those actions. The homework assignments that are used throughout CBCST typically include a written reminder that the couple takes home with them. The same process is very important for effective RP. The therapist and couple collaborate in designing and writing an RP plan that has several components and specific guidelines to follow. Even though the RP plan is written toward the end of therapy, the therapist begins identifying material for it soon after beginning treatment. The ongoing assessment reveals the couple's particular issues, barriers to progress, and changes that have contributed to their progress. RP is not a separate disconnected stage of therapy but rather a natural extension of interventions throughout treatment.

Components of the Written RP Plan

We recommend that the written RP plan include the following components. The items are tailored to the needs and experiences of each couple.

Initial sexual presenting concerns. CBCST emphasizes identification of specific client concerns and goals that are assessed for degree of progress. The RP plan including a brief summary of the concerns that the couple presented at intake, which helps them maintain perspective on where they started, what progress was achieved, and what their potential vulnerabilities for relapse may be. For example, if a couple sought therapy because the male was experiencing ED, and the couple's coping pattern had been avoidance of sex, noting this in the RP plan highlights the progress that they made and keeps the partners attuned to signs of a lapse or relapse.

Signs of a lapse/relapse. The couple list warning signs that they may be experiencing a lapse, and if the pattern becomes chronic, a relapse. The members of the couple identify signs such as "Greg gets physically aroused during kissing and manual stimulation, but loses the erection quickly when we move into position to begin intercourse," and "Greg and Laurie have decreased giving each other seductive cues that they are interested in having sex."

Potential barriers to sexual function. Based on what the couple learned through CBCST, they list key barriers to sexual function. These include (a) *negative cognitions* (e.g., a focus on sexual performance), (b) *an absence of positive cognitions* (e.g., no fantasies and positive anticipation of sexual pleasure; no stress-inoculation self-talk used when experiencing an incident of SD), (c) *negative emotions* (e.g., anger at oneself for any instance of SD, anxiety from anticipating disappointing one's partner), (d) *an absence of positive emotions* (e.g., little attention to erotic feelings), (e) *negative behavior* (e.g., avoidance, criticizing one's partner for low sexual desire), (f) *an absence of positive behavior* (e.g., a deficit in expressive and empathic listening skills), (g) *physical health problems* (e.g., arthritis, side effects from antihypertensive medication), and (h) *environmental stressors* (e.g., job stress, child-rearing responsibilities). A systematic review of these factors is well worth the effort, as it maintains the couple's awareness of the multi-dimensional factors that influence sexual response and reminds them of CBCST strategies that they have found helpful and can use in the future to protect them from relapse.

Lessons regarding factors contributing to lifelong sexual satisfaction. For this component of the RP plan, the therapist can give the partners copies of a handout ("Lessons from Great Lovers" or "GES Guidelines for Sexual Satisfaction"). This is an opportunity for the therapist to reinforce the psychoeducation that has been taking place throughout the course of therapy, discussing each guideline and how it applies to them in particular. This discussion may take most of a therapy session and can contribute to a sense of closure.

General strategies to maintain gains from therapy. Based on successful experiences during therapy, the therapist and couple devise a set of strategies that the partners commit to carrying out in the future to maintain progress and create opportunities for further growth. Table 7.2 illustrates an example of such a set of strategies. The partners usually agree to alternate who leads the discussions.

Specific psychosexual skill exercises to use periodically as a "refresher." The therapist and couple review a list of all of the psychosexual exercises that the couple used during the therapy and select 2–4 to include in the RP plan as resources that the couple can use on an as-needed "refresher" basis. For example, if one or both clients are prone to anxiety, they include breathing, physical relaxation, and mindfulness exercises. If they tend to pay too little attention to physical sensations, they can include pelvic muscle training and sensate focus exercises. If a man has residual self-doubts regarding ED, the couple include further use of the "Developing Your Erotic Continuum" exercise and the "Wax and Wane" exercise.

Plan for coping with lapses. Given that the couple has identified the signs of a potential lapse that they will monitor and has developed a range of strategies for maintaining gains and responding promptly to a lapse, the final component of the RP plan is a set of coping steps. These typically are (1) whoever first notices signs

Table 7.2 Example of Relapse Prevention Plan Strategies to Maintain Therapy Gains

Item	Schedule
• Talk about relationship engagement and satisfaction	First weekend of each month
• Reminder session: review positive, realistic expectations about sex, as well as "lessons from great lovers" and GES guidelines	First weekend of each month, as part of meeting about relationship quality
• Set aside "Pleasuring Sessions"	Once a month
• Practice communication skills	Every other month
• Hold "Couple Motivation Meeting"	Every 6 months
• Date night: Schedule couple time	Every other week
• Engage in a non-intercourse erotic scenario	Monthly
• Schedule sessions for saturating each other with touch	Monthly
• Expand sexual repertoire (e.g., showering together, "quickies")	Quarterly
• Attend church couple group to maintain social support	Weekly

of a possible lapse mentions it to the partner; and they discuss what was observed, deciding whether to take corrective steps immediately or to "keep an eye on it" for 2 weeks; (2) when the partners agree that a lapse seems to be occurring, they set a time to meet to calmly review their RP plan and share their perceptions about factors that might be contributing to the problem; (3) they select one or more exercises that have worked well in the past and set aside times to engage in them; (4) after an agreed-upon amount of time (in weeks), they have a "check-in" meeting to reassess current signs of the lapse, and make a decision to continue the current strategies, shift to different strategies, or schedule a "booster" session with their therapist. Throughout the process, it is important for the couple to talk together about the growth they have experienced in their sexual relationship since seeking therapy and to remind each other of their personal and relationship strengths. CBCST emphasizes valuing desire/pleasure/eroticism/satisfaction and putting time, energy, and communication to maintain gains and grow their intimate sexual relationship.

References

Abramowitz, J., Baucom, D., Boeding, S., Wheaton, M., Pukay-Martin, N., Fabricant, L., Paprocki, C., & Fischer, M. (2013). Treating obsessive-compulsive disorder in intimate relationships. *Behavior Therapy, 44*, 395–407.

Adams, M., & Robinson, W. (2001). Shame reduction, affect regulation, and sexual boundary development. *Sexual Addiction and Compulsivity, 8*, 45–78.

Agronin, M., & Robinson, W. (2014). Sexuality and aging. In Y. Binik & K. Hall (Eds.), *Principles and practice of sex therapy* (5th ed., pp. 525–539). New York: Guilford.

Allen, E., Atkins, D., Baucom, D., Snyder, D., Gordon, K., & Glass, S. (2005). Intrapersonal, interpersonal, and contextual factors in engaging in and response to extramarital involvement. *Clinical Psychology: Science and Practice, 12*, 101–130.

Althof, S. (2003). Therapeutic weaving: The integration of treatment techniques. In S. Levine, C. Risen, & S. Althof (Eds.), *Handbook of clinical sexuality for mental health professionals.* (pp. 259–276). New York: Guilford.

Althof, S., Abdo, C., Dean, J., Hackett, G., McCabe, M., McMahon C, ... Tan, H. (2010). International Society for Sexual Medicine's guidelines for the diagnosis and treatment of premature ejaculation. *Journal of Sexual Medicine, 7*, 2947–2969.

Althof, S., & Rosen, R. (2007). Combining medical and psychological interventions for the treatment of erectile dysfunction. In S. Leiblum (Ed.), *Principles and practice of sex therapy* (4th ed., pp. 151–166). New York: Guilford.

Althof, S., Rosen, R., Rubio-Aurioles, E., Earle, C., & Chevret-Measson, M. (2006). Psychological and interpersonal aspects and their management. In H. Porst & J. Buvat (Eds.), *Standard practice in sexual medicine* (pp. 18–30). Talden, MA: Blackwell.

Althof, S., & Wieder, M. (2004). Psychotherapy for erectile dysfunction. *Endocrine, 23*, 131–134.

Ameli, R. (2014). *25 lessons in mindfulness.* Washington, DC: American Psychological Association.

American Psychiatric Association (2014). *Diagnostic and statistical manual-V.* Washington, DC: American Psychiatric Association.

Annon, J. (1974). *The behavioral treatment of sexual problems.* Honolulu: Enabling Systems.

Aschka, C., Himmel, W., Ittner, E., & Kochen, M. (2001). Sexual problems of male patients in family practice. *Journal of Family Practice, 50*, 773–778.

Ashton, A. (2007). The new sexual pharmacology. In S. Leiblum (Ed.), *Principles and practice of sex therapy* (4th ed., pp. 509–541). New York: Guilford.

Aubin, S., & Heiman, J. (2004). Sexual dysfunction from a relationship perspective. In J. Harvey, A. Wenzel, & S. Sprecher (Eds.), *The handbook of sexuality in close relationships* (pp. 477–517). Mahwah, NJ: Lawrence Erlbaum.

Avis, N., & McKinlay, S. (1995). The Massachusetts women's sexual health study. *Journal of the American Medical Women's Association, 50*, 45–63.

Bach, A., Brown, A., & Barlow, D. (1999). The effects of false negative feedback on advocacy expectations and sexual arousal in sexually functional males. *Behavior Therapy, 30*, 79–95.

Bach, P., & Brannigan, D. (2016). The impact of lifestyle modifications on erectile dysfunction. In L. Lipshultz, A. Pastuszak, A. Goldstein, A. Giraldi, & M. Perelman (Eds.), *Management of sexual dysfunction in men and women* (pp. 134–155). Bloomington, IN: Indiana University.

Balon, R., & Segraves, R. (2005). *Handbook of sexual dysfunction.* New York: CRC.

Bancroft, J. (2009). *Human sexuality and its problems* (3rd ed.). Edinburgh: Churchill Livingstone.

Bancroft, J., Herbenick, D., & Reynolds, M. (2003). Masturbation as a marker of sexual development. In J. Bancroft (Ed.), *Sexual development in children* (pp. 134–155). Bloomington, IN: Indiana University.

Bancroft, J., & Vukadihovil, Z. (2004). Sexual addiction, sexual compulsivity, or what? *Journal of Sex Research, 41,* 225–234.

Barbach, L. (1975). *For yourself: A woman's guide to sexual fulfillment.* New York: Doubleday.

Barlow, D. (1986) Causes of sexual dysfunction: The role of anxiety and cognitive interference. *Journal of Consulting and Clinical Psychology, 54,* 140–148.

Barlow, D. (1988). *Anxiety and its disorders.* New York: Guilford.

Basson, R. (2001). Using a different model for female sexual response to address women's problematic low sexual desire. *Journal of Sex and Marital Therapy, 27,* 395–403.

Basson, R. (2007). Sexual desire/arousal disorders in women. In S. Leiblum (Ed.), *Principles and practice of sex therapy* (4th ed., pp. 25–53). New York: Guilford.

Basson, R. (2010). Women's difficulties with low sexual desire, sexual avoidance, and sexual aversion. In S. Levine, C. Risen, & S. Althof (Eds.), *A handbook of clinical sexuality for mental health professionals* (2nd ed., pp. 159–179). New York: Routledge.

Baucom, D., & Epstein, N. (1990). *Cognitive-behavioral marital therapy.* New York: Brunner/Mazel.

Baucom, D., Epstein, N., Kirby, B., & LaTaillade, J. (2015). Cognitive behavioral couple therapy. In A. Gurman, J. Lebow, & D. Snyder (Eds.), *Clinical handbook of couple therapy* (5th ed., pp. 23–60). New York: Guilford.

Baucom, D., Epstein, N., Rankin, L., & Burnett, C. (1996). Assessing relationship standards: The Inventory of Specific Relationship Standards. *Journal of Family Psychology, 10,* 72–88.

Baumeister, R., Catanes, K., & Vohs, K. (2001). Is there a gender difference in strength of sex drive? *Personality and Social Psychology Review, 5,* 242–273.

Beck, A. (1993). *Cognitive therapy and the emotional disorders.* New York: Penguin.

Beck, J. (2011). *Cognitive therapy: Basics and beyond* (2nd ed.) New York: Guilford.

Bernstein, D., Borkovec, T., & Hazlett-Stevens, H. (2000). *New directions in progressive relaxation training.* New York: Greenwood.

Bergeron, S., Rosen, N., & Pukall, C. (2014). Genital pain in women and men. In Y. Binik & K. Hall (Eds.), *Principles and practice of sex therapy* (5th ed., pp. 159–176). New York: Guilford.

Bergeron, S., Khalife, S., & Dupuis, M. (2008). A randomized comparison of cognitive therapy and medical management of provoked vestibulodynia. *Obstetrics and Gynecology, 111,* 159–166.

Berry, M., & Berry, P. (2014). Integrative approaches to the treatment of erectile dysfunction. *Current Sexual Health Reports, 6,* 114–123.

Bertozzi, S., Londero, A., Fruscalzo, A., Driul, L., & Marchesoni, D. (2010). Prevalence and risk factors for dyspeurunia and unsatisfying sexual relationships in a cohort of primiparous and secondiparous women after 12 months postpartum. *International Journal of Sexual Health, 22,* 47–53.

Binik, Y. (2010). The diagnostic criteria for vaginismus. *Archives of Sexual Behavior, 39,* 278–291.

Binik, Y., & Hall, K. (2014). *Principles and practice of sex therapy* (5th ed.). New York: Guilford.

Bodenmann, G. (2005a). Dyadic coping and its significance for marital functioning. In T. Reverson, K. Kayser, & G. Bodenmann (Eds.), *Couples coping with stress* (pp. 33–49). Washington, DC: American Psychological Association.

Bodenmann, G. (2005b). *Stress and coping in couples.* Gottinger, Germany: Hogrefe.

Bodenmann, G., Atkins, D., Schar, M., & Poffet, V. (2010). The relationship between daily stress and sexual activity. *Journal of Family Psychology, 24,* 271–279.

Bodenmann, G., Pihet, S., & Kayser, K. (2006). The relationship between dyadic coping, marital quality, and sexual activity. *Journal of Family Psychology, 20,* 485–493.

Boul, L. (2007). Sexual function and relationship satisfaction. *Sexual and Relationship Therapy, 22,* 209–220.

Bowen, S., Chawla, H., & Marlatt, G. (2010). *Mindfulness-based relapse prevention for addictive behaviors.* New York: Guilford.

Braun-Harvey, D., & Vigorito, M., (2015). *Out of control male sexual behavior.* New York: Springer.

Bradbury, T., & Fincham, F. (1992). Attributions and behavior in marital intervention. *Journal of Personality and Social Psychology, 63,* 613–628.

Brock, G., McMahon, C., Chen, K., Costigan, T., Shen, W., & Watkins, V. (2002). Efficacy and safety of tadanifel for the treatment of erectile dysfunction. *Journal of Urology, 168,* 1332–1336.

Brotto, L., & Heiman, J. (2007). Mindfulness in sex therapy. *Sexual and Relationship Therapy, 22,* 3–11.

Brotto, L., & Kingsberg, S. (2010). Sexual concerns of cancer survivors. In S. Levine, C. Risen, & S. Althof (Eds.), *Handbook of clinical sexuality for mental health professionals* (2nd ed., pp. 329–347). New York: Routledge.

Brotto, L., & Luria, M. (2014). Sexual/interest arousal disorder in women. In Y. Binik & K. Hall (Eds.), *Principles and practice of sex therapy* (5th ed., pp. 17–41). New York: Routledge.

Brotto, L., & Woo, J. (2010). Cognitive-behavioral and mindfulness-based therapy for low sexual desire. In S. Leiblum (Ed.), *Treating sexual desire disorders.* (pp. 148–164). New York: Guilford.

Bulik, C., Baucom, D., & Kirby, J. (2012). Treating anorexia nervosa in the couple context. *Journal of Cognitive Psychotherapy, 26,* 19–33.

Burns, D. (2008). *Feeling good.* New York: Harper.

Buss, D. (1995). *The evolution of desire: Strategies of human mating.* New York, Basic Books.

Byers, S., & Grenier, G. (2003). Premature or rapid ejaculation: Heterosexual couples' perceptions of men's ejaculatory behavior. *Archives of Sexual Behavior, 32,* 261–270.

Byers, S., & Grenier, G., (2004). Premature or rapid ejaculation. *Archives of Sexual Behavior, 32,* 261–270.

Calhoun, L., & Tedeschi, R. (2006). *Handbook of posttraumatic growth.* Mahwah, NJ: Erlbaum.

Campbell, T. (2005). Improving physical health through family intervention. In P. McKenry & S. Price (Eds.), *Families and change: Coping with stressful events and transitions* (3rd ed., pp. 103–127). Thousand Oaks, CA: Sage.

Chivers, M., Seto, M., Lalumiere, M., Lann, E., & Grimbos, T. (2010). Agreement of self-reported and genital measures of sexual arousal in men and women. *Archives of Sexual Behavior, 39,* 5–56.

Christensen, A., Doss, B., & Jacobson, N. (2014) *Reconcilable differences.* New York: Guilford.

Cohen, H., Padilla, Y., & Aravena, V. (2006). Psychosocial support for families of gay, lesbian, bisexual, and transgender people. In D. Morrow & L. Messinger (Eds.), *Sexual orientation and gender expression in social work practice* (pp. 153–172). New York: Columbia University.

Cooper, A. (1998). Sexually compulsive behavior. *Contemporary Sexuality, 32* (4), 1–3.

Cooper, A., Griffin-Shelley, S., Delmonico, D., & Mathy, R. (2001). Online sexual problems. *Sexual Addiction and Compulsivity, 8,* 267–285.

Cooper, A., Delmonico, D., & Burg, R. (2000). Cybersex users and abusers. *Sexual Addiction and Compulsivity, 8,* 267–285.

Cooper, A., & Marcus, I. (2003). Men who are not in control of their sexual behavior. In S. Levine, C. Risen, & S. Althof (Eds.), *Handbook of clinical sexuality for mental health professionals* (pp. 311–332). New York: Routledge.

Covington, S., & Burns, L. (Eds.). (2006). *Infertility counseling: A comprehensive handbook for clinicians* (2nd ed.). New York: Cambridge University.

Cutrona, C. (1996). *Social support in couples.* Thousand Oaks, CA: Sage.

Danielsson, I., Torstensson, T., Broda-Jansen, G., & Bohm-Starke, N. (2006). EMG biofeedback versus topical lidocaine gel. *Acta Obstetricia et Gynecologia Scandinavia, 9,* 136.

Daniluk, J., Koert, E., & Breckon, E. (2014). Sexuality and infertility. In Y. Binik & K. Hall (Eds.), *Principles and practice of sex therapy* (5th ed., pp. 419–435). New York: Guilford.

Daniluk, J., & Frances-Fischer, J. (2009) A sensitive way to address your infertility patients concerns. *Journal of Sexual and Reproductive Medicine, 7,* 3–7.

Dattilio, F., & Padesky, C. (1990). *Cognitive therapy with couples*. Sarasota, FL: Professional Resource Exchange.

Dattilio, F. (2010). *Cognitive-behavioral therapy with couples and families*. New York: Guilford.

Davis, S., Yarber, W., Bauserman, R., Scherr, G., & Davis, S. (1998). *Handbook of sexually-related measures*. London: Sage.

DeAmicus, L., Goldberg, D., LoPiccolo, J., Friedman, J., & Davidson, L. (1985). Clinical follow-up of couples treated for sexual dysfunction. *Archives of Sexual Behavior, 14*, 469–490.

Dekker, J., & Everaerd, W. (1983). A long-term follow-up study of couples treated for sexual dysfunction. *Journal of Sex and Marital Therapy, 7*, 79–113.

Dennerstein, L. (2010). *The sexual impact of menopause*. In S. Levine, C. Risen, & S Althof (Eds.), *Handbook of clinical sexuality for mental health professionals* (2nd ed., pp. 215–227). New York: Routledge.

Derogatis, L., & Mellisaratos, N. (1979). The DSFI: A multidimensional measure of sexual functioning. *Journal of Sex and Marital Therapy, 5*, 244–281.

Diamond, L. (2008). *Sexual fluidity*. Cambridge, MA: Harvard University.

Diamond, L. (2013). Concepts of female sexual orientation. In C. Patterson & A. D'Augelli (Eds.), *Handbook of psychology and sexual orientation* (pp. 3–17). New York: Oxford University Press.

Dodson, B. (1996). *Sex for one*. New York: Harmony.

Ellis, A. (1975). *A new guide to rational living*. New York: Prentice-Hall.

Elze, D. (2006). Oppression, prejudice, and discrimination. In D. Morrow & L. Messinger (Eds.), *Sexual orientation and gender expression in social work practice* (pp. 43–77). New York: Columbia University.

Ende, J., Rockwell, S., & Glasgow, M. (1984). The sexual history in general medical practice. *Archives of Internal Medicine, 144*, 558–561.

Enns, C., Rice, J., & Nutt, R. (2015). *Psychological practice with women*. Washington, DC: American Psychological Association.

Enzlin, P. (2014) Sexuality in the context of chronic illness. In Y. Binik & K. Hall (Eds.), *Principles and practice of sex therapy* (5th ed., pp. 436–456). New York: Guilford.

Epstein, N., & Baucom, D. (2002). *Enhanced cognitive-behavioral therapy for couples: A contextual approach*. Washington, DC: American Psychological Association.

Epstein, N., Dattilio, F., & Baucom, D. (2016). Cognitive-behavioral couple therapy. In T. Sexton & J. Lebow (Eds.), *Handbook of family therapy* (4th ed., pp. 361–396). New York: Routledge.

Epstein, N., & Falconier, M. (2011). Shame in couple therapy. In R. Dearing & J. Tangney (Eds.), *Shame in the therapy hour*. Washington, DC: American Psychological Association.

Epstein, N., & Werlinich, C. (1999). *Relationship Issues Survey*. Unpublished inventory. Center for Healthy Families, Department of Family Science. University of Maryland, College Park.

Epstein, N., Werlinich, C., & LaTaillade, J. (2015). Couple therapy for partner aggression. In A. Gurman, J. Lebow, & D. Snyder (Eds.), *Clinical handbook of couple therapy* (5th ed., pp. 389–411). New York: Guilford.

Everaerd, E., Both, S., & Laan, E. (2006). The experience of sexual emotions. *Annual Review of Sex Research, 17*, 183–199.

Falconier, M., Randall, A., & Bodenmann, G. (2011). *Couples coping with stress: A cross-cultural perspective*. New York: Routledge.

Federoff, J. (2010). Paraphiliac worlds. In S. Levine, C. Risen, & S. Althof (Eds.), *Handbook of clinical sexuality for mental health professionals*. New York: Routledge.

Fichten, C., Specter, I., & Libman, E. (1988). Client attributions for sexual dysfunction. *Journal of Sex and Marital Therapy, 14*, 208–224.

Figueira, I., Possidente, E., Marques, C., & Hayes, K. (2001). Sexual dysfunction: A neglected complication of panic disorder and social phobia. *Archives of Sexual Behavior, 30*, 369–377.

Finkelhor, D., & Browne, A. (1985). The traumatic impact of child sexual abuse. *American Journal of Orthopsychiatry, 55*, 530–541.

Fisher, H. (2004). *Why we love*. New York: Henry Holt.

Fisher, H., Aron, A., Masher, D., & Brown, L. (2002). The brain system of lust, romantic attraction, and attachment. *Archives of Sexual Behavior, 31*, 413–419.

Fisher, W., & Holtzapfel, S. (2014). Suppose they gave an epidemic and sex therapy didn't attend? Sexually transmitted infections concerns in the sex therapy context. In Y. Binik & K. Hall (Eds.), *Principles and practice of sex therapy* (5th ed., pp. 482–508). New York: Guilford.

Foley, S., Kope, S., & Sugrue, D. (2012) *Sex matters for women* (2nd ed.) New York: Guilford.

Folkman, S., & Lazarus, R. (1988). Coping as a mediator of emotion. *Journal of Personality and Social Psychology, 54*, 466–475.

Fraenkel, P., & Capstick, C. (2012). Contemporary two-parent families: Navigating work and family challenges. In F. Walsh (Ed.), *Normal family processes: Growing diversity and complexity* (4th ed., pp. 78–101). New York: Guilford.

Frank, E., Anderson, C., & Rubinstein, D. (1978). Frequency of sexual dysfunction in "normal" couples. *New England Journal of Medicine, 229*, 111–115.

Gehart, D. (2012). *Mindfulness and acceptance in couple and family therapy*. New York: Springer.

George, W., & Stoner, S. (2000). Understanding acute alcohol effects on sexual behavior. *Annual Review of Sex Research*, 11, 92–124.

Germer, C., Siegel, R., & Fulton, P. (2013). *Mindfulness and psychotherapy* (2nd ed.). New York: Guilford.

Giami, A., Chevret-Measson, M., & Bonierbale, M. (2009). The most common barriers for clinician comfort. *Sexologies, 18*, 238–242.

Glass, S. (2003). *Not "just friends"*. New York: Free Press.

Glazer, H., Robke, G., Swencionis, C., Hertz, R., & Young, A. (1995). The treatment of vulvar vestibulitis syndrome by electomyographic biofeedback pelvic floor musculature. *Journal of Reproductive Medicine, 40*, 283–290.

Gordon, K., Baucom, D., Epstein, N., Burnett, C., & Rankin, L. (1999). The interaction between marital standards and communication patterns. *Journal of Marital and Family Therapy, 25*, 211–223.

Gordon, K. Khaddouma, D., Baucom, D., & Snyder, D. (2015). Couple therapy and the treatment of affairs. In A. Gurman, J. Lebow, & D. Snyder (Eds.), *Clinical handbook of couple therapy*. (5th ed., pp. 412–444). New York: Guilford.

Gottman, J. (1994). *What predicts divorce?* Hillsdale, NJ: Erlbaum.

Gottman, J. (1999). *The marriage clinic: A scientifically based marital therapy*. New York: Norton.

Gottman, J., & Gottman, J. (2015). Gottman couple therapy. In A. Gurman, J. Lebow, & D. Snyder (Eds.), *Clinical handbook of couple therapy* (5th ed., pp. 129–157). New York: Guilford.

Graham, C. (2014). Orgasm disorders in women. In Y. Binik & K. Hall (Eds.), *Principles and practice of sex therapy* (5th ed., pp. 89–111). New York: Guilford.

Graham, C., Sanders, S., Mulhausen, R., & McBride, K. (2004). Turning on and turning off: A focus group study of the factors that affect women's sexual arousal. *Archives of Sexual Behavior, 33*, 527–538.

Greenberg, L., & Johnson, S. (2010). *Emotion focused therapy for couples*. New York: Guilford.

Grenier, G., & Byers, E. (1997). The relationships among ejaculatory control, ejaculatory latency, and attempts to prolong heterosexual intercourse. *Archives of Sexual Behavior, 26*, 27–42.

Grenier, G., & Byers, E. (2004). Premature or rapid ejaculation: Heterosexual couples' perceptions of men's ejaculatory behavior. *Archives of Sexual Behavior, 33*, 261–270.

Groopman, J. (2007). *How doctors think*. Boston, MA: Houghton Mifflin.

Gross, J., & John, O. (2003). Individual differences in two emotional regulation processes. *Journal of Personality and Social Psychology, 82*, 348.

Halvorsen, J., Mommsen, C., Metz, M., Moriarity, J., Hunter, B., & Lange, P. (1988). Male sexual impotence. *The Journal of Family Practice, 27*, 583–599.

Hamann, S., Herman, R., Nolan, C., & Wallen, K. (2004). Men and women differ in amygdala response to visual sexual stimuli. *Nature Neuroscience, 7*, 411–416.

Hanson, R., & Morton-Bourgon, K. (2005). The characteristics of persistent sexual offenders: A meta-analysis of recidivism studies. *Journal of Consulting and Clinical Psychology, 73*, 1154–1163.

Hanson, R., & Morton-Bourgon, K. (2009). The accuracy of recidivism risk assessments for sexual offenders. *Psychological Assessment, 21,* 1–21.

Harlow, B., Wise, L., & Stewart, E. (2001). Prevalence and predictors of chronic low genital tract discomfort. *American Journal of Obstetrics and Gynecology, 185,* 545–550.

Hartmann, V., & Waldinger, M. (2007). Treatment of delayed ejaculation. In S. Leiblum (Ed.), *Principles and practice of sex therapy* (4th ed., pp. 84–123). New York: Guilford.

Hatzichristou, D., Kyriakos, M., Apostolodis, A., Bekos, A., Tzortzis, V., Hatzimouratirsis, K., & Ioannidis, E. (2005). Sildenafil failure may be due to inadequate patient instructions and follow-up. *European Urology, 47,* 518–523.

Hawton, K., Catalan, J., Martin, P., & Fagg, J. (1986). Long term outcome in sex therapy. *Behavior Research and Therapy, 24,* 665–675.

Hayes, S., Strosahl, K., & Wilson, K. (2011). *Acceptance and commitment therapy* (2nd ed.). New York: Guilford.

Heiman, J. (2007). Orgasmic disorders in women. In S. Leiblum (Ed.), *Principles and practice of sex therapy* (pp. 84–123). New York: Guilford.

Heiman, J., & LoPiccolo, J. (1988). *Becoming orgasmic.* New York: Prentice-Hall.

Heiman, J., & Meston, C., (1999). Empirically validated treatment for sexual dysfunction. *Annual Review of Sex Research, 6,* 148–197.

Helms, H., Walls, J., & Demo, D. (2010). Everyday hassles and family stress. In S. Price, C. Price, & P. McKenry (Eds.), *Families and change: Coping with stressful events and transitions* (4th ed., pp. 357–379). Thousand Oaks, CA: Sage.

Herbenick, D., Reece, J., Schick, N., Sanders, S., Dodge, B., & Fortenberry, J. (2010). Sexual behavior in the United States: Results from a national probability sample of men and women ages 19–94. *Journal of Sexual Medicine, 7,* 255–265.

Herek, G., & Garnets, L. (2007). Sexual orientation and mental health. *Annual Review of Clinical Psychology, 3,* 353–375.

Hertlein, K., Weeks, G., & Gambecia, N. (2009). *Systemic sex therapy.* New York: Routledge.

Hill, R. (2008). *Seven strategies for positive aging.* New York: Norton.

Hillman, S. (2008). Sexual issues and aging within the context of work with older patients. *Professional Psychology: Research and Practice, 39,* 290–297.

Howe, G., Levy, M., & Caplan, R. (2004). Job loss and depressive symptoms in couples: Common stressors, stress transmission, or relationship disruption? *Journal of Family Psychology, 18,* 639.

Hurlbert, S. (1991). The role of assertiveness in female sexuality. *Journal of Sex and Marital Therapy, 17,* 183–190.

Ilies, R., Dimotakis, N., & De Pater, I. (2010). Psychological and physiological reactions to high workloads: Implications for well-being. *Personnel Psychology, 63,* 407–436.

Jacobson, N., & Christensen, A. (1996). *Integrative couple therapy.* New York: Norton.

Jacobson, N., & Margolin, G. (1979). *Marital therapy: Strategies based on social learning and behavior exchange processes.* New York: Brunner/Mazel.

Johnson, S. (2008) *Hold me tight.* Boston, MA: Little Brown.

Kafka, M. (2014). Nonparaphiliac hypersexuality disorders. In Y. Binik & K. Hall (Eds.), *Principles and practice of sex therapy* (5th ed., pp. 280–304). New York: Guilford.

Kaplan, H. (1974). *The new sex therapy.* New York: Brunner/Mazel.

Kaplan, H. (1987). *Sexual aversion, sexual phobias, and panic disorder.* New York: Brunner/Mazel.

Kenny, D., Kashy, D., & Cook, W. (2006). *Dyadic data analysis.* New York: Guilford.

Kilmann, P., Boland, J., Norton, S., Davidson, E., & Caid, C. (1986) Perspectives of sex therapy outcome. *Journal of Sex and Marital Therapy, 12,* 116–138.

Kinsey, A., Pomeroy, W., & Martin, C. (1948) *Sexual behavior in the human male.* New York: Saunders.

Kinsey, A., Pomeroy, W., & Martin, C. (1953). *Sexual behavior in the human female.* New York: Saunders.

Kirby, J., Baucom, D., & Peterman, M. (2007). An investigation of unmet intimacy needs in marital relationships. *Journal of Marital and Family Therapy, 31,* 313–325.

Kleinplatz, P. (2012). *New directions in sex therapy* (2nd ed.). New York: Routledge.

Kleinplatz, P. (2010). Lessons from great lovers. In S. Levine, C. Risen, & S. Althof (Eds.), *Handbook of clinical sexuality for mental health professionals* (2nd ed., pp. 57–72). New York: Routledge.

Kleinplatz, P., McCarrey, M., & Kateb, C. (1992). The impact of gender-role identity on women's self-esteem, lifestyle satisfaction, and conflict. *Canadian Journal of Behavioral Science, 24,* 333–347.

Kleinplatz, P., & Menard, A. (2007). Building blocks toward optimal sexuality. *The Family Journal, 15,* 72–78.

Kleinplatz, P., Menard, A., Paradis, N., Campbell, M., Palgleish, T., Segouia, A., & Davis, K. (2009). From closet to reality: Optimal sexuality among the elderly. *The Irish Psychiatrist, 10,* 15–18.

Kline, G., Pleasant, H., Whitton, S., & Markman, H. (2006). Understanding couple conflict. In A. Vangelisti & D. Perlman (Eds.), *The Cambridge handbook of personal relationships* (pp. 445–462). New York: Cambridge University.

Kuriansky, J., Sharp, L., & O'Connor, D. (1982). The treatment of anorgasmia. *Journal of Sex and Marital Therapy, 8,* 29–43.

Laan, E., & Both, S. (2011). Sexual desire and arousal disorders in women. *Advances in Psychosomatic Medicine, 31,* 16–34.

Laumann, E., Gagnon, J., Michael, R., & Michaels, S. (1994). *The social organization of sexuality: Sexual practices in the United States.* Chicago: University of Chicago.

Laumann, E., Paik, A., & Rosen, R. (1999). Sexual dysfunction in the United States: Prevalence and perspectives. *Journal of the American Medical Association, 261,* 537–544.

Laumann, E., Nicolosi, A., Glasser, D., Paik, A., Gringell, C., Moreira, E., & Wang, T. (2005). Sexual problems among women ages 40–80: Prevalence and correlates identified in the global study of sexual attitudes and behavior. *International Journal of Impotency Research, 17,* 39–57.

Leahy, D. (2003). *Roadblocks in cognitive-behavioral therapy.* New York: Guilford.

Leedes, R. (2001). The three most important criteria in diagnosing sexual addictions. *Sexual Addiction and Compulsivity, 8,* 215–226.

Leiblum, S. (1999). Love, sex, and infertility: The impact of infertility in couples. In S. Leiblum (Ed.), *Infertility: Psychological issues and counseling strategies* (pp. 149–166). New York: Wiley.

Leiblum, S. (2007). Sex therapy today. In S. Leiblum (Ed.) *Principles and practice of sex therapy* (4th ed, pp. 3–22). New York: Guilford.

Leiblum, S. (2010). *Treating sexual desire disorders.* New York: Guilford.

Lemieux, S., & Byers, E. (2008). The sexual well-being of women who have experienced child sexual abuse. *Psychology of Women Quarterly, 32,* 126–144.

Levine, S., Risen, C., & Althof, S. (2016). *Handbook of clinical sexuality for mental health professionals* (3rd ed.). New York: Routledge.

Lewis, R., Fugi-Meyer, K., Bosch, R., Fugi-Meyer, A., Laumann, E., & Lizza, E. (2004). Epidemiology/risk factors on sexual dysfunction. *Journal of Sexual Medicine, 1,* 35–39.

Lindau, S., Schumm, L., Laumann, E., Levinson, W., O'Muircheartaigh, C., & Waite, L. (2007). A study of sexuality and health among older adults in the United States. *New England Journal of Medicine, 357,* 762–774.

Lobitz, W., & Lobitz, G. (1996). Resolving the sexual intimacy paradox: A developmental model for the treatment of sexual desire disorders. *Journal of Sex and Marital Therapy, 22,* 71–84.

LoPiccolo, J., & Friedman, J. (1988). Broad spectrum treatment of low sexual desire: Integration of cognitive, behavioral, and systemic therapy. In S. Leiblum & R. Rosen (Eds.), *Sexual desire disorders* (pp. 107–144). New York: Guilford.

LoPiccolo, J., & Lobitz, W. (1972). The role of masturbation in the treatment of orgasmic dysfunction. *Archives of Sexual Behavior, 2,* 163–172.

LoPiccolo, J., & Stock, W. (1986). Treatment of sexual dysfunction. *Journal of Consulting and Clinical Psychology, 54,* 158–167.

Loudon, J. (1998). Potential confusion between erectile dysfunction and premature ejaculation. *Journal of Sex and Marital Therapy, 13,* 397–401.

Love, P., & Stosny, S. (2008). *How to improve your marriage without talking about it.* New York: Harmony.

Lyubomirsky, S., Sheldon, K., & Schkade, D. (2015). Pursuing happiness: The architecture of sustainable change. *Review of General Psychology, 9,* 111–131.

Maltz, W. (2012). *The sexual healing journey* (3rd ed.). New York: Harmony.

Marcus, I. (2010). Men who are not in control of their sexual behavior. In S. Levine, C. Risen, & S. Althof (Eds.), *Handbook of clinical sexuality for mental health professionals* (2nd ed., pp. 383–399). New York: Routledge.

Marlatt, G., & Donovan, D. (2005). *Relapse prevention: Maintenance strategies in the treatment of addictive behaviors.* New York: Guilford.

Marlatt, G., & Gordon, J. (1988). *Relapse prevention.* New York: Guilford.

Mark, K.P., Janssen, E., & Milhausen, R.R. (2011). Infidelity in heterosexual couples: Demographic, interpersonal, and personality-related predictors of extradyadic sex. *Archives of Sexual Behavior, 40,* 971–982.

Markman, H., Stanley, S., & Blumberg, S. (2010). *Fighting for your marriage* (rev. ed.). San Francisco, CA: Jossey-Bass.

Masters, W., & Johnson, V. (1966). *Human sexual response.* Boston, MA: Little/Brown.

Masters, W., & Johnson, V. (1970). *Human sexual inadequacy.* Boston, MA: Little/Brown.

McCabe, M., (1991). The development and maintenance of sexual dysfunction. *Journal of Sex and Marital Therapy, 16,* 245–260.

McCabe, M. (2001). Evaluation of cognitive-behavioral therapy program for people with sexual dysfunction. *Journal of Sex and Marital Therapy, 27,* 259–271.

McCabe, M. (2011). Sexual and relationship problems. In E. Rieger (Ed.), *Abnormal psychology* (2nd ed., pp. 312–354). Melbourne, VIC: McGraw-Hill.

McCabe, M. (2016). New concepts in the understanding of female sexual dysfunction. In L. Lipshultz, A. Pastusak, A. Goldstein, A. Giraldi, & M. Perlman (Eds.), *Management of sexual dysfunction in men and women* (pp. 307–314). New York: Springer.

McCarthy, B. (1990). Relapse prevention strategies and techniques for inhibited sexual desire. *Journal of Sex and Marital Therapy, 25,* 297–303.

McCarthy, B. (2015). *Sex made simple.* Eau Claire, WI: Pesi Publications.

McCarthy, B., Bodnar, L., & Handal, M. (2004). Integrating sex therapy and couple therapy. In J. Harvey, A. Wenzel, & S. Sprecher (Eds.), *The handbook of sexuality in close relationships* (pp. 573–593). Mahwah, NJ: Erlbaum.

McCarthy, B., & Breetz, A. (2010). Confronting sexual trauma and enhancing adult sexuality. In S. Levine, C. Risen, & A. Althof (Eds.), *Handbook of clinical sexuality for mental health professionals* (2nd ed., pp. 295–310). New York: Routledge.

McCarthy, B., & Fucito, L. (2005). Integrating medication, realistic expectations, and therapeutic interventions in the treatment of male sexual dysfunction. *Journal of Sex and Marital Therapy, 31,* 319–328.

McCarthy, B., Ginsberg, B., & Fucito, L. (2006). Resilient sexual desire in heterosexual couples. *The Family Journal, 14,* 59–64.

McCarthy, B., & McCarthy, E. (2009). *Discovering your couple sexual style.* New York: Routledge.

McCarthy, B., & McCarthy, E. (2012). *Sexual awareness* (5th ed.). New York: Routledge.

McCarthy, B., & McCarthy, E. (2014). *Revitalizing desire* (2nd ed.). New York: Routledge.

McCarthy, B., & Metz, M. (2008). *Men's sexual health.* New York: Routledge.

McCarthy, B. & Thestrup, M. (2008a). Integrating sex therapy interventions with couple therapy. *Journal of Contemporary Psychotherapy, 38,* 139–149.

McCarthy, B., & Thestrup, M. (2008b). Couple therapy and the treatment of sexual dysfunction. In A.S. Gurman (Ed.), *Clinical handbook of couple therapy* (4th ed., pp. 591–617). New York: Guilford.

McCarthy, B., & Wald, L. (2013). New strategies in assessing, treating, and relapse prevention of extramarital affairs. *Journal of Sex and Marital Therapy, 39,* 493–509.

McCarthy, B., & Wald, L. (2015). Strategies and techniques to directly address sexual desire problems. *Journal of Family Psychotherapy, 36,* 1–13.

McCarthy, B., & Wald, L. (2016). Finding her voice: First class female sexuality. *Sexual and Relationship Therapy, 31*, 138–147.

McKay, E., Kaufman, R., Doctor, U., Berkova, A., Glazer, H., & Redko, V. (2001). Treating vulvar vestibulitis with electromyographic biofeedback of pelvic floor musculature. *Journal of Reproductive Medicine, 46*, 337–342.

McKee, A., Albury, K., Dunne, M., Greshaber, S., Hartley, J., Lumby, & Matthews, B. (2000). Healthy sexual development. *International Journal of Sexual Health, 22*, 14–19.

McKinlay, J., & Feldman, H. (1994). Age related variation in sexual activity and interest in normal men: Results from the Massachusetts male aging study. In A. Rossi (Ed.), *Sexuality across the lifespan* (pp. 261–285). Chicago: University of Chicago.

McKinlay, J., Longcope, C., & Gray, A. (1989). The questionable physiological and epidemiologic basis for a male climacteric syndrome. *Maturitas, 11*, 103–115.

Meana, M. (2010). Elucidating women's (hetero) sexual desire: Definitional challenges and content expansion. *Journal of Sex Research, 47*, 104–122.

Meana, M., & Steiner, F. (2014). Hidden disorder/hidden desire: Presentation of low sexual desire in men. In Y. Binik & K. Hall (Eds.), *Principles and practice of sex therapy* (5th ed., pp. 42–60). New York: Guilford.

Meisler, T., & Carey, M. (1991). Depressed affect and male sexual arousal. *Archives of Sexual Behavior, 20*, 541–554.

Melnick, T., Soares, B., & Nasello, A. (2008). The effectiveness of psychological interventions for the treatment of erectile dysfunction. *Journal of Sexual Medicine, 5*, 2562–2574.

Meichenbaum, D. (1985). *Stress inoculation training.* New York: Pergammon.

Meston, C. & Buss, D. (2009). *Why women have sex.* New York: McMillan.

Metz, M. (1993). *The Styles of Conflict Inventory for Personal Relationships.* Palo Alto, CA: Consulting Psychologists Press.

Metz, M., & Epstein, N. (2002). Assessing the role of relationship conflict in sexual dysfunction. *Journal of Sex and Marital Therapy, 28*, 139–164.

Metz, M., & Lutz, G. (1990). Dyadic playfulness differences between sexual and marital therapy couples. *Journal of Psychology and Human sexuality, 3*, 167–182.

Metz, M., & McCarthy, B. (2003). *Coping with premature ejaculation.* Oakland, CA: New Harbinger.

Metz, M., & McCarthy, B. (2004). *Coping with erectile dysfunction.* Oakland, CA: New Harbinger.

Metz, M., & McCarthy, B. (2007). "The Good Enough Sex" model for couple sexual satisfaction. *Sexual and Relationship Therapy, 22*, 357–362.

Metz, M., & McCarthy, B. (2010). Male sexuality and couple sexual health. *Journal of Family Psychotherapy, 21*, 197–212.

Metz, M., & McCarthy, B. (2011). *Enduring desire.* New York: Routledge.

Metz, M., & McCarthy, B. (2012). The Good Enough Sex (GES) model: Perspective and clinical applications. In P. Kleinplatz (Ed.), *New directions in sex therapy* (2nd ed., pp. 213–230). New York: Routledge.

Metz, M., & Miner, M. (1998). Psychosexual and psychosocial aspects of male aging and sexual healing. *The Canadian Journal of Human Sexuality, 7*, 293–320.

Metz, M., & Pryor, J. (2000). Premature ejaculation: A psychophysical approach for assessment and management. *Journal of Sex and Marital Therapy, 26*, 293–320.

Metz, M., Pryor, J., Abuzzahab, F., Nesvacil, L., & Kozner, J. (1997). Premature ejaculation: A psychophysiological review. *Journal of Sex and Marital Therapy, 23*, 3–23.

Metz, M., & Siefert, M. (1993). Differences in men's and women's sexual health needs and expectation of physicians. *The Canadian Journal of Human Sexuality, 2*, 53–59.

Metz, M., & Weiss, K. (1992). A group therapy format for the simultaneous treatment of marital and sexual dysfunction. *Journal of Sex and Marital Therapy, 18*, 173–196.

Milheiser, R., Helmer, A., Quintero, R., Westphal, L., Milki, A., & Cath, R. (2010). Is infertility a risk factor for female sexual dysfunction? *Fertility and Sterility, 94*, 2022–2025.

Miller, G., & Bradbury, T. (1995). Refining the association between attraction and behavior in marital interactions. *Journal of Family Psychology, 9*, 196–208.

Miller, S., & Byers, E. (2009). Psychologists' continuing education and training in sexuality. *Journal of Sex and Marital Therapy, 35,* 206–219.

Miller, S., & Byers, E. (2010). Psychologists' sexual education training in graduate school. *Canadian Journal of Behavioral Science, 42,* 93–102.

Mitchell, W., DiBartolo, R., Brown, I., & Barlow, D. (1998). Effects of positive and negative mood on sexual arousal in sexually functional males. *Archives of Sexual Behavior, 27,* 197–207.

Mona, L., Syme, M., & Cameron, R. (2014). Sexuality and disability. In Y. Binik & K. Hall (Eds.), *Principles and practice of sex therapy* (5th ed., pp. 457–480). New York: Guilford.

Monson, L., & Fredman, S. (2012). *Cognitive-behavioral conjoint treatment for posttraumatic stress disorder.* New York: Guilford.

Morrow, D. (2006a). Sexual orientation and gender identity expression. In D. Morrow & L. Messinger (Eds.), *Sexual orientation and gender expression in social work practice* (pp. 3–17). New York: Columbia University.

Morrow, D. (2006b). Gay, lesbian, and bisexual identity development. In D. Morrow & L. Messinger (Eds.), *Sexual orientation and gender expression in social work practice* (pp. 81–104). New York: Columbia University.

Mosher, D. (1980). Three psychological dimensions of depth of involvement in human sexual response. *Journal of Sex Research, 16,* 1–42.

Munjack, D., Cristol, A., Goldstein, A., Phillips, S., Goldberg, A., Whipple, B., Staples, F., & Kando, P. (1976). Behavioral treatment of orgasmic dysfunction. *British Journal of Psychiatry, 129,* 493–502.

Nelson, T. (2008). *Getting the sex you want.* New York: Quiver.

Nezlek, J., & Kuppens, P. (2008). Regulating positive and negative emotion in daily life. *Journal of Personality, 76,* 561–586.

Nichols, M. (2014). Therapy with LGBTQ clients. In Y. Binik & K. Hall (Eds.), *Principles and practice of sex therapy* (5th ed., pp. 309–333). New York: Guilford.

Nicolosi, A., Laumann, E., Glasser, D., Moreira, E., Paik, A., & Gingell, C. (2004). Sexual behavior and sexual dysfunction after age 40: The global study of sexual attitudes and behaviors. *Urology, 64,* 991–997.

Nobre, P. (2009). Determinates of sexual desire problems in women. *Journal of Sex and Marital Therapy, 35,* 360–377.

Nobre, P., & Pinto-Gouveia, J. (2006). Dysfunctional sexual beliefs as vulnerability factors for sexual dysfunction. *Journal of Sex Research, 43,* 68–75.

O'Donohue, W., Dopke, C., & Swingen, D. (1997). Psychotherapy for female sexual dysfunction. *Clinical Psychiatry Review, 17,* 537–566.

O'Donohue, W., Swingen, D., Dopke, C., & Roger, L. (1999). Psychotherapy for male sexual dysfunction. *Clinical Psychiatry Review, 19,* 591–630.

O'Farrell, T., Choquettem K., Cutter, H., & Birchler, G. (1997). Sexual satisfaction and dysfunction in marriages of male alcoholics. *Journal of Studies on Alcohol, 58,* 91–99.

O'Sullivan, L., & Pasterski, V. (2014). Sexual problems in adolescents and young adults. In Y. Binik & K. Hall (Eds.), *Principles and practice of sex therapy* (5th ed., pp. 511–524). New York: Guilford.

Padma-Nathan, H., Helstrom, W., Kaiser, F., Labasky, R., Lue, T., Holton, W., …, Gesindheit, N. (1997). Treatment of men with erectile dysfunction with transurethral alprostadil. *New England Journal of Medicine, 336,* 1–7.

Paikoff, R., McCormack, A., & Sagrestanol, L. (2000). Adolescent sexuality. In L. Suchman & F. Muscarella (Eds.), *Psychological perspectives on human sexuality* (pp. 416–439). New York: Wiley.

Palace, E. (1999). Response expectancy and sexual dysfunction in couples. In I. Ikrsch (Ed.), *How expectancies shape experiences* (pp. 173–196). Washington, DC: American Psychological Association.

Pascoal, P., Narcisco, T., & Pereira, N. (2012). Predictions of body appearance and cognitive distractions during sexual activity in men and women. *Journal of Sexual Medicine, 9,* 2849–2860.

Perel, E. (2006). *Mating in captivity: Reconciling the erotic and the domestic.* New York: HarperCollins.

Perelman M.   (1980) Treatment of premature ejaculation.   In S. Leiblum & L. Pervin (Eds.), *Principles and practices of sex therapy* (pp.199–233).   New York: Guilford Press.

Perelman, M. (2009). The sexual tipping point. *Journal of Sexual Medicine, 6,* 629–632.

Perelman, M. (2014). Delayed ejaculation. In Y. Binik & K. Hall (Eds.), *Principles and practice of sex therapy* (5th ed., pp. 138–155). New York: Guilford.

Perelman, M. (2016). Psychosexual therapy for delayed ejaculation based on the sexual tipping point model. *Translational Andrology and Urology, 5,* 563–575.

Perelman, M., McMahon, C., & Barada, J. (2004). Evaluation and treatment of the ejaculatory disorders. In T. Lue (Ed.), *Atlas of male sexual dysfunction* (pp. 127–155). Philadelphia, PA: Current Medicine.

Peterson, C. (2006). *A primer of positive psychology.* New York: Oxford.

Pfaus, J. (1999). Revisiting the concept of sexual motivation. *Annual Review of Sex Research, 10,* 120–156.

Pfaus, J. (2009). Pathways of sexual desire. *Journal of Sexual Medicine, 6,* 1506–1533.

Pretzer, J., Epstein, N., & Fleming, B. (1911). Marital Attitude Survey: A measure of dysfunctional attributions and expectancies. *Journal of Cognitive Psychotherapy, 5,* 131–148.

Regan, P., & Berscheid, E. (1995). Beliefs about the state, goals, and objects of sexual desire. *Journal of Sex and Marital Therapy, 22,* 110–120.

Reinisch, J. (1991). *The Kinsey Institute new report on sex.* New York: St. Martin's.

Rellini, A. (2014). The treatment of sexual dysfunction in survivors of sexual abuse. In Y. Binik & K. Hall (Eds.), *Principles and practice of sex therapy* (5th ed., pp. 375–398). New York: Guilford.

Revenson, T., Kayser, K., & Bodenmann (2005). *Emerging perspectives on couples coping with stress.* Washington, DC: American Psychological Association.

Reynolds, B. (1991). Psychological treatment of erectile dysfunction in men without partners. *Journal of Sex and Marital Therapy, 17,* 136–146.

Reynolds, M., Herbenick, D., & Bancroft, J. (2003) The nature of childhood sexual experiences. In J. Bancroft (Ed.), *Sexual development in children* (pp. 156–185). Bloomington, IN: Indiana University.

Risen, C. (2010) Listening to sexual stories. In S. Levine, C. Risen, & S. Althof (Eds.), *Handbook of clinical sexuality for mental health professionals* (2nd ed., pp. 3–20). New York: Routledge.

Rosen, R. (2007). Erectile dysfunction. In S. Leiblum (Ed.), *Principles and practice of sex therapy* (4th ed., pp. 277–302). New York: Guilford.

Rosen, R., Miner, M., & Wincze, J. (2014). Erectile dysfunction: Integrating medical and psychological approaches. In Y. Binik & K. Hall (Eds.), *Principles and practice of sex therapy* (5th ed., pp. 61–85), New York: Guilford.

Rowland, D., & Cooper, S. (2011). Practical tips for counseling and psychotherapy in premature ejaculation. *Journal of Sexual Medicine, 8,* 342–352.

Rowland, D., & Slob, A. (1997). Premature ejaculation: Psychophysiological considerations in theory, research, and treatment. *Annual Review of Sex Research, 8,* 224–253.

Rust, J., & Golombok, S. (1985). The Golombok Rust inventory of Sexual Satisfaction (GRISS). *British Journal of Clinical Psychology, 24,* 63–64.

Sands, M., Fisher, W., Rosen, R., Heiman, J., & Eardley, I. (2008). Erectile dysfunction and constructs of masculinity and quality of life in the multination men's attitudes to life events and sexuality (Males) study. *Journal of Sexual Medicine, 5,* 583–594.

Sbrocco, T., Weisberg, R., Barlow, D., & Carter, M. (1997). The conceptual relationship between panic disorder and male erectile dysfunction. *Journal of Sex and Marital Therapy, 23,* 213–220.

Schar, M., & Poffet, N. (2010). The association between daily stress and sexual activity. *Journal of Family Psychology, 24,* 271–279.

Schein, M., Zyzanski, S., Levine, S., Medalie, J., Dickman, R., & Alemagnos, S. (1988). The frequency of sexual problems among family practice patients. *Family Practice Research Journal, 7,* 122–134.

Schnarch, D. (1991). *Constructing the sexual crucible: An integration of sexual and marital therapy.* New York: Norton.

Segraves, R., & Balon, R. (2003). *Sexual pharmacology*. New York: Norton.

Segraves, R., & Woodard, T. (2006). Female hypoactive sexual desire disorder: History and current status. *Journal of Sexual Medicine, 3*, 408–418.

Seligman, M., Rashid, J., & Parks, A. (2006). Positive psychology. *American Psychologist, 61*, 774–788.

Shamloul, D., & Ghanem, H. (2013). Erectile dysfunction. *The Lancet, 381*, 153–165.

Shifren, J., Monz, B., Russo, P., Segretti, A., & Johannis, C. (2009). Sexual problems and distress in United States women. *Obstetrics and Gynecology, 112*, 970–978.

Shindel, A., Nelson C., Naughton, C., Ohebshalom, M., & Milhall, J. (2008). Sexual function and quality of life in the male partner of infertile couples. *The Journal of Urology, 179*, 1056–1059.

Siddi, A., Reddy, P., & Chen, K. (1988). Patient acceptance and satisfaction with vasoactive intracavernous pharmacotherapy for impotence. *Journal of Urology, 140*, 293–297.

Simms, D., & Byers, E. (2009). Interpersonal perceptions of desired frequency of sexual behaviors. *The Canadian Journal of Human Sexuality, 18*, 15–25.

Snyder, D. (1997). *Manual for the Marital Satisfaction Inventory-Revised*. Los Angeles, CA: Western Psychological Services.

Snyder, D., Baucom, D., & Gordon, K. (2007). *Getting past the affair*. New York: Guilford.

Snyder, D., Castellani, A., & Whisman, M. (2006). Current status and future directions in couple therapy. *Annual Review of Psychology, 57*, 317–344.

Spanier, G. (1976). Measuring dyadic adjustment. *Journal of Marriage and the Family, 38*, 15–28.

Spector, I., & Carey, M. (1990). Incidence and prevalence of the sexual dysfunctions. *Archives of Sexual Behavior, 19*, 389–408.

Spector, I., Carey, M., & Steinberg, L. (1996). The Sexual Desire Inventory. *Journal of Sex and Marital Therapy, 22*, 175–190.

Stuart, R. (1980). *Helping couples change: A social learning approach to marital therapy*. New York: Guilford.

Stith, S., McCollum, E., & Rosen, R. (2011). *Couple therapy and domestic violence*. Washington, DC: American Psychological Association

Sugrue, D., & Whipple, B. (2001). The consensus-based classification of female sexual dysfunction. *Journal of Sex and Marital Therapy, 27*, 221–226.

ter Kuile, M., Bulte, L., Weijenborg, P., Beekman, A., Melles, R., & Onghena, P. (2009). Therapist aided exposure for women with lifelong vaginismus. *Journal of Consulting and Clinical Psychology, 77*, 149–159.

Thoma, N., & McKay, D. (2015). *Working with emotions in cognitive-behavioral therapy*. New York: Guilford.

Tiefer, L. (2004). Sex is not a natural act and other essays (2nd ed.). New York: Westview.

Turchik, J. (2012). Sexual victimization among college students. *Psychology of Men and Masculinity, 13*, 243–255.

Verschuren, J., Enzlin, R., Dijkstra, P., Gertzen, J., & Dekker R. (2010). Chronic disease and sexuality. *Journal of Sex Research, 43*, 153–170.

Vigen, R., O'Donnell, C., Baron, A., Greenwald, G., Maddux, T., Brandley, S., …, Ho, P. (2013). Association of testosterone therapy with mortality, myocardial infraction, and stroke in men with low testosterone levels. *Journal of American Medical Association, 310*, 1829–1836.

Weeks, G. (2004) The emergence of a new paradigm in sex therapy. *Sexual and Relationship Therapy, 20*, 89–107.

Weeks, G., & Gambecia, N. (2015). Couple therapy and sexual problems. In A. Gurman, J. Lebow, & D. Snyder (Eds.), *Clinical handbook of couple therapy* (5th ed., pp. 635–656). New York: Guilford.

Weeks, G., & Treat, S. (2001). *Couples in treatment*. New York: Guilford.

Weiss, R. (1980). Strategic behavioral marital therapy. In J. Vincent (Ed.), *Advances in family intervention, assessment, and theory* (pp. 229–271). Greenwich, CT: JAI Press.

Whisman, M., & Beach, S. (2012). Couple therapy for depression. *Journal of Clinical Psychology, 68*, 526–535.

Wiederman, M., & Sarin, S. (2014). Body image and sexuality. In Y. Binik & K. Hall (Eds.), *Principles and practice of sex therapy* (5th ed., pp. 359–374). New York: Guilford.

Wilhelm, S., Buhlmann, V., Hayward, L., Greenber, J., & Dimaite, R. (2010). A cognitive behavioral treatment approach for body dysmorphic disorder. *Cognitive and Behavioral Practice, 17,* 241–247.

Wincze, J., & Weisberg, R. (2015). *Sexual dysfunction* (3rd ed.) New York: Guilford.

Winton, M. (2001). Gender and sexual dysfunctions. *Journal of Sex and Marital Therapy, 27,* 333–337.

Witkiewitz, K., & Marlatt, G. (2007). *Therapist's guide to evidence-based relapse prevention.* Boston, MA: Elsevier.

Wood, J., Koch, P., & Mansfield, P. (2006). Women's sexual desire. *Journal of Sex Research, 43,* 236–244.

World Health Organization (1975). *Education and treatment of human sexuality: The training of health professionals.* Geneva, Switzerland: World Health Organization.

Wylie, K., & Hallam-Jones, A. (2005). Female sexual arousal disorder. In R. Balon & R. Segraves (Eds.), *Handbook of sexual dysfunction* (pp. 123–154). New York: Taylor and Francis.

Wylie, K., & Kenney, G. (2010). Sexual dysfunction and the aging male. *Maturities, 65,* 23–27.

Zilbergeld, B. (1999). *The new male sexuality* (revised ed.). New York: Bantam.

Zoldbrod, A. (2015). Sexual issues in trauma survivors. *Current Sexual Health Reports, 7,* 3–11.

Index

Page numbers in *italic* indicate a figure on the corresponding page